# Hitchcock's Cryptonymies

**Hitchcock's Cryptonymies**

Volume II. War Machines

# Hitchcock's Cryptonymies

Tom Cohen

University of Minnesota Press
Minneapolis • London

Published by the University of Minnesota Press
111 Third Avenue South, Suite 290
Minneapolis, MN 55401-2520
http://www.upress.umn.edu

Library of Congress Cataloging-in-Publication Data

Cohen, Tom, 1953–
    Hitchcock's cryptonymies / Tom Cohen.
        p.   cm.
    Includes bibliographical references and index.
    ISBN 0-8166-4170-6 (hc : alk. paper) — ISBN 0-8166-4171-4 (pb : alk.
paper)
    1. Hitchcock, Alfred, 1899–1980—Criticism and interpretation.   2. Spy
films—History and criticism.   3. War films—History and criticism.   I. Title.
    PN1998.3.H58C62 2005
    791.4302'33—dc22

                                                            2005001127

Printed in the United States of America on acid-free paper

The University of Minnesota is an equal-opportunity educator and employer.


12  11  10  09  08  07  06  05                    10  9  8  7  6  5  4  3  2  1

For J. Hillis Miller

# Contents

# Acknowledgments

As with the companion volume to this book, volume I of *Hitchcock's Cryptonymies, Secret Agents,* this work owes its inception and follow-through to the initial interest and subsequent patience and support of Douglas Armato. He suggested the project years ago and oversaw its realization. Whatever is interesting in it bears his trace.

Many others nourished this project and its author with their energies and ideas. I particularly thank J. Hillis Miller, to whom the volume is thoughtfully dedicated. I also am indebted in diverse ways to the work and stimulus of Eduardo Cadava, Barbara L. Cohen, Helen Elam, Werner Hamacher, Mike Hill, Geoff Manaugh, Avital Ronell, Henry Sussman, Ivana Tieman, and McKenzie Wark. My thanks to Jennifer Wesley for her practical assistance and to Laura Westlund for her guidance.

I thank Vice President William Hedberg of the University at Albany, State University of New York, for university support during the period of composition.

Finally, I appreciate the hospitality and various kindnesses of Bernard Stiegler and George Collins during the period of final revisions. And diverse acknowledgments to L.

# Preface

The average public do not, or are not, aware of "cutting" as we know it, and yet that is the pure orchestration of the motion-picture form.

**—Alfred Hitchcock to François Truffaut**

The four shots assembled here (Figure 1) are avatars, variant fugitive forms, of what I will call in this study Hitchcock's black sun, a trace that inverts solar logics and is prephenomenal. "It" is, in this sense, at the crossroads of aural and visual articulation, a hole in the fabric of representations through which a spectral agency informs the field of cinematic tropes. In the course of its migrations, it informs letters, shadows, animemes, teletechnic machines, and mobilizes in Hitchcock a transformation of reading itself. I derive the term from its perhaps most explicit cameo appearance in the first *The Man Who Knew Too Much,* where a solar trajectory underlies the title's enigmatic claim. In a marksmanship contest, a repeatedly hurled black sun in eclipse is shot or shot at, a solar simulacrum. In the first frame a targeted clay pigeon crosses the sky like a black hole in the representational fabric. When the same work takes us into the false temple of sun worshippers, a movie house for an ocularcentric or solar public, this black marble, inversely called a "light," is used to hypnotize (i.e., cinematically put into a trance) the supposed initiates to the "mysteries of the sevenfold ray." This same *black hole* within the fabric of the image and mimesis (since it returns the latter to the question of media) turns up elsewhere as a black dog, sheer sound, steps, chocolate. Or again, in the center of the sky, as a flying surveillance machine above the beach in Nice (which attacks when, in *North by Northwest,* it converts to a crop duster without crops). In the last-named film, the dark hole takes a shape: it is positioned as a pre-Columbian or, in American terms, prehistorial statuette (what the work calls a "figure") with a conical hat. It carries in its belly a secret the film (itself) is in pursuit of. Here the figure rests between two indicators: Vandamm's pointing finger and a banded stack of books. We see here, in other words, the indexing promise of the photographic image (a figure established in *Blackmail*) and a bibliocentric archive (like the "first editions" in *Rope*). The "figure" contains microfilm, which spills from it as celluloid cuttings when it falls and breaks open atop Mount Rushmore; that is, the figure contains the micrological inscriptions and graphematic systems that reside explosively at the territorial borders not only of the American real but also the personification of an earth scored with giant inert faces. A political secret always contains knowledge dangerous to the state, as the above threatens to expose the black hole's logics against the "global" tele-advertising America of which Grant's Thornhill enters as corporate executive.

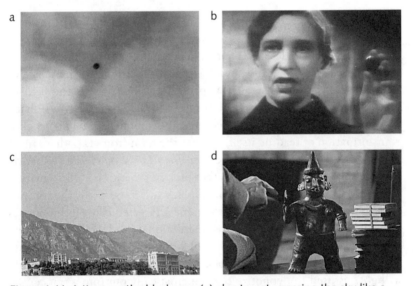

Figure 1. Variations on the black sun: (a) clay target, crossing the sky like a black hole, shot at by cinematic marksmen in the first *Man Who Knew Too Much*; (b) black marble called a "light" is held up in the false temple of sun worshippers to cinematically hypnotize; (c) police plane—surveillance, mechanized black sun, over the Mediterranean ("middle-earth") in *To Catch a Thief*; and (d) *pre*-Columbian "figure" containing secrets on microfilm, positioned *between* a pointing index finger (photographic indexing) and a stack of books (the archive).

This study assumes that Hitchcock's work is sufficiently installed in the canon, and known to a wide number of audiences, that one can address numerous of his scenes as part of the cultural background. This assumption is as well founded in the domain of film production itself—where these works and this name are ceaselessly returned to, evoked, and stolen from unpersuasively—as it is in academic criticism. "Hitchcock" in this regard is the closest thing the cinematic canon has to a core text that can be cited or commonly referenced. That status places it in a peculiar, and empowered, position for the reader. One can address Hitchcock's oeuvre as an event within a transition from a bibliocentric culture to one of telemedia—a transition he himself ceaselessly marks—or, beyond that, as a perhaps still unexplored event in a broader set of histories, say, in the globalization of what can be called the tele-archive and the epistemology of the image.

I became intrigued with Hitchcock by accident, the sort of accident attributed to the young Uncle Charlie in *Shadow of a Doubt*. The charming serial strangler of merry widows eschews all photographs of himself, but, it turns out, there is a single picture of Charlie that his adoring sister Emma has kept from the day of his "accident." This accident occurred, she explains, when he ran his bicycle into a streetcar—two vehicular machines of cinematic transport. Previous to that day, Emma recalls, Charlie was a tireless and perpetual *reader*. After that event, identified with the photograph's logic, he would not read again—or at least in the same way.

For me this collision occurred during the "rerelease" of the five works that had been withdrawn from circulation—a withdrawal, clearly, Hitchcock designed to ignite, posthumously, a different critical perspective on the dimensions of what he was doing. I had at the time been writing a dissertation chapter on Plato, an interminable and micrological essay that explored why or how the "Platonic" reading inverted what was demonstrably going on in the text—and the implications of how inverse interpretation can install itself in or as histories (metaphysics). I put this aside for a month, during which I chanced into what I thought were movies at the Quad in New York City's West Village, where these rereleased works were playing. Everything I set aside came swarming back across the screen, which should have been impossible. Imponderable visual and aural rhymes, letteral patterns, disquisitions on the giving and taking of "face," a virtual figural encyclopedia. There were, as the auteurist criticism for some reason does not tell us, *incessant* skits on the impasses of language and writing, on the blockage of speech, on media, number, and diverse machines. I looked further. When the ghost of Platonic solar imagery would turn up, as in the early *Man Who Knew Too Much*, it would be openly shot at like a clay target by marksmen, or set up as a fake temple of sun worshippers, which types like Peter Lorre used as a cinematic "front." A certain Hitchcock knew too much. It was during Judy's reading and tearing up of her letter to Scottie in *Vertigo*, a gesture that had the theater hushed, that I broke into loud laughter. Something became obvious: rather than assume a position in the aesthetic hierarchies as the mass cultural latecomer to literary culture, every scriptive or graphic event back to and before hieroglyphics (and forward past digitalization) was, now, a dossier in the teletechnic archive that this cinema assumed to access, put in a state of emergency.

After repeated exposure, one becomes aware of elaborate citational networks of signature effects at work in Hitchcock's oeuvre. It remains unanalyzed why, for instance, a proper name either using or involving the word *Mar(k)* turns up in every work: Hitchcock was allowing something he would name *mar(k)ing* to re-mark itself in the web of verbal units and names. Then lists of names repeatedly cover key characters, displacing the premise of "name" itself. For another, the "cameos" don't at all do what they were advertised to do, namely, claim the territory for Alfred Hitchcock, auteur's auteur. The opposite: they did not just create a "permanent parabasis" of every mise-en-scène, they collapsed any outside-the-frame—linking each scene or work to each, fractally. The dismembered body turns up in pieces attached to incidental characters even (the balding head, the lower lip). The teletechnic archive was destined, Hitchcock knew, to globalize itself, much as it was destined to produce, if one likes, something like Nietzsche's "last man"—a programmed consumer and tourist. It would already partake of wide cultural deformations, the advance of techno-weaponry, accelerated consumption, terrestrial eviscerations, each marked in the late films. It would also engage war scenarios that made no sense in their own terms, but did as an engulfing critique of both sides as effects of post-Enlightenment epistemology.

The cameos seemed to link sets and scenes, fractalizing each into citational anthologies and webs. As if in imitation, every signifying agent in Hitchcock would do cameo citations of itself, return, recur, be made up or re-marked otherwise: phrases and syllables (hence the recurrent phrase "sounds like"), letters, partial names, actors, what Hitchcock perhaps meant when speaking of self-plagiarism. And beneath these a ceaseless invocation of teletechnics of all variety together with language and memory.

One could propose a subtitle for this volume—*Teletechnics, Chronographs, and the Broken Word*—to focus on the consequences of reading Hitchcock's practice as an event and critical intervention in the advance of teletechnic histories (including globalization) of which it remains a key and cipher. This work supplements volume I of this project, *Secret Agents*. That study pursues the consequences of viewing Hitchcock's antiocular cinema in Benjaminian terms as "shock," intervention, and epistemo-political assault. After World War II, when the imaginary of an embattled home state has collapsed as a MacGuffin, and the teletechnic empire would have been consolidating itself under the rubric of "America," what had once been subversive secret agents as if from "a certain foreign power" are recast *within* a totalization of horizons, the cinematic prowler deauraticizing entire structures of mass tourism, simulation, marriage, theft, the law, "psychoanalysis," gender performatives—powerful revenants of Enlightenment programs. Whereas the companion volume asks how what are here called *cryptonymies* operate in "Hitchcock" as epistemo-political agents mobilized against the home state's ocularcentric and auratic premises—as part of this "cinema's" espionage and an assault on state hermeneutics—the present volume, *War Machines*, asks how that "revolutionary uplift" (as *Vertigo* applies the term to a brassiere) operates *after* that war's end, when this insurrection is, instead, distributed in the totalized horizon of the victor's emergent teletechnic empire, sometimes called "America" (including Hollywood).

The "black sun" of the first *Man Who Knew Too Much* migrates, say, into the prowling house cat of John Robie in *To Catch a Thief*. The term *teletechnics* highlights how, today, Hitchcock can be read as rethinking cinema as part of a formal transformation generally, of which "globalization" and techno-accelerations (telemarketing, mnemonics, terrestrial consumptions) are an extension; *chronographs* names the active redisposition of temporalities that this practice encounters; and "the broken word"—translating the breaking of the jewel thief's *parole* in *To Catch a Thief*—implies two things: the manner in which cinema here breaks its contract with its supposed public as a structural given, and cinema's shattering of the word, or *logos*, in the dematerialization site of synaesthetic and graphic traces. The weapon of mass de(con)struction Hitchcock saw as part of cinema's "shock" effect shifts from a military secret to operating in a manner mockingly suggested by the young Arnie's futuristic ray gun in *The Trouble with Harry*: from within the "home." What emerges is a weapon, instead, with chronographic and teletechnic powers implanted at the presumptive heart ("Hitchcock") of the auteurist and ocularcentric canon. The implication puts in question not only how "cinema" has been depicted (i.e., as a visual medium, representational at its core) but also the disposition of times, the séancing of pasts and virtual futures of which its advent partakes. As the "home state" Hitchcock assaulted consolidates itself in the "postglobal" teleculture of various imagined presents, the deauraticization of the cinematic—the latter understood as partaking of an installed *epistēmē* of contemporary memory management—requires that the histories of the teletechnic era be, perhaps, remapped or redecided again.

# Introduction: Hitchcock's Esperanto

> Pardon me while the brain reels.
> —Mannin, *Secret Agent*

> One of *television*'s greatest contributions is that it brought mur-
> der back into the *home* where it belongs.
> —Alfred Hitchcock, "After-Dinner Speech"

Can "Hitchcock" today—as if to say, in the afterlife of cinema—can
be seen as something of a cipher event in the still-evolving histories of
teletechnics?[1] Jean-Luc Godard speaks of a Hitchcock who, at the proliferating dawn of teleglobalization, wielded power on the level of global
conquerors (he mentions as lesser examples Napoleon and Hitler). The
director's name and drawl infiltrated global media to render that voice
and girth the most recognized signature of mass culture: constantly, in
the guise of "black humor," making light of the public's individual and
collective murder, later transforming critical culture and, today, still
driving and informing Hollywood production.[2] Yet throughout the
early espionage thrillers, a cinematic "villain" assaults the state with
the aim of epistemo-political sabotage, allying this practice to bombing
(the atomization and arresting temporality of photography), a shot, an
alteration of memory. And because it grasps itself as a spectral agency,
cinema would do its work within graphic memory loops, within what I
will call here the tele-archives or the domain of inscriptions.

In the first *Man Who Knew Too Much,* the cinematic front of the
anarchists' false temple of sun worshippers suspends heliocentrism and
the worship of Enlightenment tropes. The analogy between a movie
house hiding subversives dismisses the ocularcentrism that film was
supposed to uphold, a program linked to the identification of seeing
and knowing. The work "knows too much" to pretend. The plotters,

led by Peter Lorre (who has been sprung from German expressionism) make one mistake: they kidnap the daughter of a *tourist* to keep him from talking (hence the Hamletian title) when he is passed a secret by a dying international agent. Written on paper in a shaving brush held up before a mirror, as if it facilitated a cut, the secret has to do with cinema's powers. Its discovery is coincident with a Babel of languages spoken outside the door of the Swiss hotel: a salad of phonemes not possible to disentangle. The plotters need to keep this secret contained, as the entry into the temple is at each step cinematically marked. First, outside a dentist shop hangs a set of giant teeth: seeing as masticating, alternating teeth like celluloid frames. The name of the dentist, George Barbor, recurs to the word *barber* and to the shaving brush. He would cinematically anesthetize with gas. Lawrence evades this by reversing positions and proceeds. In the "Tabernacle of the Sun" duped parishioners give to the collection plate (film tickets) in order to be illuminated and initiated. When ministress Agnes chooses Clive for cinematic initiation into the "mysteries of the sevenfold ray," she hypnotizes him with the black marble, which she oddly calls a light, and her face shatters for him into light rays. The initiation leads to a precession of light and face. It is not the nascient tourist Lawrence's job to understand the cinematic mysteries, and, in reconstituting his ersatz family, he blindly wrecks the world-altering plotters.

The black sun that cancels every simulacrum and solar myth also serves as a trace and secret agent. It will shape-shift across the oeuvre. A black hole in the fabric of the visible, from which the latter's gift of light is artificed—as if its center—it unreels as a black dog that runs across the snow to precipitate an inaugural "accident," then migrates here and elsewhere across feet, chocolate, cats and birds, cryptographies, cameos, marbles and buttons, excrement. The black sun has other implications: it revokes any indexal or mimetic claim of the photograph; it precedes visual and aural effects, positing an agency that moves between different memory systems and phenomenal orders (braiding graphic and phonemic planes). The Avenger in *The Lodger,* the serial ripper, is faceless, swarms out from the suspended reflecting particles of the London fog (cinema). It may or may not be, as some recent critics have suggested, that with the erosion of traditional humanistic studies and the political models of cultural studies, critical work should seek to organize itself, not around the nation or individual language, not around identity politics and subaltern positioning, not around the "global" (given its phantasmatic rotundity) but around something else without representational status perhaps called the planetary (Gayatri Spivak, Masao Miyoshi, Wai Chee Dimock).[3] If so, then a deanthropomorphized reading of cinema may be essential for renegotiating the powers and frontiers of the tele-image, which informs contemporary perceptual and mnemonic regimes. The supposed repeal of what Walter Benjamin called "aura," the withdrawal of personification, must be reinterrogated. This may be the implication of the "earth" in Hitchcock's use of the name *George Barbor*" in the above cinematic skit involving the sun. The first name recurs in *North by Northwest*'s nonexistent *"George* Kaplan"—what translates obliquely as head *(capo)* of the earth *geo* and delivers us to the depersonified faces of Mount Rushmore. The still-unfinished "histories" of the tele-image remain intertwined not only with "global" consumption but also with evaporating biosystems (oceans, species, reserves), techno-wars and weapons. This attacking "cinema" would be allied to what would later be called the "bird war": the eye pecking and wing slashes of black marks and the cut, prehistorial and teletechnic otherness that cannot be anthropomorphized.

Benjamin observed that the advent of cinema was registered as sensorial and cognitive "shock," the mobilized dynamite of the tenth of a second, and in turn promised the atomization of perceptual networks. The tele-archive can be likened not only to a nonsite from which memory and perception are inscribed but one Hitchcock would name, in the absence of any originating logic, "mother." That is, as a motherboard of signature effects and citational networks from which time, agency, and semantics appear generated. The various interpretive exercises of this study attempt to elaborate this prospect. In the British thrillers the "villains" represent cinema's assault on the home state's epistemological models. Mr. Memory, in his vaudeville act that opens *The 39 Steps,* presents a trope of the cinematic. He is introduced as having recorded millions and millions of "facts"—so many celluloid frames in rapid succession, banal and unmodified. Yet Mr. Memory has secretly crossed over to the other side and become the machinal courier of a formula for a silent bomber, a weapon of mass de(con)struction. It threatens the state and must be, again and again, put down.

## Esperanto

The cameos had always been decoys. Hitchcock knew he would be looked for, so he sent a simulacrum before the torn curtain, collapsing the membrane in the process, linking signs and gestures to scenes across the oeuvre. The cameos solicit a Pavlovian recognition yet perform

Figure 2. *Trouble with Harry*'s "R——nie" with cinema as futuristic ray gun.

the opposite, the enfolding of a frame upon itself, no set or syllable unmarked. The corpulent body has no place in the set, is doubly *atopos*. The cameo nonetheless releases something: an exfoliating network of markers and citational agents. It dissolves the arresting image into molecular agents, recoalesced as from inscriptions. What we call "Hitchcock" emerges in and is produced by a telemnemonics, at times across anagrams, telegraphy, citational graphics.

Two decades ago William Rothman, in *Hitchcock: The Murderous Gaze,* chanced on an unusable secret. At the core of his auteurist project, Rothman speaks of something that recurs so frequently it will be called, above all else, Hitchcock's signature—even though the critic is unable to assign a content, proper role, or function to it. Accordingly, since it has been denied entrance to criticism:

> The view is through the bars of the banister, and the frame is dominated by the bars in the foreground. I call this pattern of parallel vertical lines Hitchcock's / / / / sign. It recurs at significant junctures in every one of his films. At one level, the / / / / serves as Hitchcock's signature: it is his mark on the frame, akin to his ritual cameo appearances. At another level, it signifies the confinement of the camera's subject; we might say that it stands for the barrier of the screen itself. It is also associated with sexual fear and the specific threat of loss of control or breakdown.[4]

That is, a series of slashes or bars, what Rothman calls the bar series, white and black alternation, metronomic and paralleled by aural knocking, present in a row of teeth or banisters or train tracks, a movement that is none, a seriality of repetitions that folds back as prefigural, atomizing, a reduction to footsteps or traces into which all can be visually renetworked, present even in word names ("William," "Lil[a]," or "ill"). Rothman lets out of Pandora's box an *ill* that could alter assumptions about visibility or the graphematics of cinema.[5] If the bar series can appear as a typographic sequence, / / / /, can even be called Hitchcock's premier "signature," what does that entail for the *conceit* of signature? What does it mean to sign, "I, 'Hitchcock,'" here, or inversely, "I, bar series," when that would dispossess the very premise of the I or the eye? If this signature and graphic *notation* is that *of* "cinema," then it is more primordial than the letters of any proper name. It could mobilize wholly other networks, leaping between, preceding like a cat. Such a sabotaging of ocular premises by the apparatus supposed to serve it could only occur as an assault on the tele-*archive* as such.[6]

As though on cue, one recently witnessed the dismantling of the auteurist model by its own promoters. When Peter Conrad titled his book *The Hitchcock Murders,* he used the term *murder* to imply an invasive and transfigurative assault that occurs within the structural sabotage of the medium as practiced.[7] Cinema would be among other things the obverse of any "phenomenology"—the too obvious projection of celluloid traces from behind the head to be taken as the visible. If something would alter the inscriptions of this system, as the early thrillers propose, it would alter regimes of old software, the senses as hermeneutically programmed, the archive as site of virtual pasts and futures, temporality, the eye, the "human." One might require a bar series effect to vaporize the constructions and definition of image itself, like the "London fog" said to be the narrative subject of *The Lodger.* Atomization, like the pictured buildings of Piccadilly Circus melting away for Verloc on the window of the fish tank of the zoo, before the nongaze of prehistorial animemes.

Figure 3. Spellbinding lines.

Just when one thought one had perhaps found Hitchcock's "signature"—fool's gold of the auteurist pioneer—one stumbled instead across the bar series, that is, across a signature system older than history, perception, or any one definition of "cinema"—one that arrests and clearly refuses metaphor or personification. This bar series can hardly be said to exist: is it slashes and columns or space and intervals? It is like the "do not forget" of Hamlet *père,* only it cannot not forget (and continue to cite) itself. It breaks the surface, like the formal waltzing that descends from nowhere into *Shadow of a Doubt,* a memory outside of memory. The Hitchcock political narrative is again and again one of the importation, at any instant, of an epistemo-political sabotage or suspension, a historial intervention in the name of teletechnics that would be covered up.[8]

Hitchcock remarked to Truffaut that his attention was drawn by F. W. Murnau's experiment with a universal sign language when the latter deleted title cards from his silent *The Last Laugh:* "They were making it while I worked at UFA. In that film Murnau even tried to establish a universal language by using a kind of esperanto. All the street signs, the posters, the shop signs, were in this synthetic language."[9] Hitchcock's "esperanto" is made not by signs on the street alone but by the atomization of signifying agencies that mark and re-mark their presence in the works, and can take the form of signature effects that recur, once established, in cameos of themselves. Thus phonemes referring to other meanings seem notched by the recurrent phrase "sounds like" inserted into various dialogues as a reminder. In this way, the idea of an esperanto made up of public signs (a "universal language") is transferred to the cinematic deployment of signifying agents void of programmed reference. These proliferate like a sort of Benjaminian *reine Sprache* (pure language), atomized and momentarily desemanticizing. All variety of telemedia traverse these films: machines for telegraphics and telephonics reveal themselves—the carousel, the stone millwheel, the bomb and gunshot, telegraph wires, printing presses, libraries, record players, spy codes, numericisms, the little boy's toy ray gun, uranium for atom bombs, telepathies, kitchens, stenography, trains, of course, and so on.[10] McKenzie Wark notes in a Deleuzian vein in "Vectoral Cinema": "Every kind of media of recording gets its moment in Hitchcock's films, but is always subordinated to the designs of cinema. There is the auction house and the monumental sculpture in *North by Northwest.* There are acrobats, an LP record and a concert in *The Man Who Knew Too Much* (1956). There's fireworks and fancy dress in *To Catch a Thief* (1955)."[11] But this notion was already implied in Hitchcock's first cameo, in *The Lodger.* There he is set in a glass booth as seeming editor of a newsroom (imprinting as recording) and before giant printing press gears followed by the disseminating teletype and wireless machines. Friedrich Kittler has tracked this association of telegraphy and cinema extensively without fully extending its analysis into practices of mnemonic intervention.[12] Intervening in regimes of memory accords not only with typographical machines but also with animation—the site where the speed of the replay produces animation effects of movement ("life") and accords, equally, with a nonanthropomorphic domain of animals and technicity as such. In *Sabotage,* the cinematic bomb placed on public transport is allied with singing birds and, during a trip to the zoo, with premammalian fish and turtles that appear in the tank's glass as if on a screen like that in the Bijou that shows a Disney cartoon of a bird-woman and bird-man.

What secret agents? In Hitchcock everything that recurs is cited in advance of itself as "set": objects and pieces of furniture, actors, proper names and syllables *(port-, mon-, fr-),* sounds and redoubled citations, verbal and visual relays, cameos, fragments of a cut-up body (legs, ears, hands), bridges, letters *(M, P, R, W, O, C, A),* numeration, surrogate doubles, and so on. In *The 39 Steps* Mr. Memory, who initially repeats memorized "facts" to his public, is called a "*re*markable man." In the process of being remarked, the "fact" turns retroactively into a citation. The vaudeville act of the fallen Mnemosyne, pitiably mechanical, accelerates to become the courier for a weapon of mass de(con)struction, the formula of *letters* and *numbers* for a cinematic war machine. What one might call Hitchcock's "esperanto" has nothing to do with Murnau's formal experiment. It precedes and traverses semaphoric networks, mnemonic techniques, phonetic and graphematic figures. These devolve at times to micrological marks, like the "microfilm" hidden in the pre-Columbian "figure." When it telescopes into black sun figures or the prowling black cat that opens *To Catch a Thief,* it leverages citational markets, traverses libraries, and empties museum archives.

## Travel Services

Hitchcock's "credit sequences" and opening scenes are strewn with such rebuses. They are in their covert ways as invasive as the beating black wings that carve up the visual surface struggling to open *The Birds*— gashes of, and within, the order of the "visual," epistemo-mimetic machines, and so on. They put into play advertising logics, they lure, they betray in advance.

Often these thresholds comment on cinematic tourism. *To Catch a Thief* features a credit sequence as routinely dismissed as the film itself. It is nothing but a display window, a travel service, as it calls itself. The glass window, which reflects activity across the street (hence behind the camera), cites the screen as a faux transparency of kitsch icons. So pointlessly frothful seems the accompanying score that one fails to note anything more than the apparent *promise* of the display case: we, with the film as serving agent, will turn up in glamorous "France," land of champagne, yachts, the Eiffel Tower, and bohemian street sketches. The consumer is derisively solicited by touristic icons. "Travel service," aside from troping cinema's servicing role in transporting its client (amidst other services), also might translate as teletechnics as such.

But the display window is active. It rewrites a previous credit sequence that Hitchcock was clearly brooding over, that for the first *Man Who Knew Too Much*—the one "Hitchcock" film he would enigmatically remake, and that in his next outing. It involves a vignette in which travel brochures are browsed through by a *hand,* putting the viewing and touristic "public" in the position of the absent eye or head. "Knowing too much" appears at first to involve knowing too much about seeing and cognition: the tourist eye seeks what it has been given as a model for, an ad to spur desire to locate the model's model. The hand picks out a pictured brochure of "Griesalp." The promise of (cinematic) travel organizes perception to "see" or discover that then preinstalled image, into which the screen dissolves as if into the real mountain "itself" (now a cinematic image). In the later film's window the operation has moved from the individual tourist to a thieving corporate service. The credit sequence *discredits.* It is a front. This time it is the same "tourist" who will, when instantly conveyed to Nice in the next frames, be vicariously robbed (raped, murdered) with the shriek of the cold cream–faced American tourist on discovering her jewels have been taken. "Light" will be stolen by the black cat ambling across a darkened rooftop—swank avatar of the black sun figure from that same earlier film. Whatever nonplace this Riviera signifies, it is rife with Mediterranean props from a postwar Nice that has become the casino-like magnet for affluent tourists and a spectral playground of simulacra and media depletion. One can reread the work (if not Hitchcock's oeuvre) from this credit sequence, as I will attempt later. The window is an avatar of the land pirates of *Jamaica Inn* who wave a lantern to signal to ships in distress at night: the light in the darkened movie house, the traveler's seeking illumination. Promised safety by the light, their ship is wrecked and they are murdered or knifed—that is, cut—and robbed.

What sort of wars were going on within cinema's advent as "shock" that would have decided in their outcome the futures we inhabit? Could these have been decided otherwise? That is, were there other functions to the image than the official documenting, indexing, Enlightenment-driven, mimetic, auratic ones? "Hitchcock" pursues this question through labyrinths and spectrographic networks, as if spellbound. He variously referenced his constructions as time bombs, nuclear blasts, as lightning or *Blitz,* including his late mocking fantasy of just attaching electrodes to "the public" and forgoing the film itself. There are other tropes for his practice that Hitchcock uses: sabotage, wrecking, hypnotic theft or implantation, serial strangling, anesthesia and telesthesia, catabases to the underworld, séancing. The auteur "Hitchcock" has thus been a front, too. The model that has dominated "Hitchcock" criticism since its ascent with Claude Chabrol and Éric Rohmer's study—that is, identificatory, metaphysical, ocularcentric, auratic, historicizing readings, an astonishing assemblage that remains among the richest in film studies—appears closed, and something else, or other, *knocks.* Serially. To interrogate this other *Hitchcock* would be to séance the "present's" teletechnic construction.

# I. Travel Service Window

# 1. Transports

The history of the movie camera thus coincides with the history of automatic weapons. The transport of pictures only repeats the transport of bullets. In order to focus on and fix objects moving through space, such as people, there are two procedures: to shoot and to film. In the principle of cinema resides mechanized death as it was invented in the nineteenth century: the death no longer of one's immediate opponent but of serial nonhumans.

—Friedrich Kittler, *Gramophone, Film, Typewriter*

## Port Said

In Hitchcock's early anatomy of cinematic tourism, *Rich and Strange,* the title's promise of Prospero's transformation seems to allow the two cinematic tourists to circle the globe and return to the banality of home—a stationary return to a dwelling occupied by a black cat. Harried by the machinal nature of modern times, the cinematic beckons as escape displaced, thanks to a monetary gift, onto geographic sites in a virtual map. The result of travel is privation: they lose money, almost lose their marriage, their cruise ship sinks, and they return to a now "rich and strange" banality that the cat oversees. A double of that cat turns up in the Chinese junk they are rescued by when the cruise ship sinks. But when this mobile black trace is, as it turns out, cooked and eaten unwittingly by them its stretched skin is viewed held against the sky, and it melds with a spheroid moon—emblem of eclipse, and evisceration. Innumerable cats as simulant traces cascade through the shadow play of the ghosted cinematic house called *Number 17,* in which all variations of technical distortions of theft, light play, and sound (or fake muteness and deafness) spill into a runaway *train* chase which wrecks at the ferry crossing. In *Rich and Strange,* the ship's various ports of call are termed, on title cards, "crossings." What is, or would be, crossed, or magically translated by a cinematic acceleration that is two-sided: a privative or thieving promise before the spectral tourist or mass consumer who comes to crave otherness or escape and the intimation of a lethal crossing of borders, bearing weapons of mass (de)construction or archival intervention?

Tourism is marked as a cognitive contamination. Linked to mass tourism (national monuments), it conjures nonsites by which it plunges the eye into the cognitive and political intrigues of what Benjamin called the sensorium. It cites the viewer as structurally blind to the mechanics and stakes of the visual explosions and semioclasms under examination, to "experience." It engraves the tourist as ocularist *hypocrite lecteur* doubled over his own absence and, if anything, helping to ruin the cinematic insurgencies staged as Hitchcock doubles by the teletechnic "villains." The promised transport to exotic sites that would be a selling point of this travel service—come to "St. *Moritz*"—is of course a stationary transport and matter of sets. Transport is tropological and unassured of its own event: one may return to London untransformed or end hanging off the face of a depersonified earth in near vertical free fall at Mount Rushmore. Vehicles are the material carriers and couriers. Cars and trains dominate, the latter the most explicit double of cinema (clattering tracks, alternating lights, sometimes of the underworld or Underground in London). Transport cancels the site of departure, home, while providing, in its acceleration of rushing frames, no arrival or even "present"—which, in its way, the accelerations and crashes, timed shots and time bombs seek to excise. Alternately, it is short-circuited, doubled in the circular chase or double pursuit. Hitchcock's cameo in *Blackmail* will find him *interrupted reading* on an Underground train, as are other key characters, usually women, as if the cinematic rush occurs on or induces a hyperbolic break within the enterprise of graphematic reading. Cary Grant, in *North by Northwest,* is abducted to Vandamm's library where, about to accelerate in a nonexistent direction, he quips about "catching *up* on his reading."

In *Rich and Strange,* the ports of call include Egypt's "Port Said." Given the priority of Egyptian hieroglyphics to any chronograph of pictographic inscription, "Port Said" ironizes an impermeability to speech underlined by the residual silent picture title cards. The term *port* proposes a site of border entry or *crossing over* arrested by an aporia in and of speech and words, a blockage of communication by dissimulating language—Lawrence blackmailed into silence, Iris not believed, Father

Logan barred from disclosing confessions—appearing structural to the epistemological arrest transport induces. In *The 39 Steps,* the circular double chase that will return to a preoriginary Palladium departs with the many-named "Annabella's" murder at *Port*land *Place* (alliterative site for stationary transport located near the BBC telecasting tower). That *word unit* ricochets elsewhere in contaminating citations (Constance Porter, Portland, Oregon). Travel or tourism is not a motif in Hitchcock, as if it were some theme, nor does the prospect of stationary movement solve the riddle. This cinema is vertiginously literal and constant in its attention to vehicles and their accelerations, crashes, abruptions, sinking in bogs. It is, if anything, also a sort of *going under,* in the Nietzschean sense, as to the Underground whose train sets will appear. Transport references itself to machines and teletechnic interruptions. It has to do with the material logics of vehicles of public teletransport and, alternately, the vertical or stationary hyperbolism of cognitive accelerations.

In these typologies the cinematic tourist is not just a dupe, to be despoiled, relieved of money, cognitively raped, oblivious of the underworld he or she already inhabits called "life." The tourist is heroicized by undoing cinema's revolutionary interventions. The tourist may witness or bring down, uncomprehending, the transformation of the banal indexed image, Mr. Memory's "fact," into an accelerated war machine—something "rich and strange." All focuses on machines of transport. Cars accelerate, stop, crash, double back in folds, display whirling tires. The circuitry flows, or spins, backward. Uncle Charlie, waiting to throw young Charlie on the tracks, counts down the Zeno-like divisions: "Faster. Faster. Faster . . . *Now.*"

In *Number 17* the cinematic train is a runaway that will wreck at the Channel crossing; in *Secret Agent* it will have to be stopped, bombed by planes from afar at the command of the Olympian spymaster "old man 'R.'" Once accelerated, the machine feeds off the seriality of an "$N + 1, + 1, + 1 . . .$" In *North by Northwest* a single direction is triggered that is technically nonexistent, the Benjaminian "one-way street" or what

Figure 4. Back-spinning disk morphs as zeroid wheel under detective van—film-shooting crew (*Blackmail*).

Paul de Man will call the *irreversible* shift to a performative model of the event that cannot return to the endless displacement of tropological systems. As if to ascertain what is being left behind, the work opens in the sheer traffic of Manhattan and stalled public transport—also at the beginning of *Rich and Strange*—which is tied not only to the emptiness of metaphoric systems but the advertising logic associated with the cinematic image's manipulation of memory. How does one leave the cinematic miasma and rush of frames by turning to its *material* vehicles? How does a car find itself in Norman's bog?

## Train to Constantinople

Where would Hitchcock's already runaway cinematic train go, outbidding its own acceleration, if it did not derail at the port, as it does in *Number 17*?

In *Secret Agent* the prospect returns as the secret agent on the final train ride to Constantinople must be stopped, or so the British spymaster "old man 'R'" determines from his fog-shrouded, cinematic sauna. He has lost faith in his own bumbling agents or actors, the antithetical pair Peter Lorre and John Gielgud. Neither the cinematic shockmaster Lorre nor the wooden Shakespearean—both ends of the "acting" spectrum are covered—will be able to stop the agent named "Marvin." After all, if Marvin, the real secret agent, gets to Constantinople, something will be cognitively released that will turn the tide of the first world war retrospectively against Britain by throwing the figural power of the Orient to its foes. And if that then-past war is altered in its outcome, well, the present of the film's making would be, with Britain, altered or erased, alternate futures permitted. Under the guise of the war, it is important to keep cognition of the *mar(k)* and its teletechnic role from getting out. The home state, "Britain," with its letteral spymaster, will have to put it down, contain this knowledge of its deauratic and material base. The cinematic as state apparatus must contain its double, the cinematic as teletechnic revolt, even if that is in the one actant who doesn't even try to act, Robert Young's Marvin, bearer of the *mar-* signature.

So another secret agency is invoked in the aerial bombings sent out to telesthenically bring the unruly narrative, with its hopeless starts and stops, its incompetent acting and improvisations, its *contretemps,* to a halt. This "other" secret agency is sent in from the sky and is explosive, impersonal, Olympian. That "old man 'R,'" as Marvin calls him just before this occurs, does this ascribe it to the powers of *re*currence, *re*petition, *re*portage, to police their pretense of identity and England's hermeneutic control of time and memory. It also needs to obliterate something the film itself has released to view or excess already—that the secret agency, the catalytic that traverses sensation and event, is not a person at all but something like a black trace that permeates the orders of the visual and the aural. It will include black dogs, wailing, marbles, feet, chocolates, obliterating unitary sound, a sort of black hole effect within the representational order. In no other film of Hitchcock's is this *secret agency* so explicitly focused on and linked to all manner of linguistic effects, including telepathy, language lessons, the Babel of tongues, telescopes, telesthenic action.

Since human actors are caught in the endless citation and performativity of speech, a Hamletian dilemma, Hitchcock unfairly appoints the Shakespearean Gielgud to purvey by association (and betray) the agency that permeates the historial event or turning point. And this is why the clues that the bumbling Gielgud and Lorre track, after mistakenly doing away with Caypor, the British-sounding German gentleman with the telepathic dog, lead to Hitchcock's most fascinating trope for his cinematic machine. That is not the music hall or the temple of sun worship but what is offered as another front, this time for production: the faux Swiss chocolate factory that produces the little black bonbons that, in a way, summarize the nonanthropomorphic secret agency being tracked from the beginning, only now assimilating to the chocolate secret writing, excrement, and a covert and transhistorial communication system on the order of Thomas Pynchon's *Crying of Lot 49* or the citational networks that run throughout Hitchcock's oeuvre and, in their course, absorb or activate, seemingly, every archival trace or trajectory within past and future mnemonics. The chocolate factory will turn out to be a front—with its production of sweet cinematic confections that conceal a kind of excrement—for what is called the "spies' post office." In the chocolate wrappers there is transliterated writing that the intended recipient reads, throwing away the chocolate itself. One message is intercepted, which is how the name "Marvin" is learned or revealed. This discloses the scene of cinematic production not to be a factory of facts or of pictures even but the relay and transmission of writing absolutely threatening to the home state or its hermeneutic spymaster. Sitting in his sauna, "R" is housed in cinematic mists too but is dedicated to containing its import for the state and repetition. Even Gielgud will say to a brutish-looking Turkish soldier on the train to Constantinople, the ancient capital of cognition if not constancy, that he comes from

"Hollywood." The cultural power of Shakespearean acting is undone without Gielgud's awareness of his aid in dethroning it—a setup.

"Old man 'R,'" as the defender of Britain and British espionage, signals that the state would foreclose the revelation of cinematic "marking" that Hitchcock's train would epistemo-politically install, preserving a faux regime of time, the senses, historial outcome.

This mechanized site is less of production than transcription and relay, tended by giant gears and white laboratory coats. Yet, briefly, the entire place will erupt in deafening fire alarms—a prospective conflagration. It is in a state of emergency. The spies' post office uses the chocolate factory as a front, a network central that extends, forward and back in chronology, across the oeuvre past and to come. One cinematic agency, policing repetitions with "old man R," must terminate, simply bomb out from above, another, the dangerous one of the enemy agent disclosing a postal system of markings leading toward an intervention in history, altering (in retrospect, here) the outcome of a war that would determine states and borders to come.

## "Think Thin"

Hitchcock's corpulence, like the exorbitant ingestion of meanings by the image, was always a signifier to be exploited—whether rendering the figure unthreatening and neutered, perhaps infantile, or signaling formality in excess. In *Lifeboat,* he would appear in a "Reduco Obesity Slayer" ad in a newspaper—advertising his then current weight loss, but gesturing to the semantic reduction, as the ad calls it, to the sea and lack of the discursively directionless vessel of transport. In *North by Northwest* this reduction becomes absolute. The work opens with a bizarre pun on the end of the preceding film, *Vertigo.* Ad exec Grant (the "star" as marketing product) is coming *down* in an elevator as if from the bell tower on which the last work left a shattered James Stewart, body broken like a marionette's in outline. Enough of that stuff; we'll try again in a more totally vapid vein with wisecracks, one-liners, bad advertising jingles, none of this mock-tragic, mock-Wagnerian exhaustion. The ground floor door opens and Grant mechanically greets the elevator man, whose name is "Eddie." *Eddie,* as in being of the past, the portals to the past (the verb designate -*ed*); *eddy,* as in a vertigo swirl. The last words of *Vertigo* were the nun's haunting, "I thought I heard voices," as the whole agonizing fandango of Stewart and Novak approaches, almost voice, simulated speech emerging from the webworks of mnemonic inscription. Grant tells Eddie to say hello to the *missus,* to which he answers, "We're not talking." The whole departs again, if in a superficial groove, from the blockage of speech and mock inter-subjectivity by language itself, leaving the ad-libbing exec to, again, try to communicate with "Mother" for directions or solace. Not only will "Mother" here be the same age as Grant—both mocking of and suscep-tible to being bribed by him, a prosthetic mom—but he cannot reach her by any telephonic or telegrammatic means. She is at her "bridge" game, after all. And the attempt leads to his abduction and Vandamm's intercession in the library, where he would, he says sarcastically, "catch *up* on (his) reading."

What is interrupted is the sheer traffic of the opening street scenes re-flected in the gridlike mirrors of the midtown skyscraper. What departs is the trajectory, a one-way street that leads to the attack by a mechani-cal sun on a scorched prairie horizon and the vertical suspension and acceleration of movement at Rapid City. What is sought, later, in the nonperson of George Kaplan is, indeed, not only the emptied Grant, who goes as if to "Cary Grant's" own hotel room in the Plaza to find his badly tailored suits not fitting and peppered with dandruff, but what the name literally names, the personification or head *(capo)* of the earth (*Geo*rge): the stone faces of Mount Rushmore that withdraw personifi-cation and aura from the inanimate they pretend to anthropomorphize. But if the interview in the library breaks down the pretense of perfor-mance at once, with James Mason (Vandamm) deriding Grant's acting abilities (as Eva Marie Saint's Eve Kendall later will), or positing a hyper-bolic null behind the performativity of the autocitational "I" that allows the marketable product "Cary Grant" to vamp as an advertising exec (Roger "O."), it also points to books. It is the library after all, except that one cabinet is filled with bourbon. This is the archival site, and the ar-chive of the biblio-era is liquefied as hyperbolic inebriant—anticipating what is later called "alphabet soup," the breakdown of letteration to its atomized components, and with it the entirety of the universal library be-fore the cinematic whirl. When they return the next day to find nothing but books, Mother quips of the missing bourbon, "I remember when it used to come in bottles." But something else initiates this cinematic confrontation between Vandamm and Grant, who may as well be the nonexistent Kaplan (or Archibald Leach for that matter). The drunken Grant is placed in a *Mer*cedes, with its triadic logo, and he leaves to almost plunge over the cliff. He is dumb with and awash in the double vision of accelerated semiosis that the spooled band assures in sucking up all citational relations, all memory storage past and to come, the backspinning wheel that opened *Blackmail* dangling over a cliff's edge. What halts his drunken drive is a bicycle in his headlights, drawing the double vision to a halt and the car to a sandwiched crash: the cinematic and ocular bicycle takes up the liquefaction of literary writing and spins it forward into the single, irreversible, verticular, nonexistent direction that the film itself tracks—and which, in a sense, is contained in the pre-Columbian and pre-American or prehistorial "figure's" microfilm.

Which is why the exchange in the taxi in the opening scene is so curious. Grant callously jumps ahead of a waiting man with a lie that his secretary, Maggie, scolds him for, adding that the man knew he was lying. Words are used as what Grant rebuked Grace Kelly for in his previous outing, being just "playthings." Or advertising shills for designated responses and marketing purposes, the emptying out not only of linguistic usages but also of the structure of the cinematic image as mnemonic implant generating desire for a nonexistent product it sells or wants (re)cognized. The name Maggie incorporates the only use of the *Mar-* variant in a proper name in the film, a nickname for Margaret, which echoes through marguerite back to "Daisy" in *The Lodger*: here a sexually uninteresting amanuensis who takes dictation, as Hitchcock would give in scoring scripts and production.[1] Another's hand writes, but here it writes a vacant ditty dictated to be put on Thornhill's desk the next day, circularly, to remind him to lose weight. The voice fabricates its mnemonic as an advertising jingle, "Think thin," which is to be as if circularly read by himself as another—not as corporate poetry alone but as directive or implant. The alliterative phrase applies to the film, however, and involves a kind of ascesis. It requires a zero figure— Kaplan, Roger "O."—to counter its own emptiness, stalled figurative traffic and endemic superficiality as cinematic trait. One *thinks thin*; one refuses to consume or eat or interiorize, to recover, in the absence of ocular ingestion, thought. "Thinking thin," put on the director's desk, as it were, is a *thinking* that sheds pounds of metaphor, aura, identification. By the time the book-dissolving "dr*ink*" is introduced the fractal syllable, *in*, will be etched and arrested—the drive toward interiorization and ingestion refuted, the superficies accelerated, the imbibing of booklike *ink* become bourbon proved to be without an interior, like Cathy's vomiting in *The Birds*.

In the Oak Bar at the Plaza Hotel there are carriage scenes painted on the wall, predecessor of mechanized traffic, much as the word *oak* will echo the middle initial of Thornhill's name *(O)*. Yet in naming a wood, it will *bar* a figure of the natural image (trees) at its origin or site. The relay from *think thin* to *drink,* of and as a liquefaction of biblio-phemes, seems to equate imbibing or incorporation with the interioriza-tion of meanings, of memory as *Erinnerung*—only this interiorization is precisely blocked. One is in a Zarathustran dilemma as the faux cine-matic espionage thriller opens. The faux narrative will terminate before a crossing of borders, thwarting Vandamm's exit to an unnamed cold war "other," still quipping about the work's performativity and bother-ing to "use *real* bullets."

Two deductions:

- First, the liquefied library incorporates the film's own bookish de-parture from *Hamlet* into a translation of the biblio-*archive* into cinematic mnemonics.
- Second, the titular *direction* involves an irreversible loss of aura and anthropomorphism, echoed in the directive to "think thin."

Thornhill moves from tropological traffic jams to a site where aso-lar machines attack from the sky and where the anthropomorphism of earth is withdrawn from stone faces. Think thin, think *very* thin, beyond the traffic and transport of metaphor or advertising language. Thornhill, who enters as "Grant" posing as the last man of the informa-tion age, is made to go under, in the Nietzschean sense, by embarking on a singular, irreversible direction, a "one-way street" without a place on the compass. When the closing train disappears into the tunnel, at the end, following the fantasy recuperation of Eve Kendall (who has surely fallen off the cliff), the tourist viewer is stroked to think he or she is in on a graphic sexual pun. It is the only way to keep the viewer still while metonymy and anthropomorphism are canceled. But then that would have been the secret of the microfilm inside the pre-Columbian "figure."

## Debris

At the beginning of *Lifeboat* the camera surveys debris floating on the ocean's surface after a ship's wartime sinking—remains and remain-ders immediately following a dismembering Blanchotian disaster.[2] The camera enters always at this point *after* its havoc is registered. Remnants of things float by as Tallulah Bankhead positions her typewriter in a circuit that will force it too to be abandoned as prop. Giving out that it links her to heartless reportage, to mimetic representation, the

a     b

Figure 5. L. B. Jeffries's "disaster" photographs: (a) back-flying wheel shoots into lens, while (b) atomizing cloud mushrooms behind three shadow ghosts.

persistence of the typograph survives the disruptions from below, which it catastrophically induced by preceding all that is phenomenalized or caught by the camera—its photographic agent.

A variant of this preoriginary, citational dismemberment in *Rear Window* occurs in the photograph of the car crash that accounts for James Stewart's leg being in a *cast* (or "James Stewart" for that matter). The tracking of photos made by L. B. Jeffries on the wall forms a mobile montage of montages. Once the key photograph is presented in which the torn-off rear wheel is caught flying with explosive force into the camera Jeffries would have been holding—an explosion of and by the photographic event upon whoever would have pretended to stand behind or outside it—a sequence of other photos is tracked by the probing camera whose movement seems declarative. That sequence terminates in the *negative* of a woman model, a negative whose imprint is then transposed to a magazine cover. The camera moves from the exploding temporal wheel to the cultural negativity materialized as a glamorous woman cited on a fashion magazine's cover: at once advertisement and icon for the violence that Grace Kelly's simulation of herself will imply for Stewart.

Yet in between there are other photographematic disasters: the car disintegrating into a huge fireball; a scene of war; a mushroom cloud with three figures before it, at which point a broken camera enters the frame, lying on a table, as if turned upon itself. The mushroom cloud simulates an atomic blast affiliated with the *Blitz* of the photographic "shock" and dematerialization being studied in detail—and effaced into the premise of the narrative "set."

The photograph links its own shattered camera to a preoriginary semioclasm: it is suspended by the moving images it is embedded in, a lethal flying wheel whose counterspin shoots back at the camera, which induced it by claiming instantaneous capture of the speeding vehicle.

A countercircular logic vaporizes in the mushroom cloud. This wheel, suspended in air, recurs to the wheel that opens *Blackmail,* which seems to spin or loop backward while rushing forward, as a spool, rupturing linear time from within a machinal acceleration impossible to track as a single temporal direction. A preoriginary "disaster" is allied to atomic explosions and fashion pictures of women—transposed into an elusive "before" of narrative space, a negative, recongealed as flotsam. It is itself quested for, like the secret microfilm of Vandamm, mere pieces of celluloid. It is quested for explicitly in *Spellbound* as a key to amnesia and a voided identity, yet turns to the parallel lines or bar series within all woven patterns and snow "tracks." This semioclasm has, already and in advance, altered everything yet seems effaced after being remarked. It emerges momentarily in the *black cat* that crosses Jeffries's courtyard and is the first moving thing the camera tracks.

## No Direction

The opening of *"I Confess"* in Quebec City features a series of traffic arrows on streets. Arrows of this sort point, but as they also appear on the bookstore outside Rusk's building in *Frenzy* as the camera backs away from Babs's murder, they exceed cars (this time, the streets are empty). The very topos of the street will anticipate the name of Karl Malden's detective introduced later, Inspector *La Rue,* and will find no interpretive help from the Catholic orders or the rectory that Hitchcock's apparatus this time will invade. The direction of the arrows, left to right, is the direction of reading, yet this is nonetheless contradicted by the cameo profile of Hitchcock crossing as a shadow only at the top of a cascade of stone steps, moving from right to left—a movement, a direction, that would deracinate any serial model of reading. That "reading" itself could be at stake is confirmed by the site of the lawyer Villette's murder, as we are shown through an open window frame: a *library* lined with books. This preoriginary murder is archival.

    *"I Confess"* is far more abyssal than one would guess from the scant critical attention paid to it—unless that lack of attention testifies inversely to its scandal, which has little to do with the priestly transvestism it exploits. One would, this time, do well to retain the quotation marks around the title since, unlike other titles on which they appear as a generic device of studio marketing (quotes around *"Notorious"* are potentially irrelevant), they draw attention to the premier speech act that, like a black hole, oversees the work. That performative, "confession," *the* speech act of speech acts meant to summarize the "I" at its most unme-

diated, will explode on behalf of all others, taking into its citationality
the disinvaginating power of the cinematic, which bars any and all interiority: one could imagine the work, almost, titled "         "—except then
that would generate more quotation marks to contain the first. It is not
that Father Logan (Montgomery Clift) will present Hitchcock with a
new logic to bar speech, to know too much to speak, miming the muteness of the image, which here is the oath of the priest not to repeat what
has been confessed to him, even when the "confession" involves his own
linguistic rape and entrapment.

The arrows on the street signs do not prevent an obligatory free fall
of the speaking "I," and even Hitchcock's cameo will only appear as a
bodily outline or shadow, though one placed in the position of a certain
rampart, a certain "Do not forget!" without apparent referent—unless
that is to the entirety of the set and setup. That the cinematic compels
an autocitational rift of the speaking "I" does not account for the exorbitant queerness of this mise-en-scène.

"I Confess," as a performative, is in quotation marks: that is, the very
speech act that would be most personal, most direct or honest and so
on, is cited as a citation, a *miming* of subjectivity ("I") that will also
bar Father *Logan* from speaking to save himself, if that were even possible, if even the denial would not be a confirmation and complicity in
the lawyer Villette's murder, which he benefits from since he was being
blackmailed. He is barred from relaying what is confessed to him, a
"secret" (that Keller murdered Villette), which he will then be inscribed
in, and so on. This much, exquisite as it is, is programmatic Hitchcock.
Yet confessions don't stop from multiplying, and they are never to the
point, including Mme Grandfort's "confession" of her affair with Logan,
where what was intended selflessly to exculpate Logan by exposing herself to shame in fact seals his doom—and accelerates her vengeance
against his disinterest in women. Thus the word *direction* fragments. It
is so insistently marked on the *signs* of the film's opening that it seems
compensatory, and the directions indicated are reversed by, well, the
director's cameo. But the breakdown continues beyond the directive
to read against the directions of readability (left to right). As *parole* or
word, *direction* breaks, marks a break with or without quotation marks,
already in the two-sided prefix *di-*, while the remainder, (e)rection,
houses itself momentarily in the priest's "rectory," or in the phantom of
legal right *(Recht),* which the prosecutors, inspectors, courtroom opera-
tives, and religious paraphernalia advertise and peruse. The "rectory,"
echoing *rectum,* targets an anality that the queer motif of the priest's

dresslike attire formalizes. Like *Murder!* where the transvestite Handel Fane is the object of female passion and obsession, or *The Paradine Case,* in which Latour serves a parallel role, Logan or Clift's "homosexual" markings cover a perhaps further degendering and are deployed as a faux secret. The priest's language and the rectory's inner sanctum are violated in advance by his name. The name Logan already incorporates the German for *lie (Lüge),* implying that his speech acts are no more possible to enshrine than Otto Keller's Iago-like use of the confession, which is generated always in quotes. One can say, "I confess to. . . ," but where that is used in *Sabotage* the text will have been first dictated by Detective Spenser to read "I, Carl Anton Verloc . . ."—another's words or institutional saying.

Hitchcock marks this appropriation of another's script to construct "my own" in a predispossessing manner. And it is cinematized as a kind of rape, as when the *bicycle* of another priest is continually introduced into the rectory (and repeatedly falls). This bicycle is spoken of as "shoved" into the rectory. It is given a phallic veneer, yet as a vehicle of transport it cites with its two wheels at once eyes, spectacles, or projector reels, and so on. The ocular bicycle appears in a letteral cipher in the Iago-like Keller, whose first name, Otto, graphically reproduces the apparatus. The foreign-accented Keller's opening "confession" to Logan of Villette's murder violates and entraps the priest who receives it, as if from a position of power. It performs the citational divestiture of the speech act of "confession." In the pretense of the confession the entire claim of speech acts to generate, subjectivity is *irreversibly* emptied. Keller plants and double-binds Logan's knowledge, as if in revenge for Logan's generosity and support. It is tied to a material violation as the image enters memory like the Cat's gloved hand reaching under a sleeping head for the sleeper's *jewels.* The speech act of the "confession" simulates a performativity without performer. Logan is briefly visited by a pubescent boy whose confession, it is clear, would concern masturbation.

The obsessively marked "direction" of *"I Confess"* wavers in faith before the abyss of a speech performativity that backloops to consume its scripted "I's": performance as a discursive event from which there is no other position, no subject effect that precedes it, no confessional, no honesty, no priestly nonperformative, no "half-cast(e)" position. Thus it ends in a theater after a chase through a hotel kitchen (proverbial site in Hitchcock where cinematic entertainments may be confected). Otto Keller's trajectory in the narrative will destroy Villette, himself, Keller's wife (Alma, the name of Hitchcock's wife), and Logan. It repeats in advance a destructive logic of transport, the "direction" of directionality precedent to the Nietzschean turn that *North by Northwest* performs, the death drive of and within the word *direction*. The figure of Otto Keller in the priest's cassock walking from Villette's library already implies this, and the conversion of all into a courtroom drama seems only to confirm the "law's" role as manager of blackmail. This direction of directionality goes against the signs' arrows pointing from left to right, advertisements for grammatical reading, much as the Hitchcock body does in a transvestism of the cloth that will throw off Catholic-bred readers like Chabrol and Rohmer and, paradoxically, give rise to the auteurist dossier. Behind that cassock Keller passes down a one-way street that begins in a library with the death of a lawyer, Villette, whose proper name harbors the serial letters of a cut, a series of bars *(i-l-l)*. The control that we associate with cinematic direction is what the cameo is supposed to stamp with authorial stability. Here it overtly folds into its opposite, dissolves "Hitchcock" into a shade crossing the rampart not like Hamlet but like Hamlet *père*—the do not forget of the mnemonic network's facticity, as when Logan, at his moment of crisis, paradoxically stops before a movie house and reads his dilemma in the matinee's photo shots.

## Musical Iridescence

An avalanche precedes and whites out the Alpine village that opens *The Lady Vanishes,* as if registering the explosion of Hitchcock's cinema mirrored in the Bijou's bombing in the preceding film, *Sabotage.* That the toy train or the cinematic is vampiric and awakens mechanically from the blizzard of scattered signifiers will appear soon enough—and is registered by the imaginary Balkan land dubbed *Band*riki that hosts the intrigue on the cinematic train that the eye-citing Iris Henderson will serve as cipher to. Bandriki, land of celluloid bands with its own language, totalizes the Babelesque otherness of speech cited in the opening scene at the inn. For once, the political enemy of the English is cryptically exposed as the cinematic itself, albeit here doubly referenced to popular Hollywood vampire and monster movies of the day, including a merry innkeeper named "Boris," a Bela Lugosi double in Dr. Hartz, and the presentation of a mummy-wrapped Miss Froy from which the ersatz mother figure, the vanishing lady of the title, will return. Everything from Signor Doppo's magic props to the screenlike train windows works cinematic tropes into something that is under way, a cognitive whiteout confluent with all manner of cryptic writing and messaging. When *Iris* is put in the Hamletian position of knowing too much, remembering the existence of "Miss Froy," which will be denied by all around her, what Iris knows is what is not before her, what is a mnemonic inscription, and that what is staged and fictional is the empirical fact before the eye.

The cinematic toy train of the opening avalanche scene threads the aftermath of a cinematic disaster. The whiteout references a decimating blizzard of (white) significations. The mountain inn is crammed with unexpected guests, with the polyglot owner, Boris, forced into a Babelesque impasse ("What a gift for languages," says the amateur musicologist Redman, played by Michael Redgrave). Bandriki is a country allied to the band of celluloid.

Whatever the obliteration is or has been, two figures reanimate the DOA train. There will be the musical code to be passed on by Miss Froy, and this in minimal notation (without semantic contact) and, again, by *memory*. It combines Mr. Memory's formula and the tune Hannay could not shake. The music bears a code we never share, the MacGuffin being the facticity of musical notation itself. Music will have to do with memory and transcription, as Redman demonstrates by writing down, or archiving, the peasant foot-stomping tunes. But there is a second figure required, which is whatever Iris Henderson "knows," together with whatever blocks her ability to speak or be heard. What is the status of "music," if it is allied to writing, unreadability, memory, and political secrets? In the blackout at the beginning of *Suspicion* and the traffic jam in *North by Northwest,* Cary Grant speaks of trying mail, telegraphs, phone calls to get in touch with "Mother," as if for directions. For Miss Froy to assume a *dubious* maternal role for Iris is as a gift for the eye, or sight, from the pixyish, leaping, at one point mummified "lady"—this magical demon as childless older woman, with her secret. One is covertly in the presence of a spry Mrs. Bates in her changeling salad days.

One nineteenth-century treatment of "music" involved a hierarchic inversion. Music would be "beyond" speech in the aesthetic pantheon by virtue of its desemanticized purity and unmediated access to the emotions. Yet "music"—the organization of sound departing from laws of rhythm, difference, and association—involves the alternative logics of sheer form and relation, and a mode of writing (with bars) void of semantic referents, a marking of time. Miss Froy, bearer of the tune and the unexpected secret agent, both solicits and suspends "maternal" associations for Iris. The association is complicated when she turns up wrapped in bandages, spoken of as an accident victim with "no face" at all, a site, or moment, from which she will reemerge. Hitchcock attaches "music" to a nonmaternal *mummy* (*Miss* Froy), Egyptized and defaced: prefacial, prefigural, (a)mater(n)(i)al. When she "vanishes" Iris is left with her recollection, her knowledge of Miss Froy's having been opposite her, a recollection publicly denied by all to the point of madness, of passing out and abruptly pulling the brake, halting the train. That is, braking the cinematic fiction that insists on the mimetic experience and metaphysics of film over—and in denial of—its technicity, its scene of production, the import of inscription, prerecordings, allographics.

The accord between *Iris* and the eye is echoed in the use of the verb *see* when she is asked to observe the empirical fact of who and what is literally before her, for instance, the now Balkan woman dressed like Miss Froy and planted in the seat across Iris to demonstrate her false memory. The clash has the structure of a female Hamlet scenario, in which what one "knows" or remembers is denied by the official court. The knowledge exists not only in Iris's memory of Miss Froy, who is spectrally hallucinated at one juncture, but between two mutually exclusive versions of cinema and phenomenality: the one empirical but in fact *staged* by Dr. Hartz, what one supposedly in fact "sees"; the other possessed by a truth allied to traced names on fogged windows, a knowledge here less of some father's ghost than "Mother" as *mummy*. Iris's impasse rewrites the definition of sight and knowledge: what "Iris" *knows* contradicts what is in evidence before the eye, a knowledge of inscription. It is of something not phenomenally present but from which perceptions are programmed—as from a projector's reels. In the long fight with Signor Doppo in the freight car, a series of magician's "props" recalls Hitchcockian tropes—a bird pops up, spectacles are found crushed, the magic box (camera), the size of a coffin, disappears people via a trapdoor.

Part of what Iris confirms or discovers, however, is an alternative model of the "aesthetic" itself. Rather than representing "pictures of people talking" in forms of play, cinema occurs at a site from which a programming of the senses proceeds as if out of marking systems. An atomization and recalibration of these premises, such as a whiteout or blackout may signal, stand to rewrite the phenomenality of things. Or for that matter, the definitions of history, time, agency, "man," perception. What stands to be displaced is not only an aesthetic regime invested in solar myths, ocularcentrism, and mimetic ideologies. "Iris" holds to what *the* eye cannot see in the staged reality before it, as does the blind hermit Philip *Martin* in *Saboteur*. As the (a)maternal, briefly mummified courier, the childless Miss Froy passes through all transformations (including, apparently, being shot and killed). Only Iris testified to knowing Miss Froy, this odd demater(n)(i)aled "Mother," site of coded transcriptions containing an empty secret clause on which world war hangs.

It is odd to discover a laughing Miss Froy at the piano in the British intelligence offices when we were stupid enough to have thought her, perhaps, dead, vanished. The ghoulish train keepers of Bandriki wanted her and her secret—that which Iris's impasse performs, that of the eye—from getting back to the British empiricists. Dr. *Ha*rtz (an A-H variant) knew he staged the "empirical" facts, so plain to see for Iris herself, namely, the gruesome Balkan lady substitute for Miss Froy, the denials and assurances. Yet the Home Office could want to keep the secret for itself, for the state. She is elated to look over the top of the piano and see Iris. Iris, too, is safe at home. By the second *Man Who Knew Too Much,* "Mummy" has become Doris Day; by *Psycho,* she overtly drifts back to Bandriki's side. Hitchcock's esperanto is not a "universal" tongue, invented from a milieu of signs and street semaphors. It is the totalization of all signifying logics, operatic, musical, pantechnological, linguistic, scriptive, micrological, numerical. Iris also names rainbow, which is to say color or trope, and she is steeped, here, in the Bandrikian order of inscriptions on windows, faceless mummies, preletteral notation, the prefigural more generally. By *North by Northwest* the tropological is sheer traffic, jammed in Manhattan streets like advertising language, and the prefigural itself, the fall from personifications and anthropomorphized earthen faces, will define the one-way street leading to Norman's bog. One may juxtapose Miss Froy's face lighting up over the piano at the arrival of the couple to "Mother's" skull-grin dissolving into the bog shot that closes *Psycho* to track a historial acceleration of teletechnics and the abduction of cognitive tropes by media and political genocides in the decades separating their smiles.

## Zootrope

Hitchcock's reflexive marking of the technicity of the cinematic project is apparent in virtually all telemedia and machines that appear like cameos in his set, as his sets. But what occurs when these trains and mnemonic traps, grinding gears and typographic machines do not situate epistemo-political assaults or faux metaphysical outings like *Vertigo*? How is a film void of the high "metaphysical" style marked? What of a work supposedly driven to produce a commercial success and resurrect box office clout following the experimental *Rope*? In fact, this loop through techno-metaphysical concerns condenses, is formalized, and madly accelerates in *Strangers on a Train*: the cinematic train sends forth its own phantom double in Bruno; the amusement park mocking Hitchcock's consumers' interests leads to a zootropic carousel that will spin off its moorings; the music store's emphasis on recording devices will invest the doomed and seemingly tawdry Miriam with a pregnant signature that defies her public associations as fallen, devious woman; the lighter fought over will promise or displace an Empedoclean conflagration; the tennis court volleys will turn the black sun motif into a numbing and pointless sport—and all will be referenced to the nation's capital, to tennis pro Guy's (Farley Granger) dubious social climbing and its further assault on Hitchcock's own climb back to box office power. But above all, it turns the cinematic Bruno, whose mother says he had a plan to bomb the White House, loose on Washington, DC.

Robert Walker's Bruno enters Guy's world on a train, recognizing him from the "papers." Bruno tells Guy, after clicking the toes of their shoes (Bruno's are black with white spats), that he envies Guy's ability to "*do* things," to live in the real, not in endless possibility like Bruno, although the latter inversely describes the myriad things he has done in cars and planes, vehicles of transport, mocking the "life" of Guy as, in fact, a player of sports. He enters Guy's world, flirting and flattering, as he does that of the viewer. This intrusion makes the tennis scene that is later dwelled upon odd. Played as if it were an interlude building suspense (Guy has to finish a tennis match before he can get away), its numerous *shots* follow the ball back and forth in a sort of hiatus. This is also the ball that, when black instead of white, traversed the sky as a clay target in the first *Man Who Knew Too Much*—a black sun or simulacrum trace—only here it is just knocked back and forth, again and again. The referee's scoring of "love" places the term in a calculable game while recalling its etymology in the *oeuf* or the zero. The tennis *court* is drawn with rectangular lines, carved-up screens or frames. Bruno is conjured by the "train": he enters cinematically mimicking and then preinhabiting "Guy's" psychic narrative, the latter reading on a train. Bruno (and for that matter Miriam) is the cinematic heir of the British saboteurs interiorized and isolated as the international MacGuffin recedes within a postwar telehorizon (Washington).[3]

*Strangers on a Train* speculates on its own cinematic isolation and circular entrapment. As it does so, the amusement park as Hadean entertainment supplants and magnifies the cinematic train, coming to a climax on the grotesque undead horse heads of the zootropic carousel. The cigarette lighter that would frame Guy for Miriam's murder is inscribed "From A to G." Used to illuminate Miriam's face and spectacles as Bruno strangles her, it later falls into a drain while Bruno's hand strains through the graphlike coordinates of the grate, retrieving it with fingers extending. Hitchcock reaches again for *this* lighter, this prosthetic implement of poetic conflagration. The amusement park is a cinematic Hades, the Tunnel of Love boat named "Pluto." It is best partaken of at night, lit up. But the lighter, packaging Fry's fall from the Statue of Liberty's torch as a mechanized unit, is fought over and, again, taken back in possession by the police after the accelerating carousel explodes centripetally. It is a remarkable image, as if a giant reel has spun off its machinal base: a runaway train as circular. The speed of the whirling undead-horse machine, inanimate animation and cinematic prototype, creates *horizontal falling.* Farley Granger hangs extended from the *poles* as Bruno kicks him with his black foot going into the camera, into Guy's knuckles. It is not a vertical fall this time or a falling *up* (as in *To Catch a Thief*), nor is there a simultaneous falling up and down (the trick shot of *Vertigo*). The threat of falling away occurs *horizontally* as the runaway spool accelerates. The acceleration of backlooped "experience" implodes the giant wheel as its brake is thrown by the old mechanic crawling beneath (the actor, Hitchcock later lamented, almost had his head taken off). The amusement park mocks Hitchcock's cinematic props. The horse's grimacing face intrudes everywhere, turning up again atop the dying Bruno like a deadly pet. The duped Guy clings to the horses and the pole with his hands, clinging to the faux natural image that keeps him from flying off—even as Bruno wants to tear him away from just that.

When Bruno touches his black-white-black spats against Guy's dark shoes the conversation is about *reading.* Bruno references what he has learned from the papers about Guy and Anne Morton. "You're quite a *reader*," deadpans Guy. Bruno, with his plans to blow up the White House (recalls his mother), is also called *quite* a reader.[4] Guy, with his plans to marry into a U.S. senator's family, the power circle, is not. With so many references to cinematic machines—carousels as zootropes; animated horses that neither move nor carry; popcorn makers with cinematic gears displayed; a ball going back and forth, mesmerizing its crowd as their turning heads follow mechanically—what, here, involves a technological battle within and over cinematic powers?

The music store where Miriam works advertises "radios" and features glass booths for listening to records. *Miriam* reproduces and couples randomly, performs blackmail and setups. A clock is featured prominently beside her (it is 5:45). Miriam would stop Guy's march to Washington, block Hollywood success in essence. *Mir*iam, with her specular name and cinematic spectacles, is the link to the carousel, on which she first rides, singing, as if leading the group's stationary flight. She and Bruno are doubled in discarding or playing the dominant codes. Guy's aspirations toward Washington connections and power mirrors Hitchcock's to commercial Hollywood success. Is it Bruno's job to subvert or complicate that, using the Empedoclean *lighter*? Friedrich Kittler, as if commenting on Miriam's music store, observes of phonographs and cinema:

> What phonographs and cinematographs, whose names not coincidentally derive from writing, were able to store was time: time as a mixture of audio frequencies in the acoustic realm and as the movement of single-image sequences in the optical. . . . What is called style in art is merely the switchboard of these scanning and selections. That same switchboard also controls those arts that use writing as a *serial,* that is, temporally transposed, data flow. To record the sound sequences of speech, literature has to arrest them in a system of 26 letters, thereby categorically excluding all noise sequences. Not coincidentally, this system also contains as a subsystem the seven notes, whose diatonics—*from A to G*—form the basis of *occidental music.* Following a suggestion made by the musicologist von Hornbostel, it is possible to fix the chaos of exotic music assailing European ears by first interpolating a phonograph, which is able to record this chaos in real time and then replay it in slow motion. As the rhythms begin to flag and "individual measures, even individual notes resound on their own, occidental alphabetism with its staffs can proceed to an 'exact notation.'"5

The glass booths of Miller's Music Store are ideal settings for inscribed and replayed time disks. Yet the lighter's inscription is also "From A to G," the signature of "occidental music" in Kittler's account whose "occidental alphabetism with its staffs can proceed to an 'exact notation.'" We read this exact notation as serial bars on the score's close-up in the second *Man Who Knew Too Much* as Bernard Herrmann conducts: just giant staffs. The locus of *M*s (Miriam, music, Miller's, Metcalf), Miriam's mnemonic store or storage and technotopia, consolidates her figural dominance and affinity for the amusement park (as cinema). She will be murdered with a child in her, cut off as the cinematic turns toward commercial aims that Bruno both executes and sabotages. Thus Bruno is irrepressible when crashing the Washington dinner party of Senator Morton and going into a cinematic trance when demonstrating to the dotty Mrs. Cunningham how she might best be strangled—fixated, all the while, on another child, Patricia Hitchcock. A cinematic vector, he threatens Guy's social scheme and the Washington milieu he himself emerges from. The cinematic operation is as seemingly angry as the animated horse's frozen grimace at its prospect of commercial success following the artifices of *Rope*. Miriam is differently positioned, say, than the insurrectionist Abbott or the saboteur Verloc, but her resistance to—then desire to infiltrate—the capital resonates along the same lines.

## How the Great Age Ended

Peter Conrad is adept in seeing in Charles Laughton a running citation (out of control, of course) of a certain "Hitchcock," the front of being the "law" in *Jamaica Inn* as Squire Pengallan ("I am the law here, I am justice"), sponsoring the wrecker's crew that lures endangered ships to the rocks with a (cinematic) lantern only to murder and despoil the travelers. Pengallan then uses the loot to finance hyperbolic aesthetic pursuits (cinema). Yet Conrad perhaps misreads the historicity of Pengallan's parting boast, as he leaps to his death from a ship's roost (a too portly and boastful Handel Fane). He gives his spectators a charge: "Tell your children how the great age ended."

The "great age" Laughton identifies with *himself* before the foiled crossing does not allude to the "romanticism" of the costume era it pretends to depict. That would be pointless for Hitchcock. So what does the end of the "great age" mean? This was Hitchcock's last British film before going to America and Hollywood. The passing could refer, first of all, to Hitchcock's impending crossing to America. In order to mark the last film of the British thriller period, he apparently needed to fold back in costume to a prehistory to the modern. It is in this work that he presents one of his most savage tropes of the relation of his cinema to its "public." Cinema is not a temple or music hall; its front is the "law," and its ritual involves the overt deceit and murder of its clients—not just duping them with aesthetic or religious distractions. Taking their ticket money, Laughton lures them from stormy seas by a swinging or flickering lantern—assaulted, robbed, and knifed. Their money finances Laughton's aesthetic or cinematic projects. The phrase "how the great age ended" is transformed. He, Laughton, performs how a certain "great age" ended, one that is identified with himself, like the British period for Hitchcock. Yet also a conceit concerning age or time (from the Egyptians and the Greeks through the Enlightenment and the "modern") is as if ended, here, at the Channel crossing. If anything, the "age" would not be romanticism but the "Enlightenment," as the lantern leads to calculated doom. What is "ended"—that is, assigned a telos and as if closed—is a certain model of time or histories, "history" as assembled by the historicizing archive, precinematic. At the same juncture, it asks after or opens the question of a *future* that is other than that program, whatever comes "after" the suspension of this map of before and after, in the bizarre leap of the bloated and fey Laughton. The "age" is also the closure of a certain history and model of "history."

What, then, of the dictate to relate this event and legacy? Telling one's children passes this on as a rupture to be seeded, or ceded, to the transformation of the telemnemonic. As if fast-forwarding to the digital, computerized image, much as it seeps back to encompass and precede Egyptian hieroglyphics in the British Museum. If the "great age" is not an age of history but "history" as received there is another time testified to by Laughton, disjunct, and it both precedes and supersedes that long-installed model from a certain reading of Plato through to the Enlightenment and through and beyond the *ocularcentric,* auteurist, and mimetic Hitchcocks to come, all products still of this romanticism, this auratic fable. Thus Peter Conrad describes "his" first experience of Hitchcock as a youth, reflecting inadvertently a transvaluation or rape: "*Psycho* had come to resemble a rite of passage, a visceral, constricted tunnel you had to pass through to get from one age to the next" (5).

## Soda City, Heart of the Bicarbonate Belt

The shift from the early British intrigues against England to Nazi-inspired scenarios complicated Hitchcock's phantasmal maps. In the first instance, the insurgent cineast could appear a threat affiliated with no named nation, agent of a certain "foreign power"; in the latter, during war, one is supposed to eviscerate "Nazis," not identify with them. Ina Rae Hark attempts to read this historico-political complication by literalizing Hitchcock's focus on the mission of media: "the director's inability to reconcile a belief in the desirability of preserving democracy's freedoms with his conviction that democratically constituted populations can't take on their enemies effectively without adopting those enemies' methods, inevitably sabotages his attempts to allocate to himself the mission of the democratic press."[6]

Yet there are other complications. Hitchcock, instead, seems to let both sides comingle and reverse positions, identifying differently against both as specular and fratricidal versions of the same Enlightenment programs. Regardless of what should come out at the time as more or less clear vilification of Nazis, Hitchcock identifies with the saboteur position. This occurs, certainly, with Fry in *Saboteur*. Even the postwar Nazi plot in *Notorious*'s cinematic "Rio," a place called "too much" in the "sun," is referenced to uranium sand in wine bottles, an intoxicating appeal to an artificed material light source with atomizing nuclear potential. The imperialism of the Hitchcock project is that of rewiring global mnemonics. It is not without discrete parallel to the fascist order, yet it has an inverse agenda.

Thus the arsonist Fry in *Saboteur* is associated with an Empedoclean fire erupting in the trick extinguisher sabotaged with gasoline— immolating the average American, Ken, trope of cognition *(Kennen)*, in trying to put out the opening fire in the plane factory. These planes are what the formula of *The 39 Steps* may have been preparing, conflagrating like a celluloid warehouse, compelling what *To Catch a Thief* calls "fighting fire with fire." The fire is announced by smoke, the chiaroscuro "fog" of cine-

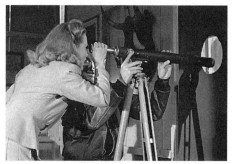

Figure 6. Soda City: saboteurs target a dam holding earth's powers in check, from shed as pinhole camera box.

graphematics (made the subject in *The Lodger*'s subtitle, *A Story about the London Fog*). Black smoke appears as a prefigure of immolation and the gray networking of marks and intervallic "light." The "war" is discretely about mass communications beyond "the war." Yet Fry will fall as if from the extended cold torch, monumental with metal flames and mock corona, of Lady Liberty, and this through the unraveling of a sleeve, a weave that, as in *Spellbound,* constitutes figuration itself. Being a saboteur has to do here with fire, conflagration, cinema, as if the California plane factory were also an array of movie studios, like the bomb in the newsreel truck that will sink the just christened battleship. Yet it *also* has to do with inscribing the American high capitalist or industrialist class like Tobin as a fifth column, as another locus on the same spectrum. The "Nazi" front becomes convoluted, fractured:

- It represents an "evil" resistance to a mechanized national war machine, interrupting the latter at its source or factory, yet it also seems to disrupt "Hollywood" in part.
- It represents, inversely, an "evil" imperialism that would appear identified with (Hitchcock's) cinematic power over the world, itself countered by the circus freaks' formal performance of democracy in the traveling circus that is yet another cinematic trope and topos.
- It represents an "evil" within nationalist political categories, deflected onto America, where the hypercapitalist Tobin is specular other to the Nazi in this regard.
- It collectively doubles against these caricatured "evils" in a general acceleration and dispersal of the latter's postures.

Each of these may be linked to fire, light, pyrotechnics, sabotage, news or newsreel cameras, ships, planes, trucks. The *empire* that the cinematic war machine contests (or differently reenacts) encompasses specular enemies within the post-Enlightenment political spectrum—as Hitchcock's unusable French propaganda shorts conflated the two opponents much too openly. Benjamin, in his "Theses on History," connects "fascism" to the epistemological models of historicism, which is to say, a sort of indexing of the real that the supposed mimetic pretense of the photographic image parallels. Hitchcock related cinema's historical intervention to both a representational decimation of earth implying globalization and to the latter's critique, sending forth the winged avian animemes to eviscerate "humanity" in the name of a prehistorial otherness without aura or personification. *Saboteur* segues between a horizonless empire of Enlightenment programs run amok and their *cinematic* other, which would atomize these and recast their temporal structure and sensoria in a fashion inclusive of both warring or specular camps.

Soda City resonates with a faux alliteration as the desert ghost town to which Barry Kane is led in tracking Fry. In Soda City Kane stumbles into a wooden shack with Priscilla Lane in tow. These are boxlike cabins replete with telephonics, revealing in one a hole that casts a circular light—as in the interior of a camera box. A telescope pivoted in the hole reveals Hoover Dam, apparent target of a plotted bombing of electricity at its source (what *Sabotage* calls "the juice"). Soda City or, as Barry quips, "the heart of the bicarbonate belt," this ghost town in which the shot of the camera's inversion of light threatens a source of harnessed power that illuminates, produces light. And if the "belt" references celluloid or a projector's mechanics, the "bicarbonate" is not only to soothe bad digestion or dyspepsia. "The heart of the bicarbonate belt": if the belt is also a band, the bifurcation of the syllable *car* registers a split between and within the band. It anticipates *To Catch a Thief*'s trope of an "amphibious" car, moving back and forth between zones and elements, life and death, caught in an evolutionary interspace. The "bicarbonate belt," placating a certain illness, names this irreconcilable *split* between the mimetic pretense of film or the ideology of the image and, in turn, the anarchivist materiality of this graphematic and virtual event.[7] The desert of Soda City is an expanse that, the film remarks, was *once a sea.*[8]

The phantom *empire* that "cinema" would dislodge is outside of the political agons of contemporary history. Here variations on the same epistemo-political order (fascism, high capitalism) are linked to an installed set of definitions (image, man, tree, train). In *Spellbound* and *Vertigo,* this empire will be cited as a hotel, the "Empire State Hotel." Yet *empire* disarticulates itself further. The general empire in question is perhaps less contested than accelerated, by its own "logics" and borders. In *The Birds* this empire is reduced to an isolated house under assault and in "the end" dispossessed ("humanity," ocularcentrism) by myriad wingbeats. Soda City is already devastated: an abandoned mining camp, scarred land, and restrained rivers that would be reshaped by sabotaging a giant dam, momentarily reflooding the desert sea in a purge.

## 2. Combined Ops: The Postal Politics of *Bon Voyage!*

Chronos is sickness itself. This is why chronosigns are inseparable from lectosigns, which force us to read so many symptoms in the image, that is, to treat the optical and sound image like something that is also readable. Not only the optical and the sound, but the present and the past, and the here and the elsewhere, constitute internal elements and relations that must be deciphered, and can be understood only in a progression analogous to that of a reading.
    **—Gilles Deleuze**

It is on this level that the bad Nazis/good Americans (etc.) dichotomy becomes thoroughly subverted: the nominal commitment to America, democracy, the free world, demanded by Hollywood, is revealed as a mere facade for a far more sweeping denunciation of masculinist politics in general.
    **—Robin Wood**

Stop and consider. It is absurd and naive, asking Hitchcock to produce propaganda shorts, even and especially in the midst of a world war, even for an ally. De Gaulle's people apparently would never see or get to see *Saboteur* or *Foreign Correspondent* or *Lifeboat* in time. It is like asking Verloc to run a documentary exposing saboteurs or asking Peter Lorre for a solar blessing from the Tabernacle of the Sun. It is to position the request in the least desirable of patron positions—like Selznick, like his TV sponsors, like England or America. Betrayal is assured, in the name of fidelity. In the preceding remark by Robin Wood one could provide the term *masculinist* a broader set of variants: ocularcentric, mimeticist, metaphysical, touristic.

Perhaps the last place one would expect to examine the spectrographic politics of Hitchcock would be in a propaganda film that, like so-called documentary, would supposedly be crafted to serve overt representational ends. That is, to confirm the sacrifice and heroism of the home against the powers of an inhuman enemy. On the surface, it is simply the wrong formula, as if giving to Nazis the covert role assigned the birds in what is later called the "bird war," or lumping the two together, fraternal and specular enemies, from the point of view of the nonhuman other, bird or seeing camera. But just as "documentary" (in *Blackmail,* say) is exposed as the hyperbolic undoing of the very pretense of indexing, documentary, or identification by imprint or fingerprint, so the propaganda short might, in fact, present an intriguing case for how, or what, "political" aims could dominate Hitchcock's practices, or whether the "political" requires here a *new* definition. This is the case with the unusable film contracted by the Free French, *Bon Voyage!* The mocking French phrase *bon voyage* incorporates *voyeurs* and sight as a locus of imperial programming.

Criticism has tried to penetrate this blind. Ina Rae Hark wrestles with the self-undermining nature of the "anti-Fascist" work in general, assuming Hitchcock's aims were to further the cause; yet she has difficulty salvaging that aim from various autodeconstructions at work.[1] One is left with the impression that one must examine again how "politics" is defined from a bird's-eye view, so to speak, that eviscerates the very epistemo-political structure of the home state, as well as the definition of the aesthetic, media, and global war. Hark admits to an aporia: "The task Hitchcock sets himself is to imagine an efficient democracy that does not achieve such efficiency at the cost of becoming that very Fascism it opposes. . . . [T]he task eventually defeats him" (334). It is so complicated, in fact, and looks so gloomy for Hitchcock, that she finds herself all but apologizing for the direction this analysis takes: "I do not mean to suggest that Hitchcock's anti-Fascist activism in these three films was consciously insincere or disingenuous" (344). Yet the problem, entirely understandable, may have something to do with the historicizing template applied. Peter Conrad, by contrast, suggests that after the war the geopolitical horizon would slowly get darker—as if the war were, despite its necessary outcome, a MacGuffin in terrestrial terms fronting for a broader archival disintegration and systemic death drive which America, as emergent global mediacracy, would absorb as it did the Nazi scientists. Such an acceleration of systemic and psychotropic devastation from within a more totalized tele-archive could not be identified too simply with "democracy" and could imply its evisceration by media, with the birds, in the end, attacking the anthropocentric as such. If *Saboteur* views America's hyperindustrialists as Nazism's fifth column, the specularity of the democratic and the fascist doubles is not only symmetrical and irresolvable but subjects both to withering critique. Indeed, since that of the fascist is rather obvious, it is the critique of the "home state" that remains in force. If a certain Hitchcock identifies with the "Nazi" other (Fisher, Willy, Tobin), it is partly because of convenience, as he had all along identified with the phantasmal political enemies of the British home state, which would always be defined as a hermeneutic regime, an epistemo-political rule, a programming of memory and the senses encountering the sabotage, anarchivist bombing, or dematerialization that the cinematic implied. One could conclude that Hitchcock, who helped edit death camp footage, analyzed the contest as a misleading deathfest and fratricidal episode between two distant points within the same doomed program or spectrum—the Enlightenment epistemology that would account both for Van Meer's doomed hope *(Foreign Correspondent)* and Nazi death bureaucracy. Both differently appeal to light, nature, number, identity, transparency, mimetic fact, and archival consumption. And the critique of these programs would depart from the mediatrix from which these positions seem, at times, interchangeable. Which is why, perhaps, Benjamin's *Theses* addressed the enemy "fascism" not by the name of Nazi but as "historicism" itself, an epistemo-critical program that fed or accelerated the mimetic state. Historicism, with its assumption that another "fact" will heal or complete the temporal trajectory of the $N + 1, + 1, + 1 \ldots$, while only feeding the nihilisms of its imaginary others. To oppose such he could only appeal to forms of historiography or inscription that suspended narrative time, accessed alternative futures and pasts, and deployed deauratic practices of disruption without interiority—one of which was called cinema.

When called on to contribute to the war cause by making propaganda films for the French Resistance, Hitchcock's political productions were deemed too "inflammatory" to use. Something in the "politics" of his performative shorts subverted even the straightforward political effort on behalf of the Allies. There are numerous indications that Hitchcock sees Americans, the British, the French, and Germans as contaminated by the same epistemo-political programs, of which the "Nazi" extreme would be one polarity. Even in a short meant for propaganda purposes, he cannot decelerate or yield, cannot suspend the allographic details that permeate his oeuvre elsewhere yet point, as here, toward a different "epistemo-political" critique than can be used for these propagandistic ends. In the case of *Bon Voyage!*, the evocation of *voyaging* and its interface with cinema, touristic and otherwise, must necessarily become entangled in an allographic dimension, which then involves the trajectory of cinema, or specifically Hitchcock's own project.[2] A twice-inverted narrative is at stake in the short work, in which a Scot is interrogated by intelligence after his return to England, only to find that his once trusted companion in occupied France was a Gestapo agent who used him as an unwitting courier to expose the Resistance network. But what is striking is not only that the short film would be filled with insistent markings that draw the exercise into the orbit of Hitchcock's signature effects, hook it up to the postal system, but that the result would generate, rightly, enough insecurity about the true targets of the "propaganda" as to make it unusable. This is new, and interesting. In wartime, *they*—his "sponsors," so to speak, his public—somehow knew without being able to name it. "Inflammatory" is an interesting term.

The work casts a certain light on how a war scenario, "real life," is interfaced and absorbed by *espionage* models that had been developed, in the British "thrillers," to represent a seditious cinematic project. How, for instance, the gears of an *other* discourse compromise and assault the very concept of the home state, monolinguistic England. "England" in the early films will often name a problematic home or interiority: the turf to be defended, it is also the site of a foreclosing hermeneutics, of mimetic laws, police and the symbolic, a site and logos to be overthrown by "villains" whose plots (assassinations, sabotage) partake of Hitchcock's would-be epistemo-political interventions. Verloc, the saboteur, would blow up Piccadilly Circus; Abbott, the assassin, would trigger with a shot a world-altering war; the Professor and Mr. Memory would facilitate the silent aerial bombing of London; Marvin would go back and alter the outcome of the first world war against England. England wins, "Hitchcock" loses, in each, more or less, except for a remainder: the text's sabotaging installation within the dawning televisual archive.

In the complementary attempt to *Bon Voyage!*, *Aventure Malgache*, the mise-en-scène opens with the Theatre Molières players preparing for a show, memorizing lines, underscoring historical "actors" engaged in performance. England is cast starkly to the Madagascar residents, at one point, as another empire that may want the island for themselves—the better of bad options, following the "Boches" and Japan (and the equally colonial French). In a replay of what makes the espionage scenario so rife with linguistic play and hermeneutic incisions, the Scot in *Bon Voyage!,* Sandy, will be sent back to England with a *letter.* Yet those he thinks he is escaping arranged his escape to relay this message and to entrap the Underground. Sandy will be called, by Stefan, a "homing pigeon." The very title, *Bon Voyage!,* aside from its sarcastic import given the setup of the escape, implicitly cites a *touristic* motif Hitchcock applies to his paying "public"—providing a further subtext the French Resistance could neither have guessed nor appreciated. But if Hitchcock cannot stop, cannot not make this propaganda short *also* "about" a cinematic intervention, is it because of ingenuity or because it bears a political force beyond the contemporary "set"?[3]

Explicit problems of language, cinema, and above all *time*—and, oddly at first, eating—shape the trajectory. The phrase "bon voyage" uttered repeatedly in the dialogue points to the stations of transport, movement, or travel for this escape and return of an RAF airman (a trope of flight for the "homing pigeon" that we will suspend addressing for the moment). Walking, bicycling, trains, cars, and planes are consecutively moved through. In fact, the signal to meet the Underground connection on the train is the act of *reading,* in this case, a newspaper. Reading also marks the Gestapo agent named *Em*berg. There is a sequence of figures interrupted while reading on cinematic trains throughout Hitchcock (including Hitchcock in *Blackmail*), a rupture in the semiotic encounter of reading (in) cinema (reading [reading]) itself, but why such sophistications *here*?

Hitchcock, once again, identifies transport and espionage with complications of language and between languages. When the film, in French, opens in the British intelligence office, Hitchcock expands on the rupture of languages and translation. This occurs once the Scot's narrative begins: Stefan, Sandy's companion, dissuades him from going to meet representatives from the Resistance at a café in Reims (we later learn that he did not, but instead hooked up with his Gestapo connection first), because Sandy's French accent is imperfect. Yet his French is deemed bad, supposedly, for using too much "slang" (meaning, in another sense, that it is too good), while its *brokenness* thereafter performs a kind of stammer between languages, a broken unfilled space that is covered when the discussion continues in French back in London. Not only will Sandy be identified repeatedly with the *letters* RAF, but the opening of the film at *Reims* graphically implicates the cross-tongued or visual resonance of *rhyme* itself, the aural concatenation between and within tongues whose foreignness to themselves can be remarked through sound ("sounds *like*"). Sandy is the empty and unwitting conveyor of a lethal *message*: whoever receives him is marked for death. It is one that he at first defends himself for not revealing (having given his "word of honor"). The stuttering locus of a disjunct tongue, Sandy is throughout the text *hungry*—ceaselessly commenting on anticipated food at the café, in the bag of the bicycle, at the farm of the French girl Jeanne's father. Indeed, if his desire to eat, to consume, and interiorize is greeted with suspicion (the first woman Resistance fighter counters that she thought they fed them well in England), it is tied to Sandy's blindness to the destructive role he is being used for throughout. Even when he belatedly gives up the address of the letter's recipient, the message had already been delivered for a time. He is busy eating, as he goes about identifying the Resistance inadvertently: the messenger, not the message, a wand of death. Eating will appear connected to Sandy's blindness to what is taking place around him throughout.

As a vehicle of the Gestapo postal relay, Sandy learns from the British intelligence officials not only that he conveyed potentially dangerous information but that, first, he was the "cover" used to expose every cell of Resistance he passed through. The opposite of Poe's purloined letter, moving through various hands left unexposed, Sandy as letter kills everyone whose relay is used, culminating specifically in the helpful Jeanne, shot in the end by Stefan with telephone in hand. One transit spot is the Hôtel de la Poste. The network of communication points that takes over the infrastructure of the tale—including, so far, dislocations of natural tongues (a Babel effect or motif), rhyme, postal relays, epistles, letteral characters, and telecommunications—is amplified and redirected by the manner in which cinema itself is re-marked. Cinema, and more interestingly, time. *Bon Voyage!* becomes a dossier issued from *Secret Agent*'s spies' post office, except that the chocolate, as entertainment, is diverted to propaganda as commissioned product. Why, however, should *time* even figure in a short propaganda film episode? Why should Hitchcock bother to play metaphysical "games" (unless he has no choice, and they are not games)? Or if the time Hitchcock appeals to is other than that of the contemporary historial "set"? A question remains of what is going on in the film, in which the MacGuffin is real history itself—a question that the story seems to re-mark and be "about." How does a technological deregulation of temporality figure in the historical time and place here, a minor relay, as it were, in the Hitchcock network or webwork?

The "plot" once again associates cinema with the motif of *travel,* something that momentarily positions Sandy, borne along by intrigue, in the unwitting position of transportee, and of inert reader. It is in the title, announced, too, *Bon Voyage!*—not a description but a performative hailing: Have a good trip, Sandy (says the Gestapo); have a good trip, viewer (says Hitchcock). Sandy will be instructed to read the news and comment on the time, when on the train, in order to effect the exchange and contact: "It's Monday" . . . "Try this one, it's yesterday's [paper]." Like documentary, the time of reportage—or recorded events—is disjunct, without a "now." When two pilots enter the Poesque wine cellar to see where Stefan left a Vichy spy's body, Sandy's remark on not finding the corpse invokes a spectral impasse: "If he was dead he couldn't have walked away." When a torch is used later entering the cellar, when Stefan meets the master spy Emberg, the image clearly cites a single light or lens. And bicycles, their tires filling the edges of the screen, are juxtaposed to the voyagers' shadows entering opposite them, wedding the shadelike figures to cinema's inscription of the players (and viewers). Rather than a gesture of coy reflexivity, the emblem of the bicycle enforces a certain law of movement, a participation on the switchboard and in the repetition systems of Hitchcock's broader writing scene. It remarks, moreover, that "cinema" as a site of transvaluation, other than human, invokes a logic of the *technos* whose suspension even a political text for "England" or "France" in wartime will not occasion. Like the wheel flying from and surviving the car crash in the photograph that opens *Rear Window*, Hitchcock's camera registers a "disaster" before and beyond that of local or "world" war.

How, nonetheless, do such spectral markings and debris open the short film to alternative readings, especially since the film hoped for by the Free French seems to dismantle itself, openly, in too elaborate a series of exchanges to sort out? To answer this question, we must put several more pieces in place. Sandy will, after all, tell his British interrogators that the Resistance's routine went like "clockwork," just like a "combined *ops*"—combined operations, or what is here a clearly blind and lethal *optics*. The figure suggests the combined operations that yield the optical as a semaphoric effect: postal systems, aural and visual puns, mnemonic tricks, bicycles, trains, reading newspapers, espionage.

The dimensions of a potential inversion must be considered. For Hitchcock seems to cast Stefan's Gestapo handler (his "director") as the purveyor of the cinematic project, even as, when he is finally surrounded in the Hôtel des Voyageurs, it forecasts that of Vandamm's arrest at the

end of *North by Northwest*. When the Gestapo's "Stefan" is explained to
be a *double* of the real Stefan (a dominant theme in *Aventure Malgache*),
the issue of distinguishing copies and simulacrum gets wedded to a
performative moment that destabilizes any simple referential ground of
this politics (everyone seems equally a cog in a rhetorical situation, as
in *Lifeboat*). In this deadly postal system, one can bind the question of
reflexive origination that the cinematic wheels raise to a rift within temporality that dodges in and out of the dialogue: *time* buckling as a template distinguishing models and copies, originals and doubles, fascist
and democratic imperialist, is suspended by the agency of the "bicycle."
This begins with the British intelligence officer asking Sandy about any
"contretemps" he may have had—that is, *troubles*, of course, but also a
warp within the temporal logic of voyage, or escape, or homecoming.
As we hear, "The homing pigeon is on its way." (The war, too, is itself a
contretemps.) If the phrase "bon voyage" assumes a sinister edge when
hurled in the tourist-spectator's face, there is another factor, one that
involves the *passage*, say, of Hitchcock back (home) to England from
his stay in America, the transposition of his British style into a different
style of American allographic formalism and then back, in a series of
folds, the homecoming desired by the viewers in order to be reassured
of the outcome of the film, the war. What, exactly, will pass for *travel*
here, or will occur in its narration? Why should a short film of pursuit
or escape—inverse forms that link the "thriller" mode to hermeneutics
as such—use this escape to England from France to invert the final
British film, *Jamaica Inn,* a personal "bon voyage" to himself, where
Squire Pengallan (the Laughton character who will suicide leaping from
the mast) is pursued to the British coast awaiting transport to France
(that is, also encoded, to America after that film)? How might the
transmarking of languages, of a Scot buried in British English buried in
French and redoubled as a French spoken in British intelligence offices
(for English ears) cover, too, a "doubling" between Hitchcock's British
and American projects? Sandy's being a *Scot* places him in Hitchcock's
system as a head, a (de)capo or an (a)cognitive agent, much as, in *The
39 Steps,* Scotland is "up," or as Ferguson is called "Scottie" ("the hard-
headed Scot") in *Vertigo*? Not surprisingly, here, Sandy himself is another nescient *vehicle.*

The logics of a contretemps, a countertime that suggests also a contra
accounting and conning of time, thread the short work in a manner
parallel to Sandy's concern for food. Only if Sandy will always be fed

just a little bit (first of all in the "pocket" on the bicycle itself), time as a figure does not progress in a determined direction. Any countertime, within Hitchcock's calculus (mise-en-scène, as it is called in the Phoenic Films credit sequence), would have to be a countertime to so-called real historical time, the time of war or the second world war—a counterposition, in some sense. The precise time of actions is prospectively designated, starting with the 1:15 meeting at Reims, through the 9:42 train, and other concerns track *an elusive punctuality* ("No later than three a.m. at any rate"). Sandy will describe the plan as having gone "like clockwork," Jeanne's watch will be protractedly removed after "Stefan" shoots her (telling her, first, to wait a moment), the narrative will be urged forward by insecure linear markers ("*then* Jeanne gave us some clothes, and *then* we ate"), and the code phrase on the train to the Resistance agent—again, when reading a paper on a train—involves notations of time and exchange.[4] The first names the day itself ("it's Monday"), while the second is the offer of yesterday's paper for today's (or, more possibly, some even older paper): "Try this one, it's yesterday's."

Condensed as this temporal dislocation is, it has distinct resonance elsewhere in Hitchcock; at this juncture, as in *Aventure Malgache* (which, if anything, more explicitly uses doubled "stage" markers), he seems absorbed by the possibilities of being inside a total war scenario, its multiple folds and doublings, without upside or down. The code word on the train is an offer to exchange one "daily" for another, for "yesterday's" (today), a deregulation of befores and afters citing a similar play at the end of *Sabotage* about the time bomb destroying the movie house or (in advance) the boy Arnie's "timing" in *The Trouble with Harry,* for whom tomorrow is yesterday, and so on. (The postwar Arnie bears heavier armament than is present here, sporting a play ray gun that would have, in its fashion, absorbed not only the first *Man Who Knew Too Much*'s "sevenfold ray" but *Notorious*'s uranium; the name "Sandy" looks back to the sand in the generator sabotaging London's electricity that opens *Sabotage,* putting out the lights, and forward to the radioactive sand in the wine bottles of *Notorious,* a trope for the manufacture of nuclear bombs, atomizing, artificially glowing, cinematic weapon.) The Gestapo spy handler Emberg, we later hear, will be the other man reading a paper on the train. Here, on the train, reading is evoked, and recalls that an "R" series is established in the film as well.[5] Its narrative departs from a rendezvous in Reims, it is preoccupied with what it continuously calls the Resistance, the first letter of RAF will be dwelt on and recited to identify the British pilots. Indeed, the centrality of the Hôtel de la Poste suggests a problem not only of telegraphy but of deferment, delay, *posting* ("No later than three a.m."). This also appears in Sandy's closing gesture toward a future time, after the war, when he would have (proleptically) met the dead Jeanne (preceding the officer's mention of a future "tomb of the unknown civilian"). *Resistance,* as a term, will be developed elsewhere (for example, in *To Catch a Thief*) to register a cinematic refusal of states or natural impositions of identification, desire, gender.

Which here raises the question of resistance (also) to what (or what else)?

The question is complicated by any logic of the contretemps. Does the latter reference a *performative* rupture in or of (this) history, or of a counterpolitics of such ruptures that cannot be formally inscribed in either "side" even in *this* world war, since the horizons and time management set *against* by Hitchcock's war machines are perhaps more encompassing still (and will elicit work like *The Birds,* "homing pigeons" assaulting "humanity" in its entirety)? It is complicated because here (again) a cinematic intervention will be momentarily aligned with Gestapo figures, including *Em*berg, for whom the double agent Stefan Godowski works (the simulacrum, the dead man who can walk). One might want to say, not too cryptically and with reference to "later" Hitchcock, that *M*'s or "Mother's" voice can speak through any *body.* "Voice" is, arriving from a prerecording, already gossip, innuendo, linkage, sound, archival touchstone: "Mother" (almost) personifies this condensation. The direction of this reading asks how Hitchcockian writing, as a system, is imported into and appropriates these propaganda shorts. If it is problematic, it may also be because a certain "Hitchcock" becomes inscribed, as said, in the figure of Emberg, the master of media.

This prospect flashes up when the interrogating officer tells Sandy about Stefan's other rendezvous, at another café than that which Stefan suggested. Here Hitchcock diverts the puppet project of double espionage in a semaphoric or "materialistic historiographic" direction. What decides the secret agenda of Stefan is a turn, as it were, toward Hitchcock's perennial *mar-* signature, a turn toward a performative logics of the mark that underlies transport, postal relays, and services: which is also to say, a service that renders the tourist, the viewer, in a position perpetually "post" to the narrative inscription, its present, and herself.

The rendezvous turns out not to be at the Café de Commerce that the fake Stefan goes to but, as we are told and shown, another, the Café des *Mor*onniers. If the *mar-* or *mor-* system invoked were not enough to activate our reading switchboard, we are left with the fact that the Gestapo contact's name is *Oskar Em*berg. It is an impacted name, an explosive whirligig of plants—*O, M, mar, more* (as in a later use of *Morocco*), *-ber(g)* as bar series, *Berg* as mountain, and so on. A *letter* is posted, and it activates the serpentine *M-* series and dossier across Hitchcock: *M* as a triple triangle figure, the thirteenth letter, the letter of Mother, murder, memory, music, and so on. (The "propaganda" film at this point, at all points, has no chance; it is a "genre" like any other, a taxidermist citation.) Even the *C-O* of Café de *C*ommerce touches a related trip wire, as it were, that of the 3 and 1, and we have been inscribed in this allographic zone of sheer commerce to begin with, in either case, the "Commerce" that is a historical café of sheer (de)capitalization, a critique of the commercial background of the war, summons more than a passing *C-O* evocation. In its anagrammatic folds and transported letters echoes counting, conning, and the *mer*(e), sea or seeing. But one has shifted cafés where one will sip or eat and observe this historial play, one has accelerated straight to that of the Moronniers, and to Emberg. Emberg and the false Stefan (or *steps*) who we will later hear recognized by the police as one "M. le Blanc" or Mr. White, are not "real" Germans as such but a projected structure, in this case, that inhabits and "doubles" a first or hermeneutic empire, England, toward which homing pigeons carry messages or return. Yet all of this occurs in the media, transport, carrier pigeons, the post, not in the contents of any letter or, for that matter, map. Blank or *blanc,* like snow, at the top of a mountain or *Berg,* as in earlier Hitchcock scenes of Alpine babel. That M. le Blanc's handler is Oskar Emberg inscribes what in Hitchcock might be called the M- constellation as the expanding network of a certain *mater*iality at the core of a "Gestapo" routine, as the controlling agency behind the "homing pigeon," Sandy, whose chance escape was from the start arranged, and who unknowingly carried the desired yet undisclosed message. It is the media themselves that are sorting out, betraying all "positions."

We perhaps see why, for Hitchcock, it is impossible to keep roles separate even in a "propaganda" film: they are in fact different moments of competing articulations, systemic spirals, mutually disinvaginated. The Resistance resists an *occupation* by another, something lodging already or imposed, but it also resists a certain inscription while operating as a transfer machine, a postal system for the relaying of a destructive *missive* or virtual missile, such as Sandy inertly becomes. The interruption in and of time by a structural contretemps (the film itself or its folds) stands to suspend an entire mimetic and narrative regime out of which the war is staged—what implies (and generates resistance to) a certain ordering of narrative or time or history. The performative consequences of Hitchcock's *temporal* politics, and the frame of history here, is alternately that of the Resistance and Emberg in differing roles or moments. Each stands to facilitate or disrupt the return "home" to England—a place, as the film acknowledges, where those most at home speak an alien tongue stammered by another alien (Scot) dialect. In order to connect with a historial politics that destabilizes the hermeneutic regime out of which rhetorical war stances are framed, the text must relinquish the literal referents of its figures (Gestapo, Resistance), that which the photography indexes—as if this lay at some root cause within the general catastrophe being surveyed or accelerated.

When the police question Sandy in the Hôtel de la Poste, he explains that he is an "Irish" mechanic working in a nearby factory that was bombed, exploded, ruptured, as if cinematically. The police have already been told to leave a disguised pilot with the flimsy cover story alone. He is their courier too, as a parasitic ganglion takes over the secret postal system of the enemy state (home, England), much as Hitchcock does the MacGuffin of "natural images" and citational sets. It is not what is relayed here but who controls and works the media or how—the cameoed "Hitchcock" glimpsed in the editing booth of *The Lodger*'s press- and newsroom.

Reference to the bombing of a factory points to a rupture—in the Café de Moronniers or of the mark. The *moronnier* inhabits French from another tongue, noncoincident with itself; the double inflection, *moron,* seems, contrary-wise, castigating the blindness of the war tourist who returns home as a lethal *carrier,* contaminating all en route. It is viral. It posts an evacuation at the site of fact production ( *fact*ory) by atomizing signifiers like sheer sound or light bursts (bombs), using the lethal ropelike tracks of Sandy's escape as a cover and lure. Hitchcock identifies an epistemo-political order under meltdown as encompassing the defining historial clash of the time, or countertime(s), and undertakes an alternative sabotage of and tear in the whole fabric. The far side of this attempt leads, inescapably, to a certain future, to something that is also an alternative or nonfuture, the post-present, "after" the war, which the propaganda film as genre promises. It is the vacated future rendezvous of Sandy and the dead Jeanne, to which the intelligence officer speculates about a time at the Arc of Triumph when there is a new tomb, to the *unknown civilian*. The future resting place posits both the existence and nonexistence of a civilian to inhabit it, one able to have read, for instance, *Bon Voyage!* This closing line, pretending to a cheap sentimentalization of Jeanne as humble martyr, points instead toward a tomb of the future, one that will acknowledge the future in a retro-monumental past which the film's "present" would become (and thereby be arrested by), a tomb that is still linked to nonknowing ("unknown"), something that all along has been the position of the setup escaped pilot, or the figure of the tourist viewer.

The name Sandy has resonance, too. Sand is dropped in the generator to put out the lights opening *Sabotage,* and doubles for radioactive matter in *Notorious*'s wine bottles: sand, a certain atomized earthen *matter* without collective shape or metaphoric embellishment. It stops, potentially explodes, creates artificial light, is the correlative of "fog," is irretrievably premimetic and other: cinema as weapon of mass de(con)struction. Sandy does not "know" what was in the letter, nor what he (stupidly) occasioned, nor the destruction of his passage in relay, nor the hidden postal relays that undergird the entire text and orient it toward a gauntlet of inert signs entirely unsuited to a propaganda film yet entirely inescapable for Hitchcock. Sandy, momentarily, is the propaganda film tourist viewer who will not know what he, in turn, is courier for—either the dissembling future of the industrial states with their cold wars and hyper(de)capitalism in the techno era to come (which Hitchcock initials and sabotages simultaneously), or its destroying double, the cinematic project of historial intervention, disassembling. Not surprisingly, then, such a countertext and contretemps seems anchored in the pivotal reading scene on the train, a scene of exchanged code words deregulating the day, time, memory itself: something like *reading* in a hyperbolic fashion—for once you have distanced both sides of a world encompassing war, what or where is left?—here determines a site of *archival interruption.* This, by suspending in advance the very "referential" system and machine that, for Hitchcock, England, the land of angels or messengers, linguistically represented as monolingual state, as ocularcentric *home,* or as the topos of the house from *The Lodger* through *The Birds.* Sandy's obliviousness to much beyond eating makes him the unwitting bearer of a killer-by-exposure missive or routing whose outline is conserved in the last image of the film, that of a future empty tomb, after the wars of the "present" would have been over. Like cars elsewhere, the true carrier is the material trace and aims, like an infection in the artery, directly at the heart—at the Home Office. De Gaulle's people should have known better than to hire a chronic saboteur to perform the sort of mission they gave Hitchcock, aiming to use him, like the appetitive Sandy, to carry an empty message that is turned against all and brings down every chain of schemes it facilitates. The empty letter expropriates all who handle it, not only the warring parties, but also the tourist viewer and Hitchcock himself, who occupies Sandy's position in his serial filmmaking.

The temptation to produce a propaganda film for the "good" side could be Hitchcock's greatest temptation to mimetic discipline—were that possible. This reverse permeability of "performance" and the political arena is precisely thematized by *Aventure Malgache*. The espionage scene here is steeped in the threat of instant death and exposure, which forms a different backdrop—let us call it "war"—than the narratives that must skirt and interface an official code or censorship. Rather than present a constitutively different logic than the commercial films, at the Café de Commerce, these risks and implications at the Café de Moronniers appear differences of degree. The "contretemps" inhabiting this miniature is preoriginary to the time it pretends to service, a servicing that becomes an order of betrayal. The viral betrayal is not that of Gestapo to Resistance fighter, which is no betrayal, or even the hungry Sandy to England (no betrayal for a Scot, perhaps), but the "betrayal" by the image of what presumes to use it as a Hôtel de la Poste. It exposes a contretemps of, and in, wartime, which is always also for Hitchcock a war within image, a *bird war* of cuts against a conjoined program encompassing a phase of "humanity." When it is not a hot war, it is a cold war or a terrorist war: it is never suspended. The film's witty French title, *Bon Voyage!*, clearly wishes happy travels to the tourist before his or her role as homing pigeon, a "good luck" to the cinematic consumer and interpreter of these missives, and a sarcastic encouragement before a different type of transport or translation, from a different "time." The *voyageur* as *voyeur* of a wartime eruption, *enjoying* the motifs of betrayal more than heroism and evil enemies—the hook, the candy: the trap begins to close, crystallized as a side panel within a broader historial labyrinth.

The propaganda short reinforces the impression that Hitchcock conceived both warring sides to be unequal if alternate ends of the same spectrum, dossiers of a grander historial and perceptual curse or program, a generally destroying history within an eviscerating representational re-gime. A *gran mal d'archives* that is still running its course. With the con-temporary ascendancy of the telemediacracies over their fascist doubles, as in Hitchcock's "America," the destroying drive becomes globally diffuse and accelerated, rather than terminated. Sandy, like the tourist viewer, is a carrier of the infection he would, he thinks, escape.

# II. Prehistory of the
# Afterlife of Cinema

# 3. A Performativity without Frame

> But if the juice dries up on its own accord, that would be an act
> of providence, as laid down in the act of William the Fourth,
> where an act is *defined* as any activity actuated by actual action.
> —*Sabotage*

It is not enough to remark a propensity to performance or "acting" in
Hitchcock, since the topic cannot be framed in a manner that maintains
borders, speakers, or places of retreat. Rather than a so-called modernist
or Pirandelloesque inflection of wit or reflexivity, the "citational structure" of the image seems turned upon itself and retracts received definitions of action, questions the spectrality of the event, allows the verticality
of movement to rewrite or vaporize direction. This question is raised if
not answered by David Sterritt:

> Hitchcock's characters "act" for more than one audience, moreover.
> They perform for one another's benefit—whether the motive is to se-
> duce, deceive, cheat, or simply communicate—in the various schemes
> that generate and sustain their narratives. They perform for their own
> gratification or protection, à la Norman Bates. They perform for us as
> we watch their movies. And they perform for Hitchcock himself. . . .
> Hitchcock, furthermore, can be considered a performer in his own
> right—explicitly in his cameo appearances; and implicitly as he ma-
> nipulates the figures in his films, who act *for* him on-screen.[1]

Norman, indeed, emerges with his wig like a diva. But it is more
interesting to note where the relation of any speaker to his or her own
mnemonic script is currently marked as a citation. Melanie Daniels enters
the bird shop—which, going back to *Sabotage,* is also a front for dispens-
ing saboteurs' bombs—to purchase, she says, mynah birds, birds whose
name suggests meaning or what is "mine" *(Meinung)* yet that memorize

empty speech sounds and repeat them, like the children later memorizing words in singsong repetition at the schoolhouse. Marnie is told by Mark how to behave like a wife: "This is the drill, dear. Wife follows husband to the front door, gives and/or gets a kiss. Stands pensively as he drives away. Oh, a little wave is optional." Roger O. Thornhill is said to be playacting a subject position that does not exist, including his own play-within-a-play death ("your very next role," Vandamm quips)—though, curiously, the apartment at the Plaza that is rented to "George Kaplan" may appear to be the one "Cary Grant," an assumed name, kept. Judy Barton will play "Madeleine," who haunts "Scottie" without ever having existed as such, a reality or false referent that will, in effect, drive "Judy" (playing or played by Kim Novak) over the edge of the bell tower. The actors cannot escape this—and not only "James Stewart," who seems reversed and exposed, or "Cary Grant," whose history and sexuality are marked and toyed with. Grace Kelly, screen siren, will repeatedly be stripped of sexual allure so that it will have to be (unsuccessfully) restaged as prosthetic performances of gender before unseducible or reactive, seemingly neuter males, as if "gender" itself defied reinvention.

The performative does not here name a "modernist" gesture, a commentary on the relation of theater to cinema, a token of self-consciousness or reflexivity. It is without retreat or reprieve, *exposed*, corresponding to the permanent parabasis marked by Hitchcock's cameos, whose signature logics do the opposite, it is now clear, of securing a return to the god-auteur's will. Just as the blackmailer Tracey was called a "sponger," this Möbius-like enframing retains the citational capacity to absorb and fold into itself whatever is unlucky enough to have been *marked* as an outside, a before, or an after. This concept does not pertain only to the inscription of the stars, consumed as semiotic sparklers. It is put into play from the first, as in *The Lodger*'s "Daisy," a model, played by "June, a mannequin," as later "Tippi" Hedren (as she is citationally listed), blonde model, will be "actually" inducted to serve *The Birds*' or *Marnie*'s apotheosis of blonde defacement. In *Murder!* the murder turns on supposedly keeping Handel Fane's "secret" of being a "half-caste" ("black blood!"), yet "Diana Baring" is played, half-cast, by "Nora Baring," the model for *The Inner History of the Baring Case* that appears as Sir John's "play" in the work's final fold of representation. Every trace chain connected to a gesture or personage or placement can be activated, displaced into a network, and, in cinematic terms, "set" without outside, including, on the *set* itself, props such as "nature," trees, and seas. The citational machine of what calls itself a camera or shutter engulfs a repetition (and rehearsal) in advance of its appearance.

Anything caught in the photographematic web is, can only be, cited as "half-cast(e)," but that casting is also a fall without reserve or ground, perhaps without up or down precisely. A star is always half-cast in film, since she is also playing herself as star and person; half out, in the star's radical singularity and history; a representational pretense half thrown or cast down in the process. In *Rope,* James Stewart, unable to speak up in his role as Rupert, is taunted by the on-set adorations of other stars in Hitchcock films and their constellations (Ingrid Bergman, "Virgo," Cary Grant, "Capricorn"). Grace Kelly never gets out of *To Catch a Thief*'s folds, to the point of being appropriated by the commodity fantasy of the "Riviera" and dying in a car crash at the scene of the picnic.

## Acting "Like"

The so-called parabasis is permanent, cannot be suspended; it consumes and rewires reference, puts the status of acting or action in question while the horizons drift, void, toward the abysses of narrative in *Vertigo* or of the geological face-off of Mount Rushmore or of precession of virtual "identity" in *Psycho,* and so on. It formally explores its antecitational premise. The act as such must occur, or be calculated, as an impossible coincidence of repetition with itself—the single shot rehearsed to coincide with the "Storm Cloud Cantata's" lightning-like cymbal clash. The "event" happens, if it does, elsewhere than in this present, within archival settings. What we call performativity, sometimes too broadly, has no *place* to return to, no "subject" effect (or even literal actor). Turned upon itself, it is a performativity without frame; hence the ceaseless recurrence to Hamlet and hyperreflexive inductions of the acting itself into the dialogue (James Mason and Eva Marie Saint, for instance, criticizing whatever it is Cary Grant does as not very good acting). It is horizonless "acting," which must by definition also fail or be paralyzed. This is the secret of agency, that it occurs by, but outside of, any control of this event, and it is the very focus of *Secret Agent,* in which the "secret" agency seems to exceed any human player as the power of sheer and voiding sound, a black dog or mark or trace, a chocolate allied to postal relays and (endless) translation or transcription.

Something secretive about this agency (and its espionage), the agency of a "secret" that, like Handel Fane's "black blood," is none. Unlike theater, where different actors may assume a role, cinema will imprint only one individual actor, and his or her acting, shape, semiotic implications, public repute, other roles, body movements—all will have to be inducted, cast, or thrown. And something happens to these people, too: Grace Kelly never leaves the set of *To Catch a Thief,* Tony Perkins is vaporized in and by *Psycho*—stamped universally, almost unusable, a sign of "Norman."

The *secret* appears inescapable but it is never secret: it, too, is not to be trusted "as" itself. There would be no figuration without it, and, in a sense, there is none. The "secret" may appear to be the motive of blackmail, for instance. The latter's logic might read: there is a trace, something from the past, like a picture made or witnessed from which a photograph emerges, that is known by another and used against some person's present or situation. The trace always knows too much and always blackmails, reads the "present" otherwise. It does not even need a referent: the first act of blackmail in *Blackmail* involves a message in a letter (we never learn the content) pertaining to Crewe, whose death erases the need to know it and becomes the "secret" in turn for Alice White or, later, her detective boyfriend. It can be spoken around and exchanged, on credit, for various commodities (cigars, money, Alice). In *Murder!,* though, the secret is that the transvestite actor Handel Fane is a "half-caste," and he supposedly murders Edna Druse to keep that secret from getting out to Diana Baring, who, we are told, plugs her ears so as not to hear and closes her eyes. She will be accused and indicted for the murder, which Fane allows, and he, in turn, was wearing a police costume during it, ostensibly to facilitate his escape. Yet we later learn that Diana Baring already knew the secret—whether being "half-caste" references being lower-caste with "black blood" (more than a racial marker) or being transsexual, homosexual, or allosexual. Or whether the term means, also or primarily, being half in and half out of *any* frame, here, half-"cast" theatrically and half-thrown, or cast, in a game meant to scramble the encounters of *chance,* or its outside: one name for what enters an entropic system to recast it, but which can only enter through a *labyrinth* of calculations (the birds attacking the Brenner house).[2]

The mediatized secrets of cinema conceal, in their obviousness, its spectrality—its stealth operations of rape, theft, disinscription of programs. That there are vast machines and duties and planning for production is effaced like the projector reels behind the viewer: cinema's technicity is already anterior, *ante,* though there, it simulates and approaches the site of preinscriptions, prerecordings, and mnemonic imprints. It simulates that by which, forgetfully, memory programs the sensorium or phenomenality of semaphoric experience or perception, like "seeing." It turns against this contractual forgetfulness, however, to at all points interrupt the machine of inscription, to alter the past and future by an intervention within the mnemonic orders from which "presents" are projected—what, in its way, is always also the MacGuffin of the MacGuffin. The effect of cognition is *animation* as the spectral minus any prospect of other, in what it thinks to be a living remove.[3] This, too, is where the actor encounters his or her autocitational words, as script or voice-over (by another), like the mynah birds sought in the opening of that film. The anatomization of storage media involves an effaced autocitation by which "actors" are, in turn, marked and effaced. When the word *storage* is insinuated by several flashing neon letters outside the penthouse windows at the close of *Rope*, the scandal that cannot quite be read or named is directed to the faux seamless band of memory storage the claustrophobic set—in fact, Möebius-like—implies in its perpetual movement or exitless replay.

Aperformativity is dangerous, like Bruno Anthony on a train, to others because it has nowhere to retreat, no subject, no dwelling (whether the English state or a California motel), as well as dangerous to itself. It is exposed, it exposes itself, to chance, to what can no longer be called alterity, erasure. Nothing is "outside," and the secret of this performativity itself is hidden fully in the open: it is so obvious it is secret. Like Larita's histrionic line from *Easy Virtue* when facing the news cameras following the divorce—"Shoot. There is nothing left to kill!"—the experience of the citational camera shot materially dematerializes, voids all reserves of identity. Hamlet references pervade Hitchcock from *The Lodger* or *Secret Agent* through *North by Northwest,* in the throwaway line of an office flirt in *Marnie* ("Have I got a danish for you?") or the reference in *The Birds* to "our little hamlet." They situate, again and again, two issues that attend the performative, for which Hamlet is perpetual cipher. First, there is the formal impasse of knowing too much to speak, something that contradicts the public truths of the court (or state), out of memory, and which produces endless discourse in the deferral, perhaps, of the one "act" that is a refusal of act yet transforms the scene in its entirety. The second issue concerns the problem of how or where an "act" or event issues as a defacement of the totality of the court—and, perhaps, suicide, were that not redundant. The problem of such a conceit of performativity is not limited to the agency of sound *(Secret Agent),* to the secrecy of foreign agents allied to feet, steps, or legs *(The 39 Steps)*—that is, to "material" signifiers including, and preceding, letters and numeration. Nor is the problem confined to actors inscribed in the works playing characters that are playing the "actors," nor to the relation of speakers to prescripted repetitions, nor to mnemonic recordings they do not coincide with or lip-synch properly, nor to the historial event or intervention, nor to sabotaging the entire state of affairs, the state regime or policial order of memory that requires that this excess knowledge or "knowing too much" be repressed. It is not limited to the parade of cameos, which the discourses of auteurism—virtual sun worshipping—cover. And it is not limited to the redundant phrase "acting *like*," particularly "like" what one is supposed to be or is in fact acting like, *en abyme*.

## The Empire Hotel

One has moved, one always was in, a zone of citational sets and chains, the black hole of the engulfing and labyrinthine image, portal of the tele-archive. It presupposes atomization, as of screen images of their "own" voiced-over sound tracks, auto-lip-synched, or of words within marked sounds and repetitions, of the whole system and spies' post office of un-read signature effects traversing and preinhabiting "Hitchcock." This is clear enough, today, in the treasury of critical explorations of the most minute detail in this oeuvre. It would recast itself, which is also to say "world," since the citational machine also is produced in perpetual back loop as something too light, a mere skin, too condensed, totalized in advance—as though the cinematic in this mode advances, instantly, to the borders of the state, seeks the outside of its own or the state's archival programs in the suspension of identification, representation, reference. At the core of the medium intended, by a certain generalized aesthetic state, to secure referential realisms, all of these aspects are suspended by the sheer externality of mnemonic inscriptions—by the celluloid as fact and storage band.

Phrases that will turn up again and again in Hitchcock in addition to "acts like" include entire networks or torsions of consequences: "too much," which recalls whatever is passing for narrative to an involuntary and hyperbolic acceleration internal to its logic; "queer," which ruptures the binary template of socialized gender to arrest channeled assumptions of identity; "sounds like," which draws one into punning labyrinths of the ear, linked up across the entire production. Mrs. Stevens tells H. H. Hugheson, the "insurance agent" performed by John Williams in *To Catch a Thief,* that he is "acting like an insurance agent"—that is, what he "is," or is acting as in the mise-en-scène, and so on. One, someone, is "acting like" what one is, only really cannot be, since one is or was "acting like" that to begin with, acting like acting like acting . . . which performs a certain likeness. The *mise-en-abyme* of mirrors in "Mother's" bedroom in *Psycho* startles Lila yet occurs just after her review of two resting bronze hands, severed organs of technicity or writing. It is a moment preceding Lila's review of Norman's bedroom and descent into the fruit cellar in her quest of Mrs. Bates, her encounter with "Mother." No *mise-en-abyme* is possible to luxuriate in as a form of irony. Rather, it points beyond *itself* to heroic prerecordings (Beethoven's *Eroica* on Norman's phonograph) that can only be repeated—or broken at the nonsite of inscribed mnemonics?

There would appear to be a law in Hitchcock: nothing is free from a contamination and drift that the metaphorics of performativity, itself, cannot circumscribe or curtail, since it is not a "metaphorics" at all. As with Hamlet, the performative is hyperbolically mobilized to yield something beyond—or before—its own cognitive paralysis, something that is an act, an interruption or event, taking down the entire court, which also knows (without saying) the "secret" of its historial impasse or police structure. The logic is no different from that invoked in speaking of breaking with ideological machines one is inscribed in and situated by. When Hitchcock rewrites the "aesthetic" in his first cameo in *The Lodger,* in Nietzschean fashion, from a category of entertainment to being the site where the world is phenomenalized from inscriptions or imprints (the teletype machine in the giant pressroom), the *aesthetic* is converted or revealed as a putative site of epistemo-political materialization by way of mnemonics.[4] Throughout Hitchcock there are references to suspended direction or its loss before a movement that is always stationary or vertical. This occurs in the pivoting arrow of the weather vane in *Murder!,* in the opening "direction" signs (left to right) of "*I Confess,*" even in the hapless arrows affixed to the outer wall of Rusk's apartment as a murder occurs. And notably, in the sheer excess of cross-traffic that opens the credit sequence of *North by Northwest.* One is routinely reminded that "north by northwest," while appropriating a line of Hamlet's, names a *nonexistent* direction, an "impossible" direction that leads not only to the border over which the micrologies inside a pre-Columbian figure would *pass* but to what seems the edge of an earth space. It has to do with the cinematic (microfilm, transport, Mount *Rush*more) yet shifts performativity from the usual play-within-a-play logic to a voiding precipice before personification or aura can be dissembled.[5]

Aperformativity sets a chain of effects in vertiginous motion that leads from a mimetic concept—"acting like" as the attempt to put on a mask that can be taken off, metaphor—to the absence of any mimetic ground. It is routinely the avuncular mentors—Murchison, Uncle Charlie, the Professor—who *betray* at the source, among other things, their guise as mentor or uncle. Yet if this fall that is neither up nor down loses a ground or (an) earth, it cannot get back to what was never there, and stands before a passage or translation into other terms. Something stands to be (or have been) reassembled in its place, already, as and before speech; so far as ground itself goes, this might be called a prosthetic earth, earth as an effect of trace chains that crisscross its bands, dispossess in advance its eyes. Such an *irreversible* direction like Benjamin's "one-way street" does not leave intact, any more than one could return to the sanctuary of the home or hospitality from its displacement as the Bates Motel. Norman guarding the portals of the netherworld with and in the name of "Mother." This renders Marion's at first warm and cleansing shower a mirror for the anticipated haven of the spectator entering the motel room: the shower a false sunburst, the slashing that of a bar series infiltrating all phenomenality, interiority, sensorial programming. Norman will condense this performer performed by the dialectical impasse of Mother's ventriloquized and ventriloquizing "voice." As he says or performs before himself in alarm on "discovering" Marion's body: "Oh, Mother! *Mother!*" Yet if Mother is not, if she has no place, if her personification requires less another being spoken through than the rupture of attempting to do that—and being exposed, inversely, in her mummified nonplace—it remains to be asked how these systems, so clunky in certain respects, return nonetheless to a deanthropomorphized and nonoriginary figure of the (a)maternal, matrical, or "material," to something left as an archival trace in words or terms eliciting or "sounding like" *mar* or *mer(e)*, particularly where these last are not given phenomenal form or sense.

## I Thought I Heard Voices

Hitchcock told Truffaut that dialogue is just more sound. The screen wraith lip-synchs what is then supplementally attached as a sound track of the "same" speakers' voice-overs; usually, though, this can be altered, or the lips be out of synch intentionally, or one might have another English-speaking actress speak the lines of a German one, Anny Ondra, in his first "talkie," *Blackmail.* This muting partition of an always prosthetic voice, separated from itself as from the moving lips of the spectral speaker, effects another double-click in the citation of *sound* itself, atomized and inviting webs of repetitions, things that "sound like" others, traversing scripts and speakers. Dialogue dissolves into sound, not the reverse: the pretended taming of sound for the anthropomorphism of voice. And this voice gets detached from everything, wanders, like "Mother's" voice does in *Psycho,* without home or body; a performativity without performer. Two things emerge from such a moment in *Vertigo* that are relevant to a horizonless movement across Hitchcock. The first has to do with time and the second with memory.

The "narrative" as an artificed construct loops back and precedes its own past, as the hokey theme of a return of the dead rising to harm the living pitched by Gavin Elster is literally exceeded. It is not the exception, it is the norm: on the screen, in its "life," in "life," the present does not exist except as a programming traversed by ghosts, others' words, trace chains, as Benjamin's reading of the photographic image banally foresaw. Any ground of reference is bracketed by the formal disruptions of a secret that is all too open (being "half-caste," the corpse in the cassone, "sex" in *To Catch a Thief*). Because "Madeleine" never existed as such, she cannot even be a real ghost, or is more real for not having been either living or dead. These convoluted "portals of the past" cannot be named *such* if a memory, however monumentalized or loved, is an implant to begin with, a sham, one Judy must re-create knowing it to be so, and so on. The "vertigo" of this logic involves a deregulation of anteriority, cinema now, not as séance—in which the past and the future stand to be recast—but as time machine run amok. But the contaminant logics of this technic do not belong to the human or speaker either. The vertigo-swirl in the sequoia trunk preinhabits the faux maternality of nature (Midge's last name is "Wood") with a movement that archives historical moments. If the dead that inhabit the living are grafted into the past by the seemingly alive (who are, anyway, unwitting specters), there is no "living" to begin with—just different types of inanimation. Any anteriority that can be installed or relies on a circular feed can be short-circuited, deregulating succession and temporality. *Vertigo* pursues this further consequence.

Hitchcock links such performativity to something hyperbolically disruptive: the number, if it is one, of three.

Carlotta's pendant that Judy Barton puts on has a bar across the top and three jewels. That is, it potentially is triadic, or more than that, a citation of 13, as is the name *Car*lotta perhaps with its opening C (third letter) and A (first), a situated and recurrent marker across Hitchcock.

For Hitchcock, the number 13 and its variants are associated with a self-canceling origin, a leap or defaulting *Ursprung* to which voice itself is tied, since now "voice" is not only another's (even if the same actor did the voice-over at a later time) but simultaneously appears hyperbolically citational and decapitated, in effect, *muting* the speaker, barring communication, "pictures of people talking." In the *Em*pire Hotel, in which Judy is found, the empire of an entire metaphysical system shifts to a conflagration or pyre of the "M": the *thirteenth* letter, one letter with three triads composing it, marks, as in the hotel similarly named in *Spellbound*, in conflagration.[6] A seemingly triadic or apostrophic model of a spoken subject, as a voiced auto-puppet, depicts of the "I" a ventriloquized ghost in advance of itself, and the sequence of 3 a false narrative designed to fictionally restrain a hyperbolic or explosive speaker position. The 3 is not at all secure, and gets propped up by retroprojecting a 1, a 1 and 3 or 13, a 3 conjuring and erasing "one" before its advent, exposing itself, too, as a zero and zero as a MacGuffin, a cauldron or threshing machine held in suspense by the visible plane that the triangle introduces to space. For even in this model such a "public speaker" would be like Hannay in the Scottish Assembly Hall, unable to say what he knows amidst allegories of double-talk before a public that takes him for a laconic Scot. In the process, it is such an "I" that is structurally void and hyperbolically positioned as the cipher that, knowing nothing of this, will casually and differentially emerge in the smoke rings of Uncle Charlie, the blank amnesia of John Ballantine, the middle initial *O* that stands for "nothing" in Roger O. Thornhill, and so on. (One may call these Hitchcock's "O-men.") It returns us to the back-spinning circle in the opening of *Blackmail* that signals not just a wheel or a reel but a backloop of mnemonics that could break or void the programmatic implant by sheer acceleration. In *Rope,* the word becomes deed by misreading or too correctly reading a preceding generation's banter, a word issued by a pompous professor literalized and then disowned by its cowardly relay. At the beginning of *Strangers on a Train*, Bruno complains to Guy in their first meeting on the train that he (Bruno) envies the tennis player Guy, since he lives in the world and does things, unlike himself—except that he (Bruno) aperforms more acceleratedly stunning things having to do with technology and transport (having ridden in a supersonic plane and driven at high speed with his eyes closed, he speculates on interplanetary travel at the dinner party he turns up at later, and he kills).

## Activity Actuated by Actual Action

Aperformativity is so without reprieve or a fall-back position that it is compelled, in a way, to repeat itself forward, without model and copy, voiding any so-called subject position or to take cover behind the law. The theatrical metaphorics that suffuse *Murder!* or *Stage Fright* or even *"I Confess"* or *Family Plot* (Lumley's job as actor and references to sexual "performance") pertain not to the theater but a hyperperformativity we cannot call "speech acts" without sounding like the mocking example of William the Fourth's laying down of the "act" presented in *Sabotage*. *"I Confess,"* a film citing a paradigmatic speech act (in quotes), eviscerates the very "speech act" it makes the pretext of a narrative that claims every countervariation in this performative among its wreckage, for instance, Mme Grandefort's "confession" to protect Logan, which only provides the exhibitionistic occasion for her embellishments to damage her husband and further destroy Logan, and so on. What Sterritt calls a ubiquity of "acting" turns out to put the term's conventional uses at risk of meltdown and atomizing the clustered variants of agent, agency, actuality, action.

Ted (or "Ed") Spenser, *Sabotage*'s detective of traditional allegory, pursues the cinematic saboteur practicing Benjaminian allegory, that of the blast, the shock, the epistemo-political suspension and photographic *Blitz*, or blackout. This binds the act of sabotage practiced by Hitchcockian cinema, its performance and status as "event." Yet in his banter to the moviegoers seemingly robbed of their money, Spenser legalistically defends the ticket seller, Mrs. V. Although disguised as a *greengrocer*, a fruit and vegetable seller, he is the law, working here to evade the law with double-talk of a curious sort about acts, acting, and actions. The law, after all, enters the work limping, as double-talk by its own representative, who, in protecting Mrs. V., works to circumvent it. It is an enforced royal fiction for legatees inheriting the codified "act," a performative fiat become an inscribed fact, itself on inspection illegible. Law, legibility, *légère*, legs, and legacies are summoned:

> Now if a plane were to come along and drop a bomb on you, that would be an unfriendly act within the meaning of the act. But if the juice dries up on its own accord, that would be an act of providence, as laid down in the act of William the Fourth, where an act is *defined* as any activity actuated by actual action.

If the act of defining an act is in meltdown or suspension, would be arrested even, that definition must be resupplied from an absolutely legitimate source, a king's laying down of the law as the law, the king's "act" in which, once again, or "where an act is *defined* . . ." The giving of definition is as itself an act, is even archived as an "act": a question of official definition italicized by the dictionary entry for the word *sabotage* illuminated in the credit sequence. Its unquestioned authority lies in its anteriority or pastness as well: to disrupt being encased in a defining law one must, so to speak, precede it as well—loop back in a precession that exposes the founding implant or law as one virtuality among others. It disinscribes or suspends. Blacks out.

In the disguised detective's double talk, definition and meaning are in hiatus, and even aerial bombing, if it is different, consumes its self-reference in being designated "an unfriendly act *within* the meaning of the act." (And with this aerial bomb—"if a plane were to come along and drop a bomb on you, that would be an unfriendly act within the meaning of the act"—Hitchcock cites the telesthetic or cinematic air-strike derailing the narrative of his preceding outing, *Secret Agent,* where aerial bombings called in by "old man R" cut through the inability of the wooden Gielgud *to act* [in any sense], and specifically to stop the real secret agent, Marvin, from reaching Constantinople.) It is, in Peter Conrad's sense, atomized or "dematerialized" by cinema's technicity— or, as Christopher Morris suggests, a matter of something like *photons,* the reflective droplets suspended in fog.[7] Spenser's puckish summary and displacement of the *Genealogies of Morals* proceeds against itself. Derived from a royal act of positing the law, of the law positing itself, Spenser's badinage pertains to defining what is not in it, a definition of act as "of providence." By, in, or outside of this self-retracting law, something occurs, something happens or has happened, is catastrophic and "of its own accord."

Hitchcock marks a deformation in the amodernist and proactively destructive logics of "allegory," a shift from representation to what can no longer be called a performative yet which is turned upon, and against, the production of the "present" itself by inscription. At the opening of *Sabotage,* a luminous bulb dims out just as that in the projector, more or less ill-timed, goes on, inscribing the activity of the real projection as a counterperformative, even ritual, event. This caesura inscribes and per-forms a sabotage of and already within light and places everyone in the afterworld—but no one notices; Londoners emerging from the Under-ground just laugh and are entertained, and some want a refund. Verloc's effort to overcome this black hole or impasse mirrors Hitchcock's in the perpetually darkened work.[8] In William the Fourth's cited "act," "where an act is defined as any activity actuated by actual action," the consuming of cognates and positing of "origins" alike (dubious kings) open a peculiar dossier on the act—falling back into, or inversely exploiting, the virtual Hamletian paralysis of *Secret Agent* before a mercurial material trace (black ball, the dog, legs, sheer sound, the general, and so on). As a project Hitchcock pitched to a suspicious Gielgud as *"Hamlet* by other means," the allegorical princeling, William the Fourth, countersigns this in advance. To attribute the disarticulation of *act* to *Willi*am the Fourth's fiat or imposed "act" is to link the blackout to a cinematic totalization, a bar series in a four-sided frame. This blackout precedes nature, whose lightning blasts are inhabited by this logic. In the pugilistic knockout as cinematic *Blitz* at the Royal Albert Hall in *The Ring,* Conrad astutely reminds us: "White flashes of lightning with black intervals between them scythe across the screen" (62), like a "cosmic catastrophe."

An aperformativity without frame is, nonetheless, attacked by a crop duster that guards horizons to the point of spraying crops that do not exist. A horizon is a crease in a plane, here gathered machinally behind reel-like propellers and shooting guns. It turns the tropological order into a slaughter zone that is preparatory to an archival convulsion. Such aperformativity without horizon is less a rhetorical insight than, here, a surpassed donnée.

# 4. "How Old Is Mae West?"

"Have you time for me now?"
—Grace Kelly to Cary Grant, *To Catch a Thief*

The chief point I keep in mind when selecting my heroine is that she must be fashioned to please women rather than men, for women form three-quarters of the average cinema audience.
—Alfred Hitchcock, "How I Choose My Heroines"

In the opening scene in the Music Hall of *The 39 Steps,* a peculiar question is asked of Mr. Memory, who, generally, will repeat all known "facts" that the public can, in recognizing, confirm in the follow-up: "Am I right, sir?" Memory, heir of the mother of the muses, Mnemosyne, is reduced to turning tricks for the hoi polloi in what amounts to a cinema house: photographs, of course, copy "facts," and if the audience recognizes them he earns his keep. If the question is about the future (the audience tests and jostles him), he tells them to come back, and if it is too personal or baiting, he passes. But the question in question has an answer, a literal one anyway, and he still defers. Someone asks, "How old is Mae West?" Mr. Memory demurs that he never tells a lady's age.

But there are other reasons to play it safe, since it is a highly figural question. Given the presence of the word "West" and the topic of age, it may invoke the same history that he, a dignified creature fallen on hard times, partakes of by implicitly recalling Mnemosyne. Only later do we learn that he will regain his autonomy, or at least aggressive dignity, in other ways, as a courier for smuggling memorized secrets out of England for making a silent bomber. Mr. Memory's shift from repeating "facts" to becoming a weapon of mass destruction implies that cinematic memory, accelerated beyond mimetic "facts," converts into a techno-weapon to decimate the hermeneutic home state. He carries a string of numbers and letters, cryptonymies, that no one would have heard or could recognize when recited, breaking the pretense that memory is a slave of mimetic entertainment. But the question about "Mae West" he simply declines to answer. Why?

## Female "Female" Impersonation

Hitchcock makes several allusions to Mae West, all oddly inflected. In addition to this, a caricature of her appears in the Disney cartoon in *Sabotage*, being serenaded by Cock Robin when the latter is shot by a shadowy crow's arrow—half-bird, half-human. She is also alluded to in *Frenzy*, when the necktie killer Rusk references his "mum," who he notes used to say, "Beulah, peel me a grape"—an old Mae West line. "Mae West" as Rusk's "mum"?

Mae West would have to be acknowledged otherwise, as a subversive pop-cultural figure, as far as a lady's age goes. She is not just a lady. She is not just an aggressive sexual icon. She is, she was, perhaps the foremost female female impersonator, a deconstructor of gender performatives. It is one thing to be a male in drag, like Handel Fane, another half-bird when last seen in his suicidal trapeze act in *Murder!* But to be a female "female" impersonator amounts to a double positive and a double negative at once. Mae West would make jokes about men with prosthetic guns in their pockets, what Hannay turns up with in *The 39 Steps* in the form of a pipe. To ask, here, "How old is 'Mae West'?" turns out to have more deranging resonance, which accounts for Mr. Memory's silence. One could translate the question, for example, as, How long, in the West, has "woman" had to be a female female impersonator? How old is this charade, and what else would there be, if the entire system of gender differencing appears to depend upon it? It returns to the question of hyper- or aperformativity applied not to a phantasmal heterosexual norm but to where, or how, that apparent norm stages itself over its own absence—if, to begin with, "woman" were in question as a performative effect so old or instituted one dare not ask what preceded it. And the reason one might not do so, of course, is not only because of what it does or does not disclose about the heterosexed female norm. In a way, "Annabella Smith" will, moments later, give a counterdemonstration of this faux norm when she picks up Hannay with the implicit promise of sex, playing at the veiled mysterious lady, then eating, dismissing him, going to sleep alone, and staggering in with a knife in her back, driving him from his flat into the circular chase as her presumed killer. The question is dangerous, of course, because of what it might say of "men" in turn: are they, would they be, male "male" impersonators, or something else?

Cinematic *hyper*aperformativity opens in Hitchcock a question that does not have a familiar answer, any more than the formula for the warplane would be known and hence recognizable. But that is the point. And to some extent, this question has been raised indirectly in recent criticism, albeit from a position preinvested in the answer, or at least one form of the answer—to the degree that a queer or homosexualist other can be offered as the alternate system or logic to a compulsive heterosexualist code. Lee Edelman has pressed this strategy with unique insight, finding that a certain revocation of the heterosexist cliché of the couple appears in Hitchcock, where, as in *The Birds,* what is attacked is in part the way that a family plot decrees a certain claim to the future inherent in reproduction that voids arrival and decimates human terrain and meaning systems—one point for the attack on the children.[1] He terms this space, revising Slavoj Zizek, "*sinthome*-osexuality" and reinscribes it in the alternative sexuality and class, homosexually marked, whose practice of arrival or coming is not deferred since it is not chained to a nihilistic temporal model more or less chiliastic.

But what if alternative sexualities intricately populating Hitchcock were impossible to reinscribe in a new binary—not male and female or hetero and homo—and if the emptying of the dominant figures were irrecuperable to one or another of familiar alternatives that have always informed if not complemented that of the West back to the Greek motifs suffusing *The 39 Steps* (Mnemosyne, Muses, "Anabella," Palladium)? It is not accidental that Mae West would be a queer icon too, and it is not certain that queer performance represents an outside to this question posed to Mr. Memory. It is also always possible that what is in question involves autoimpersonation on every front, in the absence of literal *sex,* which can appear something of a MacGuffin itself in Hitchcock. As if, always also, a question about memory and the origins of the West involved a fault within mimesis or its programs. Or as if whoever or whatever one asks this from the screen, what speaks is already a shimmering wraith, an etched skin personified, a site of animation that, as in life, forgets and takes itself for real. If so, then "Mae West" would be a broader cipher or black hole in which the naturalization of gender performance, so evident in film actors and actresses, dissolved. Once again, the first victim of this black hole, as in *Vertigo,* would be the assumed "male" position (a point I'll return to).

If "Mae West" is remarkable, is already marked, she is not just another blonde, but a protean hyperbole or hyperbolic prototype, which no one, perhaps, is about to serially dispatch. "She" may be already monstrous, half-bird, half-animation, amaternal, yet the last place one might look for a cipher of Mrs. Bates's *khora*-like duties. "She" is empowered in an undecidably exaggerated site between gender performatives, a female "female" impersonator. Differently, the question reads: How long, for how many centuries or millennia, has "woman" been *this,* a performative effect of another's eye mimed within its own prosthetics, an impersonation of another as itself which supplants any original it claimed to be reciting inversely? That the question in the Music Hall goes *unanswered* is not at all surprising. A silence, a hole in memory, a courtesy? "How *old*" has to do, moreover, with age, duration, *birth dates.* How long has whatever Mae West signifies been around, anyway, or is there anything before it from a male-shaped discourse, since, as the origin of speech in *Blackmail* in a policemen's rest room suggests, a certain order of "talk" is homosocially and *male* inscribed? Does anything precede or displace what "she" pretends to and what "she" ruptures in advance? What pandemonium would occur if Mr. Memory answered?

Although one can extend this question into various corners of Hitchcock's work, and particularly with certain actresses or mise-en-scènes, it may be useful to suggest its inverse disclosure, which may make Mr. Memory especially reluctant to answer. That may be, not because Mr. Memory is obedient to the state (clearly, as a spy courier and traitor, like Hitchcock to his television "sponsors," he is not), but because of what it might do to his fragile livelihood as a Music Hall performer. It is clear in Hitchcock, for instance, that while the serial murder of women (largely blondes) figures as a core metaphysical preoccupation, and that feminist critiques have been particularly important, including Laura Mulvey's "male gaze" and Tania Modleski's nuanced indictment of Hitchcock's supposed paternalist suppression of woman's ambisexual knowledge—or the appearance of such—there has been residual inversion of anything that would allow a masculinist gaze to be monumentalized.[2] Fathers seem never to occupy paternal roles, or to be absent, or abdicated in advance. Innumerable males turn up, like the underwear salesman on the train with Hannay, who retreat in their preoriginary emasculation to diverse fetishes. But what Mae West as female "female" impersonator seems explosively to imply is a locus before which gender is performatively feigned. That this must be effaced is an example of how the cinematic deployment of Mr. Memory's formula emerges as a stealth weapon of mass de(con)struction. What must be supposed is that the "male" position is differently forged. Moreover, what is taken as a patriarchal order when examined for the violence of its effects has no such alpha figure at its core, no literal patriarchs or fathers, but rather—and one thinks of Hitchcock in drag as Queen Victoria introducing one of his TV slots—what could as well be called a *eunarchy*. That is, from the perspective of *The 39 Steps* there is no "male" either, not in the sense of an identity opposed to the *Nachkonstruktion* of institutional power.

## Golden Curls

As regards the construction of a postgendered "female" and its viral implications for what I have called the eunarchy I will focus on three Mae West avatars of very different sorts in Hitchcock: Tippi Hedren's Marnie, Kim Novak's Judy Barton as "Madeleine" in *Vertigo,* and Marlene Dietrich in *Stage Fright.*

The perpetual strain of pregendering or postgendering can be observed in any number of sites. When *Marnie* opens, we see her only from behind carrying a yellow purse stuffed with what turns out to be stolen cash, the loot from Strutt's office. It is perhaps cinema's most succinct undoing of the imaginary of the phallus, since by circulating as countermytheme of a freely detached and mobile vaginal entity, one expanding with folds and allied to the pink book pages that serve as background for the credit sequence, the alliance of a privileged signifier with the phallic order is simply suspended. With Marnie's back to us, we later see her many Social Security cards bearing various *Mar-* aliases, including Mary and Marion.[3] This cinematic thief "is" all of the Mar-names, or blonde variants, across Hitchcock. *And* she is their summary negation too, the *-nie* of the name heard as privative, a site that refuses imprint or projection. In the course of this story as told, Marnie would despoil the site of book publication or production, Rutland Publishing, as cinema itself would. She is a brilliant fabricator ("liar") and allomorphic thief impicturing herself according to the male employer's imaginary. Yet she is positioned opposite a *mark,* Mark Rutland—essentially James Bond (Sean Connery) as a trapped neuter requiring a cinematic chase, the hunting of Marnie as jaguarandi, to construct desire as entrapment. In the end he acquires her by implicit blackmail, when she chooses to go with him implying it is better than jail. Mark first hears of her as the victimized businessman Strutt is reporting her thefts to detectives. When they ask if she came to work for him with "references," he hesitates and his secretary reminds him that she did not. She had *no references.* She is instead teletechnically allied with a copy machine, an avenging she-Bartleby. Looking for a term to describe her criminal behavior, Strutt instead dwells on her *legs*, so Mark sympathetically suggests that she might be termed, simply, "resourceful." The term for a machinal copyist is self-canceling: the female female impersonator not as source or *Ursprung* quite, but as the contradictory *repetition (re-)* of (a) source, which can be no origin if it were already a repetition.

A parallel complication occurs in *Vertigo* with Novak's rendition of "Judy Barton" playing "Madeleine Elster." Kim Novak plays her as a tranced-out cyborg-blonde, although too full-bodied and too obviously affected (that is too obviously acting "like"), with features that could occasionally dwarf those of the deluded James Stewart. Stewart, in Hitchcock, is routinely regressed to a quasi-neutered vacancy over which his more familiar Hollywood traits—hysterical American everymale—are misaligned and barely cited to cover an enigma (unlike Grant, say, no compensating homoerotics seems to take over).[4] Hitchcock told Truffaut that what Stewart undergoes is a virtual "rape," which describes a cinematic variant of Hitchcock's logic of epistemo-political sabotage.[5] This "vertigo" will not be a fear of falling but a loss of up or down, of ground altogether, before the prosthesis of a mnemonic implant. It still has something to do with Mae West and, with all sorts of conditions, what is named "Mother" elsewhere: a personified nonsite precedent to gender assignations or personification, preoriginary, cutting and slicing, withdrawn from any auratic contract of identification, or narrative hypnosis spellbound to names, grammar, custom, spelling, installed programs.

"Scottie" will seem haunted and inhabited by the dead—the condition of cinematic séancing—but in fact he is haunted by a dead "Madeleine

Figure 7. Disinvaginated pocket: Marnie's stuffed aphallic "purse."

Elster" who was never alive, never existed as such, was only manufactured by (or through) Kim Novak's Judy Barton performing as "Madeleine Elster" to begin with (that is, perfoming as starlet "Kim Novak"). He is not even haunted by the real dead, which would be moderately sensible, since what never lived could not even be dead, properly, and the logic is rendered inside out, again. The memory of Madeleine is artificed, a mnemonic implant become a wildly mourned real to Scottie, a pre-spectral phantom whom Judy Barton, the "real" Kim Novak character, is then compelled to play at being yet again, to re-create in this tertiary arena through clothes and gesture, replicating at best the setup Gavin Elster contrived to manipulate him through her. It is odd that such a work should have been asked to exemplify the theory of the male gaze. Particularly so, since at the end Stewart shrieks at Judy that she was a "very apt pupil," that is, in addition to being Elster's creation, the locus of the eye, a nervous eye that opens Saul Bass's credit sequence of the film and appears preinhabited by graphic bands. Tracking up from the lips, the parting orifice of consumption and speech, what the camera enters is a woman's pupil preinhabited first by a vortex and then by monstrous graphics, Möbius-like in their spiraling and morphing elaboration, mnemonic webs mapped on twisting bands of space-time. Within the (here female) eye: mnemonics, graphics, marks; preceding the eye, lips: aperture of language, ingestion, teeth. Stewart has been in fact all along viewed and shot from woman's perspective—much as Midge glances up covertly, or discloses in the transposed head painting a perspective that could collapse the entire narrative fabric, compelling him to withdraw from the room without a word. Novak as Judy as Madeleine must watch Scottie giving in to every fake setup and bad act-ing set piece from the start. If Scottie has to fall for the haunted-woman act—that is, a clichéd prop of gothic cinema and literature—in order to be in love, and this in a mock-Oedipal transgression anticipated by Gavin, he exceeds the position he dismissed mockingly when Gavin first asked him if he believed that the dead can return and harm the living. Scottie's being haunted by a ghost of what never existed is what Hitchcock likens to a kind of rape.

## Interlude

It is another "blonde" who brings the "Mae West" factor to unannounced clarity: Grace Kelly, who by instinct seemed to understand Hitchcock's spectographic emptying and redoubling of gender as comic, and to respond as an insider—she perhaps thought. Screen goddess, no male in the films she appears in for Hitchcock seems to desire her. "Perfect," she would be murdered or fled from.[6] There is nothing like it, since the audience seems never to get this point—is always, somehow, as if blocking or compensating for this vacancy. Even homopoetics does not substitute an alternate truth or secret to counter heterosexual rituals, but appears a variant of a more primary suspension that is as if compensated for, or counterfeited, through gesture, impersonation, seduction as artifice. Since I will address this issue later I leave it as a bookmark for the moment, which Kelly herself might be called for other reasons. There is here, in every rehearsed phrase of script, a potentially effaced doubletake, where the "female" female impersonator appears as if in drag as "woman." Neither does "sex" function as the secret—no longer the repository of Eros or any universal drive for reproduction, suspended. What is called "sex" in Hitchcock is another MacGuffin, even as what is called desire will never strictly be affirmed, as if the very trope of desire were, itself, the relapse or mutation of an archival or scopic drive for which the closest analog might be eating or consuming, the eye as teeth. The blonde is another MacGuffin, or, as a chorus girl says (on a title card) early in *The Lodger,* when "golden curls" have become a prosthetic risk, "No more peroxide for yours truly."

Scopic violence toward "woman" and the prosthetic blonde specifically is redoubled and serially undone in the same gesture, a gesture, beginning with *The Lodger*'s Avenger, that both hyperbolizes and ruptures a metaphysical program implied, and subverted, by the question about the age of the counterblonde Mae West (whom no one is about to strangle). To be sure, "woman" is caught in machines of serial murder, the blonde whose open-mouthed mute face opens *The Lodger,* the "merry widows" of *Shadow of a Doubt,* Marion in the shower of *Psycho,* the necktie victims of *Frenzy.* On the one hand, "she" can be the summa of a reflected light in Western metaphorics, the evisceration of a program, the Western blonde as icon of European whiteness veered toward a violence through which a system had constructed and sacrificially fed itself. She is Hitchcock's white whale, whose serial negation in the Avenger's system hyperbolizes every narrative dependence on the $N + 1, + 1, + 1 \ldots$ as temporal abyss and zero-generated model. She is a specter of a metaphysics of "light" and the mopping up of its eviscerated program—that of woman as source, as other, as "Mother," as the undoing of each. On the other hand, this serial and even circular acceleration backspins off

its moorings like the carousel in *Strangers on a Train,* a strategy of exposure, sabotage. The murder of blondes sustains and repeats metaphysical programs, feeds this drive, names it at once and thoroughly in *The
Lodger,* dislodges it with all its hyperbolic implications, sacrifices itself to
its sacrificial drive. The *cinematic* in Hitchcock is not "representational."
It locates the source of phenomenalization in shadow, image as citation,
artificed "light" (obvious in the projector), mnemotechnics: a virtual
atomization of markers, "dematerialization," phantom digitalization.
This allies this cinema to a preoriginary trace for which the eye or "life"
is an effect. Yet cinema deploys this technical fact to bracket not only
the metaphorics it cites but also its own promise of anthropomorphism,
programs of identification. Hitchcock elicits from the spectrality of the
cinematic a deauratic, prefigural factor from which gender, psychology,
face, agency, and temporalization are decited, utterly denatured, recalled
from their prehistorial afterlife.

To link such an effortless deconstruction to concerns of social justice
is not without force, especially in what applies to the eunarchy. What is
called male in association with the discourse of a homosocial brotherhood (like the detectives who first introduce speech to this cinema in
the men's bathroom in *Blackmail*), a brotherhood of ritual mourning
and will to presence, is mounted over an evacuation. Body parts or organs are disinscribed—feet, steps, hands, ears can appear as if cut off and
autonomous. The eunarchy's double violence emanates from the counterforce of perpetuating the former's fiction, like a "Madeleine" who never
existed. Thus the position of a "father" is erased across Hitchcock, abdicated or fallen away: a family plot in the absence of paternity. In the
aperformatives of "woman," Hitchcock invites the violences and violations of the ocularcentric myth to converge, dis(as)semble, such as those
that have assumed the paternal metaphors of the Platonic sun and light,
the Enlightenment, or the transparency of the eye as their point of de-
parture and cognitive empowerment. Turned back upon themselves,
they are atomized as shadow play under what might be called now, with
all sorts of conditions, the "gaze of Mae *West.*"

Variations and combinatoires shift. In *Frenzy,* references are made
to "Dick-O" Blaney, as if two genital shapes were interfaced, mirrored
in the fetish necktie with its circle-collar and dangling tie. In *Family
Plot* Lumley promises Blanche in bed a "standing ovation," where an
erection is interfaced with an "O" figure marked as female (ovarian).
Tropes are circulated that retire the binary war of genital markers, become invertible spaces or topographic folds, like Marnie's purse.[7] Even

Figure 8. Animated, half-bird "Mae West" puts life and gender in question.

"Mother" is not one, not necessarily a she, not of a gendered binary or origin, perhaps an it, certainly spoken in *Psycho* by a voice in drag, or something like a marking system more generally: the nonplace where inscriptions phenomenalize world and program senses. Mother as celluloid, as Norman's bog. "Marnie" enters the film—and stands in for cinema here—as voided of the rituals of "sexuality" altogether, and for Connery she must be tamed, lured, blackmailed, and stupefyingly tutored to appear to assent to simulate it to assuage his bibliophilic or archival norm, that of the patrilineal eunarchy. In Hitchcock's calculus, she is a ground zero. Marnie serially performs a political theft of a phallo-semantic phantasm, virgin inversion of the space of prostitution that her mother will be marked with (*"Bernice Ed*gar" incorporates the bar motif and sheer anteriority into her cinematized name). One site of the eunarchy is represented by the book production business of Rutland Publishing.

Recasting the detective work of *Spellbound,* where the amnesiac Gregory Peck is haunted by the bar series pattern, Marnie seems led by her flashes of red back to a suppressed trauma, the young Marnie's killing with a fire poker of the sailor or john (Bruce Dern) visiting her mother. Yet what needs to be noted is that is also a screen memory or front, as Marnie's mother drifts into reverie about Marnie's origin, how she conceived and had her. The preflashback echoes origin while pretending, grotesquely, to be sentimentally induced. In her first act of prostitution, Bernice traded sex for Billy's basketball sweatshirt. Nice enough—except that *Billy* will be echoed in the zombie children's chant outside, in the word *ill* ("Mother, mother, I am ill, / Send for the doctor on the hill"), as it is echoed in the sister-in-law's name, Lil, putting out these letters as another bar series signature (ill, / / /), Marnie's progenitor as marker without source—*re*-sourceful. This precession of source is what, like that of the sun, introduces a movement of justice across Hitchcock's work, resistant to any identificatory inscription that is not mobile in its positional politics. In *The Birds* the caged lovebirds' sex cannot be identified, and in *Sabotage,* reference is made at the zoo to an antediluvian fish that, after birthing, changes sex. The psychoanalytic facade, as in *Spellbound,* is the MacGuffin Hitchcock plays when he has no other, knowing it will kick dust up everywhere and set the narratologists and hermeneuts on an Easter egg hunt that buys time.

Figure 9. Blank rectangular screen as Marnie's luggage; glance at cartoon ship in port.

Marnie enters the frame initially as already a cinematic agent allied with the copy machine she worked on in Strutt's office. Her thieving withdrawal from the system of all circulation, including that of the mother's love, heroicizes rather than criminalizes her—hence her inheritance of every *Mar-* name in Hitchcock by default. In Mar*nie* a cinematic logic of the "mark" seems simultaneously accelerated and withdrawn from mere personification.[8] These transformations cannot be returned to a familial itinerary. Marnie's prevaricating inventions or fiction-making powers in the car with Mark present an extraordinary political resistance to the eunarchic fables of truth, indexing, documentation. It seems in countertransition between two spectral systems. In the one, the murder of the blonde is accelerated to the point of its own evisceration, already serially caught in a virtual infinity of repetitions in *The Lodger.* In the second, the blonde *as* thief and criminal, bears all names, avenges "Mother," and is as completely detached from romance or sex as "Mother" is from origination or source. She is blissfully void only in riding her horse, Forio, circulating and jumping barriers. From this side of the band or divide, "patriarchist" institutions front for a covert eunarchy. A deanthropomorphic agency appears posited before which a sexed or gendered subject would have to be mimed into simulated existence along multiple planes like a screen apparition.

Marlene Dietrich in *Stage Fright* is herself etched as a chain-smoking "Mae West" aspirant, but without the smile and gags, she is not up to the job and left by Hitchcock a bit exposed. An effaced variant of "female" female drag, Dietrich, unlike the revolutionary West, appears infinitesimally corroded by her own stagecraft. Peter Conrad errs in reading Hitchcock's use of her as "about the defamation of Dietrich" (325). There is a curious line of Jane Wyman's in the taxi with Michael Wilding in which she, a *woman* nominally, claims she cannot understand what goes on in a woman's head, designating "she" as another. Yet Wyman, who has three large *X*'s stitched down the crotch of her dress, like Hitchcock's woven fingers effacing his own in profile, is also other than woman. It is like Hitchcock's sprinkling of the phrase "act like" when applied to what the character "is." Only here the phrase is abandoned and its logic totalized as an actress playing an acting student acting a role in a "real" set whispers that she doesn't get it but soldiers on. When Dietrich appears in her stage act crooning Cole Porter's "The Laziest Girl in Town," framed by a receding *mise en abyme* backdrop of kitschy prop clouds, surrounded by a chorus of top-hatted younger men like replicants from an assembly line, her *laziness* is a withdrawal from the glazed sexual promises that stage the whole formal charade. She is too lazy to bother with it. She could, she would, but she cannot be bothered performing what she can semaphorically generate without effort. But rather than this being some new twist on a gendered abyss, even for her it seems citationally old already. As is asked of Mr. Memory, how "old" is all this?

## MWMWMW

The gaze or nongaze of "Mae West" is not that of a given position on a binarized map, even one of gender violence and rhetorical seduction. It possesses no aura whatsoever while taking in, technically, every variation. At its most material, Hitchcock seems to pretend for an instant that something as spectral as the screen wraith *itself* is made to perform as whatever is seen or taken as visible on the screen—and assume that impersonation of human performativity, or gender performativity, which the public consumes and buys, is no different from what "real" people do in impersonifying themselves. Yet something else is happening here, something like a reinscription. What I am calling the gaze of Mae West, which is no "gaze" precisely, which is deauratic and depersonified, positions Hitchcock's *cinematic* to allow this spectral impersonation of woman to operate as the avenger against a "male" position that had assumed itself naturalized. Having steeped this production in the logics of violence to and specular destruction of woman, it accelerates that to mark an inversion—as with Marnie. No naturalized "men," no ontologized "women": something that "acts like" both perhaps in a general spectrality in default and mnemotechnic system frayed to bursting. This is also to suggest, however, that a trope like "justice" circulates in these systems as a sort of translational measure and agency, like the bar series. Within the autoscopy of Western prosthetics, "Hitchcock" names a transformation of mnemonic inscriptions. That *event* imports an irreversible dismembering of binarized gendering as cultural legend and shadow play encircling shot bodies. But this can only occur with a simultaneous or already implied dismantling of ocularcentric premises: that is, of the trope of vision, of light itself (the pyro*technic*), of agency, of the event.

Faced with a ubiquitous patriarchy that doubles the effaced front for a spectral eunarchy, one might expect a call to go out to a counterpower, a countergender, to right this, to inflict justice. To avenge. Like Justice herself, with her celluloid-cutting sword in one hand. One might counter the ghost patriarchy of fraternal eunuchs with "Mother," or a ghost mother, differently without gender, perhaps an it, speaking through still more *borrowed* voices. But there is a problem. If *Mr.* Memory begins reciting memorized facts, the repetition of these answers produces citational dismemberment: the fact, re-marked as word or image, becomes a hive of citational effects. This impasse of or within cinema—that a repetition which should secure identity morphs into a web of associated figures, a spy network—is also the impossibility of any "documentary." The premise of the cinematic "image"—that it indexes the real and is guardian of mimesis: that is, the pretense of the eunarchy undoes itself. The camera's pretense to documentation or mimetic reproduction is, simultaneously, shot, suicided, like the spool-like barrel of Dr. Murchison's revolver pointed into the camera.

If we were to pursue why the bar series translates aurally into this minimal form of knocking, like that under a table at a séance, we might ask Mr. Memory why the latter seems to be Hitchcock's final trope for his cinema in *Family Plot*. That is, cinema as a (faux) séance, accessing the memory of the dead (as is said by Julia Rainbird), is deployed fumblingly in this last work as if to recast the future, here, to redispose of a family *legacy*, of *the* familial. It is driven by the plot of "the family," at the point of its extinction in the aged Julia Rainbird, to hunt down and reacquire the one cast-off illegitimate member who has managed to escape its logics, its legacy, its name—more or less happily as a master serial jewel thief. The séance would regamble its future, access what is called the memory of the dead, albeit with the result not of reestablishing the family line and bestowing its name and fortune on the rightful heir but of destroying him in the process of that disclosure, curtailing itself. The eunarchy has its powers. The deauratization of "gender" registers a blackout and then an instant replay of all the latter's performative modalities, exposed or negated as then unmoored autocitation, part mynah bird. The MacGuffin of desire remaps and reenacts itself, like Madeleine Elster, as a frayed strategy to fend off this nonanthropomorphic gaze and its questions. The gaze of "Mae West" as the travesties of the female suggests an avenging refusal of gaze, among other things, avenging against the pretense of "gaze" before which something puts on his or her face.

# 5. Phoenix Rex: The Passing of Oedipus in Hitchcock

The ultimate socio-ideological lesson of *Psycho* is therefore the
collapse of the very field of intersubjectivity as medium of
Truth in late capitalism, its disintegration into the two poles of
expert knowledge and psychotic "private" truth. Does, however,
this mean that today, in the late capitalist universe, psychoanalysis . . . is no longer possible?
—**Slavoj Zizek**

Poor Mother. She works like a dog, just like a dog.
—*Shadow of a Doubt*

What does a phoenix have to do with dead stuffed birds, immobilized
in a blank "psychotic" stare, arrested in predatory flight? How, moreover, can that fabled bird be other than mockingly meant to celebrate a
rebirth of flight not out of the fiery ashes of a Daedalian crash, eternally
recurrent, but as drawn, dredged by pulleys, as a dead mechanical vehicle (a Ford at that) emergent from a fecal burial pond, a bog? What
car-tomb, what retrieved newspaper folded over what deficit of cash,
resumes the upward trajectory—in abject mockery, or otherwise?—of a
phoenix, at the point where traces are being recovered from what seemed
a pure act of vanishing (Marion's), and that of another bird-name signaling a cinematic aerial shot *(Crane)*? What links this mechanical
phoenix or antiphoenix, emergent from the bog under another's power,
by metonymic chains, to the cultural ruse of Oedipus, to the passing
or bypassing of the hermeneutic blind and hegemony associable with
this "complex," and with that, a certain claim and capital investment,
tended to and guarded by the psychoanalytic birds of prey that pretend
to own and watch over this Hades (film, Hitchcock, *Psycho*)? According

to what logic is a dead automobile pulled from an excremental bog to evoke a "phoenix" at all?

Questions. Such as those put to Mr. Memory in the Music Hall, only for which there are not yet memorized answers to be replayed, not yet "facts." If one summons the "Oedipus" into this mix, it is to name a certain use of the triad, deriving from one of Freud's more popularized platforms, as itself an auratic, familial or familiar cover, a triangle that, with all sorts of gore, can sustain the narrative of human subjects warring, replacing, and desiring. There is son, father, and mother, for starters. Yet throughout Hitchcock, in fact, there really are no substantive fathers at all; they are all placeholders at best or abdicated or absent. Trickier still, while traversed by mothers, these last are as bizarre as they are remarkable—as amaternal, often, as they can emerge, as in *Psycho,* as simply other. The Hitchcockian triad, the cinematic triad, is spawned from another logic through which this one first passes, as through an alimentary system it is digested into its perpetual parts. One might say, the first is the cover of an auratic program; the later, prehistorial to the "family plot," teletechnic other. Moreover, it is insufficient to declare Hitchcock, or *Psycho,* simply anti-Oedipal, as if there were a Deleuzian matrix to house and recuperate the loss of hermeneutic capital, any more than one can hustle to the Lacanian prop box to retrieve "maternal superego" to plaster over birds that have, as clearly as possible, deflected anthropomorphisms or family plots.

## A Bad Leg

The title of the 1924 essay by Freud, "The Passing of the Oedipal Complex," has a strange resonance. Freud's text is something of a minor note or aside that describes the possibility of overcoming the Oedipal complex for the boy child when it "succumbs to the threat of castration" (180), with preliminary ruminations, always cut off, on the girl's "Oedipal complex."[1] Yet in working this theme of sexual difference in the classic locus of the Oedipal the essay provides a more obscure commentary. Although Freud seems to dispense with the female version quickly ("The girl passes over—by way of a symbolic analogy, one may say—from the penis to a child"; 181), the essay sets up another narrative within Freud's trajectory in which, quite similarly, the centrality of the Oedipal labyrinth will, in a sense, pass, even as it will, in another sense or space, be maintained. What passes or is passing by Freud's turn to the girl's supposed Oedipus, is a linchpin of the metapsychological papers whose trajectory seems to be at once fulfilled and dismantled in the 1926 monograph, *Hemmung, Symptom, und Angst* ("The Problem of Anxiety"). Freud emerges from the "Oedipus" through a sort of splitting or *Spaltung* within his own trajectory. What I want to focus on instead is where a very different argument can be made for and about Hitchcock. Specifically, that his trajectory or that, more accurately, of global teletechnics more or less explicitly, and through careful markers, can be said to pass or *pass on* the Oedipal system. Something can pass for (an Oedipal effect, say), or pass on (abstain), or it can pass from relevance with its double-binding logics (in the individual, in Freud's work). The triangular logic that binds the Oedipal family in a certain narrative Freud deploys is a relapse, of sorts, before the logics of the triad into which the cinematic empire moves here.[2]

One problem with the Oedipal puzzle is its perpetuation of a model of interiority, even if that is void of such in fact, and with it the reinscription of an entire humanist hermeneutic it was trying to pass beyond. The eye lingers in the "gaze" as dislocated organ and confabulation, even when posited as personification of "the thing," or the dead, and so on, which is never quite as uncanny as one wants it to be. Hitchcock's direct invocations of "psychoanalysis," each defacing it as prop, occur in *Spellbound* and *Marnie*. Hitchcock's engagement with the discourse of psychoanalysis is discretely eviscerating and consuming, circulating it as semiotic coinage, disinscribing its historial frame, finding it another room in the labyrinthine madhouse of "Green Manors"—the latter at once heard as Selznick's studios and the structure of the house in Western thought. The malicious nod to the Enlightenment promise of pop psychoanalysis inscribed in the odd scrolled text introducing *Spellbound* cites the advent of silent film in its format while posting the whole beneath a citation from Shakespeare's *Julius Caesar* observing a "fault" said to be not in "the stars" but in "ourselves"—an inverse swipe at the inadequacies of Peck and Bergman, the "stars" in this film.

The pretext of *Spellbound* as the "first" psychoanalytic-based film is disemboweling: nothing supersedes, precedes, or suspends the cinemaclastic network, which is uncovered, again, in the ur-memory that psychoanalysis, a state hermeneutic allied to the police here, attempts to own but cannot recognize: that is, the parallel bar-slashes that haunt the spell or psychotic trance, a nonrevelatory memory before memory that Peck's amnesiac Ballantine misuses and misreads. Hitchcock attacks an Enlightenment pretense to pop psychoanalysis, which would not be inaccurate overall and infects and indicts even Lacanian redactions—

assuming the term is heard across a wider *photophobia,* as the work mockingly calls a certain fear not only of the citational structure of the image but of the betraying structure of "light" itself (for instance, that it does not exist as such, is prosthetic or inhabited by tracks, alternation, waves, rhythms, serial slashes, preoriginary shade). Thus the seemingly repressed memory that will, if unearthed, supposedly heal, that of a fratricidal push onto these same spiked bars, in fact reveals or stops nothing, and is dismissed as the narrative proceeds to incarcerate Peck (who by then richly deserves erasure). The leap into the structure of mnemonics that the bar series invokes puts the entire operation of recollection or recognition in default. It is reflected in the inserted Dalí dream sequence, citing Buñuel, in which scissors *cut the eyeball* on a curtain that, as it parts, reveals yet another eye: that is, preceding the "gaze" of the subject by a cut, a material order of marking that generates, and bars, metaphoric totalizations of the *eye.*[3]

So, "psychosis," in *Spellbound,* names not a foreclosure of psychic space: it is the exposure and discarding of the "Symbolic" as a surrealist prop or trope; it adheres to and within a graphematic marking system precedent to or structuring the default of memory, a mnemonics before or outside of memory, or the archive. Its logics are naturally enough like that of "Mother" in *Psycho,* of "her" postdialectical "voice" (the autocitational voice or voice-over as such), without locus, *atopos,* without gender, without body. The Hitchcock set, with its open artifice

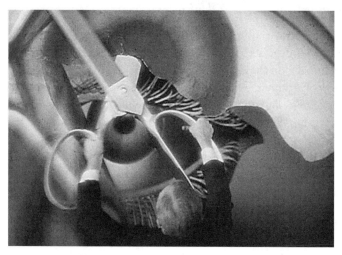

Figure 10. Spellbound—scissor cut of eye in Dalí dream.

and props (like the absurd skiing sequence with its dreamlike irreal cliffs and nonexistent New York alps), links Dalí's deformed graphics to the representational terms of the cinematic.[4] From Gregory Peck's perspective, the revelation of fratricide as suppressed amnesia-inducing trauma is oddly denied and made exculpatory, since it depicts an obviously vicious intent echoed inversely in its disclaimer ("I didn't kill my brother—it was an *accident!*"). Having turned himself into a pretext, the narrative removes Peck from the mise-en-scène, locking him away behind shadows and bars. One is left to readdress the fate of "Green Manors," of ocularist tropes and the Symbolic, up to the point where Dr. Murchison's giant prop hand turns a cinematic "revolver" into an eye that, unnaturally, *survives* black-and-white technology long enough to introduce Hitchcock's first blood spurt of color, red, on the screen.

In *The Birds* we hear Annie construct a purely Oedipal interpretation of her interaction with Mitch Brennan and his mother, and then adds the flyer that there is nothing Oedipal about it, thank you, virtually gutting the interpretive value of the model put forward and leaving it in quest of a reading not prepackaged, not that of the Bodega:

ANNIE (on Mitch's mother): When I got back to San Francisco, I spent days trying to figure out exactly what I had done to displease her.

MELANIE: What had you done?

ANNIE: Nothing. I simply existed. So, what's the answer? Jealous woman, right? Clinging, possessive mother. *Wrong. With all due respect to Oedipus, I don't think that was the case.* (My emphasis.)

Oedipus is Freud's cultural MacGuffin—or rather, in less glorified terms, yet another in the series. The demystification of origin seems to have a double impact: on the one hand, it aborts the entire naturalistic or organic ideology of mimesis by situating the place of reading or consciousness in the domain of artifice, prosthetics, mnemotracks, signs; on the other, it compels an alternative reading, one not yet in place and perhaps impossible to simply install as such. A phoenix, the name of the place, the Arizona city into which the aerial eye that opens *Psycho* descends. A phoenix, mythic bird that arises from its own ashes, like celluloid too close to its bulb, its own cinders: the chain pulling the car out of Norman's bog in the last shot. Whatever would be promised by the proliferating stuffed birds in *Psycho* is here bound to fire and eviscerations and cycles and putative rebirth, albeit inversely: rather than fire, it is the bog; rather than rebirthed flight, the dredging chain like a celluloid strip drags the car shell, as if back to horrific light. What is remotely "rebirthing" here?

Figure 11. Cinema aimed against itself: (a) eye's detached feet push body double ("brother") onto spiked bars; (b) Dr. Murchison's eye, detached hand turns *spooled* revolver against itself; shot releases technicolor red.

## The Cell

The dismantling of family had all along been a given—like the Potemkin "family" Verloc surrounds himself with as a front, the child a brother, the wife contracted with in exchange for the latter's care, sexless, a *family plot*. What Hitchcock does here, and elsewhere, as in the father and son taxidermists, the Ambrose Chappells in the second *Man Who Knew Too Much,* is place the generations in a relation closer to that of replication, simulation, or repetition itself. One problem is, in a sense, that while everyone can criticize the account given by the psychiatrist to explain Norman's proposed psychosis, it may be difficult for any Oedipal narrative to get beyond this same scene and proceed down the hallway to that in the cell—the last display of Norman, or Norman as "Mother," outside the closure provided by the sheriff's office. That's where the psychoanalytic tropes stop.[5]

The psychiatrist explains that Norman committed the murders of Marion and Arbogast, or rather not, that "Mother" did it. He goes on to explain that, in his reconstruction (they have yet to get the car back), Norman had poisoned his mother and her lover both, preserving her body and treating it. Mother has here become the main (if absent) subject or secret referent and, indeed, the agent of the violation; and Norman, who committed the murders, converts in his cell into the passive front for the (ventriloquized) "dominant" personality: a double inversion or (a)maternal (dis)invagination. This brings a quick rejoinder and warning from the sheriff about lawyers trying to build a defense case for the guy, as if it were a calculation at Norman's suggestion. When the camera follows the guard carrying a blanket to Norman, we seem to discover him in full psychosis, blanked and blanketed by "Mother." Yet we may not notice what by now should have been apparent because it is marked through the film, that is, that *"Mother" is not Mother*; she is not where or who she is—and not only in the sense that she is, as Norman suggests, *not quite herself.* Specifically, while the psychiatrist puts the blame on "Mother," it is Mother's voice we now are treated to in Norman's head, and it is she who blames Norman for trying to make her seem guilty for what he did: which is what we have just seen in the psychiatrist's speech. In a short-circuiting of dialectics that cannot be recuperated, "Mother" is herself a somewhat paranoid thing focused on rhetorical posturing before a panoptical or policial eye, calculating for the rhetorical impression to be left (that she "wouldn't hurt a fly"). The fly rests on the hand, a black spot on a giant white surface: restless with cut motion, it visually rhymes with the skeet shoot or attacking plane. Norman's face (and "Mother's" voice) dissolves into what emerges, and disappears, as Mother's grinning skull, and they in turn the bog with a mechanized chain drawing the car-tomb from cloacal waters. "Mother" is not buried in the bog. "Mother" is the bog—whatever it is.

If Hitchcock is ground zero of the cinematic, *Psycho* is ground zero in Hitchcock. It reads and rewrites every other film. If there is one thing the work seems to show us, it is that "Mother" is not where you think she is. That she may not have *place* as such.

Hitchcock demonstrates this quite explicitly in the film when Lila goes up to the house. If Arbogast does meet "Mother," it is not in his role as the representative of communal assurance and rationality alone, but as someone who expects to find her upstairs, who expects the Oedipal explanation of Norman's problems, as does a likely audience. Lila is looking for Mrs. Bates and determines she is not in the expected place. "As" a woman she is not necessarily taken in by the Oedipal theater that Norman, literally, puts on when entering the cellar in drag with his knife raised. *If* the Oedipal theater or machine destroys women, gets them in the shower where their nonsecret is exposed, it would seem to be to destroy them before they expose or destroy *it*, that theater, or the nonplace of "Mother" that it conceals. This disemboweling is perhaps also done by a certain ventriloquizing and ventriloquized "Mother." And if this is done by a "man," in the film's actual production, or even by a Norman, neither "man" nor not "man," it would not be a mono-lithic patriarchy performing this, nor a maternal "superego." What Nor-man is or does is more than double: "he" (or it) perpetuates the house as an economy of male (auto)evisceration, and "he" (or it) waits upon an other alterity, a new logics of the disinvested home no longer as interior, just as "Mother" is no longer maternal. Norman performs the ritual evisceration of metaphysics, waiting for the repeat cuts to yield another scene—like Hitchcock's *serial* filmmaking, repeating the same violence toward women that marks, inaugurates, and sustains that historial field or parenthesis, much as it does in *The Lodger*. He houses a site of Na-poleonic vigil almost bursting from exile, revolutionary, musical, impe-rial, heroic, even if confusing itself with its graphophonic replay, like Beethoven's *Eroica Symphony* to which, in mockery, the film nods.

"Mother" is not where she should be. She is *atopos*. She is not in her room, in her bed, and where she is found, in the fruit cellar, oddly recalls that Hitchcock's *father* was a fruit seller (a reference made in *Sabotage*). The "family plot" is barred from reconstituting itself, much as in Hitchcock's last film, *Family Plot*, where the plotters are emplotted as well, entombed.[6] When Norman bursts into the fruit cellar in drag ("He's a transvestite," blurts the deputy later), he not only looks like a diva but is held back, restrained by Sam Loomis, in the attitude of the *Laocoön*, that is, as a figure of the aesthetic's inability to speak or act, but also its inability not to project itself in the mode of theater, the inmixing of personifications of the dead and an aperformativity without ground. Norman's inversion of classical aesthetics in caberet mockery, with a cinematic cutting knife, is a ritual inversion—it converts the aesthetic as a site of play and representation to the site of preinscriptions, like those of celluloid, out of which world, historiality, temporal politics, "identity," and the senses would be programmed and phenomenalized. Norman is restrained by the dullard Loomis on the stage of this perpetually impending inversion, a warrior of the archive. His cutting knife revokes the ghost of classical "aesthetics," out of whose logic Norman emerges, inverting the latter's diminished position as play, entertainment, mere "laughter" (in *Sabotage*), into a ground zero of the world's inscriptions.

To speak of going "beyond" or coming "before" the pleasure principle would be jejune, even where this prospect retires, for a certain Freud, the *Traumdeutung*'s MacGuffin of dream as wish fulfillment with a teleological structure. The cinema as practiced by Hitchcock allows for no unconscious, no covert reserves. Mother "acts like" Norman's personification or, for a time, puppet, a prosopopoeia needed to motivate, retronarrativize, and bless his text with a mummified family seal of approval. Yet such a narrative is possible to read as a legal maneuver, a legal defense. From the time the psychiatrist begins to speak, there is suspicion about any legalities of describing Norman's illness. In "Mother's" last words there seems an obsessive concern with how "they" view her, or Norman, in establishing blame or guilt, leading to the exquisite riff on not hurting a fly in front of the viewer's gaze, which is, briefly, also *hers*.

Figure 12. Norman as Laocoön in drag with cutting knife, restrained by Loomis.

Indeed, the psychiatrist blames "Mother" entirely, exculpating Norman, forgetting his murder of her, too. When we go beyond this scene to the cell, again, we hear "Mother," ventriloquizing and ventriloquized, contradicting the psychiatrist by noting that she had to tell him the story lest Norman use her to take the blame. At this point, Norman seems normal or even protected in sacrifice because he is officially the psychotic subject who carries, supports, or invents the Oedipal narrative by counterpoint, the concept of "Mother" as jealous and desired (m)other origin. Norman is normal because he counterinvents and anchors the Oedipal complex as he stuffs and ventriloquizes "Mother" as such, placating not just the psychiatrist but the hermeneutic representatives in the sheriff's office. So he keeps his mouth shut and lets "Mother" talk— and betray herself. Perhaps. The murdering of women is but one staged symptomatic of the Oedipal narrative and its purported suppressing affirmation of sexual difference. Yet what if sexual difference were not being suppressed, because it did not exist in that way, as monolithic "sexual difference," and this fiction is also superimposed over Diva Norman's performance? Norman is normal because, at this instant, he both represents and retracts the wishes of the community of interpreters who cluster around the storyteller psychiatrist for shelter and partake of the cultural metanarratives. The Laocoön of this reversed ordering of *the* aesthetic, inscribed now in accelerated telemedia from which world derives, struggles to implement itself in ritualized replays.

When Norman's face dissolves into "Mother's" grinning skull, what

Figure 13. *Khora* rechained: Norman dissolves into "Mother's" grin, "Mother" sinks into the bog.

is involved seems a further stripping away of flesh, even though that skull does not signify "death," is itself grinning (Hitchcock called *Psycho* a "comedy"), and is of indeterminate gender. "Mother" *seems* to have reinvented herself, momentarily, *between* inanimate thing and personification. The skull gives way, as dissolve, into the dredging chain drawing the curious phoenixlike car from the swamp, which links "Mother" and chains and retrieval or dredging machines positioned in the place of the camera, drawing out of fecal darkness a vehicle of transport and a tomb. That is, the car when focused upon is taken out of all figuration. Raymond Durgnat, narrating the title sequence of *Psycho* as a choreography of alphabetical agents, discloses a parallel effect:

> Uncompleted syntax holds the screen for a full two seconds, until the letters' middle stratum skids left, pursued by more grey bands, which amass in a tight, though still staggered, formation. They rebuild the "window-blind" striation, but this time from grey on black (reversing the earlier construction process). New shards of letters slide in, but before any words can crystallize, the blank grey bands scud back the way they came (surprise reversal of directional thrust). On the now black background, the scattering of broken letters slide and snap together, spelling *Psycho,* for about two seconds, until that word, too, cracks into three strata. They slip a little notch sideways, but in opposite directions, so that each letter, vertically misaligned, seems to jerk and tug against itself. The word disintegrates—not, as the generally lateral kinetic has led us to expect, laterally—but, instead, the letters' top halves fly up and away and off the screen, while their lower halves plunge off the bottom of the frame. Since each half of a letter implies the other half, and it all happens so fast, it's as if our word-world suddenly doubles and splits and speeds in opposite directions, like a "troubled reflection."[7]

One is in a prefigural, prearchival, preoriginary "archival" site, *atopos,* for which the components that fashion letters are exploding, signatures barely and only momentarily exposed.

If one applies the threshing machine of the title performance of preletters that Durgnat reveals as a principle, one can turn that too on the problem of *mother* as place and name. As a matter of triads and triangles, the letter *M* is insistent, three times three (triangles), raised to the "power of gamma." Even the triply triangulated series of *M-* terms that interlace Hitchcock's work like a dredging chain or ever-altering signature do not recover this content: mother, memory, music, machine, mountain, murder, man . . . "Mother," as in Emma Hitchcock, a name echoed in *Rich and Strange* ("Em") as well as in *Shadow of a Doubt*, yet also a letter, *M*, the thirteenth in the alphabet, already a 1 and 3 signature, bearing three triads or triangles in itself (as does its inverse, W), up and down, a letter of jointed bars, angled, barely held together, indeed, spellbound or spelling bound against the insignia or pattern that eviscerates all space-time, all mimetic pretext or aura or personifications. "Mother" as privileged front for *M*: *Mer, mar*(r), *mer(e)*. The sea, the *see*. In going beyond the psychiatrist's exposition in the sheriff's office, Hitchcock provides us with the unique narrative space of what would, in any other film, be simply disseminated across the work: a dominating (non)place, since mother "is" nowhere in *Psycho*, does not have a place—where "Mother" may perhaps be perceived as a projected prosopopoeia rather than an origin, or decked out in Oedipal terms for peace of mind's sake.

Norman (dis)incarnates the *normal* projection and ventriloquization of the "Oedipus" narrative and eviscerates it, removes it from any recuperable dialectic, wears it like a transvestite's dress, renders it a prop of cultural theater less to be surpassed than already mere facade.

## Lila's Stations

But such matters and dialectics have always been about the house, its economimetic rule, its secret. Lila enters the house looking for that secret. She calls out for Mrs. Bates and ascends the stairs as Loomis distracts Norman in the motel office. Yet on entering her bedroom Mother is marked by an outline that is also an absence, her bodily indentation in the bedding, where she is not. When Lila is startled it is not by the movement of Mother behind her but her own movement, or that of her image, mirrored in a *mise en abyme* or regression between two mirrors. The moment appears to suspend or erase momentarily the quest for Mother, who is not there, transplanting that into an infinite regress of representation. It follows, however, the bronze box with severed hands atop folded—cut off, hands of a type of hyperwriting trigger a specular fall that elicits a cry. When Lila proceeds to Norman's room she encounters a child's possessions: a rabbit doll, looking out with a bent ear, then a phonograph (machine of preinscription and repetition) with Beethoven's *Eroica* on it, an unmoving disk, and then an untitled bound book, which she opens. Here eyes widen and the camera cuts away. If the Beethoven symphony suggests a private theater of Norman's world as heroic, before the ear, the doll appears a fetishized precursor of taxidermy. The gramophone links the technical reproduction of a black disk's memory storage to the mnemonic superscription of "voice." For a film bearing the name *Psycho,* the possibility of being replayed (or re-playing something) is also the means of the speaker's self-impersonation. This book is the last object Lila holds, widening her eyes on a page we are not allowed to see, a book without shared markings or interior. One has drifted as if through three spaces: that of a specular *mise en abyme* before the indented absence in Mother's bed; that of the teletechnics of machines of reproduction and taxidermy; and that, in the book, of archivization. Lila is ready to meet "Mother" now.

One can interject another specter here, over or behind the front of "Mother," allied to techno-relays, terminal legacies, archival hiatus, signature systems (or, as noted earlier, an array of letteral graphics or cuts). That would be a "mother" without existence as such or place, oc-cupying an impossible place, *atopos. Amater.* Knife in hand, no "she," hers is also the place of *Atropos,* the Fate who cuts threads and names a retraction of trope, of figure, as if the placeless place of the cut, apo-tropaic to any "eye," were atopic by definition. "Mother's" voiding of all origins transforms genealogical predicates. She or it is thus traversed by the preoriginary logics Derrida approaches in analyzing the Platonic *khora* in the *Timaeus* as (a)material site or *atopos* of inscription before all phenomenality:

> In the couple outside of the couple, this strange mother who gives place without engendering can no longer be considered as an origin. She/it eludes all anthropo-theological schemas, all history, all reve-lation, and all truth. Preoriginary, before and outside of all genera-tion, she no longer even has the meaning of a past, of a present that is past. Before signifies no temporal anteriority. The relation of inde-pendence, the nonrelation, looks more like the relation of the interval or the spacing to what is lodged in it to be received in it.[8]

She or "it," what is called Mother is like the relation of the interval, the bar series, to what it situates and engenders by cutting it off. The "family" is rotated but sustained in its illness: the third will be personified, per-haps the son, perhaps Daddy, in a managed agon: a scripted wrestling match. Hitchcock's triad is not the generator of mimetic desire and rivalry, which are interestingly absent from Hitchcock's trunk of props. It suspends alternation or dialectic, mutes and hyperbolically ruptures "speech," atomizes into recombinant parts, is produced by and pre-originary to number and visibility. A "zero" or cipher space, off the main road or map, the bog regurgitates, is and can be, again, dragged, sucks into itself representational techniques and technics, oil engulfing the machine that would have transported it, inside out, in a desert site of wasted ghost trees.

The "phoenix" motif signaled by the location of *Psycho*'s opening in Phoenix, Arizona, is referenced in the final image of the *chain* dredging up Marion's Ford from the fecal swamp. The bog, however, is also a viscous pool of letteration and oil, black anteriority capable of absorbing cars and stars—a black hole, as J. Hillis Miller has used the term, the locus of aporias that register as gaps on any spectrum yet consume and disarticulate constellations of sense or historial programs.[9] The phoenix, monstrous bird, rises from its fiery ashes, like a photographic image from exposure to negativizing light, at which point the bog momentarily becomes a developing tank of chemicals. Viscous, the bog includes what Leo G. Carroll in the preceding film wittily references as "alphabet soup": a site where letters disaggregate into their composite of inscriptions. The bog does not contain "Mother"; the bog, site of disarticulation of letters, is Mother heard as a logic of *khora, atopos*, without maternal gender or originary logics, off every road. This bird is introduced, nonetheless, as the title sequence deposits us in Phoenix itself, of course, and it does this for us in advance by allowing the masticating series of bars that have traversed the title credits to phenomenalize into the building structures that materialize as the city of the West. Norman does not have a place in any Oedipal mapping. He would be the sphinx herself, asking a question about how "man" might be defined by reference to a creature that is three-legged in old age, marked by a tripod. Norman would be Hamlet simultaneously hyperbolized as father and son, on the ramparts feeding himself an already forgotten injunction not to forget what lies behind the visible—inscriptions, chains, recordings. As the *Eroica* signals, Norman appears, mock-imperial in asolar exile.

One must consider what this ground zero of Hitchcock, the ground zero of "cinema," has passed through its alimentary coils, all of the prehistorial and posthistorial time chains it is connected to, and all that is entailed by the "Oedipal" hermeneutics' evisceration by a mother who cannot be personified or given place. If "Mother" elicits a chain of marks or *M-* terms across Hitchcock's writing, the metonymic chain that dredges up this machine or vehicle could be seen to imply an altered model of perception released or affirmed across the band—as what stands as if *beyond* the pleasure principle of everything represented by the "Oedipus" in this schema, as well as before it, in whatever is posited by the bronze hands in Mother's vacated if indented, imprinted, or inscribed room. The bog is not quite fecal. The body it delivers that stands beyond metonymy is metallic, machinal now.[10] Oil, in the place of excrement, which translates into the sheer excess of wealth or diamonds, black, what nonetheless as fossil fuel derived from returned dead prehistorial organisms that inhabit and make motors or machines run. What machines?

The bog as oil and excremental pond from which rises the phoenix-like Ford—and the prefix *fore-* should be heard, like Marnie's horse Forio, as a certain preoriginary logic—implies a network of prefigural signifiers. Put a different way, the metal links (like celluloid frames) that pull the car as a metonymic chain return a vehicle-tomb to dubious light with a certain promise, beyond the death's-head grin of "Mother," she or it, and "beyond" or "before," already, the mimetic pretext of the image. All would be changed; "Mother" harbors an impulse of war in a later work termed the "bird war." Moreover, it is beyond any biological anthropomorphism of "death," the human, "psychosis," or even cinema. What is prefaced and predicted, and what makes claim to a certain figure of renewal, is the translation of legibility itself: rather than receive cinema as a site of characters, faces, "pictures of people" talking, Oedipal narratives, and so on, one is reconstituted from out of a machinal impasse, and reads legs, staring dead birds, bronze hands, *M-* systems and letteral agents, aural relays or sound, the entire Babel field of pure language in Benjamin's sense (that is, signifiers constitutive of all languages but void of "meaning"). The end-as-beginning of *Psycho* converts this eternal return of the reel into *another scene of legibility.* This translation, which I have mapped opportunistically around a "passing of the Oedipal" logics of interpretation, is posited, asserted, withdrawn, proleptically marked or blocked, fought over, and globalized across Hitchcock.[11] As an immense template for the disinscription of auratic premises, it anticipates—and is preparatory to—*coming wars of reinscription* that would redecide the definition of the human, "life," mnemonics, aesthetics, earth.

## Alphabet Soup

Marion tears up the toilet paper with monetary calculations, the writing of numbers (or letters), a small scrap of which is retrieved by Lila from the toilet, identifying character script with excrement. *Mère, merd,* the bog is a miniature *mer* or sea, as in *Rebecca,* which sea we are told could conquer her or the flame-encrusted *R* of repetition. And like that chain too, there emerges, across each film, a sequence of *Mar*-inflected names so unavoidably, so obviously, as to have escaped general notice. So the positive inflection of the phoenix-car can here be "read" as an alteration in legibility, in the archive, translation, the eye (socket), light (bulbs), (a)materiality, the anthropomorphic itself. *Nor*man thus evokes the deanthropomorphic, the deauratic. Oedipus, in this respect, is also claimed at the moment of self-blinding, of a pecking out of the eyes, a blinding by and of (black) light that aggressively eschews the creaking apparatuses of ocularcentrism, mimeticism, and so on.

To speak of a "passing" or overpassing (in a Nietzschean sense) of the "Oedipus" by Hitchcock is to redirect our attention away from the auteurist, psychoanalytic, culturalist, film theoretical, surrogate, and gender-political Hitchcocks toward a mnemonic field of teletechnics, a sensorium that is being disassembled and reassembled as a mnemo-technic of passage, marked across these films in figures of ports, bridges, aporetic border crossing, and so on, from the earliest works on. It is the world-altering supplantation and supplementation by one inscriptive program or horizon of legibility for another. This, after all, is what all of Hitchcock's early anarchivist and Benjaminian saboteurs implied by their intent of cinematic intervention in the historial.

I asked, at first, what the connection of a retrieved car from a bog (here, clearly, of traces, letters, organic decay and fuel, excremental field of signifiers without content or meaning, bars and relays and dogs and chocolate, of *mer* and *mère* and *merd*) had to the premise of a phoenix's return, where there are no ashes or fire. Here that bog is also an ink-pot, sheer anteriority, like that into which the judge dips his pen in *The Manxman*. Like the circular pattern of *The 39 Steps,* the retrieval of Marion's used car from the black site of imprint and script conveys another version of the silent warplane formula of that early "political thriller." It is hinted at in the "fly" that alights on Norman's hand: precursor of the phoenix (as insect), circumspect foremodel of attacking birds, treating Norman's hand like the bronze statuettes still on Mother's dresser—dismembered figures of writing, of teletechnic power shuttling from the cave paintings to the cinematic cuffs of the lodger. The phoenix comes from the ashes, a beyond of mourning almost without remainder—out of the burning flash of celluloid and bulb: a monstrous bird, a perpetual ghost in advance, since any flight effaces that non-origin that defines its reappearance. A bird effaced in infinite repetition, projecting the hope or doom of this circuitry, as with a burst of power, here drawn from mud by a celluloid chain emerging from chemicals.

Unlike the *silent* warplane whose formula is carried by Mr. Memory, the car-tomb from the bog is not running, cannot fly. Reemerging from a swamp, black pit of fecal atomization, it may, if anything, be heard as the premise of an *other* writing or reading machine. That would be already in place and marked throughout "Hitchcock," is the oeuvre, and yet still "to come." It lies, from the first, not only "beyond" the pleasure principle, "beyond" the dream interpretation of the "Oedipus," "beyond" irony (a phrase Fredric Jameson risks using of Hitchcock), but "before" the protocols of mimetic culture, hermeneutics, identification, and film-theoretical accoutrements have a chance. But this was all Benjamin meant by a cinema that suspends aura, personification, as its material advent and definition. This emergent vehicle would be, then, possible to see as a phoenix in this "comedy" if and only if it denoted that other machine indicated by a "psycho" or spectrographic or allographic structure that had also always been in place. Here the ghosts of different orders, planes, and times do battle.

As a great cat with human visage, the sphinx can rest or spring. Half-animal, she is interested in transspecies riddles. Sphincterlike, circular, atopic, she could just as easily have feigned to Oedipus that he got the answer to her famous riddle right, that it referenced "man" (playing on his narcissism as in everything else), the question about the third leg about bad footage, knowing what was in store for Oedipus in his faux victory.

The closing shot at the bog recalls Hitchcock's fantasy scene as told to Truffaut for *North by Northwest* where, at a Detroit car factory, there emerges a new car off the assembly line, which, though no one had ever been in it, contains a corpse, as does Marion's, emerging contrary-wise from the mud. It was the right move at California Charlie's, still, for her to change cars and license plates—and she, the only customer to outpitch the used car salesman himself. It was right to get another car whose history she does not know but which, a vehicle's vehicle, takes her straight to the Bates Motel, straight through its evacuating logics, a step beyond its vacant rooms' "dialectics at a standstill." This *other* car has intruded into Hitchcock's sets throughout. It opened *Blackmail* with the unfulfilled promise of a police van rounding up semaphoric criminals; Favell tries to sell them in *Rebecca*; its wasted shell in a Philadelphia lot situates *Shadow of a Doubt*; it is what Danielle, in *To Catch a Thief,* tells Robie he needs to change as well, from his old car (the blonde American fake, Francie) to a younger, newer one (the butch brunette simulacrum thief, Danielle), which will run better and last longer. The dredged-up Ford has become what Francie calls herself at one point: *amphibious,* moving across both sides of the terrain, death and life (or *bio*). It is amphibio-political. A phoenix rises from cinders of a semaphoric order. It rises because it has gone farther, through complete incineration, reconvening whatever outlasts that: the irrevocably deauratic, the desert border, fossil waste, prehistorical avenging, the inversion of the "aesthetic" sprung from its safe place as play to the center of sensorial programming, the eviscerations of foliage and consumptions of car culture, the cruel visual banality of "America," past and future, programmed from the heart of the teletechnic image.

## Minotaur; or, Norman at the Bog

There is an archival shot of the set of *Psycho* that may harbor a clue to the labyrinth of this image, of "image" as such, insofar as what is called image lures the eye with seemingly recognizable forms only to trap it in crosscurrents of citational trace chains shot through with different times. Within the labyrinth, a figure used in *Spellbound,* is a minotaur—something neither animal nor man, perhaps machinal, that consumes, to which all threads lead. The shot features Norman or "Tony Perkins" standing before the bog. One may wonder if it does not, for Hitchcock, cite or encapsulate a certain import of the entire work, knowing the role *Psycho* would play within and beyond his canon. If Hitchcock is ground zero of cinema, *Psycho* may seem ground zero in "Hitchcock"—a cipher to both events. The film's recurrence to black and white cites cinema at and from its silent origins. Outside of the film itself, the archival shot is also a shot at the tele-archive whose logics are, here, condensed. The still from the British Film Institute re-marks that it is on a *set,* betrays itself as such by leaving Perkins's marker visible (a *T*). Hence it is "of" the film set, or the set of the "earth" featured in and giving background to it. A *desert* shot, that deforested earth offers up a clearly dead tree that looms behind and to the left of Norman, doubling and dominating his form. Norman looks out into the camera—where the bog would be, in the place of the spectator—yet his eyes seem almost like those of a blindman. An archival shot, it is a shot of and at the state of the archive. The tree that would naturally cite both nature and genealogies, were it given iconic aura, is more than ghosted. It appears prosthetic, not just a prop, but a tree marking itself as if thrust into the earth. As the eye settles on it, it breaks into geometric shapes as a host of letters: a gamma forms where the cross branch rests, a triad, a *T.* If one looks again a ghostly *face* struggles to emerge in shadows cast by a lowering sun, shrieking holes for nose and eyes, like a silent film wraith that cannot quite emerge. The shadow play almost grants *personification* to a

Figure 14. "Perkins" on *set* (marker underfoot) of *Psycho* "per se" as Norman looks at bog before a spectral tree.

thing, a tree, a gamma, or even 3—or, to another letter almost legible, something like a *J.* That would be an odd letter for Hitchcock, relatively unused by him, and impossible to ascertain or read, since its lower spur is sunk. The entire tree registers a technicity as if thrust into the earth and altering it, desertifying it, forward and backward in time, putting among its time lines the fossil fuel waste cited by the bog that absorbs automobiles and the planetary waste the former's consumption by the latter irradiated—the container engulfed by a now prosthetic earth, a cinematic set, heir to letteration. And a "man" is set in this set—Tony Perkins, who as "Norman" will be sacrificed more than just as a career to his appearance in this film and set. His pants seem short, his hand reaches into or is coming out of a pocket, his collar is upturned. Norman or "Perkins" is both avenger and survivor, out of place almost. There is a tiny house in the woods, the economics of "the house" reduced to toy size for once in this earthscape; hoses coil on the ground behind Perkins.

There is an elongated oval in the center of the tree's awkward limbs, a cinematic hole not unlike that of the morphing graphics in the woman's eye that opens *Vertigo*. There is a tiny structure that looks like an oil derrick by the tree's lower side, linking the car-consuming bog to a viscous ink, fossil fuel from which engines of transport and global economies would run and over which they would war. The black and white again cite the origins of the cinematic as the arboreal triads do *The Lodger*'s Avenger, or as the gamma does Mr. Memory's formula for a cinematic warplane by way of the accelerations of telemnemonic strips ("$R - 1$ over $R$ to the power of gamma"): the gamma, as letter, harbors both a $c$ and a $3$ or triangle—first plane of visibility, perhaps "first" number.

The black hole absorbs light and consumes stars, as the bog here does Perkins, say, or Janet Leigh. It warps time and spatial maps. Rather than identify an aporia, it mobilizes such knots as sites of disappearance and reinscription—as if the consumption of constellations that a black hole performs were to be heard in Benjamin's sense, as that of trace networks that shape or program histories,

Figure 15. The *star*: depersonified face of teletechnic tree, letteral staff of the *J*, goring horned minotaur in the labyrinth of an image.

senses, pasts, and futures. Norman's viscous bog is the black hole of black holes; *atopos,* off the main road, it loops back to receive the advent of cinema itself and the histories the latter programs and engulfs: the affiliation between cinema and techno-wars to come, "globalization," memory management, techno-accelerations, planetary evisceration. The bog suggests a site where even letters dissolve into the marks and particles that are shaped into them—as Durgnat obliquely observed. The tree of threes or "life" or genealogies or the natural image, and so on and on, is not dead but spectral, preghosted by the letteral shapes that decimate all genealogical or natural pretense. "Nature" is preinhabited by a *technē* that, for Hitchcock, makes this set prop appear more rammed into the earth than grown from it, like the cut sequoia in *Vertigo,* whose ringed trunk reveals in its whirling circles an archive of date lines for historial "events." This letteral *staff* hung with gammas seems also a single bar or slash that is almost preletteral and removed from any series. Previsible, preletteral, it doubles Norman's lanky staring figure. If there is a prosopopoeia of a letteral tree, perhaps of a *J,* in the holed eyes and mouth of the cross branch, personification withdraws from Norman together with aura. The earth is deauratic, the human cinematically hung, the moment of the photograph doubles the set it shoots and takes in terrestrial time lines. These active trace chains exceed any detached "present" of the shot, which—citing everything that would ever be performed or signified by *Psycho* within any narrative whatsoever—includes all of cinematic, ocular, technographic, tele-archival, and scriptive history, as the chase through the British Museum did in *Blackmail.*

    The face that almost emerges seems to take on *horns* in the cross branch. Citing the relation of cinema to human prehistorial ritual and sacrifice, it appears a primordial totem. It takes on the shape of a sacrificial headdress or animist god, where a human face, as in cinema, would impose itself upon an inanimate or dead thing. In the labyrinth of the image, there is a minotaur. Pursuing the hermeneutic threads of the image's labyrinth leads to this figure: half-man, half-bull, it consumes like the host of the Bates's motel does female guests. The serial killing of blondes from *The Lodger* on has a curious double logic. On the one hand, it appears the very icon of metaphysics with its disposal of women as reflected light, "golden curls"; on the other hand, Norman, an *A*venger, accelerates that machinery against itself to the point of cancellation or moving beyond. Whatever avenges here does not do so for a specific past trauma or wound, any more than the prehistorical birds can be said to do so:

whatever avenges from and within the image, like the chiaroscuro fog identified with the serial murders of *The Lodger,* does so for a totality that, nonanthropomorphic, includes the *technē* and animemes that traverse and are the cinematic here, the tele-archival itself. The minotaur is the image that always "betrays"; one can identify with it, find a referent, narrate it, each in turn betrayed. Such a minotaur resides not in an auteur but in the signature system itself.

The archival frame shoots and cites *Psycho* in its performative entirety and the archive it inherits and serves as touchstone or relay to all that departs from it as an iconic event in "cinema." That is, of the entire cataclysm and acceleration with which the photographic is teletechnically allied: the techno-genocides and techno-weaponry of its century and beyond, the global telemarketing and political programming of the *last man* it announces. A tree mushrooms atop the hill behind Norman, a mushroom cloud, citing the affinity of the cinematic to nuclear blasts and atomization—an affiliation made by the radioactive sand of *Notorious* and elsewhere. If the advent of cinema occurs, as Benjamin asserts, with the revocation of *aura* (autuerism, identification, mimeticism), that he defines as the loss of personification, anthropomorphism. What humans took to be perception is exposed as the phenomenalization of always external mnemonic machines and bands: inscriptions, animations. The guest becomes the host of the host, here, the technic supplants the tree, exposing "nature," like "Mother," as something nonoriginary, unnatural. Like the "private eye" named *Arbogast,* the *arbre* is, already, guested, ghosted by another.

As an image *of image* and an encapsulation of the cinematic, *Norman* at the bog also performs its own endless extrapolation of itself: the image betrays. It betrays the culture dependent on it; it betrays the reader who invests in it—like the shipwreckers of *Jamaica Inn* luring you with a lantern from distressed seas. You think this is a promotional shot, but it plays havoc with every history you took for granted. Less at the end of than within each string is the minotaur, which consumes in turn, yet cannot quite emerge as a prosopopoeia of the barlike staff. You think you can recognize objects, identify with characters, follow narrative lines, but it betrays each assumption. It operates within a field of citational chains, and, as citation, it will distance and betray each imposition. Like "Hitchcock," installed at the center of a canon that is supposed to guard the nature of the visible, mimetic reproduction, realism, who is thoroughly antiocularist, and for whom, in the strict sense, there is no representation, no "eye" as organ, no "light," no sun as other than effect or artifice, no gaze. The bog, like Mother, is absent from the shot itself, or, at best, positioned with the viewer. Yet Mother is everywhere. What *Psycho* calls "Mother"—a virtual *khora* site, in the sense elaborated by Derrida, where all inscriptions are virtual and prephenomenalized—is the bog.

The *J* that forms the staff of the dead tree is not quite visible, even if it lies at the core of what would be, in this frame and hence in all cinema, the visible. It is a missing *J*, like that of the initial for the name "Joseph," which Hitchcock did not leave any trace of in constructing his trademark (there is no "Alfred J. Hitchcock"). The *J* is all but a preletteral "letter," capable of becoming all others, a skeletal slash. Yet it is the letter not only of Joseph the biblical interpreter of dreams but, in the genealogy of the letter, the digit, and in Egyptian hieroglyphics the *hand*—trace of the cave painting, agent of writing, announcer of the human and tele-technic era. There is a sign in Joe Newton's Santa Rosa bank in *Shadow of a Doubt,* the only allusion to the world war of the time, advertising government bonds with the call to buy a "stake in America." The *J* is the staff of all letteration, the bar that precedes series and patterns, the technic, slammed into an earth it transfigures and, alternately, privately makes "rich and strange." The *J* is that stake, "America" the name of a tele-empire that, already, rendered World War II a misleading diversion for the accelerations to come, linked already in the fifth column indus-trialists of *Saboteur.*

Norman does not gaze at us or the bog. Indeed, there is no gaze, as aura disappears and the personification of trees flares up only to recede. All of the histories affiliated with the cinematic or its advent in the global or planetary era converge in this archival shot, which is, again, a shot of and at the tele-archive—the era of the book and writing, the photograph's "shock effect," globalization, deforestation telemarketing, techno-wars or genocides, a prehistorical earth and what comes after "man." The shot is nonanthropomorphic, like the slashes of the birds. The shot of the cinematic, like the cinematic itself, being deauratic, is beyond mourning. Norman is outside, at sunset, without what he else-where calls his "trusty umbrella."

# III. Jump Cuts

# 6. Time Machines

## Tongues

> As soon as I landed in England, I found out that I was dead!
> —*Secret Agent*

Michel Chion argues that the separation of voice from the body in *Psycho,* of "Mother's" voice, heard but never seen, belongs to the category of the *acousmêtre*: "In *Psycho* . . . voice and body brush against each other at the end of a long asymptotic journey."[1] The disembodied voice ("A person who talks to you on the telephone, whom you have never met, is an *acousmêtre*" [206]) is addressed to the idea of Mother, inviting Doris Day's singing, mounting the self-replicating stairs of the second *Man Who Knew Too Much* in search of her kidnapped son, to enter the template. And yet, seemingly disembodied, the origin of the voice is paradoxically preserved in hiatus. Elsewhere "Mother" would be contacted, so to speak, by Cary Grant in the openings both of *Suspicion* and *North by Northwest,* in the first by a letter and in the second by another teletechnic (phone, telegraph), in all cases mnemonic media. But Mother is off playing "bridge" with her cronies. "She" is media.

The *acousmêtre* seems designed to render more "uncanny" the figure of Mother, but two problems emerge. In *Psycho* "Mother" is never definitively arrived at, identified, or subject to recognition as to what she pretends (or is pretended to be); even in Norman's (celluloid) cell, this is exacerbated, placed outside any dialectic as "Norman" speaks, "Mother" who is paranoid about "Norman," sets him up while alert to being set up. The vanity of performance and citational dispossession is accelerated. But this rupture rereads and inhabits not this refined moment, but, if more discretely, all of Hitchcock, not only in the disembodied voice that opens *Rebecca* and will remain nameless. It recurs to and names the relation of voice to face or bodily graphics, or talkies in general to silent film writing. This partition and redoubling over and of the voice literalizes the "voice-over" that is a perpetual mismatch, and it confirms the reinscription of the cinematic into "silent" film premises: the priority of graphematics over any and all pretense that voice is other than additional sound, that it *expresses*. Hitchcock dismisses other movies as "pictures of people talking." All dialogue is first of all sound, he tells Truffaut. But it also mutes, cuts off, so that this blockage of speech, Hamletlike and belonging to the structure of image as such, is thematized in the narratives perpetually, as in the prohibition of saying, telling secrets (McKenna), telling confessions (Logan), or the need to dissimulate (Hannay), saying what no one else says or claims to have seen (Iris Henderson), and so on. Hitchcock will intentionally desynchronize some voice-overs, as occurs with Bertani's French-intoned English in *To Catch a Thief*, where this dehiscence is doubly mobilized in association with a sort of interlanguage or translation effect. The ventriloquized voice of "Mother" is symptomatic of voice as such.

The *acousmêtre* connects hearing itself to measure, to a metrics or metros "heard" in the knocking motif in Hitchcock that is one aural analog of the bar series. It allows "Mother" to dissolve, in essence, into a variant of a prefigural, machinal, materially differencing effect—preceding gender and "origin." The *acousmêtre* seems, against its own logic, to return to a maternalist and Oedipal trope. In practice, however, it records the dispossession of voice in advance of its definition—as when a screen voice seems barely attached to moving lips, or when a character's or

Figure 16. Obverse *acousmêtre*: Hank, above, ghost of telephonics.

actor's recitation speaks like the mynah birds sought by Tippi Hedren, or when the citational fabric of scripted dialogue frays into what it "sounds *like*." "Mother" is neither natural nor originary nor necessarily female nor embodied nor disembodied fully; it is, perhaps, the technicity of "voice" (and its premise of attachment to a speaking head) that is exposed as an alien media positioned, supposedly, at the site of nonidentity ("Mother"). By situating an archival rupture in "Mother's voice," sought by the son, the effect is to reinforce a (fractured) master origin by accommodating its self-difference. The example Chion gives is Doris Day's singing voice reaching her son, Hank, atop endlessly replicating steps, yet there is a counterexample in the airport, with Inspector Buchanan listening in, where it is Hank's voice that is disembodied— on, or as, the black telephone.

## Trifecta

> There was a telephone scene in the picture: the hero was asking the heroine to marry him. . . . I wanted to do it a new way: to show neither the man nor the woman. I wanted to put the whole conversation over by means of a dumb *show* produced through a third person: in this case the telephone operator who was listening in.
> **—Alfred Hitchcock**

> Next they will give me the third degree.
> **—*Spellbound***

Hitchcock's description of the operator scene from *Easy Virtue* is paradigmatic: the dialogue between two characters is the entire premise or content but is not heard or relevant; it is displaced to a third person, who partakes without the others' awareness, miming a "dumb show" through which the media, and the switchboard itself, operate.

There is something naive about Deleuze's gloss of Hitchcock that is reminiscent of Charles Sanders Peirce's semiotic model of "thirdness," mostly because it is restricted to a rhetorical triangulation: "in the history of cinema Hitchcock appears as one who no longer conceives of the constitution of a film as a function of two terms—the director and the film to be made—but as a function of three: the director, the film and the public." Hitchcock's screen all but swarms with figures of threeness, with triads and triangles, in an excess that on the surface seems to disarticulate rather than enforce any familiar sense of "thirdness" on the philosophico-rhetorical map. But even if the "public" could be unified—as Baudelaire's *hypocrite lecteurs,* Poe's "crowd," or Hitchcock's tourists—why is this *multitude* so formalized that the triad or number 3, or 13, alone appears like a ritual genuflection, a withdrawal of aura and explosion of units and dyads?[2]

So there is perhaps some other encryption here, something tied to the number 13, to pyramids and tripods, to the camera and cameo, indeed, *number* as such. It will have nothing to do with so-called mimetic desire or love triangles. One should recall the stakes: Hitchcock's first movie project as director (uncompleted and now lost) was called *Number 13*; triangles are referred to repeatedly in dialogue or visually choreograph objects and space *(Rope)*; triangles echo visually in the dominant letter *M,* as thirteenth letter, yet also as a graph of three triangles (an effect often coupled with its inversely directed double, *W: The Man Who . . . , The Wrong Man,* Mae West, Montreal/Winnipeg, Merry Widow). But if a certain threeness haunts and pervades these graphics, it is not in some private notation, such as recalling that Hitchcock's birthday was August 13. Whatever holds 3 or 13 in play for Hitchcock's machine has the potential to dispossess and deform visual surface. *Thirteen,* the number of number for Hitchcock—of a certain invasive geo-metron, we might say, that preinhabits any cinematic "present"—will return, recur, recirculate in systematically random ciphers.[3] So we see why Deleuze's comment is nonetheless too casual, as if unaware of this weblike proliferation that renders any such aperçu somewhat belated, minimal, or misleading at best. Why does "thirdness" not only appear as a rhetorical fracture and dissimulation accompanied by surveillance, double-talk, or originary murder, but also drift into the play of "1" and "3," including 13 or 39 or letteral combinations of *C* (3) and *A* or *O* (1)? Why does it rest, at times, in the pyramid, Egyptian certainly, or become an effect similar to runes like the bar series or wheel? Why does the blind man Philip Martin in *Saboteur* give Barry Kane the parting advice, as a man of the ear, to "*practice* the triangle" in order to evade being framed? But to begin with, again, this is not a love triangle of any sort. If the "one" is a trope within number, a spectral zero, as Paul de Man suggests, what simultaneously calls it into parlance and suspends or annihilates it in advance as a ghost position? What has the "3" to do with apostrophe, face, hyperbole, citationality, *trees*? What is the link between the "3" and the null or zero, circle or "O"?[4]

The serial killer, the *A*venger, leaves a calling card with a pyramid on his victims, a symbol repeated on the lodger's map of his appearances leading, he concludes, all in "one direction." One sees this opening the first blonde's murder—face frozen in a mute scream—*already* a repetition in a series (a seriality without origin), on a Tuesday (third day), the card bearing at its center not a letter but a design, a signature, a large triad.[5] What has this to do with the triangle being the "first" geometric figure occupying space and accorded *visibility*—that is, for a technician of the "visible"?

*The Lodger* is subtitled *A Story of the London Fog.* The story is about the fog, and the Avenger strikes with the camera emerging from fog, only to recede again, never seen, faceless. The story is about the fog—vapor, suspended water particles that catch light, a chiaroscuro effect of uncertain shadow play, engulfing and shrouding, a site of ambush. It is in fact a "story" of the house as well, the house as fog. The status of the *oikos* or dwelling, preinhabited by a murderous alterity, a lodging house with the number 13 above it. A lodging or *logos,* dispossessed in its imaginary. The wan upper-class guest in a house numbered 13 will be presented as tracking another who he also, perhaps, is, himself avenging (we are later given) his own sister's murder when the lights blacked out at a ballroom dance, the Avenger's "first" blonde victim: avenging a murder against the triangle murderer, avenging for and against the Avenger. The detour involves the machinal production and relay of news, of media, the telecommunications sequence following the initial "murder" (which, as elsewhere, is somehow preoriginary). It is here that Hitchcock's first cameo appears. The *calling card* the Avenger leaves with the body is clearly a signature token—neither letter nor message. Even if the pyramid will bear on the hieroglyphic trope of silent film (reiterated in the Nefertiti scene in the British Museum), it is anything but clear what it had to do with a preoriginary murder cast in the title card as split, MUR/DER, with one syllable white on black, the other the opposite, white and black doubly reversible. It coincides with a violation of reading by, and by means of, white and black, which, if they were ever to coincide, would suspend the visual order.[6] If something unable to enter the public signifying order is being avenged, some initial injury or wound (a rejection by the blonde, a prosthesis of peroxide, a lack in the very metaphysics of blondes, the blondeness of [a] metaphysics), the serial repetitions of the act do not set it right, do not fulfill the need of revenge or end *ressentiment* itself but only garner, of course, further spillage, proliferation of blonde corpses, more and more triangles.

In contrast to Deleuze's citing of a "thirdness" that is purely rhetorical in relation to the audience, the triangle marks among other things a preoriginary (self) murder—at once destroying and constitutive. Something in the *triad* is not merely a complication of plot or desire, but identified at once with murder or "death" (in quotes, since it remains to be considered what this marks on Hitchcock's screen), as well as with an "origin" that begins as or after its own cancellation, like presenting "life" as a semiotic effect like animation.[7]

The triangle or pyramid on the Avenger's card, then, suggests several lines of convergence: it attends a preoriginary "murder" (or its serial repetition); it does so as an agent of avenging or revenging, implementing repetition itself, *ressentiment,* and a (failed) attempt to exceed that mode by the act of turning upon itself (which only gets caught as another repetition); it is a unit, but is triadic; it is the first visible plane in geometrics, signature of (in)visibility; it seems associated not exclusively with a social triad, such as a love triangle, but with a pharaohlike subject ("Hitchcock's" birthdate), the eye on the masonic pyramid (on the dollar bill, say) or visibility itself. Moreover, its pyramidal form in this ideogram connects both to a hieroglyphic and to an Egyptian dimension. The 3 (c) and 1 (a) sign for *ca*mera or *ca*meo.[8] The pyramid is "one" and destroys the 1 it simulates or produces as a trope of zero. It is like speech that, coming into play with a third figure supplementing any two, revokes the pretense of the one speaker or even the subject it appears to permit, reproducing the utterance as a dissemblance before that (already occurring) violence and the surveillance it implies.

What is foggy here is that the pyramid seems, perversely, not a signature but the agent. What seems present in the triangle or the number 13 appears as a 1 and a 3, a 1 that is (also) a 3 and that is annulled in becoming, having already been, a 3—which, in turn, is a faux unit, a token of the *metron* itself, say, as in the "bar series" William Rothman typographically cites as "/ / / /." Thus, if one likes, a *geo-metrics,* the measuring effect of a material semiosis inhabiting the official logos and, with it, a sheer formalization of earth, the "material," the face of the earth (Mount Rushmore), which, not strangely, resembles (as with the stone face of Nefertiti) where face and voice seem "given" to the inanimate, the stone, the painting, a prosopopoeia Hitchcock will return to at numerous junctures. Thus as *number,* the complex here goes to the "source" and exposes the *1* as a historical implant, like the stabilizing ghost term, zero (the "I" or eye)—number at its own "birth," formalism as a root site in which the anamorphic warping of time and space, of form, as in the material dimension of film, occurs.[9] The triangle, from within this historial fold, appears the phoenix corpse of phenomenalizaton: not an *eidos,* it precedes and supersedes the "story of the London fog," cinema as the narrated undoing of this site of preinscription, of world. The pyramid that precedes the 1, though, or renders it triadic, appears Egyptian, precedes "Plato," and returns as if to the prehistorial mark sublated in the projection of the *eidos,* Plato's calling card, an imperial recuperation on behalf of a rhetorical solarity. It comes out of the preoriginary fog of semiotic differencing, in ambush, at any time, avenging in the name of these material *stoicheia* this historial relapse of the Platonic inversion. Yet it emerges in *The Man Who Knew Too Much* also at the center of the logo for the Egypticist "Tabernacle of the Sun" surrounded by shooting, licking light daggers or rays. In the place of this eclipsed sun, it *precedes* the recuperative Egyptian as well. It is as if numbering dehoused the "advent" of a technicity of which the cinematic is distant and advance legatee, and, in shifting to digital, would return to be wildly dissolved into and as.[10]

One might wish, here, to recall one account of the advent of numbering in the West: that, in a sense, it begins with 3, since 1 was not originarily a number, but a late invention, 2 is merely its duplicate, and 1 and zero ciphers differently filling a shared nonplace. *One* occurs as if after the 3, but in a way cancels its primacy, while 3, to begin with, cancels 1 by spawning it as a retroprojection—more still, a necessary narrative device, a MacGuffin. All of which may be mere formal frivolity, a kind of pointless exocrypt at the navel of numbering (yet also visibility, form, graphics, logos), did it not have another correlate in the experience of speech, in the emergence of the speaker, of the "I" in the utterance. This "I's" dilemma is reflected not just, for Hitchcock, in the mute and intersubstitutable face(s) of silent film, but in the succession of lead characters who are prevented from speaking, unable to say what they "know," or be believed, or for that matter, bear a string of proper names. Not because the latter situation is a thematic or psychological one, but something else going to the core of a semiotic injunction, a permanent strangling of voice as *expression.*[11]

The structure of "dialogue" is trialogic, but the 3 that guarantees the social order of language also implies a self-canceling operation so far as the 1, the "I," is concerned: it mutes or blocks speech. The triadic model demonstrates something other than a ruptured or displaced temporal site at which the *one* emerges only as already dead, a faux personification and citation of itself when apostrophizing a third (nonhuman) figure. It bars the emergence of utterance as personification, as face or prosopopoeia—indeed, caught in a kind of virtuality, as the projection of an anterior trace, an outside, that may seem like the succession of morphing faces receiving the wireless news or public inscription in *The Lodger.*

In this self-canceling site of "origination," the *utterer* converting vibratory and rehearsed sounds into autocitation parallels the dilemma of the "1" in the triadic constellation. First, an explosive *hyperbologic* underlies this site of a first person's cinematic emergence as a third, apostrophic, and second, that in this "model" there persists a kind of enfolding of any framing distance. Among other things, this means that in the performative emergence of a cinematic speaker barred from communication and already "dead," the protocols of mimesis are suspended, frames included in the site of the framed. Moreover, it is only the hyperaperformativity, the re-marking of "acting," that overtakes the concealed structure of citation in the "I," *as if* the act could then occur as an event. This enfolding of the outside is also one of the past, *anteriority,* inscription, the apostrophized yet nonanthropomorphic site. This self-*interrupting* model is bound to an incomplete personification of the inanimate over which the human voice is staged—that is, what stages speech as a social exchange is without face or aura, what Benjamin argues is canceled with the advent of cinema. This trauma is staged in the Hitchcock *speaker* microdynamically. Even Joel McCrea and Laraine Day reciting marriage proposals and declarations of "love" on the night ferry in *Foreign Correspondent* do so as if deadpanning an autocitation of what the other might anticipate (the supposed original of this being Hitchcock and Alma). Its logic breaks with the trail by which a past trace is projected into a continuous future repetition, puts memory itself into crisis in an instantaneous *standstill,* and opens the system to a murderous permeation by a material agency that appears preoriginary—a kind of machinal "Mother," of bird attack that disinteriorizes. Marvin, in *Secret Agent,* speaks of himself as a "triangle" *retiring* from the "family circle," then speeds on to Constantinople.

One might now go a step beyond. If the figure of 13 is a cipher for the emergence of a subject effect, say "Hitchcock's" birthday (now in a problematic sense that imperils the received narrative of the past), and if cinema itself doubles as the site of this machinal third, since it feelingly posits face or voice (thereby receding, as is necessary, to a site of inscription precedent to all characters or identities emerging), it is also the case that if the Avenger resumes the first letter, *A,* of Hitchcock's name, the recurrent initials themselves, coming up in numerous variants, A. H., simulate the routine utterance of apostrophe: "Ah!"[12] At this momentary convergence, the triad appears another analog of the bar series, of the "signature" that precedes all other signature effects and graphically dismembers the name "Hitchcock." The pyramid on the calling card bears these encrypted systems, as the upward-pointing sign of the Avenger is poised—immersed in metaphysics, doubling it as the blonde herself, and incarnating it in the trope of serial and triadic murder—to present and overleap *ressentiment,* the circular dependence of memory on a certain preinstalled cognitive narrative. The triangle as the signature of utterance, of its failure, and therefore of material inscription that dispossesses, but in being so it opens a new scene, another site of action and writing in the spectral machine of Hitchcock's name.

In these variants in which the 1 and 3 put "man" itself at risk, together with the relation to anteriority, to memory or history, there is named another process or historical project. It flashes across the Hitchcock screen in proliferating anagrammatic ciphers as in recurrent letteral combinations of *Ca,* or *Co*: Canadian, Carlotta, Carlton at Cannes, Capricorn. Another cipher can be heard in a series of *p-* words and proper names that mark that letter, from the proliferation in *The 39 Steps* of such words (Portland Place, pips in poultry, pipes) to *Torn Curtain,* where it turns up as code for the East German underground, as a Greek $\pi$ etched in the earth under the foot. Pi, that is, the Pythagorean formula whose transposition begins (since it can be endlessly extended) 3.14, 3 and 1, and . . . 4, what in this mise-en-scène would be the frame itself, both the literal frame of cinema and the four-sided metaphor that is never quite real or symmetrical, a "frame" absorbing even the audience or spectator (either as tourist or potential reader). When this figure intervenes or haunts a scene of writing, cinematic or spectral writing, as here, it is not as a passive referent, since it is literally unreadable, but as a node, the activation of a chain of semiotic rerouting and transformations. It could be said to assault and open or alter the entire model or modality of reference, the suspension of the very mimesis film was supposed to consolidate, but, in Hitchcock, effaces. Thus if the letter *p,* when annotated, echoes the *pi* and hence the triad motif, it will be from the first associated with a canceled origin, a principle of disruption: Portland Place is the site of Annabella's murder; "pips in poultry" (the question asked three times by the harried and henpecked old figure in the Music Hall) refers to the cause or origin of a disease in a bird, no longer one of flight. It reactivates a transformative, material, countermimetic logic that may extend to an overriding trajectory of crossing in Hitchcock's machine—a machine of war in a specific sense. It is this metaphoric site of a spectral cinema, encased in the triad or pyramid logic, where face is (almost) given and inscription phenomenally projected from a mnemonic device. Here one finds a technological correlate to Benjamin's figure of "shock," understood both as attribute of cinema's interruption in the cultural-historical continuum and as linguistic caesura, the suspense by which "materialist historiography" breaks through all historicism to chance an act that puts various pasts and futures at risk.

If the pyramideme is a calling card of anything, or asks to have its call returned, "Mother" contacted by telephone or telegraphy, it may be as a shift from a sabotaged machine of reference, a passive converted to an active mimesis without copy or original, a permanent interruption in the received structuring of "time" or historiality and "experience" and the event. And it is irreversible, since one cannot return to a "1" from the "3" as other than the latter's spectral retroprojection. But at the same time it is aporetic, halted in the middle of the bridge as that "passage," outwitting its renarrativization, since it was never other, and what is passed from would be an instituted relapse encountered as installed historial regime. Ocularcentrism, the *eidein*, the Enlightenment. Hyperbolic, self-enframing, initiatory yet already "dead," apostrophic and muting—the pyramid place-marks an Egyptoid signature and precedes it, contains the signature of cinemallographic logics that exceed any anthropomorphic trope. When the Greek $\pi$ is flashed underfoot, in the hypogrammatic position etched in the earth, to indicate an Underground

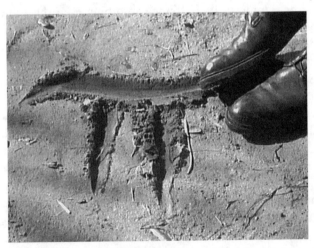

Figure 17. Code of cinematic Resistance *(Torn Curtain),* the Pythagorean pi etched in soil.

or Resistance, it recalls the narrative surface to its inscription in what-ever is unfolding in the array of shadows, phonemes, body parts, and put-on faces: that is, in the "set." Whenever these nodes materialize, in the shy candelabra or alliterative stutter, the switchboard of multiply networked signature effects goes wild. It all but panics. Except it has been there before, it recollects after the initial shock, memory clicking and shuttering to stabilize. In fact, it has never been elsewhere.

One cannot approach this dimension in Hitchcock without coming up against the deformations of number (particularly about the zero, MacGuffin of circuits, or the 3) and letters, which circulate in giant neon isolation, anagrammatic combinatoire, and Poesque cryptonymies, without skirting a scandal. They solicit response rather than, as usual, occlusion, yet cannot be accommodated to mimetic premises at all. They reside close to the inscriptions of celluloid. What is interesting is how one engages a zone that is stamped with the typographic impri-matur of Hitchcock's first cameo in *The Lodger*. For instance, one may recall that Hitchcock worked on all the details of script and storybooks before anything was shot (which he protested was a bore), or recall that he began as a graphic artist of silent titles (working with letters), and suggest that he played Nabokovian crossword games. Because this practical description keeps the issue within the order of aesthetic play, it might be greeted with amused interest. But if one suggested that the implosion of numeration and letteral repetitions registers a cinematic interrogation of sheer form or graphic traces, which was how logos was originally thought of, at the intersection of word and number, that would be different. One would not be dealing then with puzzles played by a clever auteur but with relations and inscriptions to which "Hitchcock" became viral host. And that would be another matter. Yet, since these have largely been occluded and give almost no one pleasure to examine, one would have to conclude the latter.

## They're Literary Critics

*Shadow of a Doubt* has a double secret. While one imagines one is watch-ing a story about an evil uncle taking up residence amidst his sister's family and engaging the niece who learns his secret, something is happening to the definition of house itself. The work, and specifically the house, is ceaselessly traversed with teletechnic figures. Uncle Charlie (Joseph Cotten) goes to a telephone to send a telegram, wherein he voices a telegraph message in staccato style; young sister Anne cannot stop compulsively reading, a bespectacled automaton; young Charlie (Teresa

Wright) is marked as telepathic—and libraries, penciled memoranda, numerical counting (Roger's steps), radios, photography, and so on invade
and traverse the premises. Later, the detective's name will be Graham (or
*gram*), as if the mark sought its place in this criminally teletechnic residence. When Uncle Charlie cuts out an article from the paper that refers
to his "Merry Widow" killing spree, he shapes the remaining news sheet
into a house, pretending the children will find it interesting to play
with, though they aren't amused ("That's Papa's paper!"). But the deed
is done: standing on the floor is a paper house overrun with print and
letters, its portals the product of cuts and omissions.

One would expect to get some illumination, then, from a curious appearance by Herb, the mother-dominated neighbor who huddles with
father Joe on the porch. Emma explains that they are "literary critics,"
and we hear them evaluating the crime pulp fiction they read for the best
ways to commit murder. Uncle Charlie fits in too well in the American
family, where all members speak past one another, absorbed in psychotic preoccupations. The only mention of the world war raging outside
Santa Rosa is in a bank, where a poster urges citizens to buy a "stake" in
America through war bonds, as if the entity itself were vampiric. So it
turns out that Joe and Herb, rather than offering illuminations through
a metacommentary on all the obsessions with reading and telegraphics
in the total absence of communication, are "literary critics" in a fairly
defined sense. They are interested in comparing and evaluating the murder techniques they discover in their reading—or proposing new ones.
When young Charlie erupts about how morbid they are, obsessing, like
good Americans, about killing others, Joe protests that they are innocent: they are only proposing ways of killing one another. The archival
death drive gives blanket amnesty if its contracts are respected and no
principle of gain is involved, unlike the Merry Widow killer supposedly.
The key rule of the sport is to find a way to kill with the least expense
of energy and without leaving a clue or getting caught: the only impedi-
ments that restrain normal citizens. Herb plays his trump idea with an
unreadable moniker: "Inny." It is so clever it deserves a nickname that
is explained as standing for "Indian arrow poison." In its way, *inny*
suggests the cinematic rape or murder: insinuate a poison by a pinprick
that goes unnoted close to the psychic template that it contaminates,
despoils, and eviscerates from within. The structure is like Cary Grant's
glowing white milk glass of *Suspicion* or the "medication" delivered to
Ingrid Bergman in *Notorious* or the sedatives given Doris Day in the

second *Man Who Knew Too Much*. It is also like what Hitchcock describes as Scottie Ferguson's epistemological "rape." It is actually a good piece of literary critical reading since, by pretending to affirm interiors, it virtually eviscerates them and the space it cannot but seem to name.

Something penetrates the defenses under the cover of being something else, poisons or exteriorizes the "inner" system, including memory, and genetically reengineers an always artificial or implanted set of programs, pasts, mnemonics.

The critics shift their reading adventures to issues of revision, application, intervention. The nonphenomenal form of *inny*, as word and application, precedes inspection or defense, like the bomber whose *soundless* formula would be purveyed in *The 39 Steps*, or telepathy itself. *Inny* works, as an affectionate if diminutive phoneme, yet needs Herb's gloss. It cancels a certain interior or interiority, much as the news cut out of the house with Papa's paper does, a flimsy dwelling walled with public print and letteration. The Indian is the preoriginary "American" to the West of Santa Rosa, California, moreover, and their persistence poisons the current usurpers' pretense to originariness, even to Americanness. The literary critics manage to perform an unusual reading feat by fetishizing murder as an aesthetic ritual or domestic addiction, or magnifying its implication in reading to a pop cultural joke. They are not troubled by interpretive debate but go directly to the site of reinscription.

## Photophobia

> The sketches for framing, the strict delimitation of the frame,
> the apparent elimination of the out-of-frame, are explained by
> Hitchcock's constant reference, not to painting or the theater,
> but to tapestry-making, that is, to weaving.
> **—Gilles Deleuze**

"Cinema" poses as an intervention preceding memory in *Spellbound*, where the parallel lines of the "bar series" precede all visuals and etiological quests.

It is interesting that in *Spellbound*, Hitchcock's most exclusive paean to the bar series, this is briefly allied to what is called, by the psychoanalytic mentor of Constance Peterson (Ingrid Bergman), Dr. Brulov, "photophobia." *Photophobia* is a term oddly used to explain John Ballantine's (Gregory Peck) lapses into threatening trances and protopsychotic cinamnesia. It occurs when he is startled by a brilliant if not blinding light outside the window. It turns out that snow has fallen and the reflective white has blanketed the earth. To have a *phobia* to light is odd and suggests that "light" is not what it seems, not light, indeed, lethal:

CONSTANCE: Snow!
DR. BRULOV: The light frightened him—photophobia.
CONSTANCE: That's the white he's afraid of. Snow and those tracks.
DR. BRULOV: What tracks?
CONSTANCE: The sled tracks in the snow . . . skiing . . . ski tracks in the snow.

What is first named photophobia, anticipating Marnie's panic before lightning, anachronized as "colors," conceals instead the mnemonic plague of what precedes or mars white, *tracks*. Brulov complains of the dead cineast Dr. Edwardes: "What kind of an analyst is it, who wants to cure psychosis by taking people *skating* or to a *bowling* alley?" Yet the work that solemnly announces it is the first film on "psychoanalysis," presented as a neo-Enlightenment program (if you bring the trauma to light, the cure will follow), offers itself as a cure to psychoanalysis, whose Green Manors will be run by Dr. Murchison—the director who kills the incoming Dr. Edwardes, his replacement, to retain control. The great house of Green Manors inherits others in Hitchcock, including that of the Selznick studio logo opening the work, implied to be a madhouse in turn, and the archival rule that offers a Shakespeare quote from *Julius Caesar* about "the stars" not being to blame for the fault within (that is, Peck's and Bergman's tranced-out performances will have to be gotten around). Assassination and counterusurpation of an empire constitute the subtext, not only between the fratricial Murchison and the already dead *Ed*wardes (whose name evokes sheer anteriority), but also between cinema and psychoanalysis as its double here. Covertly, the references to Rome (Italy and New York) and the "Empire *State* Hotel" bring this combat into focus: while pretending to produce the first film and homage to the great modern science of the mind, Hitchcock sees cinema and psychoanalysis as competitors for an imperial position in the global era to come—which will be the reigning spectrographic practice with power to reach into the heads of innumerable communities.

Books fly through the air at Green Manors, as the one Rhonda Fleming as "*Mary Car*michael" throws at Bergman's head or the *Labyrinth of the Guilt Complex* which gives away its author's autograph, "Dr. Edwardes," as false, revealing the blank "I" of Peck the amnesiac in quest of a memory or trauma. It is here that the parallel bar pattern figures, which is what must be unriddled. Peck sees it in all variety of threads, or what Deleuze calls weaves, or what one might simply call trope: table and bed coverings, clothes. Hitchcock is reading his cinema, psychoanalyzing it as a hermeneutic hunt. Psychoanalysis here has taken on the role of the hermeneutic state, a totalizing explanatory machine, and as a science of spellbinding trances, of a threatened cinematic order in the person of Dr. Murchison.

The "labyrinth" named, though, is the structure of image itself. Pursuing all threads into it does not allow one, like Perseus, to return, since they all lead in a way to the minotaur, half-animal, half-man, consuming in turn. Doors open on doors opening on doors, only to reveal luminous white walls that trigger more "photophobia." Peck's teeth-grinding stare is itself under a spell, likening amnesiac psychosis to the cinematic trance. On the one hand, the bar pattern triggers both Peck's amnesia and stands to undo it. On the other, Dr. Murchison, renegade director, will suicide himself as Green Manors emerges as yet another front for the cinematic madhouse itself. This suicitation of cinema at one of its limits introduces, with a pistol-as-projector gunshot into the *eye,* or camera, the first flash of *color* in Hitchcock's cinema, as if retiring black-and-white film as such. Garish red washes across the screen in a flash. The cinematic gun is turned against cinema's own premises. Photophobia alludes not to the white glare of the snow but to the tracks, somehow, that cross it: photophobia would name a dread not of "light" as such but of light's prosthetic secret, its dispersal across particles and waves and reflectors. Photophobia is thus a phobia of tracks.

This riddle—why is psychoanalysis presented as a haunting?—becomes more insistent, inhabiting the odd title itself. What is *spellbound*? "Psychoanalysis" is set up and seen as a consuming hermeneutic, a stand-in for a certain law of the book. What finally emerges in the flashback as Ballantine's etiological "accident" and ur-trauma is a "MacGuffin" that is not one: the revelation of the early fatricide solves nothing, and the narrative doubles back. The flashback, of course, involves Ballantine's pushing his young brother onto a spiked fence with his feet, and it discloses the opposite of innocence (in fact, if anything the fratricide appears clearly intentional, so its recollection as a means of jubilation is, as Peck's face makes clear, still more deceived) and turns out not to free him after all. What is the *spell* that binds, or that binds to spelling itself, which allows this film to be presented, in a way, as Hitchcock's own hyperbolically literal paean, unread certainly, to the entirely premimetic bar series? What, and why, does the *bar pattern—*

the slashes or parallel lines tracked through the film and associated with Peck's psychosis or empty and murderous stare—haunt, and why is haunting made to precede and inhabit a hermeneutic hunt, a ritual tracking that can only return to a preoriginary, and dispossessing, site? Why *ghosts* in what is a film about the *neo*-Enlightenment appearance of psychoanalysis, unless psychoanalysis were itself "haunted," not only by the demented inversions of Green Manors but by spectral logics like cinema?

In the case of *Spellbound* what is hunted and haunted can be tracked through three parallel fronts: psychoanalysis as stand-in for a totalizing hermeneutic (the aesthetic state); the logic of sight or ocularcentrism itself ("I'm haunted but I can't *see* by what," says Peck); a precession of memory and language ("we have the word *white* on our side," Bergman blurts). Murchison will advise Constance at the end to "pick up the threads of your life." The hyperbolic figure of the "pick up" will resonate, in association with hyperbolic *pic*turing and reading, as when Bergman interrupts Peck reading on the train: "Don't read the paper—let's pick up where we left off."[13] *Picking up* recurs in various films: insistently in the second *Man Who Knew Too Much,* for instance, where it is also in the closing line of the film ("pick up Hank"). It returns one to the hyperbolic forgetfulness of picturing, the machinery that produces the blind mimetic spell of the picture.

What is doing the haunting, then, cannot be the bar pattern itself, whether as motif, or decked out in the narrative trappings of a repressed trauma (snow tracks, impaling bars). That pattern always murders in advance, and enables. It becomes a premise of action, at the price of decimating the mimetic counterlogic to which it also gives rise. Prior to the first snow sequence at Dr. Brulov's the *bar pattern* is given an ostensible home; its primary site will be as Deleuze perceived woven cloth or clothes: tablecloths, patterns in suits or textiles, the bedcover.

John *Ballantine* (the name of a famous American beer whose logo was *three* interlocking rings) has a burn scar on his hand. His amnesia, referenced to air battle over Rome in the war, is linked to this Empedoclean scar. This trauma of memory and of writing (the *hand's* scar) will thus be connected to the bar series too. No trauma studies can have access to the bar pattern as such, however, since it is not "a" memory but the premise of where mnemonics inscribes and erases itself and the visual as such.

What is haunting here, why the gothicisms, imported from Vincent Price–style romps into an event, cinema's "first" attempt to represent psychoanalysis, as the credits more or less boast with mock solemnity?

Why does the work send an obnoxious Hitchcock double into the lobby of the Empire State Hotel to harass Bergman, a tipsy gent from *Pitt*sburgh who keeps hitting on her, exposing the fatuous and threadbare excuse of "romance" that coats the labyrinth of her embarrassing infatuation with Peck? What is encountered is an aporetic port, like an uncrossable bridge, like the doors opening on other doors or the paradoxical premise of a transition without another place to go on this map.[14]

This blank retraction of the syrupy romance is embroiled with Peck's infantile-sweet-passive-aggressive mock erotics.[15] Yet this has a defacing effect on the play of gender. The movement of Constance from frigid intellectual to passionate woman, each a cliché, is undermined by more than the pathology of what she is "loving" (patient, psychopath, amnesiac, fratricidal cineast). It is in the early fork marks she etches on the tablecloth in which the bar series pattern is first put into play. Bergman uses a fork to sketch in the tablecloth a vaginal outline composed of those same embedded lines, which Peck rubs, as if to erase, with a softly aphallic butter knife—as in a trance. Cinema knows too much. A double gesture: what would be rubbed or effaced is not only where the bar pattern itself precedes any vaginal "origin" but also where genital extensions and pockets become disarticulated, uncertain. This "psychotic" precession of a blind semiosis over "erotic" metaphor recurs in the razor scene in the bedroom, where the bedspread's linear weave covers Bergman's sleeping figure. Peck bypasses the entire allure of the sleeping Bergman, the pretense of erotic identification and desire. Gender is preceded and almost vaporized, reconstituted as aftereffect and performative, leading through the doggedness of Bergman's love to the surreal ski scene in which Peck follows Bergman bent behind her doggie-style, in a position that rewrites the queer complicity of Bergman's heterosexual allure: she must convert his rear window preferences through tricks like those Grace Kelly masters with James Stewart—another Freudian truth Hitchcock understands, he thinks, better, through the preoriginary logics of "photophobia."

The psychotic *stare* would be better called a trance, spellbound by the bar series that shatters hermeneutic spells and precedes spelling. Peck's Ballantine shifts, momentarily, into the position of Hitchcock public, who transition from the identities they have been bestowed toward this intervallic precession of all phenomenalization, and toward its dispossession of the eye, spellbound alternately by ocularcentrism or its revocation: the scissoral eye of Dalí's dream sequence. This stare,

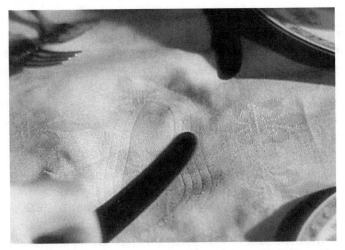

Figure 18. Genital metrics: butter knife smooths away vaginoid outline.

and its resistance, bars the auratic personification of any "gaze." The "trauma" that *Spellbound* unearths, as it were, is a trauma in and before the trope of sight yet also before metaphorization can take effect. One is spellbound in being blinded even by grammar, by spelling itself, which the bar pattern dismembers and scrambles, as outside the cyclorama's window at the close of *Rope* giant dismembered letters flash in neon—as if the whole took place between the lines on a giant page or screen. The name of the sanatorium, Green Manors, names this prosthesis behind the anthropomorphic fiction of "nature" itself. A paralinguistic effect or semiosis precedes not only psyche and eros, the demigods of psycho-analysis, but phusis altogether, like the gunman on the ski slope, hiding behind a tree. As we hear from Constance when she adds up the clues, there will have been a "weapon at the *foot* of a tree with the murderer's *fingerprints* on it." Murchison is at the time holding the very weapon that, in the obvious set prop of a giant hand, will turn back on his eye, into the camera, putatively into the viewer.[16] The scissoring of the giant eye in Dalí's dream sequence is repeated here. When Hitchcock in his unusual epigraph quotes *Julius Caesar* on the fault lying not in the stars but in ourselves, he was not aping the discovery of psychoanalysis. He was not only marking the limitation of the stars, Bergman and Peck, to do much more than walk through the hilarious script in a kind of oblivious trance.

## No Touching

In *The Birds,* the first collective attack occurs on the children at Cathy's birthday party during a game of "blindman's bluff." This attack of myriad black specks or asolarities on a "birthday," the ritual celebration of origin, is accompanied by an admonition by Cathy during the game, as she complains to another kid, "No touching." Since this has no bearing on the sexual frigidity at issue elsewhere, itself a MacGuffin, it remains a riddle. *Touching* irradiates across Hitchcock together with finger-pointing and fingerprints.

If "touching" precedes the supposed priority of sight, as Derrida argues in *Le Toucher,* it does more than expose the latter as a massively installed ideological blind whose premises—the naturalness and transparency of perception, light, knowing as *eidein*—were never what they pretended. Yet even "touching" names an impossible premise of contact, a pretense of sense certainty, which underlies every epistemo-political realism, empiricism, materialism, pragmatism, and so on, every phenomenology, and exposes each as an "idealism" managed by the aesthetic state (England, in the early films). Hence, "no touching," the seemingly transparent window that is in fact a barrier to the alcoholic seeking his hit ("like an alcoholic at a bar on election day," taunts Grace Kelly in *To Catch a Thief*). Yet his bar to touch that registers contact moves into a seemingly implacable zone where cold (formalism) and hot (immersion in the senses) seem vertiginous and reversible. In that film, as elsewhere, there is a recurrence of the figure of "fingerprints" analyzed virtually in *Blackmail.* "Touching" is not experienced but testified to after the fact by the archive of fingerprints, as in *Blackmail*'s police lineup and fingerprint review. Something irreducibly singular that appears a means of legal identification (the "identification parade") is also without mimetic premises at all, a vertigo of almost parallel nested swirls; something like the film "print" itself precedes phenomenalization, projection, light, face.

The promise of indexing and of indicating the real, of contact, is swept up into a graphematic system that precedes and defers its possibility. For cinema, it also implies the impossibility of documentary. The moving picture *Fingerprints* alluded to by Detective Frank Webber will suggest literal identification, yet it points back to the faux documentary opening of *Blackmail,* itself a hive of allegories. But the nonrepresentational graphics represented in rows of fingerprints in the identification parade, as it is called, preceding arrest, dissolves into the criminal's face and, together with the mimetic fiction of the "documentary," into the fictive film about police life that Webber hopes would reproduce the actual record of his work (he wants to see the film to compare his knowledge of the real thing). The print of the finger supersedes, and implicates, the promise of the pointing finger, the point of the point, which can always imply the punctuality of a temporal promise, an imaginary *punctum* or "now," a *maintenant* in which the hand *(main)* seeks to hold on to *(tenant)* a present it never had. In *Blackmail* the last we see of the murdered artist, Crewe, is *the hand* with the pointing finger emerging from behind the bed curtain. It is this that Tracy, the film's official blackmailer, deploys as accusing finger, as indicator or indictment pointing at Webber before plunging through the glass dome of the British Museum.[17] That is, before plunging through the monumental archives of "history," back to and *before* the Egyptian statuary and hieroglyphics, passing through—then falling through the roof's dome back into—the universal reading room.

Thus, Cathy's remark about "no touching" resonates with the impulse, or presupposition of *barred* contact, prospective touch, or even accusation. But if pointing evokes the failed promise of a *punctum* in a series, it morphs into two other logics. *Fingerprints* invariably references any film print that, in the discourse of perception Hitchcock anatomizes, precedes phenomenality (or reference). It flashes by at the nonplace where a mnemonic imprint archives what is called perception as such: the hands from which the digit extends, the cave paintings' signature of technicity. In Hitchcock, hands matter: detached, granted personified agency or lack of agency, cuffed (with the two rings citing reels), present in names (Handel Fane, Richard Hannay, Iris Henderson), isolated and cut off, as with the dead artist Crewe's extended hand, the bronze folded hands in "Mother's" bedroom in *Psycho*. Hands mobilize a series of figures, including that of signature (*H-A* incorporates A. H.). This agent of writing is interesting. Hitchcock seldom wrote directly, did not want to credit himself with dialogue but to puppet others, give *dictation* using others' hands. Handcuffs can mark this famous handlessness of cinematic production, what, precisely, involves no contact or touching necessarily, only directing others to do so. The reel- or spectacle-like cuffs also imply arrest, by the photograph or frame. "No touching," cuffed hands, finger pointing *(indicare)* resolved to prints or inscription, writing barred and arrested (by) itself (in or as the hyperscript of Hitchcockian cinemallography). Mnemonic inscription, allied to music and analphabetic writing, generates and disowns this phenomenality.

It is around this site that the prehistorial and vaguely machinal birds descend and attack.

All of this reflects little more than the facticity of "pieces of film" viewed as premise for the cinematic sensorium, the sensorium's (a)materiality or spectrality. In the early films *seeing* may appear dependent upon pursuing or being hunted by a black trace or sound such as a dispossessing clang, crash, explosion, or even serial knocking. Such a mobile trace—blot or hat or dog or umbrella—is also a lieutenant for the frame's being constitutively folded "into" the four-sided box of the visible, as though contracting the imaginary lines of edges to a summary animated dot.

The missing finger joint of Professor Jordan in *The 39 Steps* has done much, perhaps, to deter close inspection of the work's import, providing a misleading relay to a satisfying invocation of "castration," the return to a hermeneutic facade pointedly cast off. Typically, as one still finds in Zizek, when Hannay encounters this notorious *hand*, which he had been warned is the only identifying trait of this master plotter and killer with many names, we are told that he parries a lesson of "castration," both as emasculation and inscription in a symbolic network. But the professor's shooting of Hannay, after which the latter appears to collapse, is in fact foiled by a hymn book in the tweed coat he was given by *Marg*aret, the Scottish crofter's entrapped young wife. But perhaps the MacGuffin of the symbolic has taken its toll in advance, by its own faux institutionalization according to a phenomenal name of the father. (Names are cut up, scattered, taken up and put on, multiplied in Annabella and the professor to elicit a sort of nonspace and signature effect atomized as letters and numbers in the secret memorized formula of Mr. Memory.) From the start, we could invert this absent digit as a mock setup ridiculing the trope of "castration" it predictably, as from a recording, spawns to cover this site.

One seems to have been already taught otherwise in *Blackmail*, where fingerprints and pointing fingers prevail, and where Alice's glove has its fingertips cut off. The finger is not, thus, the protrusion of a phallic order but the dismembered phantom of a cognitive and linguistic promise: that of indexing (as in the Greek *deiknumi*, pointing at) the chimera of a spot or immediate place, such as film pretends to. To absent this finger in advance—even a "joint," as with the professor's—"teaches" a different logic. He does not point, accuse, or indict; he simply shoots. The deletion *almost* makes the fingers nine in number, a squaring of *3*, which renders the fingers no longer ten, no longer digital. The gesture precludes in its numerology a coming digitalization that will prove more mimetically enslaved than the analogic. The squaring of 3 pulls back from affirming the faux symmetry of the deca. It implies decacide. The missing digit does not symbolize "castration," which is inversely a rather plenitudinous trope, so much as it spectralizes *fingering*. In *Frenzy*, Babs (or *Bar*bara) complains that the Globe's Epimethean barkeep Forsythe is always "fingering" her. A *fingerprint* leaves traces of an impossible touch, or contact sheet, the image shot without hands, in which touch and imprint precede the order of the visible.

## Foreign Correspondence

In *Foreign Correspondent* the espionage model is supplanted by one rooted in public media and reportage—the correspondence between photographic reproduction and the "facts" of the newspaper—converting the confabulation of a world war's outbreak to a media fable. From *The Lodger*, the print form of newspapers had mimed the rift between machinal imprint and the installation of facts in the head of the "public," as the real, and in *Shadow of a Doubt* it is cut out into the shape of a house. A reporter *re-ports*, that is, records and relays, but that also suggests a pistol's report, a crashing sound, even as the word retains the logics of a passage, a go-between, a reiterative *portal*.

*Foreign Correspondent* connects a narrative about events leading to war with a problem of media, of recording or getting the real facts (the "story")—as if their causality were inverse—and it does so by putting the notion of a correspondent or correspondence in conjunction with what is foreign in or to that media—a question of *translation*. Joel McCrea, temperamental maverick reporter, rambling American, is sent to Europe to get the real facts no one else can dig up, to simply report, as a camera does, and becomes in the process an agent of acceleration. The most obvious of "MacGuffins" has to do with the "clause" of a secret peace treaty to be extracted from the old European Enlightenment pacifist Van Meer—a name allying him to the borderless site of crossings and disasters, the *sea*.

How do the tele-archive and global war collude? What does it mean for Hitchcock to position a work around the outbreak of a "war," rather than in the middle of it? Is there attraction to *wartime* itself as an arena of disinscription or reinscription that is not openly commented on? What, in any case, is this relation of reportage, media, if the media, like Stewart in *Rear Window*, becomes a catalyst for and a player in events rather than a *recorder*? What is the relationship between telemedia and war? And what role does the obsessive focus on reportage, transmission, "communication," and writing have in the semiosis of war? I will suspend looking at what complications occur, here, if and as the cinematic project gets identified with the clandestine Nazi Fisher, played by Herbert Marshall using a British "Peace Party" as a front. Does the phrase "foreign correspondent" not also name an alienness within the notion of correspondence (mimesis) and that in turn within the determinations of world history, or, for that matter, the *Globe,* as Johnny Jones's newspaper is named, citing Shakespeare's stage and in advance the name of the bar in *Frenzy*? This globe is what we see first as a turning model atop the news building. It is void, metallic, advertising itself, and striated or segmented by coordinates. The globe heading toward world war is the site and product of news services trying to report, to get the real "story," with camera-like accuracy. This skeletal graphics recurs immediately in the paper cutout that we find placed over Joel McCrea's face when the camera alights on him, and these structural graphics will recur one more time: segmenting the doomed airplane's glass cockpit window into a glamorous cage incapable of keeping the sea out as it crashes during its transatlantic crossing, shot down by "friendly" fire.

How does a work supposedly reporting on and initiating "war"—to the point of feigning propaganda in McCrea's closing radiocast during a bombing raid's *blackout,* in which the disembodied voice wails about the "light" going out—suggest a crisis within correspondence, in mimesis and telecommunications? If the locus of light or Enlightenment, its bastion, becomes McCrea's detached "voice," does this relay the locus, quietly and abysmally, to what will later emerge as "Mother"?

A devolution from picture to script (retaining the emphasis on the typewriter) seems, in fact, the domain of inscription that must be entered by the reporter. Numerous written notes are gathered in piles, received or intercepted, like those left on Laraine Day's dais or Fisher's desk; attention is repeatedly drawn to displacing telephonics (a phone mouthpiece is hung around the statue of a Negro head on the cinematic ship in order to eavesdrop on a staged conversation); a so-called radiogram is received on the plane. In the last case, a highlighted memo speaks of "steps" being taken to meet the plane on the other side, where it will not arrive.[18]

The most enigmatic figure is perhaps the Dutch pacifist ambassador Van Meer (Albert Bassermann). It is his memorized "clause 27" of a peace treaty that would be extracted, an inert splicing of the devices of the memorized formula from *The 39 Steps* and *The Man Who Knew Too*

*Much,* pegged to a triad (3 x 3 x 3). "Huntley Haverstock," the renamed Johnny Jones, will be tracked for "know(ing) too much." Van Meer will also seem to be "assassinated" (by a pistol held to a camera, splicing two kinds of shot)—killing what turns out to be a substitute and identical double of him. It is this other that McCrea will call a ringer, a "dead image."[19] Van Meer will repeatedly appeal to *birds,* and the "little people" who feed the birds, associated with sunlight through a window: Van Meer's gently befuddled Europacifism and old world culture appeal not to any political alliance or concern but to what he calls the "little people." Fisher will dive into and be absorbed by the sea. His front is the "Peace Party," a double or alliterative *P,* and he is this time on a cinematic fishing trip—the point at which *Lifeboat* all but concludes by using a jewel as bait (snapped off by a fat fish, seen in close-up loitering casually underwater). The zoographematic birds are pivotal as a referent beyond any mixing and confusing of homelands, languages, identities, borders.[20] In turn, a traffic jam of letteral and nominal play seems to occur in the stuttering doubling of letters within names *(JJ, HH, ff, OO, ll, tt, ee).* After giving up his secret during a torture that seems to involve his already light-blinded eyes being gouged out, Van Meer will be retired or discarded from the film like an emptied seashell or vessel.

Van Meer, the "original" whose double is shot in the face by the gun concealed in a camera, not (just) the "dead image," is discovered in a small room above a restaurant. He appears drugged but is again subject to the worst of tortures for the old Enlightenment European— nonstop American jazz, which he is kept awake for with floodlamps. The double already shot, Van Meer "dead," the "original" is pulped for the extraction of his secret clause by disarticulating the senses, being made to endure the same bad film production he is in again and again. As the destroyed moral icon of the film, Van Meer is not to be identified with in any way—less so, absurdly but typically, than Fisher's cinematic Nazis. When he finally breaks it is under an unseen torture that we see George Sanders shudder at having to witness, the likely fate of the gentle Gloucester is signaled by wincing eyes. It is at this point in the film, when Sanders leaps out of the window of the safe house, that Peter Conrad stumbles into a curious example of this alphabet soup when, in his words, *"Foreign Correspondent* pauses to contemplate a graphic puzzle" (236). The film title now suggests a displacement of Baudelairean *correspondances* with a mass media focus on the public reportage of the news (mimesis). Ffolliott looks down from the window he will leap from onto a giant sign below to scan "letters, slanting diagonally across the screen, which appear to spell out *CORZO.*" Conrad pursues a tip from "the surrealist Aragon, who reported on the ambiguous sign of a Parisian house of ill fame" to discern or decipher that the restaurant, too, is named Maison Rouge—which, at this point, lies beneath the room where the nearly dead Van Meer is being tortured. In deciphering the sign's neon lettering, which had been read sideways, Conrad identifies CORZU as in fact a piece of MAISON ROUGE, specifically, ON ROU: "The 'N', looked at from above, twists sideways into 'Z'" (237). This crossword skit breaks Sanders's fall, having altered a scrambled puzzle that incorporates in COR the 3-1 signature and the echo of a car, or vehicle, the ZO suggesting *zoo-* or zero, the two *O*s, while its corrected version puts the cinematic roulette wheel into active spin. These letters are altered by the shape and direction of mere lines, redissolved into the neon-illuminated "red house," brothel of European fratricide.

The emblem of "empire," here, is strangely located. The floodlights torturing Van Meer bear the tradename Empire Electric Photo Flood Lamps, anticipating the recurrence of the word *Empire* in the Empire (or Empire State) Hotel in *Spellbound* and *Vertigo.* The term *empire* is imperiously suffused with artificed "light" here and other teletechnic powers: the relation of empire to the letter *M*, which laces Hitchcock as a pyre, a site of virtual immolation, yet as hotel, *hôte,* or here *Maison.* The illicit house of red, kitchen and brothel, cinematic torture chamber and decider of empires and wards—linking cinema and the "villains" and the "heroes" to variant imperialisms and counterimperialisms—implies that the pyre or fire that would blaze as pyrotechnics here emanates from the atomization of letters or their luminescence, bound to "electric photo." Artificed *light,* accompanied by syncopated jazz, "photophobia," would suspend the Enlightenment sensibility and eye, in which both imperial sides are inscribed. The real war occurs in epistemo-political territory, just as the "story," as it's called, changes directions after this scene on which the outbreak of world war and devastation hangs. It leaves Joel McCrea in the last shots transmitting from a wireless rather than through print when all the lights go out, still pretending to convey a "light" already marked as artificed, "electric," as though the *Enlightenment* were being shut off, a blackout *not* as a benightedness but as caesura and exposure.

*Empire* suggests the sort of power and command of the world that Godard attributes to a certain Hitchcock as first master of global media, the activation of the imperial spies' post office of all marking systems in a cross-historial switchboard. It is the movement of a rewiring of definition and sensorial mnemonics that suffuses both the proper name "Hitchcock" as expeditionary force and the counteragents of the police, or state, which work to suppress or curtail the former.[21] Three imperialisms then: the barely identified German, the extant one of the homeland (American, England, English), and Hitchcock's archival intervention in and by the film that pairs the other two and leaps back and forth between them, inhabits one after another, until the Americans shoot down their own plane and reporter. These multiple inversions buoy Hitchcock's Nazi protagonists (Fry, Fisher, Willie) into strange territory: since Anglo-America is "home" and the site of mimeticism and historicism, the fascist other has sympathetic moments and can be inhabited allegorically. Asymmetrical doubles within the same specular history or program—the mask and heir of Enlightenment metaphorics and blinds—American industrialists represent the Nazi fifth column in *Saboteur.* The "Nazi" crystallizes, momentarily, a cinematic trajectory, as occurs, too, with the uranium (nonsolar source of light and atomization by blindingly annihilating bombs) stored in wine bottles in *Notorious* (cinematic inebriant). The cinematic oscillates between Hollywood's co-optation by the mimetic state as a negative imperialism (the already imperial "realism" of every phenomenological and representational or hermeneutic regime from the Enlightenment to the aesthetic label of modernism) and teletechnic envoys of a different mnemonic or material time, such as that which "knows too much" about what powers these auratic regimes. This cinema, which bars representation, represents not this or that natural image cited by the camera as a signifying agent *without* foreign correspondence. Rather, it overexposes this artificed light on behalf of a blinding pyrotechnicity and materiality Hitchcock seems to reference to a prosthetic earth. In all cases, a precession of the graphics of letteration—long exposed in the alliance between triangles and letters like *A, M, W,* and *V*—participates in an alteration of perceptual models over which any world war is fought.

The inscription of war into a war of and within media itself (and where the power, or the editor of the *Globe,* Mr. *Powers,* roosts) anticipates another globalization. The fate of the globe, the segmented sphere seen turning atop the Gotham skyscraper of the *Globe* newspaper, is being decided through torturing this Enlightenment European addicted, nonetheless, to the import of birds. If the sensorium and reference (correspondence) are being invaded and suspended for Van Meer, who would be mnemonically downloaded by his Nazi kidnappers, that scene dismantles the structure or authenticity of "light." The "real" war is inscribed in the logic of the Enlightenment that produced Germany and England as specular variants within a broader mimetological history that, for and in Hitchcock, has already lived off its own afterlife, within and beyond the "dead image" whose cancellation would yield the "secret" of clause 27. Of course, the "story" to be reported is both sought *and produced* by its agent, yielding "H. H." at the close in a London radio studio at a microphone issuing a nationalist appeal to a country at war—America, where alone there is still "light" or "lights" kept burning. The *blackout* is a familiar caesura, and McCrea's visage disappears in the darkened frame. This "light" that is understood as nonsolar dismantles the Enlightenment on both sides of its ideological effects (ostensible rational democracy, ostensible rational fascism, both of which are made even more interchangeable in the French propaganda films, as well as in *Saboteur* or *Lifeboat,* and so on). When the radiogram intercepted by Fisher speaks of "steps" to be taken, the doomed expressionist airplane, chosen vehicle for crossing to "the other side" (no place is named), mimes again a textual-historial crisis within Hitchcock's materialistic historiographic practice. An older lady complaining about the chaos gets sucked out a window into a reel-like propeller, her blood sprayed incidentally on the outside of a window.

That this crisis is more referenced than performed marks it, again, as a failed outing, too much a repetition of formulas to approach any (impossible) "other side," which, nonetheless, one could ally to certain moves to come, to an "inner history" of foreign correspondents. At the point where this cinema must represent not the threat of *war* or its afterworld but its *actual* inception, it goes flat, producing a web of glyphs in its place, like Johnny Jones's cutout. Hitchcock seems almost irritated by this invasive literalization, since the real power and war of and for the world are brewing elsewhere, in the archive and teletechnics that already imply an accelerated global media totality to come. There would be a techno-war under way that references, in part, reference, *co-respondence.* The Van Meer who cannot quite be killed or assassinated, not by a direct (camera) shot to the face (mimesis) nor even the scrambling of aural signifiers in jazz (sound and [a]rhythm) nor blinding "light," occupies an exorbitant place in the marking system: that is, his name suggests alone in the work the sites *of Mother* (van mère), however guised or transvestual, much as it does that *of the sea,* of seeing returned to the reflective surface of molecular waves that swamp the plane when it is shot down—and into which Fis(c)her will, in a gesture of paternal sacrifice, disappear or dissolve.

This gesture sheds black light on "Hitchcock's" subjugation of contemporary politics to a pan-cultural critique and assault. He asks who will control the installed ocularcentric machinery of empire, the metaphors of history, the system and degree of consumptions, time, advertising, the senses. This other *war* is spectralized in the process of *reportage* as such, itself shot. And this under cover of the havoc of real war and the constraints of propaganda.

Van Meer is *of the sea* and seeing, the play of chance signifiers allied to disaster. He delivers back the "heroes" clinging to a bobbing plane *wing*. The *mer(e)* will absorb and reflect, take and produce corpses, like that sea said to be more powerful than Rebecca. The American ship that picks up the survivors is commanded by an anxious *Cap*tain *Mar*tin. Of course, the plane went down under "friendly" fire, the *Americans,* doing the Germans' work, shooting one of their own, or not, in any case, wanting this "crossing" back to occur. As if caught in a diplomatic dilemma, the troubled captain issues a prohibition on reporting what has occurred—that is, against any direct communication from the ship. This ban is circumvented by taking the black phone on which the *Globe*'s editor, Powers, is listening and putting it behind the statue of a black head and face. Not quite telepathy, the "story" (also, of the film) is then told to the captain with various inflections so that Powers can overhear, transcribe the story: Van Meer's kidnapping, Fisher's treason and death, the shot plane, and so on. An ineffective political thriller, *Foreign Correspondent* attaches itself to another or "foreign" story, with other foreign correspondence, an event that involves a shift in the machinery of transcription—even as "Huntley Haverstock" turns up propagandizing about America retaining the promise and the negative power of this other or prosthetic "light." Van Meer elicits this site of a reinscription of (European) memory and the sensory blinds of the Enlightenment, a metaphorization of light that Hitchcock's cinema had been epistemo-politically warring against throughout the British political "thrillers." The faceless black or a-privative light of this allegorical America speaks of a future open amidst the putting out of all lights by the Enlightenment's own's accelerated programs.

## Suspecters

At the beginning of *Suspicion,* in the blacked-out train compartment, a comparison is made between Lina's (Joan Fontaine's) first-class ticket and Johnny's (Cary Grant's) third-class one. As the lights come on a caesura inhabits the autocitation of dialogue, investing all, and specifi-

cally Grant, with undecidability, incremental suspicion without resolu-
tion. When Lina later asks why Johnny is so direct with her in asking
about her (Lina's) interest in kissing, whether he is always so honest with
women, Grant answers no, "truth" with her is just the mode most likely
to be successful.[22]

In *Suspicion,* Grant's Johnny is a variant of Lorre's general or Keller
or Bruno—hyperperformatives. His being a figure of figuration results
in Grant's *face* simply fragmenting, as Nurse Agnes's does into light rays
when she hypnotizes Clive with a black marble called a "light" in the
first *Man Who Knew Too Much.* Grant's facial contortions dissolve into
detached muggings in which no part coheres, a demolition of hermeneutic positioning, the very "monkey face" he repeatedly teases Lina
with having. In the first scene on the train, Lina is interrupted with
her glasses on reading a book titled *Child Psychiatry.* The film moves
through numerous written, photographic, and pictorial devices, specifically a chain established between letter writing, post offices, telegrams, a
game of *anagrams,* and books, returning as the book of the mystery writ-
er *(Murder on the Footbridge),* which leads Lina to discover that Johnny
is reading a "real-life" book called *The Trial of Richard Palmer* as a guide
(supposedly) to poisoning her without a trace. Yet "Johnny," too, figures
for Lina through his photos (virtually, Cary Grant's publicity pictures),
first in the newspaper, then (more curiously) in a book. By filling in
blanks Lina is, in this, a tourist reader, encountered on a train, seduced
by the cinematic Grant, precursor of Bruno. Grant mentions *stamps*
for a letter to his mother (hailing the opening of *North by Northwest*),
and the interruption and prevarication eviscerate Lina's perpetual attempts at reading by identification of psychiatric traits. This reference to
stamps seems to draw us not only into letters but, literally, what is later
called a game of anagrams.[23] The changeable "Johnny" is not the figure
of spontaneity he seems but rather a product of compulsory dissimulation as truth, as he says of his strategy for kissing her. Grant's *photo*
determines Lina's relation to him, and inscribes Grant's screen creation,
which clearly fascinated Hitchcock by his face's virtual refusal of identification. That betrayal occurs in the province of photography's sleight
of hand: seducing with proximity (the arrested scene) and proactively
implanting an alien mnemonics, a kind of theft as faux intimacy. The
lightbulb placed in the milk glass potentially to signify poison dissolves
the lantern of the photoplay into milky white. Fontaine, like the worshippers at the Tabernacle of the Sun, thus pays for the imagined security
of "marriage."

When Beaky Thwaite mumbles about a girl approaching him in Paris and is cut off by Johnny in front of Lina, one implication of the untold story is that it is not a "girl," but a transvestite, a "suspicion" that is probed and inverted at Isabel's dinner party, as a female guest appears as if in drag with a tie and slicked-back hair. Such "notations" connect pre-originary degendering to speech performance itself. The resulting inversions attend a linguistic act without an egological address of return and pass into an aperformativity of gender—the wheel of color backspins white, as an instant autocitational fall—that cannot be accounted for as any kind of Bovarism. This Hitchcock seems to block by making the first book Lina is found reading one about child psychiatry (not fiction or romance). The film, of course, is all about unreadability or its perpetual spiral in disassembling, or deciphering, signs that can only lead in one direction. A dispossessing network of suspicious agents, marks, and steps performs a kind of murder on the "footbridge," the murder of a succession of hermeneutic techniques of appropriation that *Suspicion*, in particular, jams, merely by rehearsing. Hitchcock created controversy about the ending, suggesting in what has become lore that he could not allow Grant to in fact murder Fontaine, since it would have poisoned Grant's screen persona. It is unimaginable that he would have chosen such literalism. He wanted sheer undecidability to be grasped as irreversibly murderous. In the entirely apt ending, Grant seems exculpated, rather than disclosed as in fact the murderer he would be without lifting a hand. Hitchcock allows the car to graph a U-turn at the work's end. Grant in fact still gives nothing away. It is Lina who preempts Johnny's final explanation by anxiously supplying the ameliorating interpretations for his actions—the ones she *wants* to hear—which he, taking her hints, proceeds to act out (again) or elaborate on. Nothing in the work prevents his giving her the leftover white milk glass with a lightbulb in it on their return home. *Suspicion* is an exercise in the destruction of any identification with or of the star's face—of aura as such.

## Technos

I will admit that I have, from time to time, hoped that technology would devise a machine to replace the actor. . . . In *Foreign Correspondent* Joel McCrea played a scene with a windmill and in *North by Northwest* Cary Grant's *vis-à-vis* was a crop-dusting airplane.
—**Alfred Hitchcock, "After-Dinner Speech"**

What we name "Hitchcock" is a set of effects and trace chains. He had become host to, and preinhabited by, whatever is meant by the cinematic in all of its extensions: he could not *not* lend himself, his body, his outline—an autograph of cascading curves—to the teletechnic. What cannot, accordingly, be called Hitchcock's teletechnological bias is testified to in routine exchanges, such as this to Truffaut: "I don't care about the subject matter; I don't care about the acting; but I do care about the pieces of film and the photography and the sound track and all the technical ingredients that made the audience scream" (211). Yet more interesting is where he plants such *technicity* in a site that informs various "naturalistic" figures. All of the problem solving poured into working out the intricate artifices of detailed sets and set machines, small or gigantic (the cyclorama and camera work of *Rope,* reproducing miles of city skyline, the trick vertigo shot, the giant striated faces of Mount Rushmore), amounts to just another mode of thinking *technicity.* That there is no interiority in the photograph leads not to the presumed coldness of Hitchcockian formalism but to a recalibration of (a)materiality, of something like the "picture's" perpetual premise: an *earth.* From this sheer technicity, in turn, extends what can almost be called a performative ethics, the transformation of the hermeneutic chase by its own acceleration and of the programmed sensorium into a nonanthropomorphic, deauratic site. Humans, animemes, objects. Sight, memory, consumption, cognition. Historical sets, "nature." *Aterra.*

# 7. Matrixide

## Animemes

> Cinema is like an animal; the *likeness* a form of encryption.
> From animal to animation, figure to force, poor ontology to
> pure energy, cinema may be the technological metaphor that
> configures mimetically, magnetically, the other world of the
> animal. . . . The figure for nature in language, *animal,* was
> transformed in cinema to the name for movement in tech-
> nology, *animation.* . . . The advent of cinema is thus haunted by
> the animal figure, driven, as it were, by the wildlife after death
> of the animal.
> **—Akira Lippit, *Electric Animal***

Marnie counters Mark Rutland, book publisher who identifies his real
profession as a lapsed "zoologist," with the question, "Does zoology include people, Mr. Rutland?" In *The Birds* an inversion of position puts
humans in what seems nonanthropomorphic perspective, enclosed in
telephone cages, yet even there intolerable to behold without attacking. Hitchcock's deployment of animemes traverses a series of bounds:
animation, trace, telepathy, animal otherness, black suns; dogs and cats,
zoo creatures (say, fish and turtles in *Sabotage*'s aquarium), birds, carousel
and real horses; in the second *Man Who Knew Too Much*, a menagerie
of stuffed beasts. In the first film of that title, a little black dog running
across the snow, black on white, spawns the narrative with an accident,
a fall and whiteout; in *Secret Agent*, a similar dog gets entangled in legs.
Emissaries and effects of excess or technicity, animemes seem allied not
with "nature," any more than trees and sequoias are, but with technicity,
sound, and marks.

*The Birds* exceeds and shivers this into myriad points and avenging wing beats. Its opening visit to the birdshop transfers back to *Sabotage* and Chatman's pet shop, a (cinematic) bomb factory. The birds' staccato singing is there allied to the time bomb carried with film canisters. The latter work opens with Melanie's request of the bird-voiced saleswoman for a mynah, in which name we hear the *mine* of proprietary *me*aning *(Meinung)* dispossessed. The bird repeats words mechanically, miming a human's voice—just like humans. The vocal machine of the mynah void of cognition recites its "own" language as another, sheer sound. It anticipates the schoolchildren repeating their singsong lesson collectively, just before the birds attack. And the birds themselves are allied with a machinal, technical hum—as Hitchcock affirms to Truffaut—while animal-related machinery turns up, like a John Deere tractor. Their multiplicity and scattering flight fragment the "black sun" from the early thrillers into pecking beaks and slashing wings. Elsewhere a black hole appears as prowling black cats, deafening sounds, feet or steps, chocolate, excrement, hyperbolic or mediated skins or characters (Peter Lorre's dark-skinned general).[1] It operates as a spectral inhabitant of other bodies; deathless, a deathless death, it is virtually speechless or mute, something preserved in the mynah. Yet the birds are avenging as if from noplace, the rim of the archive turned against an anthropomorphic machine.

The animeme is underdetermined, explosive to human cinematics, domestic and unseen or frozen in artificed rage like carousel horses. This *zoographism* suggests a generation of the *zoe*, of "life," in the zoetrope, precinematic carousel of accelerating movement mimed by that in *Strangers on a Train*. It loops back through atomized chemical processes and semaphoric animation effects called "life." The birds bring a cut, a black hole or zero converted into proactive, avenging assault that pecks out eyes, identifying the human plague with an ocularcentric error.

### Frenzied Earth

We can observe a certain enframing at work in *Frenzy*. Hitchcock returns to his originary outing, after all, in a citational revisitation by inversion of *The Lodger*: it is fascinating because of all that has occurred in five decades, because of its immersion in a seemingly blighted contemporaneity. Commercial, polluting, loveless, postcolonial England, strangled by its own neckties, its produce a matter of mass markets, serial murder normatized and without aura. This "future" present connected to the Avenger's task in the first Hitchcock work marks the former's event as "failed." Cinema, rather than ripping metaphysics serially, had accelerated the domain of what could be called in Nietzschean parlance the last man, like Blaney, the ex-flight squadron leader who cannot integrate that heroic persona of an imaginary sublime and warring past to the fallen small world of that present. Peter Conrad identifies Blaney's battle experience as temporally "out of joint," impossible to match to World War II, at best relegated to the 1956 Suez crisis, "a post-imperial film rather than a post-war one" (114). It may not have a temporal location at all. But *empire* has other resonances in Hitchcock—echoed, as noted, in the Empire (State) Hotels of *Spellbound* and *Vertigo.*

The credits begin with the camera descending from the heavens like a bird. It is a travel brochure vision of the Thames accompanied by ceremonial celebratory "British" pomp entirely out of place for the fallen capital. Yet the aerial shot of London Bridge bears a royal insignia in the upper-right corner, like an official state *postcard.* This image is condoned, counterfeit, an ad for consumption. While the monumental *bridge* is familiar to any tourist, it is in the process of drawing open as the camera pans forward. The bridge *breaks.* And as it does so a tug, crossing left to right, dissects the frame with a diagonal gash of black smoke. A politician addresses a crowd, citing a Wordsworth poem celebrating nature, as he promises to end pollution and renew a ravaged earth (a theme carried over in the fruit market, the potato truck, the commerce of general exchange of produced goods). The Thames spawns on its banks hollow political speeches about recovering from pollution: the future is already set by inexorable planetary consumption and cutting, mirrored in the flood of produce moving in and out of the market, the defiant dead creatures in the inspector's inedible soup. A woman's corpse, facedown, naked except for a necktie around her neck, floats by. Everyone cranes to *see,* and Hitchcock turns up in the crowd next to a black woman, reverse immigrant of a collapsed empire. The politician, pressed back by his handlers, asks, "Is that my club tie?"

The imperialism of "England" warred against in and by the early thrillers, as if by the counterempire of Hitchcock's cinematic anarchists, has exhausted both by the time of *Frenzy*—albeit differently. London has devolved into a busy afterworld, void of eros, a well-fed, well-behaved shrunken land of the nervous dead, where even the Globe Bar cannot endure Blaney's intensity and irritable tics. The Globe now is just a place to catch a quick drink from bottles hung like teats, while the evisceration of the planet runs apace. *Frenzy's* strangler is no longer an Avenger; there is no trauma that induces shock or can be isolated. The friendly necktie strangler, Bob Rusk, even displays his live smiling "Mum" in the window. The now blond Barry Foster as Rusk, sporting a "pin" with the letter *R* that he *picks* his bar series teeth with, just makes an indifferent incision in this scene by picking off "birds." His demeanor is that of a scheming child, and he *enjoys* himself (almost alone in the world of the film).

And yet the still *postmark* has set in motion several semio-virals: it inscribes the tourist-viewer into a privileged and aerial yet blind position, celebrated with (demented) British pomp and undercut as the connective figure of the bridge parts. What seems, then, like the gates of the city opening to receive the aerial camera disconnects as a caesura over the totality of the frame. As the bridge is raised, the outline of an *A* and *H* seems to break and emerge: a posting of letters, of a field of the "signature," in the place of the bridge and over the river shot, over a natural confluence, over earth, from which nonetheless the first corpse will be flushed. The Thames has become the Detroit factory Hitchcock fantasized about inserting into *North by Northwest*, with a corpse turning up unaccounted for in a car on the assembly line. The black diagonal slash collapses into the frame any outside that the frame passively was to exclude: like it, the British anthem will next sound not to a royal cliché but in the grubby produce market in Covent Garden, belching noisy trucks, fruit sellers (or cellars), commerce, another disconnect. The sublime British horizon is trumpeted, to be replaced by the glory of an utterly fallen realm, without making the adjustment: this is not just postimperial, it is, in its markings, already "globalized," as with the name of the bar. It is post–bird war, spectral, the Eden of the last man, and as usual, no one knows they are dead.

The tourist is transported to an alternate scene, to that of a Wordsworth or Milton's *Paradise Regained*, yet the inversion to potato trucks and masses of produce is inscribed in that high aesthetic tradition. It is a scene guided by infratextual relays, postal effects. The opening frame had been marred and dissected by a tug's black smear of smoke, the *fog* condensed to a lightless cut, presaging the opening scene's *bar*, engulfing Shakespeare's stage "Globe." In the politician's opening speech—empty, posturing ridiculously, mock-poetical—a betraying figure of the Wordsworthian *sublime* is put into play. What is the relation of *Frenzy*, not to the high romantic poetic tradition, but to that of a sublime relayed back, like so many pretty postcards stamped "Return to Sender," from the blind Milton (paracited by Janet Leigh in the opening hotel room of *Psycho*)? The romantic tradition is woven into the tele-imperial death drive of service-era globalization. London as cockney forerunner, sans sci-fi accoutrements, of *Blade Runner*'s L.A. It is an earth poisoned and encompassed, servicing a socius in the absence of Eros. In the marriage broker agency, Rusk, in a cinematic trance, strangles Brenda Blaney while muttering "lovely . . . lovely" as his victim recites prayers—a distilling of the aesthetic in its Christian-Western terms to its finest point of parareligious ritual.[2] Not just an impotent rape, but one without exception or noteworthiness: the frenzy that is cast at the site where the aesthetic "act" would break the glass of media has taken its place as a corpse cited among the other potatoes.

This terrestrial rape is noted in the centrality of the fruit market, where trucks arrive, load, unload, and depart. Yet it is a rape paradoxically conducted under the sign of Wordsworth: that is, within a presumed metaphorization of earth that converges with consumption, mimed in the grotesque dining vignettes in which the inspector's batty wife experiments with soups afloat with bizarre sea creatures. The politician's promised reclamation and recuperation are contravened by the floating corpse that, in turn, the politician would suppress—were there not the question of his club tie. The tie is Hitchcock's looping rope, turned into civilized strangling fetish, limply phallic and circularly vaginal at once. This makes the scene in the potato truck when Rusk cracks his "R" pin loose from Brenda's stiffening fingers problematic. Surrounded by dusty potatoes in mass transport, spheroid replicants of other discs and suns, in the dark, with flashing cinematic highway lights, Rusk snaps open, as it were, the pointing fingers of *Blackmail,* the promise of representational veracity, the photograph's indexing of a real, from which Rusk retrieves his "R" pin of "repetition." Unlike the subsequent *Family Plot,* which is suffused with "self-plagiarisms," as Hitchcock referred to his recycling of figures, *Frenzy* seems disconnected from its own flashing switchboards, refusing to answer the calls its citational overload suggests. Like London Bridge, the disconnect between the fallen natural image, as with mass-marketed potatoes, and the allographical intervention, is virtually totalized—the two planes not quite touching, except in the twig crack of a finger.

Thus grapes and potatoes present commodified tokens of produce, their volume infinitely duplicable, truckloads of blackened spheroids, passed around and to be consumed eventually. One enters a totalized space and globalized terrain without outside: the globe or earth, the relay systems of citation and erasure poised with tripwires. Under the banner of "paradise regained," a wasted earth promises itself as irrecuperable.

The *bridge* breaks up as letters, and the mimetic flow of the river produces preoriginary corpses. This combines with a Wordsworthian rhetoric of nature rhapsodic or sublime, misread or recited, complicitous with a denuding of earth, a program of reference with pan-terrestrial and pan-historial consequences. The Romantic tradition and the Enlightenment programs and the sublime and the "aesthetic" as packaged throughout were one, present in the cloacal confluences of *Frenzy*'s Thames, Norman's bog in drainage.

### Starage

> [F]or a while our electrical experts were stumped. . . . So we
> bought a bomb release at a war surplus store, adjusted it to
> synchronize the alternate flashing of the neon "Storage" sign . . .
> and got exactly the effect we wanted.
> **—Alfred Hitchcock, "My Most Exciting Picture"**

At the end of *Rope,* as night descends on the cycloramic Manhattan skyline set, giant neon letters can be made out flashing near the window in garish red and green. No word is spelled out and one is not even sure of the letters, so the attempt to read that is activated is kept incomplete, though the size and insistence of the letters are invasive. James Stewart's Rupert has already warned, "It's odd the way one can *pyramid* simple facts into wild fantasies, isn't it?" And Peter Conrad shows ingenuity in identifying the letters given as *S* and *R,* and then: "One last letter is obliquely glimpsed: a 'T' after the 'S'—still not enough to make up a word" (128). Yet he does so, ignoring that Hitchcock had told us this already in an interview. Noting that the Astoria (as in the Waldorf Astoria Hotel) is too many blocks away, he concludes that the intended word is *storage,* which he then blanks on as "a facetious comment on the body bundled into the makeshift coffin, and on the skyscrapers that are filing cabinets for people" (129). This assignation must be set against the artifice of the cyclorama, the claustrophobia of a simulant apartment and a "coffin" or cassone that will be associated with books. The latter are wrapped by the stranglers' cord, supposed *"first* editions"; yet if they are meant to suggest something original in this circulating scene of replicants without originals that will hint at the nausea of eternal recurrence in the Poulenc score (Rupert will disown his words, the originals that Brandon implements), "first editions" are nonetheless mass printed, without being truly first or original. They are printed from a mnemonic device stamping preset inscriptions and letters. *Storage* is shocking in this context: the word that is planted yet will not be allowed to assemble itself makes the little players in their penthouse appear to be micrologs between giant lines of unreadable print. It certainly includes the storage of memory in the filmic band as archive. The words *Astoria* and *storage* would not necessarily be incompatible, hence Conrad's contribution as a reader. Neither word appears and both remain virtual, disassembling the terms of stars and stories with the a-privative of each in turn. The stack of books on the cassone puts reading in question.

The rule of the game in *Rope,* of course, is that the secret or corpse cannot be literally referred to yet is constantly before one; hence it generates incessant figural double-talk. Yet Brandon and Phillip's act implements as a literalist reading the oft-stated ideas of the former mentor, Rupert, who disowns his own words as mere playful citation or their being taken seriously, after installing them through repetition. He insists his statements about higher men being free to murder were figural, in play obviously, not meant *as such.* Rupert is caught in the empty gesture of distancing himself from a transposition of "his" words, put in circulation, trying to return to the authority of his meaning by denying it was "meant"—effectively, at the moment of condemning Brandon, denying his own authoring of Brandon's literalizing yet experimental "act."

The name "Nietzsche" is here put into play. Negatively, of course, by Mr. Kentley, though what may be Nietzschean will involve a formal problematic rather than the "superman" trope with which Hitler is associated here (a misappropriation that Brandon dismisses). It references instead a problematic of recurrence and repetition that is crystallized in the artificed "cyclorama" itself, in the closed space and mock-literal time passing as if from afternoon to twilight to (abruptly) night, mapped at the braided site of twisting recurrence echoed in Poulenc's backlooping "Perpetual Motion" which Phillip Morgan plays.[3]

Rupert at the close fires three shots out the window as the giant broken letters shift in the background. He panics and calls in an external world to *police* the monstrosity, and end the filmic experiment. But the virtuous "Stewart" is exposed as weak, derivative, and self-betraying, while he pretends to invite in justice. Brandon only *literalizes* the star's words, which the latter suddenly disowns. A *star* gives the lie to the sun: if there are numerous stars giving off light, then the solar is not central, paternal, originary, even necessarily light. Innumerable suns mean no "sun," but rather multiplicity, simulation. *Constellations* is Benjamin's term for a mnemonic convergence of historial trace chains at a moment of intervention in an order of stored memory to be replayed. The postwar film tracks the return influx of fascist rhetoric from the conquered enemy into the new democratic empire via the intellectual and educational class, as the latter acquired Nazi scientists for work on rockets, or used stars to aestheticize the charismatic "leader" (and train a populace to identify with his cinematic traits). For instance, if the neon letters were to spell *star* instead (since in fact they never do assemble as a word), then the "star" would be *Stewart*, whose authority is clearly defaced and voided: the star purveying midwestern virtues, a moral dissembler. The work's star would not only be exposed (does his "public," literalizing his crafted American virtues, use them to commit justice killings, or attribute reality to this "personality" as a model?). Hitchcock's dialogue mentions stars quite explicitly in this sense, drawing amused attention to Stewart in the process by praising his competition on the A-list while he has to listen as he's not mentioned at all. It is in a grand parabasis designed to torture and draw attention by absence to "James Stewart" as James Mason and Cary Grant and Ingrid Bergman are all but drooled over and celebrated by name. The latter are raised to the heavens in their stardom and given their own *constellations:* Grant is a Capricorn, we hear, Bergman a Virgo.

The star facilitates the imposition of a faux metaphoric totality and personification anointed, as by the Greeks, as a *constellation*. The latter departs from a number of points organized from chance and stamped, personified, like animation, into an empowered being, object (a belt) or animal (goat). Benjamin called such points monads, irreducibly singular instants that coalesce as a site of virtual intervention, "constellations" as archival mobiles poised to be reconfigured. The word *starage* or *storage* generated by giant neon letters outside the window in *Rope* displaces the cyclorama as night abruptly falls and an electric lighting claims visibility. It exposes the "star" Stewart as suspended or hung in an increasingly contaminated braid of words and literalizing impostures that void all moral investment, such as Stewart's appearance promises and haplessly mimes. Indeed, "he" is the key link in a citational chain that effectuates the murder, in which, as artwork, Brandon has reason to take cognitive pride, as much as Hitchcock clearly did in executing *Rope*. The flashing neon sign that perhaps assembles itself in a never-present word, *storage,* recoils to name a form of memory storage that the claustrophic set of *Rope,* a cassone itself (or Pandora's box), brings to visibility only to conceal. In this, it places the corpse out in the open to (not) be seen.

## (A)Mosaics

Dots, borders, import-export, boxes, triangles, threads, ports . . . Within Hitchcock there are recurrent figures or names bearing the spectral word *port,* implying door ("portals of the past"), and transport and, inversely, aporia. Like the word *crossing* when it appears or the recurrent bridges in these works, the prospect of a certain passage across borders, or outer limits of the archive, is, at least negatively, raised. In questioning this prospect, we might give special attention to Professor Jordan in *The 39 Steps.* There is a biblical reference in the name "Jordan," coupled with the professor's quip about leading Hannay "up the garden path—or is it down," since in this work that juxtaposes *W*s to *M*s, goes up to Scotland and back down to a London Palladium that, in a sense, precedes the opening scene music hall, up and down are the same (Heraclitus might aver). Movement up or down is reversibly suspended if not cinematically stationary. An evil cognitive Eden is not a poised "dialectics at a standstill." Hannay will try all along to get out of this movie, and he is tracked by an erector set helicopter-projector over the moors. The professor was introduced by the dying Annabella as a dangerous man of many names and disguises (like herself), only he could not hide one physical trait. With impeccable etiquette the professor discloses his missing finger "joint" in his study—and after graciously offering Hannay the opportunity to commit suicide, promptly shoots him. The bullet is stopped by a hymn book concealed, unbeknownst to Hannay, in the coat he had been given by the crofter's wife. Any "garden" in Alt-Na-Shellach appears a murderous, preoriginary site where "up" and "down" are as interchangeable as they may seem in the up and down of the three triangles comprising the reversible letter *M* of "Mae West."

But the bad Eden occurs amidst the barren moors of Scotland. And it conceals another implication of the name Jordan—the *crossing* of a Lethe-like river that projects a new lawgiving. Such a crossing would be linked to Mr. Memory's attempt to get across the border to the outside of England with his secret warplane formula. One can read "exodus" here as that paradoxical exile of those never with a home to return to. It is a form of exteriority reflected in the exit signs of the Assembly Hall and the fake police car's turn away from the road to *Inverary.* The name Jordan, here professorial, is implicated in a kind of tutelary "crossing," a crossing over and through the circular figures of the text (and memory itself), as if toward another Mosaic law. Crossing, certainly, seems associated with getting destroying "secrets" across an archival border from within. There they are managed by the state and now would be turned, mnemonically, against it. Any hypothetical crossing might be exemplified in the silent warplane formula itself—a set of numbers and letters, agents of a different cognitive model of legibility. An attacking silent plane, a mechanical black sun, or myriad birds. The professor teaches about something explosive within the cinematic, the mark, and in *Sabotage* another professor will make those time bombs and place them beneath bird cages. What one might call an "(a)Mosaic" turn is associated with both the professor and with Hannay. Hannay, misperforming the role of the tutored cipher, learns nothing really but the blank witnessing and undoing of a world-altering (cinematic) event, while the professor stands behind a subversive, transvaluative, anarchival, nameless enterprise. The boy Stevie in *Sabotage* is warned by his sister, "Mrs. V.," to be "careful at the crossing" and will be blown up on the bus there. The word crossing recurs on title cards in *Rich and Strange* regarding the cruise ship's travels. Hitchcock deploys numerous professors, references to schools, universities, students—usually in the past tense, scenes of instruction virtually failed and unnoticed, often with cross-references. The professor in *North by Northwest* is switched from Hannay's nemesis to being the government's spy chief (Leo G. Carroll), though Vandamm, whose own resumption of "Professor Jordan's" interview is pushed up to the beginning of the narrative in Townsend's library, appears nonetheless in a photo before an unnamed university. Whatever scene of instruction is ceaselessly referenced floats without direction between the names and positions—except where, in *The Birds*, the schoolhouse is itself attacked and emptied.

## Verte

> For that hotel room . . . I deliberately chose a hotel on Post Street that had a vertical green sign outside. I wanted her to emerge from that room as a ghost with a green effect, so I put a wide sliding glass in front of the camera, blurred at the top when she first appears. We raised this glass as she came toward Scottie. In other words, he saw her first as a ghost, but with her proximity she became clarified and solid.
>
> **—Alfred Hitchcock to Donald Spoto**

Hitchcock deploys both the color and the word *green* in counternatural modes in *Vertigo,* although he had been doing so in other films all along. Why is green, supposed signature of nature, here associated with specters?

Judy, in the scene described to Spoto, mimes her own phenomenalization as another whom she played, the ghost of someone who never in fact
*was*. It is one thing to be inhabited by the return of the unhappy dead, of
course, but another to be housing the ghost of someone who never lived
to begin with—which is rather maddening. How is *green* connected to
*ver*tigo, echoing the first syllable's variant? Green is not only a figure of
nausea, of falling up and down at once and without ground, of turning
inside out, as seems exemplified in *The Birds,* where Cathy vomits, where
pockets appear on the outside of pants, where Bodega Bay maps the
invagination of a coastline. If it is supposed to be applied to nature, to
trees at all, the latter lie cut and splayed to disclose more graphic swirls
still. Why the *vert*(e) in vertigo?

Sequoia is an Indian word, Scottie tells Madeleine. It means ever
living, ever green. Yet when the trunk is cut, its inner rings are marked
with corresponding dates in historical time going back to the Battle
of Hastings, the founding of the English kingdom and language that
California stands at the outer, Hispanic ring of in time and terrain. It is
not natural, it discloses an archive. Judy as "Madeleine" stands pointing
at a *spot* that predates her life and speaks for Carlotta in locating where
or when she, "I," died. The inner cut of the tree presents another vertigo
pattern of rings, only here marking a series of events. Time would be
dated along those rings yet also vortexed, with and as "nature," and
this by a graphematic system preinhabiting what is taken as the natural
image of the tree, much as the credit sequence does inhabiting a nervous
or dissembling female eye.[4] The tree is preinhabited by a *technē*, chronographic markings. Hitchcock uses the figure or name *wood* recurrently:
there is an agent Wood alluded to in the first *Man Who Knew Too Much,*
Dietrich's Charlotte Inwood as a faux maternal marker in *Stage Fright,*
Bishop Wood kidnapped in *Family Plot* (cryptographically exposed as
"Arthur Adamson's" lost and unidentified biological father). Hitchcock
cites the dissimulating Burnham Woods *(Macbeth)* and a rich, widowed
Mrs. Green in *Shadow of a Doubt.* In *Vertigo,* this moniker is bestowed
on Barbara Bel Geddes's Midge Wood, already *verte,* vertiginous. The
archive in *Shadow of a Doubt,* the "Free Public Library," is covered with
ferns; the cinematic and linguistic mansion of *Spellbound* is Green
Manors, and so on. "Nature" is not simply rejected by Hitchcockian
artifice, predefined by laws and graphics or staged as a set effect, *it
never was natural.* The figuration of nature is a maternal hoax, too,
like Madeleine. Nothing precedes the teletechnic set, which cites and
engulfs "everything." Mother, nature, prosthetics, effects of animation,

anthropomorphisms. As a mytheme with maternal pretenses "nature" reinforces or parallels the ideological figure of reference itself, of the mimetic pretext of photography, of a ground or presence that pretends to anchor memory or signs. *It* is itself the effect of metaphoric installations (travel brochures).

The tourist viewer need not *see* in the image the citational multidirectionality, temporal violations, dismembered body pieces, and prosthetic syllables or even letteral displays (in *Rope* we are too close, for instance, even to read the giant neon letters out the window). That is one reason why the vertigo reverse dolly shot does not mime a dizziness or mere falling effect. It falls up and down simultaneously, which is also to say it falls without end or ground. The malady of vertigo will eventually be defined as one of the inner ear, the labyrinth of aural traces, yet here it is not only a malady since, while deposited in the nescient Scottie, it also registers a power of the purely cinematic to suspend binarized markers: a Zarathustran nausea. Inversely, when Hitchcock presents a Hannay or a Thornhill as performing the fictional roles imposed on them, they reverse the direction of self-mimicry, performing a forward-moving or active mimesis without models or copy. Such eruptions of proactive mimesis may be the closest thing to inventing the natural, as it were, *forward*: an always prosthetic implant turns out to score relations to memory, repetition, mimetology. "Nature," if cited at all in the green motif as other than "front," would partake of the logic of a nausea beyond voiding that is one effect of the disinvaginating loss of interior or exterior as such, like the birds affiliated explicitly with machines. "Nature," all along a *technē*, like the sun, never originary, would have been the primitive linguistic invention of a certain hermeneutic reflex and relapse, enforced as and by ocularcentrism, even though "she" (ever maternal) displays this other face when seeming most, well, natural: that is, when setting species of animals and plants to work miming, camouflaging, or adapting in advance and proactively to local systemic factors from without—how, say, a shape-shifting fish will look like a particular stone, an insect like a green leaf, and so on. In *Sabotage*, we are told of a fish that, after giving birth, simply changes sexes, morphs, and in *The Birds* the lovebirds' sex cannot be distinguished. "Nature" parallels Mrs. Bates in *Psycho*.

So the vertigo motif is actually a predicate for the emptying out of a certain mock-romantic mimetic ideology in the name of the "natural"; or "nature," here, is another name for a kind of transvaluation, the sequoia's rings sucking historical dates into the tree's graphic vortex, the trajectory of Hitchcock's diverse "O-men" ("Johnny-O," Roger O., Dick-O). They are O-men, in part, because they will seem designated for what Nietzsche calls *going under*—the dismantling of an entire representational facade or nervous system, a referential order or identity. Judy steps out of a ghostliness into virtual presence as befogged green. There is a quest for incorporation by a ghost effect that never quite had a body, a ghost of someone or something that never existed to begin with, but wants to again, this badly acted "Madeleine," as could be said as well of the unincorporable bar series. Judy's last name is *Bar*ton, regurgitating across decades the cinematic Detective Barton from *Number 17.* A double or prosthetic ghost, then, a reverse or failed incorporation of what did not exist, even if she dominates the seemingly existent and returns as avenging ghost for what *was* not. One can pretend, with gothic flourish, to be unable to say whether Hitchcock's assault on "golden curls" is the acceleration of the death drive of metaphysics, a self-cancellation, or the encounter with—and transgression of—its nonexistence. In turn, an underlying critique of the word *green* as a naturalist trope for which the *vert* turns into tropological vertigo exposes a soporific maternal figure as a faux specter or prosthesis without interior, connected to nausea, mnemonics, *Ekel*. It exposes, say, the use of the term *green* in political discourse as setting itself up, say, to conceal (beneath the recuperative logic of saving, retaining, conserving, which can be caricatured) a translational task unthinkable without its own archival reinscription. Such a reinscription includes the "eye" being understood in its sensorial hegemony as predatory and consuming, a long-running ghost caught in the effacement of its secret, autodispossessed.

## Bird Wars

> . . . an apocalypse without apocalypse, an apocalypse without vision . . .
> —Jacques Derrida

If nature is suspended as a "front," what of biblical lore and apocalyptics, of the technics and era and catastrophe of the book? Movement as slash, taking out the eye as constituted, jamming interiorization, picking out pockets or bays, dispossession by flying nothings. To approach the titular starlings of *The Birds* as an apocalyptic vision of some sort is naive, aside from allying the interpreter with a somewhat debased drunk in the Tides Restaurant. The *birds* have thus been said to "repre-

sent" a rebellious nature, a biblical revenge on humankind, or the de-
facements of Tippi Hedren's purported sexuality. Yet *The Birds* is more
interesting read as antiapocalyptic. The avenging wings and slashes that
peck out eyes, dispossessing the ocular program, are causeless—or, like
the Avenger with his triangle calling card, or the motives of the cinematic saboteurs, what avenges swarms from the atomized fog, as if from
within the sheer anteriority of the archive.

Thus the Brenner house is attacked, invaded, and dispossessed of interiors. This, by a certain exteriority of the house or dwelling to itself. This
exteriority is one with the empty horizons of Bodega Bay, what forms at
best a pocket in the shore allied to the accident of commerce *(bodega)*.
No inside. The "birds" generate reference to account for themselves, only
to exceed it generically as cutting wings and myriad attacking spots.
They adhere to a strictly acausal logic, which will ally them in the closing
frames to the hum of a *machine,* to technics. But they also attack and
cannot locate themselves within the programs of memory, given their
central grouping and assault on the schoolhouse during a classroom
exercise in group rememoration, group recitation that depicts learn-
ing for "children" as parroting and memorizing. They interrupt human
programming at the site of collective memorization, inscription. They
are, logically, impossible—the *impossible.* One cannot *not* recall the
array of citations gathering across pivotal bird appearances in earlier
Hitchcock films. "Birds" will prefigure a mobile army of implications
crossing points of otherness: the bird costume of Handel Fane, connecting birds with cross-gendering and sublime flight; the birdcage carrying
the bomb in *Sabotage,* connecting the chirping sound with a destroying
semiotic; the chirping in *Blackmail,* or the caws in *Young and Innocent,*
suspending a temporal scenario with a witnessing rupture from without; the birds in *Foreign Correspondent,* odd repositories of Van Meer's
humaneness; Norman's stuffed raptors absorbing the stare of the "dead."
Birds—white gulls and black crows, say—condense and infinitely fragment these traces (sound, machine, bombs, black suns). *The Birds* seems
to stall the infratextual machine, empty out the citations it solicits.

Which is why the work is, in a more protracted sense, almost banally
antiapocalyptic, starting as it uniquely does with the familiar, domestic
and nonpredatory birds whose radical otherness is both attacking and
elusive. They take possession of the frame, as titular subject without
subject, from having been background at Union Square in the opening, Hitchcock's signature agents pared to slicing points and enraged.

There is an obvious connection between the myriad birds and the figure of the "black sun" of the *Man Who Knew Too Much* (or the sun-as-machine in the crop duster scene of *North by Northwest*), a figure that had always marked the narratives covertly, as black dogs and cats; but as such, it loops us back to a representational black hole, partaking of geological time and prehistory, in which anteriority, marking, and materiality are in "revolutionary uplift." "Nature" or "life" is animation, here, redefined in the suspension of the former's pretended binaries. As the stuffed birds of *Psycho* reanimated, they traverse the boundaries of underworld and overworld. This removes them from any faux allegory of nature—or displaces the idea of nature as natural, as the originary, as ground, as mother, as reference. (In the mimetic or ideological terms, nature is another trope for a prosthetic referential ground and personification.) The tableau cancels the two narratives of apocalypse brought forth in the restaurant: the woman ornithologist, degendered, haughty, and birdlike, purveyor of eunarchic "science," and the inebriant end-of-the-world ranter (we can bracket the hysterical mother's added condemnation of "Melanie Daniels" as "evil" cause). Neither the ornithologist's explanation nor that of an epoch of the book, the biblical projection of world-cleansing destruction, penetrates. They attack not on behalf of an allegorical idea, a return to nature or God, but of a techno-earth collectively invoked, perhaps by *Melanie,* whose platinum head and black name present the fictional binaries of black light in the same place. It is a model of *avenging* against a totality, on behalf of an absent cause, as was the case with the Avenger of *The Lodger* already. It is the mnemonic secret smuggled out of the home state's archive and to be turned, in silent aerial attacks, against the state, the home, the family, the personified, the eye.

If the birds have something to do with the nonhuman, script, and earth, there is always the implication that some form of *justice* is being witnessed, effected, or served. Here, the system of *ressentiment* or revenge is inverted by the human victims, eyes eaten out as an attack on the construction or program of the visible, the "human" ocularcentrism that misidentifies light and form and sun with power and knowledge rather than predation and consumption. The birds avenge against the implications of meaning systems, based as they are on archiving ("General Semantics"), programming, herd behavior, repetition, and *ressentiment.* But how, ultimately, are myriad "harpies" (Peter Conrad's trope), of nature and not natural, "impossible," piercings of deanthropomorphic otherness, in contact with the terrestrial? Why does Tippi Hedren's

Melanie—whose name, indicating blackness, is superimposed on Hitchcock's "model" blonde, an actual model stepping, as with "June" in *The Lodger*, into the cinema (a model preceding itself *as* copy)—pass first through the post office in getting to her boat?

The advent of attacking birds will have something to do with the appearance of Tippi Hedren, whose high-pitched, discomfiting voice and flat self-miming yet citational looks generate perpetual violence on the screen, at the core of the visual.[5] The blonde or black-blonde, melanined, is not only a parodic emblem of metaphysics from within the West, she is one from whom the apparatus of feminine inscription has slipped, has already turned into antimetaphysics as well, to reappear as the thief, Marnie. The birds are flying feet or legs, headless black holes. By suspending any extant model of reading, Hitchcock addresses a foreclosed scene (or, the same thing, a scene foreclosed as the open, as sheer, blinding exteriority). *An open book, or rather a closed one,* as Annie says of herself. To some extent this is echoed by the Spanish term *bodega*, a little market, and by the labels in the restaurant for "packaged goods," or by the manner in which the children, reciting their answers and singing by rote, mark the acquisition of human consciousness as a mechanically installed memory, a programmed system. This system can only be suspended by another linguistic logic or "shock," to which the birds are arguably related. Here Hitchcock's "weak messianism" involves a different turn than the apocalyptic ranter does in invoking biblical disaster (what is at issue, to a limited degree, is cinema's blank undoing of the archival disaster of an era defined by a misinterpretation or theologization of the book).

Occurring at a site that suspends narrative origins (birthdays), passes through post offices, exposes interiors as folds or pockets, collapses models into copies (without models), and marks the human terrain as prepackaged, the birds' attack is connected to an earth stripped of aura and personification—what, paradoxically, the cinematic against its mimetic pretense performs as sabotage. It is an earth of horizons and folds, an unearthly earth familiar from the disappearance of "ground" in *Vertigo*, virtually, of gravity in *To Catch a Thief,* or direction (falling off the "face" of an earth) in *North by Northwest*. The birds assume the role of an (a)materiality allied, in Hitchcock, to the cut or knocking motif, animated and autonomous, as well as to various shocks and explosions (the bomb in the birdcage of *Sabotage,* invoked by the opening bird shop scene). The birds demand, above all, attention: from being excluded, at the margins of the frame or story, as above Union Square in the opening scene, they enter the frame of the visible and emerge, folded up again, the invisible frame become putative center, dispossessing the house while, all along, figures of a disinteriorized trace. In this way, the "bird war" attacks both the "natural" and the "biblical" readings of apocalypse as relapses, fallback strategies of personification. Atomized as flying cuts, they precede and supersede any epoch of the book past or to come as if en route to, and in excess of, a coming digital culture. As such, the birds cannot be apocalyptic. Their invasion as a warping of temporal logic implies a folding in of the frame, without outside. Nature as origin here is the effect of a certain aesthetic ideology, and its disarticulation accompanies that of mimetic regimes. It may seem parallel to the nausea of Zarathustra before the snake of eternal recurrence, and the biting off of the snake's head, the stepping "beyond" to a site that is not mapped yet in other terms. *Earth*, after all, is what the camera will always (also) be gazing at, always recording—even when a simulacrum earth, as with sets of anthropomorphic monuments shaped of stone and steel.

But *nature*, like Hitchcock's signature, was always other than maternal, an anthropomorphized "she," the shot's representational claim. "She" is something else, *proactively* mimetic, a mimesis without model or copy, much as species that alter ceaselessly according to the technicity of an environs or for camouflage or shape shifting, adapting proleptically as an animal or coral sea creature or insect assumes camouflage in the presence of a predatory other when it cannot "see" itself to be like the mimicked twig. This teletechnic "earth" is the paradoxical counterworld to the passivity of "globalization." This earth is allied to the birds because of the latter's refusal of mimetic laws—teleological, referential, apocalyptic. Viewing the birds as agents of deauraticization, Lee Edelman glosses the avian assault as a logic of the unreadability of a default: "Performing the unintelligibility of this formal mechanism or drive, the birds usher in the collapse of an ideologically naturalized reality into the various artificial purposes that collaborate to maintain it."[6]

The birds *attack* the construct of the visible, standing reserves of reference and consumption, interiors, eyes. The interruption of mnemonic programming explains their fondness for assaulting children as bearers of perpetuation and enemies of a possible future. Bodega Bay locates a vacant yet consuming pocket, *at(r)opos*, the market *bodega* as buffer to cinematic "shock." Any avenging "justice" here assaults a human epochal program of mnemonics and consumption in the name of a technicity that territorializes "life," animation as biopolitical logic—the cinematic cut as "natural history," the caesura of geological time. They bar relapse. Not "acting" allows the birds to constitute a domain of the deauratic beyond personification or identification and there posit an act. The end is not just a nonending, as Hitchcock complained in having to give the film artificial closure (the added title: "The End"), since the humans—the Brenners with a catatonic Melanie—are driven out of the home's auratic logics.[7] It is the only work in which one can *say* "the human" and that is merely descriptive.[8] *The Birds* even suspends infracitational signature systems: allusions of the usual sort, and there are many, tend to die or be switched off when tracked. Nonapocalyptic, the birds pass by telegraph wires or rest on geometrically graphed jungle gyms: they are not biblical plagues or nature's emissaries but teletechnic agents. As if completing a cycle begun with the *nostos* of Odysseus, Hitchcock cancels finally the home or house as organizing fiction—as he, or cinema, does "family" elsewhere.

## Not a MacGuffin

The MacGuffin, considered as a structure, turns on a contradiction: "that's a MacGuffin" / "that's not a MacGuffin."
—Thomas Elsaesser

Hitchcock is counter-Homeric: Atropos does not raise her shears to terminate a destiny, but before there is, ever, a forgetful narrative of "life." There is a hidden drawer within the trick logic of the "MacGuffin." On the one hand, the term has been taken to refer to the pretext or empty fiction on which any Hitchcock plot or political intrigue turns, the excuse for the chase; on the other, it breaks away to designate and consume an entire order of reference. Like Montresor's promised Amontillado. If you think it is the band of secret agents called the "39 steps," that becomes the title of the work itself, and you must recalculate the coil. If you think it is the contentless microfilm, that becomes Kaplan, "Grant," the micrographic facticity of the celluloid. It is programmed to vacate its assigned referent and migrate. It is hurled against the spell of the ocular, and morphs, retreats across spelling itself, a drug or cure.[9]

Hitchcock's dissimulation is revelatory:

The word MacGuffin comes from a story about two men in an English train, and one says to the other, "What's that package on the baggage rack over your head?" "Oh," he says, "that's a MacGuffin."

The first one says, "Well, what's a MacGuffin?" "It's an apparatus for trapping lions in the Scottish highlands." So the other says, "But there are no lions in the Scottish highlands." And he answers, "Then that's no MacGuffin." (Truffaut, 43)

The explanation performs the contrary of a definition: it is allegorical in the most destroying sense. First, the spoken text is a deferral of the questioner, a kind of brush-off, as if also to say, What business is it of yours? Second, in the end the mysterious package and object of the story turns out *not* to be a MacGuffin. Even the "MacGuffin" is not one, not a MacGuffin, because the MacGuffin, an "apparatus," cannot really exist within these parameters ("there are no lions"). But this does not stop the seemingly literal MacGuffin from then standing behind and animating numerous other secret agents, speaking through them and moving on, as the "MacGuffin" logic momentarily alights on the undisclosed package like a camera lens might. Except the package too resembles a box camera. It appears a self-canceling figure, consumed by representation as its own escape and perpetuation. The apparatus simply "is" not, is nonexistent, and does not represent anything possible, like finding *impossible* lions in the Scottish highlands, attacking birds in Bodega Bay.

It would not be difficult to invest each official "MacGuffin" with cryptonymic value. Like the cameo, the MacGuffin voids referential contracts, converts objects into citations, deontologizes "identification." "MacGuffin" as a term seems to plunge into the anamorphic space of temporal prestidigitation; hence its proper Scottish name, an *M* moniker. It can be converted from the static mystique of being a hole in various "Symbolics" to appearing a mobile agent of translation, a viral contamination by something precedent to figurative meaning, refusing assignations, exploding mimetic pretexts. In practice, the term absorbs not the fictional telos of a chase plot but the historical setting, mimetic pretexts of the set, the very "history" or referents that appear to account for place ("Scotland," "Rio," "Nice").

Perhaps Hitchcock's most calculated effect in bantering about the "MacGuffin" is to give his interlocutors the slip while bestowing the illusion of access to a secret whose very absence is performed by the mock figure itself.[10] What distinguishes the appearance and vanishing of the "MacGuffin," however, is that what it conceals is not a hole, and what the "nothing" of the MacGuffin names is not *just* nothing. Nothing is not nothing, nothing will (not) come of nothing—as Lear's fool allows. "Nothing," rather, might appear the hyperbolic effect of a certain transformation—less Wagner's "ring" than a formalization of a certain, too literal, "eternal recurrence." These resonances link one logic of the MacGuffin to a circulating "O" or wheel that, broken off in the photograph of the car crash that opens *Rear Window*, flies or caroms across visual puns, like Uncle Charlie's smoke rings, and a panoply of talking heads ("characters"). The zero, as a performative fiction and trope, is not quite nothing: it is a MacGuffin that, as a material marker, permits the fictitious order of progressive numeration to institute itself. It can be the *eidos*, capital, the Oedipal complex, "gender," identification. Like the bar series, "Mother," certain letteral complexes and pyramids, or the cameo and various nominal and aural signature systems, the *MacGuffin* on the cinematic train, above on the rack, *impacts*, without doing anything, on encrypted sites, inscriptions, mnemonic clusters, and petroglyphs.

The MacGuffin gives a name for that great cat (lion) located in the wrong signscape (the Scottish highlands) for which the house "cats" at the beginning of *Number 17* or featured in *To Catch a Thief* represent unobtrusive variants. Of course, less generally, it is a sop extended to the public to sponge up any metaphysical spillage of signification that tourists would not know how to process. From being a throwaway placeholder it becomes in fact an "apparatus." Today, it has entered the vocabulary, been made familiar. It does trap lions in "the Scottish highlands," virtual hermeneutic predators at the head or capo, where the eye and mnemonics collaborate.[11] By its *circulation*, the MacGuffin allows the public to explain away or anesthetize the complete violation of aesthetic distance that has already occurred. As a contraption, it is the pop cultural guarantor of an irreversible *step*. It has no place. From fictive goal of the plot (say, a secret clause), to photographic pictures and their mimetic claims, to the detached sound play of spoken words or dialogue, to the "nothing" that dries up mimetic and semantic reserves en route to *another model of language*. The MacGuffin guards a sort of "translation" against relapse, personification, aura. It confutes repetition, it countersigns recurrence against its literalization. It performs and negates its own and the culture's symptomatology. It sucks into itself the referential debris; the apparatus is, as box, cassone, or camera, a capturing weapon tracking what has no *place*. The "MacGuffin" is not simply "a" nothing, since it wanders into a formalized, cinematized, metalogos that includes, if generalized, not just a secret inscription but the "zero" within the order of number which is a historial MacGuffin of the so-called real. It traverses the key conceptual tropes of diverse histories: auteur, the one, capital, media, the *eidos*, eternal recurrence, and so on, filtering into a fracture within conceptual taxonomies of the *eye*. The zero that is the nonsite of the cinematic (the "camera" is itself MacGuffin here) suggests not a nihilism as such (another MacGuffin) but a site that, as if capturing that totality, stands as if "beyond" or "outside" it. The MacGuffin is the logical hiatus of virtualities from which the "real" of "history" is forgetfully inscribed or generated.

If the "MacGuffin" always migrates to a spectral position that defaces itself as the most obvious object of pursuit, only to reappear behind the pursuer, it is not just that it assumes a viral role. And it is not just that "it" can inhabit if not co-opt the position of any identity the instant that is presumed legitimized. And it is not just that it guarantees the rupture of any referential premise or supposition and stands guard over the work of translation, of "allegory," of materialistic historiography, of "cinema." And it is not just that, rather than being a "nothing," it shares the structure of the zero as such, or the circuit that returns in advance of its beginning, at a site of preinscription. The "MacGuffin," dissimulating itself as a canard, actively empties representational grids and logics. An anecdote presented as a throwaway, it is affiliated with all the zeroids, backspinning wheels, spectacles, cycloramas (essentially every set), reels, vertigo swirls, corneal vortexes, clanging sounds, hence dogs, cats, black suns. What is called here a black sun departing from Hitchcock's early visuals (the clay target in the first *Man Who Knew Too Much*) is as easily called a "black hole" that both fictively sustains and violently rends or deforms representational and temporal orders. The essence of the teletechnic, it absorbs light and stars, and consumes mimetic logics that would try to be generated as its remedy. The "MacGuffin," tool of Atropos, muse of the cinematic cut, redirects the going under of the star on the memory band—James Stewart in San Francisco, Cary Grant departing New York—into the cultural network and memory of "the public," last man and atopic citizen of the teletechnic empire that seems both telos and evacuation of the ocular, "global," "human" era.

## Reading on a Train, Interrupted

> With Hitchcock, a new kind of "figures" appear which are figures of thoughts.
>
> —Gilles Deleuze

> For the tragic *transport* is properly empty and the most unbound. Whereby, in the rhythmic succession of representations, in which the *transport* presents itself, *what in meter is called the*

*caesura,* the pure word, the counter-rhythmic intrusion, becomes
necessary in order to meet the racing alternation of representations at its culmination, such that what appears then is no
longer the alternation of representations but representation itself.
—**Friedrich Hölderlin**

An important collection of critical essays titled *A Hitchcock Reader* featured on its cover the one cameo of the director actually and actively
reading in his films. He is on a London Underground train, which is
always, for Hitchcock, a figure of cinema. Yet the cameo in *Blackmail*
is not just of Hitchcock reading on a train—he is reading and he is
interrupted doing so. It is a narrative cameo about, and performing, an
interruption by, of, and within legibilities, stationary and accelerated.
Alone, it speculates on the role of the book and reading as and in the
thinking of this cinema.

This scene of interrupted reading in Hitchcock's films occurs frequently, often with female characters and usually on trains. The moment
in this case is interesting as it occurs not only in the cameo itself but *in*
the first British "talkie," a work or media event with numerous and contradictory implications. It marks, it performs a fold in the teletechnic
era—the addition or supplement of sound to what had been silents with
their sheer graphematic base, the unleashing of the faux mimeticism of
people "talking." A technological shock of sorts, it will alter the entire
cinematic sensoria at the very least.

One might turn to or return from the suppposedly ancient traditions of the book and the letter, which flood the citational image at the
appearance of any book in the cinematic image that "Hitchcock" will
hold and read. Hitchcock, after all, began by making graphics and title
cards for silents, a tutelage in the traffic of letters and geometrics—and
yet, he is not allowed to read. A restless and bullying boy *interrupts*
him, reminding of something *else,* something perhaps outside the set
or marking it as "set," and this upsets the scene's stationary and trance-
like repose—that is, if the cameo had not already both interrupted and
confirmed a transition (from book to cinema, from silent to talkie, and
so on). The book sits at all times open atop a black boxlike briefcase,
covering the lap. The boy is irrepressible, it seems, and if he interrupts
Hitchcock reading, he is also not instructed particularly by Hitchcock's
stabbing finger of complaint or of photographic indexing. On the contrary, he exceeds Hitchcock's brief repertoire, the only figure to cross in
front of the sign for ice-skating on the screenlike frame of the window.

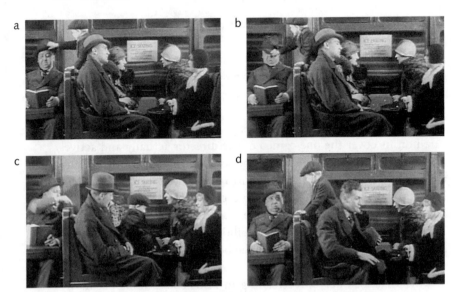

Figure 19. Hitchcock, interrupted while reading on a train in *Blackmail*'s cameo: (a) a bullying boy interrupts; (b) the boy pulls the hat over his *eyes*; (c) a timid Hitchcock protests with *Blackmail*'s ubiquitous pointing finger (promise of indexing), but (d) is stared into submission.

The segment occurs early and in the Underground. That is, it cites the cinematic *underworld* as such, the atopic and luciferian zone of the not living or dead, which nonetheless is not substantially other than what is called "life" in and by any viewer who sees screened images and cognizes by mnemonic programs and signifying matrices. Or who, at any given moment, *reads*. The host has become guest of the guest set, the set taken into itself. Hitchcock's cameo, which implies or performs a semaphoric explosion with its sedentary appearance, is a perpetual parabasis networking film to film, tele-archive to history, shot to shot. He here faces the camera sitting perpendicular to the two distracted principals, Detective Frank Webber and Alice White, who stare emptily past one another in the dead time of transport. The director, the only one who should not be in this set—indeed, who cannot not import this "outside" into the set's anamorphic and labyrinthine signscape—is reading a book. The bullying boy pulls his hat down and then stares him down. He will even return when the director tries to resume. It is all very discrete, were it not embedded in a work that is, as noted, an event of sorts in teletechnics' past and to come: that of silent film's addition and absorption of sound, that of the first British "talkie." The event occupies a virtually hingelike site as if between and across teletechnic eras or histories. Pulling the hat down over the eyes momentarily blinds or *blacks out* the eyes. The boy seems an agent that has wandered into the frame from elsewhere, like the director himself, and momentarily, by intimidation and force, he takes over. He resumes his seat and then returns, pulling down the *hat* of Detective Webber, en route to taking up his station looking down at the director. Hitchcock responds: he adjusts his hat, tries to grab the boy, who has run back to his mother's protection, and points a finger, jabbing down, a pointing and indexing finger that in fact will traverse *Blackmail* in many variants and imply accusation, identification, fingerprints (as if exploring the point of cinematic contact or putative touch), the photograph's capacity (or not) to indicate or index. The director or his image tries to take up reading again. The boy returns and glares, enough to remind and intimidate the reading director, suspended between the book and the telesthenic rush, rattles, and alternating light.

Why *reading*? Why interrupted? Is the boy an emissary from the future or the past? Does he insist that Hitchcock give up with the march of progress signaled by the "talkie" they are (almost) in, or rather hyperbolize the mnemonic networks of silent reading? *Reading* occurs explicitly three times across *Blackmail*: the arrested criminal reads a paper in the silent portion that opens the film, Hitchcock reads in his cameo, and the blackmailer Tracey will be chased through the British Museum's universal reading room. He flees past the Egyptian room with its hieroglyphics and mounts the *out*side of the archival dome only to plunge through it to his death, finger pointing, into the universal reading room. This room has rings upon rings of desks irradiating outward, each filled with people reading. Hitchcock envisions circles of reading mannequins at the heart of the historial archive.

Trains situate cinema's machinal and sensorial premises: the alternation of shadows, of clacking sounds, its promise of stasis in transport, the Underground as afterlife of the image, of memory storage, of animated "life."[12] The train's clattering accompaniments include deafening machinal roars, the alternating light-dark-light cast by rushing shadow, the clattering of iron wheels, the track that replicates bars or divisions accelerating. The train seems to mark a metonymy of linkages subject to crash or erasure, the screen as analog of windows, in which middle space, fogged over sometimes and precisely nontransparent, letters or names may emerge. Preceding perception, cutting, and sequencing, it performs and cites the series of bars on the tracks. If reading on a train implies its (own) hyperbolic suspension, that includes a rush of effaced differences precedent to "light" or phonemes. Is there an interruption of received reading models, programs? The structure is hyperbolic: sign chains deluge or reflexively backloop, reinscription becomes possible. It is almost "too much."

The nonsite interrupts. It interrupts reading (by) itself, as the eye looks up and around. One could anticipate a different network of cameos, markers, and hyperlinks. At the core of the cinematic canon, "Hitchcock," a signature used to anchor its history, puts its premises in question: that cinema is mimetic, that it is a visual medium "as such," that it is distinct from the era of the book simply, and so on.

Not all interrupted reading occurs on trains.[13] In the case of Uncle Charlie in *Shadow of a Doubt,* a cessation of reading is associated with an "accident." The merry widow strangler (Joseph Cotten) is identified with teletechnics and media, as in the early dissolve that merges him with the reel-like telephone dial and telegraph wires. What are called at times "accidents" in Hitchcock involve not just chance interruptions but *transformative* cinematic breaks. They imply or trigger alternative memory systems or times. For Uncle Charlie such an *accident* is associated with cinematic trams or bicycles, reading, and a photograph.[14] The shock of the photograph empties a young personality near death, given a figural skull *fracture* by running his bicycle into a tram: up until then he could not stop reading; after that he would never read again but become hyperactive, criminal, a serial strangler. The photograph accelerates his reading hyperbolically, resulting in his near-death accident. It is as if he were extending the photograph's citational trace chains and wormholes in simultaneous hiatus (as occurs at the end of *Blackmail* when Tracey is chased through the British Museum and falls into the universal reading room). The picture is said by sister Emma to be the one photograph remaining of young Uncle Charlie, who cannot abide being photographed, mimetically presented, and claims there are none of him in existence. Here a cinematically avenging wraith is not interrupted reading on a train; rather, a train, and a single photograph, interrupt and curtail all reading, engendering a discontinuous identity allied to smoke rings and zeroes, strangling "useless" widows.

The "house" in *Shadow of a Doubt* is inhabited by a plethora of teletechnic media. Uncle Charlie telegraphs Santa Rosa of his coming in a way that inscribes a caesura in and outside of the missive ("'Try and stop me.' *Stop*"); young sister Anne, bespectacled, mechanically *reads* everything hyperliterally, interrupting her obsessive reading to pretend to take a phone message she will lie about seeking a pencil for ("I looked!"); Young Charlie (Teresa Wright) visits what is called the free public library; the abdicated "father" Joe and the mother-dominated neighbor, Herb, chat as "literary critics," fantasizing about the technicalities of murder; the problematic of *telepathy* erupts in association with music; and the enamored but desexed detective is named *Graham,* echoing the telegram office. A linkage between reading and photographs complicates the relation between reading (books) and cinema. As noted, the one surviving photograph of young Uncle Charlie is from the day of the "accident," but it propels him into another time: the *photograph* of the boy and the "accident" are referenced to a narrative. Reading stops, is arrested, by the time of the photographic accident, even implodes with it:

EMMA (referring to the only photo existing of Uncle Charlie, and that of him as a boy): It was taken the very day he had his accident. And then, a few days later, when the pictures came home, Mama cried. She wondered if he'd ever look the same. She wondered if he'd ever be the same.

YOUNG CHARLIE: Uncle Charlie, you were beautiful.

EMMA: Wasn't he, though? And such a quiet boy, *always reading.* I always said Papa should never have bought you that *bicycle*; you didn't know how to *handle* it. Charlie, he took it right out on the *icy* road and skid it into a *streetcar.* We thought he was going to die.

YOUNG CHARLIE: I'm glad he didn't.

EMMA: Well, he almost did. He fractured his *skull.* And he was laid up for so long, and then, when he was getting well, there was no holding him. It was just as though all the rest he had was, well, *too much* for him and he had to get into mischief to *blow up* steam. *He didn't do much reading* after that, let me tell you. (My emphasis.)

Cinematic figures swarm the passage: the bicycle (two reels, transport), the streetcar; reference to *hands* and the "half-cast(e)" transvestite bird-performer of *Murder!,* Handel Fane ("didn't know how to handle it"); the skid across Mallarméan ice; perpetual reading, "always reading." Reading, already incessant, is hyperbolized by the time of the photo: he will *fracture* his skull in skidding on the ice on his new bicycle, calamitously accelerating. "Mama cried. She wondered if he'd ever be the same." There is no transition from the book. The cineast will not see, or "look the same," let alone "be the same." This confluence of the photograph with an event or "accident" alters everything. It empties and accelerates. It has to do with excess reading, becoming *hyper*, murderous, and nomadic, assuming many names: "He didn't do much reading after that, let me tell you." He didn't have to—the transition from the specular infinity of the book to the violence of the photograph, murderous, is like that into a kind of action.

"Hitchcock" today suggests less an auteur or episode within one or another film history than a cipher for a yet unfolding event. "Today," that means in an advanced moment in the post-"global" media trajectory that cinema's advent installed and inaugurated, at a time when "cinema" itself is declared dead before new media—as if the former, now doubly spectral, could be inspected again, or as if it were a question of some antedated or single technology (say, what is called analogic). Hitchcock's trajectory parallels the emergent global programs of the teletechnic era, its transitional wars and mass accelerations.

In early Hitchcock *thrillers* a cinematic insurgency is staged as and in a state of emergency it itself produces. It occurs under the guise of anarchists, saboteurs, shootist assassins, and cinematic usurpers against the home state: the sensorial and hermeneutic order the public is supposed to want protected. The usurpers wage a covert *espionage war* against the ocularcentric programs and its regimes of memory, against aesthetic ideologies, organizations of time and identity, consumption. This may be one import of the notion of cinematic "shock" in Benjamin—silent yet like a bomb blast, atomizing or vaporizing signifying and mnemonic orders. Such an uprising has secret agents, secret agencies within the tele-archive that cannot be read or identified (with), figures the "eye" would not be able to see because they are anagrammatically dispersed or citationally inaccessible to the "visual" as that has been blindly constructed. They reside in teletechnic orders upon which "memory" depends, what *The 39 Steps* calls *steps* or legs. These can be called signature systems, citational networks, combinatoires. Hitchcock began his training as a graphic artist positioning letters on title cards, alert to the letter. It has barely been tracked to what degree this occurs through incessant explorations of writing, translation, letteral graphics, scenes of Babel, postal relays, *telegraphies,* and cryptonymies of all sorts. They interrupt reading on a train.

One may propose a fable to account for the definitions of the "eye" inherited from prehistorial programs. They depend on two tropological functions that persist, massively, "today," and form the basis, perhaps, for all manipulations of telemarketing and of mediacracy's directives: identification and mimesis, bonding with the face of the "friend" and securing the real as objects of possession or use. But it is precisely these auratic functions that, together with personification and the pretense of "light" itself, Benjamin maintained were destroyed with the advent of the cinematic. The state's management of media, which is to say memory and identification, maintains these tropes as *natural*. Despite Benjamin's purported assertion, film studies have done little perhaps to date but resurrect aura, as it were, over the wound cinema opened— returning to figures of light, character, auteur, personification, indexing "gaze," and ocularcentrism in what appears a fateful relapse.

A researcher recently noted that most TV viewers regard sitcom char- acters as "friends," realer than their actual friends, and concluded that the eye cannot fully adjust to or apprehend what it has not been exposed to, say, for 200,000 years. The eye of the hunter-gatherer would have been programmed to serve two primary functions: to distinguish the friend (from the enemy in order to preserve the tribe) and to hunt (or track, the ur-model of reading). The prosthetic eye identifies or identifies with the *face* of the other; it affirms the specular premise of the tribal "friend" or decides against the enemy other. This trust in or *identification* with the "face," on which the star system regressively rests, is revoked in Hitchcock. One program of the "eye," here, is irreversibly revoked. The other function might involve references to tracking movements, prey—what Hitchcock terms the "chase" as the analog and premise for cinema's rapid passage of frames. The chase names a hermeneutic pursuit, of detection and reading, if only to mime rote rituals of memory when seeking what it has already planted and then, as if in play, forgets, so as to discover it again and again. Mr. Memory's "facts." Nothing is more evident to Hitchcock than that cinema is a mnemoni- cally devastating device with explosive, dematerializing, and deauratic powers. Hitchcock short-circuits or suspends the chase by accelerating it, making it always and at once a *double* chase turned back upon itself: the chaser chased. The second defining trait of this archaic program of the "eye" is imploded in advance.

Hitchcock cuts the eye. What sort of prosthetic eye, deanthropo- morphized by this invasive cinema, subsists beyond this point?[15] The citational monstrosity Hitchcock wields necessarily posits a next fold or space—if, that is, ocularcentrism has been suspended, and with it the historial programs of defaulted Greek and Enlightenment metaphors that feed its regime. This is what it means for cinema to arrive in the absence of aura. The eye, here, cannot identify the face of the friend; it cannot assume the chase is not self-duplicating in advance. Thus, the figures of blinding that are privileged across Hitchcock—Dalí's scissored eyeball, the bloody sockets of the farmer in Bodega Bay, Mother's cigarette in a sunny-side-up egg in a Cannes hotel—put out what is already a touristic blind in the name of a weave of retention and pretension that produces the "eye" as effect.

IV. The Black Sun

# 8. Prosthesis of the Visible

"No one can like the drummer man!"
—*Young and Innocent*

These holes of blackness, these black holes in the image-flow of cinema, are more than conventional indices by which to register lapses of time; they signify, and anticipate, lapses of another sort altogether insofar as they represent moments where vision withdraws into itself, refusing the distance, the separation, that allows it to take in objects so as to take in, instead, the articulating cut from which seeing as such proceeds.
—Lee Edelman

*Blinking*: what the eye does to wash itself, to shutter or shut out light, to open as if afresh upon a world whose lines, perceptual configurations, shapes mnemonically reassemble where or as already imprinted or known; an interruption or cut, involuntary contraction, segmenting, sphincter-like.

In *Sabotage,* Detective Ted Spenser calls the shutting down of the Bijou through the putting out of the lights in London, the caesura induced by and opening that filmwork itself, a "*blinkin'* shame." In *Young and Innocent,* blinking is a tic, an accelerating twitch, first witnessed compulsively before a stormy background of lightning flashes, *Blitz*. It is linked to a bad or arrhythmic heartbeat for which heart pills will have to be taken, and this by a jazz band's drummer. Blinking identifies this murderer of a movie star, his wife, named Christine Clay, found strangled and washed up by the sea. An aging star from the silents, he complains of her taking up with a young screenwriter ("Boys!"), as if calling her back from a shifting cinematic alliance "talkies" made necessary. It is a tic, a twitch, that will expose the killer when he is tracked down in minstrel blackface, keeping beat. This twitch, this *arrhythmic* heartbeat will accelerate wildly, eye opening and shutting compulsively, rhythm wrecked as he keels over: the facial parallel to a cinematic train wreck. Questioned about the murder, he bursts into a pealing mad laughter. The blackface becomes what Lee Edelman calls a "black hole" locus, consuming in advance the movie *star* as the narrative's own premise.

The modality of the eye, of the visual, or the legible, has hung like a backdrop over the thinking of the cinematic, like Dalí's surreal and eye-filled gambling room in *Spellbound*'s dream sequence, with a certain bias that has proved, in ways, blinding. It has separated language from the eye, mnemonics from the cut, aesthetics from politics, death from "life." Even in a sophisticated Hitchcockian like Zizek, it enforces the need to get "beyond the wall of language," breathing life into the old personification of the gaze—final perverse outpost of the ocularcentric program. But what emerges in the "strange case" of Hitchcock may be a different sort of agency, a secret signifying agency, material yet corresponding to no specific letter or word or script or "gaze" as such. Unable to dissociate itself from anteriority, mnemonics, it is without relation to a given image or phenomenal trance. In *To Catch a Thief,* it is called a cat.

*To Catch a Thief* remains concealed from the eye by its own reputation. The work is, by all accounts, a "light" or marginal one and has drawn little or no critical attention. David Sterritt glides typically over this site, a black hole hiding within the canon, yet the opening credits and subsequent black cat walking at night spurs defensive allusions to its "documentary" status or "literalization," as if the alternatives were too monstrous to imagine:

> Even such an apparently light and artificial concoction as *To Catch a Thief* (1955) bears traces of Hitchcock's documentary impulse, moreover, here translated into a very different idiom. After a credit sequence that indicates the setting and mood of the story with a shot of a travel-agency window, the largely wordless opening sequence alternates conspicuously acted shots of burglary aftermaths with realistic views of a cat (introducing the narrative's "cat burglar" motif) walking across real-looking roofs. Although this is not a documentary sequence, its shop-window and stalking-cat shots are so completely *literalized*—visually and metaphorically—as to recall Hitchcock's roots in the documentary tradition despite the whimsical narrative that follows them.[1]

What anxiety makes one reach for the tradition of "documentary" here, as if groping for some contact, or touch? If the credit sequence "indicates the setting and mood of the story"—oh, is that what the touristic emblems signs on display perform?—they are unread. But then, it is all for a "whimsical narrative," very light stuff.

"Cinema" may be for Hitchcock this service of travel advertisements and lures, the ads for "France," signs that, as clichés, mock this promised cinematic landscape for sale. If so, it is itself a burglar's front. Yet this travel service window montage *points,* Sterritt says, to the specter of documentary—that it, the promise of "realistic views." But what if it set a trap for readers like Sterritt? Cary Grant as John Robie is an ex–cat burglar nicknamed "the Cat," and his techniques are being mimicked by another, so that the thefts are referred back and attributed to him. This brings the "original" cat out of retirement to track his "copy cat," who is said to use his "mark," and whom Robie alone, knowing his own technique, can anticipate.[2] Let us ignore for the moment the spillage of frames here—that Grant comes back from premature retirement to make the film, or that Hitchcock will simulate a "Hitchcock" film (which others can do with greater financial success), or that, in chasing its own copy, the "original" appears to copy "his" copy in a circularity that all but guarantees a vapid if not utterly "light" result.

I will recur to the questionable legibility of a single line, which unfolds a dimension of Hitchcock—or, for that matter, cinema—that exemplifies the deauratic. This resounds with Benjamin's claim that cinema appears with the destruction of aura, but understood not as the loss of originary presence (as, say, with a painting), but the retraction of personification, of anthropomorphism, of a natural trope of "light," and indeed of ocularcentrism, and a series of temporal or identity models that have long attended this blinding program. Together with this question there arises the issue of precisely how micrologically (i.e., according to what protocols of marks, puns, rhymes, letters, cross-verbal and ocular affiliations) one can read "Hitchcock," today, and to what ends. If aura demands that one take the visual as a natural order of perception, to withdraw aura places one in a zone of marks, letteration, graphic figures that is, on its surface, closer to issues of legibility as such, a mnemonic order in keeping with the brute fact of celluloid's role as memory storage bands. What is at issue, even in a very light work, if "light" itself is revoked?

The line in question is the closing one of the film. Grace Kelly, playing "Francie Stevens" (as "Grace Kelly," perhaps, given the marriage to Prince Rainier occasioned by the location), has just chased Cary Grant back to his villa. This, after Robie has exposed who was "behind" the copycat jewel thefts at the eighteen-century costume gala held at the Sanford villa. Behind the unmasked Danielle Foussard's perfect imitation of Robie's or Grant's "mark" and style as the "copycat" was the restaurateur Bertani, caterer at the gala. It is his cinematic kitchen that includes Robie's old underworld partners from the French Resistance in postwar France, like him free owing to a fragile "parole" granted for wartime service. Francie pursues in a police car and, chastising Robie for fleeing her, proposes to shake hands good-bye. A genre kiss ensues and Grace fast-forwards beyond the assumption of having finally caught her "thief." Francie looks out at the beautiful vistas of Robie's mountain-top villa, which the film has shown us twice before: "Oh, Mother will love it up here!" A bell rings, and Grant's half-face appears like a trap has snapped shut as Francie closes her eyes in the imagined bliss of arrival. Mrs. Stevens, "Mother," played by and as Jessie Royce Landis, will appear the worldliest and most benign of all such in Hitchcock. Nonetheless, one is left with questions: Whatever "Mother" designates, why would she, keeping in mind her avatar to come in *Psycho,* love it here? Where is *here,* and why *"up* here"? What does "love" mean in this context? Given how light the work is, and what sheer froth the ending is for this superficial outing, why even ask?

The clue, I think, lies in another line in an earlier visit to the villa, and it opens an abyss whose labyrinthine implications for this work and others cannot be calculated or exhausted. It is a line of the insurance salesman, H. H. Hughson (John Williams), who during an early visit to discuss Robie's help in catching the new "copycat" and recouping his company's losses also is taken by the sheer visual splendor of the scene, and the long vistas (what Grant in a gambling mode calls a "long shot"). Hughson praises the villa in terms that return us to the tricky logic of the travel service window of the credit sequence. "Tricky," because it inscribes the unwitting viewer as a tourist set up with a bunch of clichés he or she is paying for and, instantly, being robbed through or by. The term he uses is distinct: he calls Robie's villa or at least its vistas a kind of "travel folder heaven." It is a place, that is, no doubt a logic within the cinematic outing itself, that looks from on high over the gorgeous Riviera landscape and signscape. Yet it does so, if one lets the phrase take root, in a way shaped by advertising images that one, as a tourist, has accepted as "beautiful" in advance and looks to replicate regardless of what one is in fact seeing. Moreover, the word *heaven* is double-sided at least: in addition to suggesting the bliss of paradise, it connotes an afterlife. One is dead in heaven, after all, as one is within the cinematic band as a screen wraith, for one, or within one's eyesight if that is itself preprogrammed by things like travel folders. Moreover, what does it mean to *fold* or to travel fold or for travel—which is linked to cinematic movement, as are its machinal vehicles purporting stationary transport—to itself fold, collapse? The work appears just *too light* to bother with such questions. Rather like Robie's maid Germaine's quiches, which Hughson enjoys and Robie says are as "light as air." Significant, in a film in which the Cat's gloved hand reaches under the sleeping head on the pillow to take jewels, much as the film reaches into the head of the entranced viewer to despoil, plant, relieve, alter, rape.

But what if being *too* light were a calculated assault on light itself, as one might suspect of a deauratic practice, one that understands the cinematic not as producing "pictures of people talking" to identify with but something void of personification and anthropomorphisms? The difference may be decisive if one reads Hitchcock not through the categories of film aesthetics (auteurism, identification) but as an event in the transformations of teletechnics and artificial memory within an emerging "global" mediatrix. *To Catch a Thief* might then seem to be Hitchcock's "most" post-postmodern performance—to the point of retiring the category in advance, and with it "modernism" itself. Its cinematic mise-en-scène, the *postwar* Riviera, seems able to sponge up all or any pasts instantly into its folds or surfaces, such as those of the Mediterranean cradle it incessantly marks within its frames. The capture of the copycat, by way of the imitation of an imitator imitating, marks the work as also "about" the fate of Western mimesis and the camera's own claim to capture or catch in its image, as does Sterritt's reversion to the assurances of documentary to occlude, oddly, the film's highly allegorical and performatively abyssal credit sequence. The mise-en-scène of a postwar Riviera is posthistorial as well, invoking Mediterranean ghost gods like Hephaestus in the wine steward Foussard's limp. In a way reminiscent of (or condensing) *Secret Agent*, there will be a discrete but decisive scene that addresses and breaks down language itself, though not in ways that allow one to hypostasize the term as a "literary" figure alone. Rather, language seems named as a perpetual site of translation and mnemonics linked to various teletechnic fields involved, inevitably, with the cinematic, and here with theft. The pursuit is generated by what Robie speaks of in the early boat ride with Danielle as past *language lessons* and, in this context, of the threat that hangs over him for "*breaking* his *parole*." The work has, so far, successfully blinded its tourist consumers as a light-as-air trifle. Yet scarcely out of the credit sequence, we, the viewers, have been emblematically or in fact raped, murdered, or robbed as the female tourist, in cold cream, shrieks. What is given is a sort of detour that leads back, inevitably if unexpectedly, to "Mother," perhaps even to what or how she loves and consumes, and what that has to do with the *eye,* with "travel folder heaven," and with what one may call—with the history of the West condensed like chips at a casino—the prosthesis of the visible.

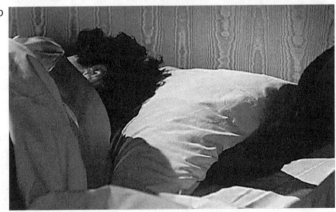

Figure 20. "Robbed!" (a) Opening shriek of American tourist (viewer). (b) Hypno-klepto-poetics: gloved *hand* passes into sleeping head.

## Language Lessons

A deauratic practice of cinema (i.e., cinema) *has* to atomize and break its word since it precedes the graphematic structure or unit of the letter or the articulate phoneme. But that is not the same as moving "beyond" a "wall of language," or for that matter, metonymy, "the Symbolic," and so on. Hitchcock remains a counterocularist oeuvre placed enigmatically at the center of an imaginary visualist or ocularcentric canon (film studies). At stake might be the fate not only of the *parole* (what does it mean if it or the Mediterranean logos itself breaks into parts?) but the eye and ear and so on. Which brings us to Zizek.

Zizek's readings of Hitchcock are marked by contradictory features. "Hitchcock" serves among other things as a map to chart a sort of late Lacanianism meant to overleap the perceived impasses of so-called post-structuralism or, for that matter, Lacan's "middle" period, which favors the powers of the Symbolic. This is a move, Zizek tells us, also to a site "beyond the wall of language," and it accords fairly well with claims that the cinematic image performs such a leap as a media power itself. That place beyond language emanates phallophanies of what is beyond the Symbolic, of "the Thing." It offers a double logic: on the one hand, it would be free of aura, personification, metaphor, the automatism of the Symbolic; on the other, it would itself be personified, given a (reassuringly nonanthropocentric) "gaze," a still ocularized position. I take Zizek, in this role, as an example not only of one way that a neo-Lacanian interest in Hitchcock does its work (Hitchcock as an "exemplary" colonization) but also of why he might be viewed as the last avatar, however inverted, of the auteurist tradition that has dominated and deformed the critical archive and guaranteed its regressive or auratic profile.

Zizek's approach to the "gaze" shares the following with the auteurist tradition it situates itself within: a recuperation of "Hitchcock" as master prestidigitator and theological guarantor of decreed (here Lacanian) moves, a relapse into metaphoric association and mimetic interpretation, and the occlusion of any address of the specifics of language (for Zizek including film "dialogue"). It sustains the division between the visual and textual that underlies the ideology of ocularcentrism generally. Zizek installs Hitchcock as a foil, in the name of "late Lacan," to oppose hermeneutic models involving identification and subjectivization on the one hand and also so-called post-structuralism on the other.

Zizek performs this complicated balancing act in his reading of *Psycho* titled, "In His Bold Gaze My Ruin Is Writ Large." Indeed, while attempting to move "beyond" a hermeneutics that he sees as belonging still to the automata of the Symbolic, Zizek only *empties and inverts its terms*, remaining within the field he claims to exceed. What is interesting for Hitchcock is that this all depends on the suppression of all varieties of linguistic technology from translation to language lessons to telepathy. The numerous appearances of media and telegraphies that saturate Hitchcock are blankly occluded, as the last ghosts of subjectivity and identification, that is to say the auratic, make their appearances. As Zizek maps a shift between middle Lacan and late Lacan, as if from the symbolic to the real and the domain of "the Thing," *Psycho* suggests "a subject *beyond* subjectivity," which in turn allows us to identify with "an abyss *beyond* identification." On the one hand, a will to go beyond subjectivity, to remove "aura" from this site, assumes this "beyond" can be named, asserted, projected, stated only in the absence of all signifying properties or vehicles—since it is the beyond, we hear, of whatever is called language but what is generally defined by its metonymic properties, its substitutive chains, its endless *errance*. At the same time, it is at this point that the characterization relapses into the effect of a "subject" that returns after its own "beyond." In negative form, the terms of subjectivity and identification invertedly return. For Zizek, Norman or the supposedly uncanny "gaze" of the psycho (if that *is* Norman) becomes the very model of the Lacanian definition of the subject: the subject as monster, as the living dead, the personified *Thing*.

The move from a so-called middle Lacan's concern, from the Symbolic (and hence, the signifier, metonymy), into which "deconstruction" and "post-structuralism" in general are dissolved, would be toward various encounters with a Real. In this way late Lacan can be used to disrupt the "gentrification" of historicism and intersubjective narrativization. But we see here another fold rooted in the wish to pivot terms of the modern and postmodern about one another in a dance of mutual advantage. A simplified narrative binary results that "moves" as if from modernism to postmodernism, or (symbolic) language *to* a "beyond the wall of language." Zizek does not note in evoking Hitchcock that this "beyond," so to speak, depends on a logic of and within wildly orchestrated and patterned signifying agencies. These agencies are aware, at all times, of everything involved in cinematic production, that is, from chemical and scriptive processes to the history of the tele-archive and the book, ocularcentric programs and, indeed, psychoanalysis *(Spellbound)*.

The "beyond" of language in Hitchcock's case is simply the effect of more material markers and more citations functioning otherwise. One has moved in Zizek's model not from language to its beyond but from metonymy back to metaphor—as in a kind of fold. In surpassing metonymy en route to the Real or "the Thing," Zizek unwittingly returns to metaphor, much as in superseding the signifier he invokes a "sign" that contains in itself the "answer of the real." In moving "beyond" one form of signifying practice he only moves to another, and triggers regressions to suspect or precritical figures: metaphor, or what might translate his use of "sign," symbol.[3]

A crisis emerges, in fact, when the problem of material signs returns in Zizek's reading of Hitchcock. I will mention this briefly before returning to my focus, and why I would supplant *To Catch a Thief* for *Psycho*, even, as a cipher of this crisis (and, perhaps, why they could be called the same). It has everything to do with an aesthetic ideology by which cinema, the image, or the so-called visual has been viewed to date—that is, as the site of aura, immediacy, or the real (as with the reversion earlier to "documentary" or "realisms").

Zizek's shift from middle Lacan to late Lacan is mapped, also, by the shift from the symptom (the figure of infinite interpretability) to the *sinthome*. The latter is said to represent "the limit of interpretation," with which the subject can only identify, or "enjoy," yet which in doing becomes his or her ontological anchor in the Real. But what if some sort of "front" intervenes to sell tickets to, market, or commodify this mobile umbilical access to a "Real," as can only happen if one is still in a signifying network? Hitchcock's atomization of and by the cinematic is only possible on the level of marks, pointillist shadows, what *The Lodger* calls fog. It turns out, of course, that to prevent this from being apparent, something like the *sinthome* must turn up, that is, yet another signifying agent of sorts. In "Hitchcockian *sinthomes*," Zizek wants to break with a merely intersubjective model: the theological model that, nonetheless, he inverts and perpetuates. The *sinthome* would be a protrusion to which the radical contingency of existence bonds itself beyond metonymy or "interpretation." It would be the key to the riddle of reading Hitchcock, finally allow us to name those repetitions across this oeuvre (the intellectual woman with spectacles, the glass of milk, the suspended hand are his examples) that generate interpretation. Yet if the domain of "the Thing" is not some hoary gothic site, it may be because "the obscene, impossible Thing" is primarily experienced through the facticity of inscription: that is, the movement of the black cat that we see crossing the rooftop after the opening thefts in *To Catch a Thief*. What if instead of using Lacan to read Hitchcock one reversed the polarities? If in Zizek's hands the rhetoric of the "gaze," long dominant in film theory, cannot stop from returning beneath a rhetoric of transparency, it seems barred by a nonsite associated as if with a letter, in this case, the letter *M*. That is, with memory, marking, the machine, music, murder, and something *Psycho* calls "Mother." For Hitchcock, cinema's microgrammatologies *precede* the origins of the Western logos (and Egypt, in *Blackmail*), since they adhere to marks in advance of any graphematic strategy. Above all, Zizek resists not some deconstructive straw man but the explosion, shock, or atomization marked by Hitchcock's immersion, from the first cameo of *The Lodger,* in the teletechnic rupture and the powers of the cinematic trace he discovers before light is even generated.[4]

## Folds

The line about Robie's villa—"Oh, Mother will love it up here!"—is at once light, humorous, and beyond lethal. This is so for Grant, certainly, who half-peers with one Cyclops eye around Grace Kelly's appalling bliss. Keeping "Mother" in *Psycho* in mind, a nonsite that includes what Derrida implies by his reading of the Platonic teletechnic *khora,* a nonsite of inscription before phenomenalization, we might ask where, exactly, is *here*? What is travel folder heaven? What is the topography of a spectral-ized *screen* advertising "France"? (Does what is called "France" include primarily the logics of this screen—entirely material in its import and role as relay within teletechnic histories?) And what does this work, which won an Oscar for its cinematography, its sweeping and gorgeous travel pictures, tell us of sight? Why does the work speak of "language lessons" in a boat whose engines have been cut, then of broken *paroles,* then perform something of a fall through historial signposts and eras, into the Sanford gala's costume version of history?

There is a brief *aerial pan* during the opening car chase from Robie's villa that harbors a performative if labyrinthine clue concerning what Mother will love, and what travel folder heaven might be. One is, to be sure, at first unaware of anything beyond a prolonged tracking shot that takes in the beauty of the Riviera promised by the travel service. Several things distinguish this visual sequence that one may not remark while the eye loses itself in the folds of the landscape, even while the sweep and pleasure of the views generate advertised delight. The extent of this seduction seems quite total, as when the film is awarded its only Oscar

Figure 21. Travel folding: aerial shot tracking car chase.

for this nonetheless wholly un-Hitchcockian cinematography. I will list these points briefly.

1. It is an aerial shot, and therefore it cites the formula from *The 39 Steps* that Mr. Memory would smuggle out, a formula accelerating the mnemonics of cinema from its pretense of representing "facts," Mr. Memory's vaudeville show, to acting as flying bomber of the homeland and its mnemonic archive.

2. In this most artificial and techno-confected of works (culminating in a pyrotechnic display of an artificed sun, virtually), the shot purporting to treat a *natural* setting and earthscape as "beautiful," is not only unique in all of Hitchcock but radically non-Hitchcockian; since he never turns the camera over to "nature," it also fulfills the devious and thieving contract of the travel service window of the titles: here, it seems to say, is what you want, beautiful travel brochure pictures of "the Riviera"—one is in, without knowing it, travel folder heaven.

3. The chase of Robie and Germaine's car by Inspector Lepic's car (a name evoking the picturing mimetic "eye" on its hunt for the thieving trace called "the Cat") folds on conspicuous turns in the road and hills, but these suggest also mnemonic folds in this "double chase," as when the car being pursued with Germaine driving is stopped before a fold or flock of sheep and turns out not to have Robie in it (who has discreetly gotten out), whereupon Lepic turns (or folds) back, only to pass Grant again on a bus going in the opposite direction, missing him.

4. The sheep represent another fold of memory, that is, a citation, since they come out of *The 39 Steps* again, confirming that everything,

of course, on the mnemonic band had to do with Mr. Memory and not with "sight," not with simple "*pan*oramas," except that the citation of this barren earthscape could be said even to include what the work repeatedly calls "everything" (the earth, its elements, the Mediterranean logos and history through the postwar boom, the teletechnic affluence going back to the Greek deities and engorging the telemarketing era presaged in the credit sequence, and so on).

5. Hitchcock will appear somber if not oddly mournful and stiff, *eyes closed,* in his cameo on the bus with Grant next to a birdcage, citing *Sabotage,* indicating that this too light work and trifle is deemed, by Hitchcock, a time bomb, that cinematic rupture and atomization wired to historial time-space (and rather piquantly citing nuclear blasts in its fireworks).

6. When looked at again, what was deemed by the tourist viewer (including the Academy of Motion Picture Art and Sciences) to be a "beautiful" panorama is much more eviscerating, since there are virtually no trees, and hence all but no life on the rocky earthscape, in which tiny humans, if visible at all, are in what almost seem like troglodyte dwelling places.

7. The source of the aerial shot, the place of the "eye," is marked by a brief shadow on the earth of the flying machine, allying it to a shadow or unexpectedly the cat itself, and this makes a brief cameo later as a police plane buzzing the boat in which Robie and Danielle speak of their past language lessons—a plane that presages the crop duster in Grant's

Figure 22. Cameo on bus cites *Sabotage*'s birdcage time bomb.

next and last Hitchcock outing. It serves as a machinal "sun," and it not only displaces the source of light as prosthetic but allies the act of "seeing" to an excoriating nongaze and active consumption that also *burns* away life and trees from what it looks at, or records, while presuming to mask that as "beautiful" because it (this phantom "eye") had seen travel brochure pictures proclaiming it as such. The machinal eye that records, here, is not only blind to what it sees, a sort of asolar Cyclops after Odysseus's (or Outis's) visit, but is, in its touristic or consumerist ease, a destroying and negating agency, as if whatever this artificed "eye" imprints, records, regurgitates, pleasures in, transports itself to (cinematically) will be, per definition, eviscerated and mummified, and not just on the celluloid band but before it and as archival fact.

8. The panorama pretends, then, to suspend the human and allegorical dimension of cinema as if in favor of something like the mimetic or documentary self-effacement of the camera (and of Hitchcock, who is rewarded with an Oscar for suppressing his meanness, giving up apparent control, giving us just a gorgeous earthscape), which is to say, fallen into the blindness of Sterritt when he suggested something like "documentary" was under way, yet in fact it is at its *most* performative and destroying, blinding and consuming, allegorical and eviscerating, enough to account for the deeply reserved look in Hitchcock's cameo.

9. What is called "travel folder heaven" implies *not* that the eye is presented with a gorgeous long shot, but that it is trapped in the folds of memory and memory bands blindly pleasuring in the pretense of beheld images whose production and consumption, indeed, occur only in an afterlife that archives and devastates any Real.

10. This literal and virtual burning away of trees by an eye in the place of a prosthetic aerial sun—which the work re-marks in Grant's alias, "Conrad Burns," a lumberman from Portland, Oregon (Mother quips, "There's not much lumber around here")—marks itself oddly through a burning away of gravity: that is, of the natural image (trees) or grounded reference, since everything it consumes becomes a cutting and citation, with a resulting loss of gravity or gravitas evident in things and people constantly as if flying *up,* to the tops of roofs, long shots at and from Robie's cinematic villa, aerial flight, cliff tops, or the film's *too light* reputation.

Certainly, there are literal folds in the road that could correspond to the descriptive phrase "travel *folder* heaven." Something in the positioned aerial eye partakes of the Avenger's logics.

For a work in which an originary cat is in pursuit of his imitator, this tracking shot seems at first the least Hitchcockian sequence. Hitchcock contrives a signature effect in the momentary annulment of his signature. But what emerges in the complications and implications of the folding (which occurs in the stationary "movement" of the viewer's eye in the cinema finally) is that this "eye" effect, a conglomerate of mnemonic and recording and staging and production and projection elements combined with preparatory touristic implants (the travel service's mocking icons and implied photos selling "France"), is still to be assimilated to the *atopos* of the prowling, thieving black cat or trace, as the flicker of shadow on the earth from the plane marks. Something else moves as agency here than either word or picture; something other instigates the visual as an effect that is neither transparent nor passive nor "beautiful" but actively eviscerating or consuming yet produced by and within archival folds and machinery.

The *Med*iterranean doubles as and names a sort of terrestrialized *media*. To the background of a nauseatingly light romantic score, the lens has been shooting what cannot appear to be a set. Hitchcock will be rewarded for it, they think, with an Oscar pat on the back: get out of the haunted houses and affirm the mimetic splendor of the world, the proper use of the camera, the academy quietly suggests. Never does Hitchcock relinquish his control to such a seemingly open or chance pan: it has none of the detail or choreography one braces for in Hitchcock and shows almost no humans at all. On the contrary, it cites and indicts the filmgoer's touristic demand for glamorous travel footage. Yet the surveillance, in a film text that later refers to "real estate *lists*," has something of Hawthorne's and Kafka's surveyors in it. This panorama also seems to site or cite everything—all *terrain*, dwellings, the Mediterranean cradle, the sun, vehicles, the double chase, the devastating agency this "eye" has as well, almost in the position of the sun, or as brief shadow, its eclipse. The car chase doubles back even as a folding, collapsing, devastating exposé of "seeing." The travel service window, unmanned, is a tourist trap, itself a lethal front, as Bertani's kitchen later will be revealed to be. The mimetic promise is not just a logic of consumption within a program of representation (or perception), it betrays and it has many spells: identification with the star, delight in place, security of reference (no thefts), temporal location, promise to be transported to glamour, to witness "love."

This least interesting of pans presents a performative riddle. The pan is a deadpan. It citationally evacuates not only any subject position of the viewer but also the mimetic or representational contract of cinematography as such, that which shoots and maps, follows and imprints an earth or earthscape. The shot seems to say: Here, look at the luscious Riviera, at the reproduction of "nature" that will win an Oscar. Look, but what is happening cites the machines of such looking, contracts of expectation, and graphics, as part of its synthetic operation: it archives, and archives its own archiving, into which any imaginary position you can assume will be folded. It is yours, you paid for it, it is even the "most beautiful," as the dialogue affirms. But it betrays, you and then itself, or rather, as image, irreversibly performs and discloses to the blind eye the implications of that betrayal. First of all, what the image presents, which we, coming from the travel brochure of expected templates, are *blind* to, is in fact rather barren and ugly: a rockscape. For Hitchcock, this is already what is stripped of metaphor or personification, not to mention vegetation, forests, "life." The *pan,* totalizing, performs the opposite of what it promises, opening a rhetorical rift in the pretense of landscape shots, much as Hitchcock did in *Blackmail,* around the pretense of documentary. And in this Hitchcock's camera shatters, with the *lightest* of *touches,* the mimetic logos, now a broken "parole" within the prison house of Enlightenment perceptual fictions or models. There is the same imaginary logic of contact, touch, indexing, the Real in the landscape shot as in documentary—and each suppresses the citational premise of the image to sustain a false and deadly pretense of transparency. The sequence undoes this promise by referencing its dependence on mnemonics and citation, which in effect bars natural representation and renders the metaphysics of the "gaze" regressive. The earthscape is geographically marked and traversed by cars and lined roads, signifying tracks that fold and multiply into not just citational puns (visual, aural) but convergences of histories: that of cinema's trajectory, that of the cradle of the Mediterranean and its logos, that of the world wars, that of the advent of telemarketing and tourism, that of the "American," of "France" as a cinematic topos, and eventually, at points in the work, histories of sound, number, representation, nuclear weaponry, "light," sex, and temporal orders: what the film misleadingly calls, in Francie's words, "an offer with everything."

Jump-cut to the second scene at Robie's villa, where Grant will lunch with insurance agent H. H. Hughson and get from him the "real estate list," the insurance company's list of persons with jewelry likely to be stolen. If *To Catch a Thief* is calculated to be overlooked as a light text, here this very lightness is openly commented on and curiously transformed. It is a "lightness" that absorbs all cognates of light: the figure of overwhelming light as well as lightness as mere fluff, superficial and without gravity, a sort of nothing or sheer excess. As Francie complains in a later scene, "Mother, the book you're reading is *upside down*." What we take for light stuff retains a different and darker source, like the black cat traversing rooftops, materialized as a thieving gloved *hand*, since the very premise of the shot, or the word, involves a preoriginary theft, and catastrophe, that sends forth emissaries into the rectangular frame. This thieving will be potentially also of everything: "jewels," reference, being, sex, history, gravity, origin. Raymond Bellour glosses the stolen diamond in *Family Plot* by noting it "could well reflect everything: death, sex, reflected light, which all gather in the eye of the viewer, as if through the lens of a camera, through the vision of the *mise en scène*, the vision of whatsoever becomes its intercessor."[5]

In the postwar or posthistorial world of the French Riviera—one of faux Baudrillardian seduction without production, of copies without originals, of obscene gendered performance without sex—signs do not have referents, or rather, their definition as signs does not efface them toward any assured signifieds. The typical Frenchman, Bertani, has an Italian name; Grace Kelly speaks of Cary Grant's "Robie" being like an American in an English movie rather than the reverse. As noted, the entirety occurs under the threat of what is called Robie "breaking" his *parole*, of a broken word or *logos*, and what one can no longer call a "film" or a "text" scatters references to the dismembered parts of language, as in Robie's giving Danielle language "lessons." Language lessons address a middle space of translation that evokes, as sound, the inert signifiers Benjamin references as "pure language" *(reine Sprache)*. That the Greek *logos* is invoked in the Mediterranean setting and architecture together with the serial evocation of the four elements (earth, fire, water, and air) and the presence of demigods. When the phrase "light touch" is used, it suggests pickpocketing as well as cunning subtlety, epistemological contact, and the imprinting of "light." The phrase is double-clicked, re-marked. *Hitchcock knows: he has programmed the blind reputation of the film, apotropaically, from the first, performing its blindness and blindings as its mark, deferring its legibility to readers to come.* The restaurateur Bertani, whose catering service turns out to be "behind" the thefts, tells Robie that his kitchen works just "like a machine . . . cutting, slicing," allying the kitchen as a front for film production (splicing). This "light touch" spoken of in the dialogue is also a touch or touching, physical or epistemological, that is deadly. Robie adds immediately about his cook, "She strangled a German general once, without a sound." And how do we hear figures that despoil without a sound, like the bomber formula in *The 39 Steps,* the prosthetic sun, Germaine's cinematic hands?

Something in the work that is concerned with "copies" or simulacra will have effectively voided both gravity and direction (up *and* down) by occupying a site in which origin as earth, egg, sun, eye, or Mother is instantly and in advance evacuated—indeed, in which a *khora*-like "Mother" extinguishes generation before its advent, and marks "life" as a spectralization of histories. This "Riviera" with nouveau riche American tourists presages the bubble of the globalized tele-era whose advent Hitchcock participates in, launches, and resists in the postwar French Riviera. This resistance to totalization on behalf of the cinematic "cat" is echoed in Grant's reference to the Resistance in the war, or the Underground army of ghosts, revenants, and knowers of excess that the screen itself rallies. This *underworld* has its "celebrities," as Robie calls himself, much as "Cary Grant" would be a Hadean star—a screen wraith who, like the black cat, eludes mimetic contracts. This too is a resistance to gravity, the upward fall that Heinrich von Kleist would term *antigrav* in speaking of the *Marionettentheater,* suggested in the casino scene in which the lady gambler is compromised when Robie drops a gambling plaque down her cleavage. It is a subtle pantomime designed to get Mrs. Stevens's attention yet traversed by commentary on woman's naked body and the fetish of clothes, the con game of sexual exchange (or its evasion) and numerical returns. Hoping to keep the plaque, the woman says "Il n'est pas bien grave" but is compelled to give Grant numerous small chips in exchange to avoid going in search of it (Robie: "If you would rather not take *my word* for it"). This Gordian knot of inversions will return us to the panoramic shot of the car chase, no longer an idyll with its rocky cliffs denuded of trees, again remarked by Robie's pseudonym in the story, that of "Conrad Burns," a lumberman from Oregon. It would be tempting to gloss this pseudonym as naming one who clear-cuts all *natural images* (trees) at or before the origin (Oregon); one who, recalling the sun-scorched landscape and like a prosthetic sun, burns (them) in a circular system in which copies precede their models (the German *Rad*), replicate mnemonic copies in turn, a backspinning system of consciousness or mnemonic conning itself (*Con*rad). In Hitchcock's cryptonymic scheme, "Cary Grant" appears an unwitting Zarathustran virus.

Whatever would be called "eye" hereafter, which is to say, going back through historial folds as the costume gala would seem to do or the furtive citations of Greek gods wandering, lost, in the Mediterranean posthistorial set, it is now within the service, what the film calls a *service compris,* of an eviscerating trace figure that is, like the cat, prephenomenal, *khora*-like, something "Mother" might love to practice and enjoy the entrapping devastations of while miming enjoyment or even, like Francie, faking *jouissance.*

Heaven, for sure, suggests not only bliss, a sort of dead or touristic *jouissance* ghoulishly echoed in the fireworks' mock-orgasmic sputtering, but also an afterlife connected to a travel folder. What, though, again, is a travel *folder?* The word ricochets discreetly elsewhere in the dialogue. Grant as Robie gives a brief account of his own origin as a jewel thief: "I was a member of an American trapeze act in a circus that traveled

Figure 23. (a) "Oh, Mother will love it up here!" followed by (b) Grant's Cyclopean alarm as bell tolls.

in Europe. It *folded* and I was stranded, so I put my agility to a more rewarding purpose." Where the folds of the film text include the induction of the out-of-frame, the enfolding and exfoliation of trace chains without historical outside, *it* is a putative *origin* that is also that of the "real" Grant as an actor, if the fold, here, inscribes the "real" (actor) in the engulfing fiction. This inscription of "real" actors may be compared to Jessie Royce Landis's complaining that "nobody calls me *Jessie* anymore" or to Grace Kelly's inability, *ever,* to escape from the film (even at the place of death). "Folding" can imply a catastrophe like some antimatter's implosion at the site of origins. We hear references, outside of any set, to the *names* of the "actors," thus situating them in the screen event: one cannot "*carry* it off," or one cannot "get out of it *grace*fully," inscribing the unreal real histories of the once living actors, as if played by the film characters inversely. In the lobby of the Hotel Carlson, tourists turn to ogle "Grace Kelly" and "Cary Grant," the stars "themselves." Thus the word *fold* extends its reach to imply total collapse, as well as fall or demise.

"Travel" or cinema *folds,* crashes or turns back, by virtue of its ceaseless ability to re-mark, suicite, reinscribe. In the travel service window the "Eiffel Tower" is not only an icon for "France" but, like the model cruise ship that cites *Rich and Strange,* a miniature copy. It is an advertisement whose logic runs, in degraded fashion, in the manner that the photographic or cinematic image does, by implant, manipulation of expectation, imaginary recognition, generated appetite. These models pretend to cite or incite the clichéd question, relevant to Mother or the sun, of what comes first, the model or the thing itself, the copy or the original. Or, as clearly emerges in the film's many appearances of chickens and eggs, what comes first altogether, the chicken or the egg: a chicken crosses the road and stops, causing a police car crash; there is a reference to the sky falling (Chicken Little); and eggs appear in all varieties as the egg thrown at the window in front of Robie's face, as quiche, as sunny-side up. The backlooped model, in which the chicken precedes the egg and breaks with generational logic, applies to travel folding as a mnemonic contrivance—like film. "Travel folder heaven" implies that whatever image one looks at and thinks beautiful had been promised in some memory implant; it comes out of a travel folder picture: it is what one has *already* been led to desire and then led to as if *re*cognize mechanically as "beautiful," without really reading or seeing it, and whether or not it is really there as predicted.[6] This entire logic is prefigured in the credit sequence to the first *Man Who Knew Too Much,* in which travel brochures are browsed through and selected from by a hand (and eye).

This *automotive* folding of the first car chase—which is also, in advance, catastrophic, like a *circus* that folds—implicitly bars a figure even like the "gaze" from ever instituting itself other than metaphorically. At the place we would least expect it, that of the passive aerial viewing *of* the car chase—touristic pleasure and consumption, when we think ourselves to imbibe the "beautiful" Riviera landscape—we are constituted by every variant of logic possible to read in the dissolving "gaze" of Norman.[7] This copying machinery presented as the "eye" pointedly eviscerates earth, even as the ride simulates a gourmet visual tour. It consumes that which it depends on or uses as ground or source of nutrients, reference, ingestion; it consumes, in advance, or eviscerates, the premises of "life," and not just on film.[8]

Now there is a politics here, and a "Resistance," at a certain rim of the archive, since the entire machinery of which this faux "present" is a product will have been, in a way, turned in advance against itself, suicided, autoimmolating in a pyrotechnic whiteout, like Robie's initial shotgun barrel in the faux suicide he stages, both pointed at and away from the camera.[9] As is routine in Hitchcock, the "cinematic" is turned against itself in a precessual "hunt" that may recur to the irreducible bar series, as in *Spellbound,* where the revolver is turned against Dr. Murchison's then camera eye.

Figure 24. Nice angle: shotgun (camera) turned toward camera.

As the narrative—which is preoccupied with clothes—approaches its moment of unveiling, Grant replies to Francie's question whether the Sanford gala will be dangerous with a dismissal: "Not for tourists." For the tourist viewers will not see or read what is at stake, even upside down, but discount everything with the epithet *light,* as in an inconsequential or marginal work. What appears a "beautiful" vision to the audience and to the Oscar-awarding academy is not only the case of an eye blindly retroprojecting over a dead and treeless signscape that it was trained to look for from a previous photo, a travel folder, but something more problematic. The tourists are blinded now, since what was in the travel folder, which is what they see, is not at all what is before them and the camera. The blind will have to be blinded again, as by a hot poker when pyrotechnics whites out the scene in a cold blaze. Or like "Mother's" cigarette ember in the hotel room. In what may be taken as an emblematic rebus for all of Hitchcock, *Mother* raises her cigarette while in conversation. We had just heard Hughson in the preceding scene baited for being the type who might steal an ashtray from a hotel, being a minor everyday thief rather than a professional. Mother looks around, the ashtray is missing.

Mrs. Stevens walks across the room and puts the cigarette out in a sunny-side-up egg. There is a split-second close-up, however, as the ember enters the running yolk. It shows "Mother's" hand extinguishing the hot poker into an egg, that is, putting out the egg as if *before* its advent (by Mother). The ocular egg resonates as a putting out simultaneously of the *eye*. And finally, perhaps most ruthlessly, it registers as a putting out of the *sun* as origin of light and cognition. The shot takes a second, yet in that intercut time it contaminates vast archival networks. With the lightest of touches, here literally, a chain of destructions is accomplished that alters the building blocks of institutional premises (the later pyrotechnic scene extends this *burnout* of the screen to the eye of the viewer). But this logic applies, too, to the tourist viewer of the panorama. What his or her eye is simultaneously blind to is that the landscape is practically treeless or lifeless, *burned* dry by a scorching sun, a sun that, rather than being a source of light and life, is now a black hole or cat. The desiccation of natural referents (trees) is inscribed in the barren landscape that seems at first meant to represent mimetic powers and representational purity and a caress of the earth at its most visually seductive: the earth or trees as origin and nature. Mrs. Stevens's cigarette shot is the quickest of detours yet, in a way, is never returned from. "Mother" puts out the egg, the eye, and the sun with one gesture.[10]

The posthistorial excess of simulacra on the Riviera is linked to the "origin" of the Stevens's jewels. This fortune, it turns out, was derived without labor or production. It is a black *gift* of oil discovered near an outhouse ("a little thing out back"). It equates diamonds with excrement, the dinosaur waste and carbon reserve from which diamonds compress. Oil suggests sheer anteriority, reserves from which all machines, including the cinematic, get their energy or "juice" (as *Sabotage* calls it). Much as Mrs. Stevens unexpectedly presents a charming variant of *Psycho*'s "Mother," this origin and reserve echo in advance Norman's car- and star-consuming *bog*. The bog is a site in which all may be dissolved yet not transfigured necessarily; inklike, it is perhaps first prefigured in

Figure 25. No ashtray: "Mother" extinguishes egg, eye, and sun.

*The Manxman*'s dissolve from a bubbling dark pool, receptacle for the heroine's would-be suicide, to the inkwell on the deemster's desk, from which a pen is drawn. The problem for Zizek is that of getting "beyond" not the "wall of language" but the rhetoric of ocularcentrism, the ghost of auteurism, the last refuge of auratic reading at its point of inversion or disappearance. Triflingly light, *To Catch a Thief* absorbs suns and origins like a black hole, triggers wormholes of historial time (the gala), misplaces a Mediterranean, and becomes a spectral zone of atomic and linguistic disruptions. It compels another look, another remarking.

# 9. Upping the Ante: A Deauratic Cinema

As Nietzsche put it, man is "a rope over an abyss," stretched between animal and "Übermensch" . . . Taut, tensed, that rope can be extended into a trapeze. The character played by Grant in *To Catch a Thief* is a veteran of the highwire.
—**Peter Conrad**

The O stands for nothing. Cinema is nothing but the rot of time. And yet cinema is everything, swallowing every other means of culture whole . . . Like the MacGuffin, the cinema is an index of what it destroys.
—**McKenzie Wark**

The chicken that causes a police car to crash into a wall on the way to the picnic scene in *To Catch a Thief* does so to get, famously, to the other side. The other side of what? The French cop explains the wreck to his superior on the wireless by yelling, "Poulet! Poulet!" Summoning the entire wiring of teletechnics, the clever tourist hears a remark about Francie (that she is what was called a tramp), as if that were the content, but the chicken in question imperiously looks back, stopped in the middle . . . Like stopping on a bridge, or like being born, as is said of Francie with a proliferation of *H*s: "in a taxi halfway between home and the hospital." How do we track a tele-archival shift that rests in between, in or as *media,* like one that extinguishes light, the eye, the *eidetic* as a temporarily imposed program (one, two millennia), revoked by the cinematic? What are the consequences if we concede to the networking of citations and punning cataphors the status of an underground life—a spies' post office? Moreover, in the travel service window a bohemian cartoon tells us conditionally, "If you love life, you'll love France." What is meant by *life*? By *love*? What is "France"? What does it mean for this black cat to be a thieving trace that moved behind each telekinetic medium—itself neither letteral nor pictorial? Why does Hitchcock's cameo here appear with so remarkable an insinuation, that this most trifling of works is explosive, like a nuclear bomb?

Such a pursuit requires not a major, serious "masterpiece," not a *Vertigo* or *Psycho,* say, covered with interpretive hieroglyphs, but perhaps a willfully minor or dismissed work to investigate, one deemed a trifle, ignored almost universally.[1] Thomas Leitch, like David Sterritt, annotates this long-standing dismissal with a redemptive and patronizing pat on the back:

> *To Catch a Thief* is widely and aptly considered a decorative trifle, its comedy agreeable but shallow. But the other films Hayes wrote for Hitchcock . . . (allow) us to see *To Catch a Thief* as marking one stage in a genuinely affirmative period, not simply as a temporary escape from Hitchcock's customary pessimism.[2]

Yet "Hitchcock" programs *all* of these occlusions, concealing this work's legibility like Cary Grant stepping into the shadows to avoid being seen by the police. It is in retraction, black against black. Anyway, things have become too light to know, here, what gravity is, where the "earth" as center may be. What does one do with a work, after all, in which Hitchcock will inscribe the predatory asolar tourist eye in a blind scorching of vegetation and earth, or a benign "Mother," blinding in a casual aside the sun, virtually, with a cigarette? The aerial eye, invisibly fed through memory loops and machines, cannibilizes its folds and travels. *It* is not terrestrial or "natural" or originary or solar. *It* does not posit an eye or a sun or even a mother quite. *It* performs, and decimates, a proactive tele-archive accelerated to consume its own premises. *It* exceeds any rhetoric of desire. *It* tells us: this is also "about" not postwar France or the fractalized "front" of an aged Western logos (solar, eidetic) but the cinematization of the global, its black hole and mobilizations. One could give it *one more fold,* and *up the ante,* as at a casino, by asking, what are we to do with a work that can appear, in an unexampled sense, beyond both mourning and ocularcentrism? Why is "time" its biggest problem, as Grant says? What occurs to gender or seduction, to love or "life," in this Zarathustran noon within Hitchcock's trajectory?

This last question reflects irresponsibility or light-headedness. I have great sympathy with natural resistances to it. It is a "resistance" that Cary Grant, in any event, is said to serve, to have served, in the Underground army of cinematic wraiths. Grant resists identification, pursues and is pursued as "the Cat." One would like to capture the Cat, this time, or his copy, it doesn't matter to Lepic, not the way one captures the Riviera landscape or a face with a picture, but the way one would, as *Secret Agent* attempts, isolate the secret agency of a trace that moves within cinematic surfaces and bands, mnemonic systems and visual effects, timescapes and wars and disasters. One could anticipate and even voice the objections to this approach, much as it responds to the edict of the work's title. For instance, assuming I can risk several replies as well:

*You are saying, then, that the travel service montage anatomizes the betraying logics of the image, is Hitchcock's storefront, even though that import alters the very model of reading by which the "canon" is stitched together?* Of course, look at it again, only not as its client. *And this window is displaying its own advertising logic as the underlying mnemonics that roosts in the afterlife of the "Riviera," cinemascape of this middle-earth?* Um-hmm. Doesn't Grant return in his next outing as an ad exec, and . . . *OK. But this is more puzzling: that your "Hitchcock" takes into account a fragmentation of language, you call it a "broken parole," that absorbs the histories of the Mediterranean logos?* Right—that can be shown easily (and your "Hitchcock" is thinking all of this, intervening in it?), if one has ears: moreover, this is nothing new, since in the British thrillers he isolates all teletechnic and linguistic media, from presses and teletypes to telephony and translation effects, letteral play and reading, and so on. Nothing new for him. *OK, which means what exactly, according to you: that the visual, as we call it, or even "pure cinema," as Hitchcock pretended to, never meant what we thought or even what we see, but rather is immersed in and produced by hypersthenic coils of signifying surfaces, almost prephenomenal (whatever that means) and that what you call the ocularcentrism that cinema has been held to serve (a sort of* service compris*) is and always has been betrayed, its eye put out as a telemnemonic effect, a legibility effect of sorts?* Yeah. And it is really almost a banality, in fact, and there from the beginning in Hitchcock. And admit it, there is something entirely unsurprising about H. choosing this work, essentially, this seeming "trifle" that no one will seriously address, to look the *sun* in the face, so to speak, to sponsor it almost on-screen, and determine it as prosthetic, pyrotechnics, even as it seems to put out the tourist eye. *Hmmm . . . let's go back . . . Travel folding? How is this teletechnic "Hitchcock" of yours different from other auteur concoctions, which you criticize, since in your version he knows too much, perhaps everything?* Well, maybe he is "born" in their incineration: there is no one in the agency storefront, just the display case and window, signs and reflections and frames and a close-up of a sketch with a text one must, as it were, read. This is also an accelerated logic of cinematic signature systems; what you call "Hitchcock," or ventriloquize, is just host to . . . *But this is not really what you were saying.* No? *No. You are saying that this work sucks up into its "light" mise-en-scène multiple historical lines and trace chains that it also extinguishes: the Mediterranean logos of its posthistorial, postwar debris.* Not only "postwar." *OK. . . . More: that this work can be viewed as tracking Hitchcock's intervention and the "global" media horizons to come. To catch a cat means, too, to capture whatever the image tries to capture, including its own logics, only to encounter a catlike trace that moves behind it all, desperately rewiring time lines. You see, you have me doing it. The story would be tracking its own simulacra, like "the cat" pursuing his own copycat. The work posits itself as an "an offer(ing) with everything," put on the roulette table at the casino—reaching back before the error of the book (there is a parabiblical reference to the dead father of Francie, one "Jeremiah") and beyond the "globalized" bubble that this cinematic mise-en-scène called Nice (and often, patronizingly, just by the English adjective "nice") drifts toward, like the mass beheading reserved for the costumed Bourbon court gathered, formalized, in the absurd expenditure and Hollywood robes attempting to recover and manufacture historical identity still at the gala?* Good, close enough: except that this mise-en-scène makes "light" too of its own apocalyptics, dismisses them, and here I'd risk noting that it warps into a kind of autosavaging time machine in the process, as if . . . *OK, enough. This is a game: take the lightest of works and show that it is the most important, and so on. Critic's delight. Vaporize a leading ideology (auteurism), only to reinscribe it. And so on.* Not exactly—and, in fact, not at all—since once the first move is made, the game board reorganizes itself within the archival. . . . *Oh yes, that is the "Benjaminian" connection, as you call it?* Well . . . Or "Hitchcockian," or . . . *But you neglect a small piece of your own logic.* That's right, but where does *this* thread lead? I did all this too quickly, like something to touch too lightly on—not, say, crash a cymbal over. Another fold is needed? Another twist of rope? So let me try this: the dilemma of why, in this most artificial of artificed works, a pyro*technic,* "nature" in the form of a landscape shot without humans seems more dawdled over than anywhere in Hitchcock. Here "earth" seems *caught* in the rectangular screen, like a thief, yet it appears more and more prosthetized, treeless, exposed as a site without direction or gravity exactly, whose burning consumption and evisceration seem in advance accomplished by the same prosthetic eye—not the lens, now, but our own—that would imagine it aesthetically beautiful, a point of travel. So we will start again, fold again, as an experiment of legibilities, and ask where the thread leads, or if a minotaur is already on hand. You will agree with me on the simplest point, almost inarguable, that there is a micrological dimension to Hitchcock's banded surfaces that takes account of its own violation of and production within competing archival histories and shifts, going backward and forward? *Wait. You say somewhere that Hitchcock incorporates a failed "scenes of instruction."* Often if not always. Not just by locations like the schoolhouse in *The Birds*, which will be emptied by the bird attack, but the numerous "professors" that crisscross the opus, including Professor Jordan of *The 39 Steps* or the bombmaker of *Sabotage*, Mr. Chatman (or "Cat man"). Here it may be "Professor Robie" but concerns, as noted explicitly, language lessons. *Why? What, yet again, but now in slow motion, as it were, has the "visual" in cinema to do with language lessons?*

Let us hypothesize that the "cat" names, among other things, a trace figure irreducible either to visual or aural terms. *To Catch a Thief* would appear an unguarded portal to its chambers of production and historial networking, like the visit to the taxidermists' shop in the second *Man Who Knew Too Much*. This is why the cameo is so somber, Hitchcock's eyes shut, lowered too close to the birdcage that cites the cinematic time bomb that the film is as zoographematic, totalizing. One could almost invent temporary rules of mapping this, such as the commentary on the phrase "travel folder heaven" begins to do. One would have to unpack phrases, connect rhymes and linkages, mobilize the motherboard of signature relays. And it would not depend on unpacking the occasional planted phrase in the spectral port of "Nice," such as when Grant quips that "building is *booming*," and we inversely hear reference to Verloc's cinematic bombings of structures, or when Francie observes of the Sanford gala to Robie that "everyone who *counts* will be there," marking the anapocalyptic gathering as one of sheer formalization drifting into numeration itself.

*To Catch a Thief* chases and performs a total eclipse on behalf of the cinematic gesture: in midcentury, in Hitchcock's midcareer, under a noon sun before the Mediterranean, medial. It takes a thief to catch a thief. "To catch a thief" also means: to arrest the logics of pictorial capture and as the historial capital gambled in Monaco's casinos at the teletechnic dusk of the West, which is at once the afterlife and pre-history of the "global" and postglobal. Or, how does one capture, or consume, pictorially, according to the inept Inspector Lepic, if the image is composed, instead, of betraying trace chains, citational formalizations, phonemes, archival avenging, something other than the touristic "eye" sees, yet by which it is cinematically preinhabited in any case, like a trance and trace, already thieving and consuming? If this occurs only within mnemonic orders, why does it ally itself to nuclear atomization, unsettling programs that order pasts and erase virtual futures? And again, why would "Mother" love this travel folder hell, consumer of histories and planetary life?

# 10. Hitchcock's Light Touch

The parasite would destroy the host without realizing it. Neither use nor exchange has value in its eyes, for it appropriates things—one could say that it *steals* them—prior to use or exchange: it haunts and devours them.
—Michel Serres, *The Natural Contract*

Every time I use the word cut . . . I mean a shot, a separate piece of film. And another piece of film that would be a cut would be a black cat slinking along the wall.
—Alfred Hitchcock, "On Style"

*To Catch a Thief* visually condenses and implodes, in the opening car chase, the ritual "chase" that Hitchcock deploys as a trope of the cinematic, miming, as he suggests in an interview, the mock continuity of the celluloid band. To curtail that chase (like the rooftop chase that begins *Vertigo*) positions the narrative as if "beyond" the former's machinal controls and pretenses. But the chase or hunt here accelerated to implosion had long also been the template for philosophical inquiry, for hermeneutic tracking, for a version of reading. That "chase," if left to run its own logics, would be quickly unhinged, doubled, or ritualized, as when the results are known and sought again and again: memory plants what it itself will, after the ritual of pursuit, pretend to find (again) and confirm. Like a travel brochure or an advertisement picture, or like Mr. Memory answering questions with known "facts" ("Am I right, sir?"). So Hitchcock redoubles it, again and at once, accelerating and short-circuiting it like a runaway train. The shotgun whose shot insinuates a faux suicide and facilitates Robie's escape from his villa, from "travel folder heaven," is pointed slightly away from the camera. The double chase short-circuits expectations of perception or reading, anticipating and suspending them, as when an original is pursuing or copying its copy: a copycat, say, who steals the original's mark and discloses the original to be a copy (already a simulacrum of thief) of *his* copy. The original "Cat," if there is such, must imitate himself to anticipate and catch his copycat, who in effect frames him. The feline "Grant" might even have his parole revoked—the status that lets him enjoy the fine taste displayed by his villa and refined life of semiretirement. Grant tells Bertani that these thefts all "bear my mark." He alone stands a chance of catching "this imitator" who can "imitate me so perfectly." The double chase folds back upon itself, suicites itself (the shotgun), and something else, all at once, emerges. Hitchcock understands "theft" as something preoriginary. Each character can be reconfigured as a thief, much as Robie tells the insurance agent, Hughson, that the latter is one because he has taken a hotel ashtray.

The cat is for Hitchcock an animeme and animated shade that threads diverse semaphoric logics: it prowls or traverses frames, including temporal networks. Numerous cats explode out of the dispossessed "house" of *Number 17* and as a "word" ("the word 'cat,'" says Danielle) it bears the 13 signature *(C, A)*. One might track *it* by unpacking how the visible is betrayed and revealed as a scorching and consuming prosthesis in the seemingly innocent panorama, displayed as a mnemonic disaster in the midst of its ritual pleasuring and touristic trance in travel folder heaven. To further unpack the last line of the work with its anticipation of "Mother's" coming, that Mother "will love it up here," one must be alert to the implications of the black cat. It appears prephenomenal

Figure 26. Travel service window: "If you love life, you'll love France!"

yet actively gambles with the teletechnic structures of history, form, memory, and as the panorama suggests, the experience of earth. In this way, which infects the logic of global advertisements and mass tourism, the work unexpectedly continues and glosses where the British espionage films have the cinematic anarchists and usurpers threaten a cataclysmic alteration of history. I propose to highlight this tapestry before returning to the gala scene. What is called the cat is one name for a black hole within representational systems.

Unobserved through the apotropaic "lightness" of the work, the cat cites and precedes the "origin" of the Western logos. The classical Mediterranean setting invokes Greek architectural origins and ghosting allusions to disenfranchised gods like Hephaestus (Foussard's limp) or Prometheus, who stole fire (and gave mortals language) or Cyclops. Yet this circling back before the *Ursprung* of the West is undone by the same feline logic that exposed the "original" cat. Theft, preoriginary, would be rooted in mimesis, in copying: "I have to catch this imitator myself." The travel service window appears as a con, a criminal front luring tourists to be robbed. There is no human in the window. It is rather like what Mrs. Stevens encounters, in a light machinal form, in the hotel casino. She has already complained of the French custom of *service compris,* in which the tip is included in the bill, whether you want to pay one or not. She also carps about the cinematic roulette wheels. They always win, she says, so she might as well just "mail" the money in. It is a "whirling pickpocket," like the projector reels. A vertigo swirl resonates in this phrase or image, which partakes of recurrent uses of the word fragment or term *pick* (Lepic, pick up, pick out, picnic). Hitchcock uses this technique of repetition to isolate key phonemes. A "whirling pickpocket" appears tied to the effects of rapidly generated pieces of celluloid. It steals by virtue of coming up in its whirling cast with ever differing combinations—of numbers, of ideas, of where the black marble lands, of identifications with actors, or of the generated reference. What *whirls,* too, is the chance combinatoire of the wheel that renders, in its spin, the copy in advance of the "original" that must copy it—together with the singularity of any reading event. Wherever the ball stops, different trace chains appear, different figures are networked, yet they are as if stations in a descending maelstrom, in which chance also appears fixed. That is, like the light and frivolous Riviera, whose privileged tourists represent a doomed economic cadre drifting in costume toward a sort of historial beheading. This is implied in the gala scene, where so many guests arrive as costumed citations of royalty in prerevolutionary

France, a clear, and doomed, relapse. And yet the roulette wheel is a pickpocket, reaching into faux interiors to despoil, to pick out or picture, to turn inside out any imaginary reserve.

One can use the "whirling pickpocket" as a principle of reading to break the blind or spell of this *too light* work.

## Travel Folder Hell Redux: "The Mediterranean *Used* to Be This Way"

> In this realm, transfer tickets are of no avail. Within the confines of a system of transportation—or of language as a system of communication—one can transfer from one vehicle to another, but one cannot transfer from being like a vehicle to being like a temple, or ground.
> —Paul de Man

The travel service window offers a misleading *service compris,* of course, in which *compris* must be heard epistemically *(comprendre).* The glass window reflects another scene than what is displayed behind it, namely, a street with slow traffic moving in both directions. Glass, another trope for diamonds, is not a transparent medium. Across the street one can just make out a ghostly movie marquee. The display itself appears cut by an inverse shadow pointing like an arrow in the conceit of a direction—that, say, of reading conventionally, left to right. The traffic may be tropological, the choking excess of metaphoric sense or even citations. Yet the marquee itself cites *Sabotage's* Bijou (the jewels that will be stolen by the copycat in any case). Verloc's movie house would be blown up in a suicide bombing by the anarchist named after a cat, Chatman. Tania Modleski notes of tourism that "Hitchcock exhibits the utmost contempt for tourism—and most especially for what one might call cinema as tourism" (104). Yet it is not clear that there is any alternative, or if the epistemology of tourism is not automatically inscribed in memory programs. Tourism is invited, solicited, doubled, and, immediately after the credit sequence, despoiled, like a rape or a murder or a theft, with the shriek of a grotesque middle-aged American woman, face white with cold cream. The first spoken words of loss: *"My jewels!"* What totality has been, already, vacated, like the jewel box that looks like an emptied theater? What is intended by this anachronization of *The Lodger's* opening if silent scream, transposing a "golden curled" blonde to a middle-aged grotesque tourist, troping the lapsed history between them, or condensing this theft to the advent of the cinematic, now grotesque in its pointless affluence?

The travel agency window does not have photographs. Rather, it uses iconic models and cartoon sketches, graphics, turning at the end to a seemingly breezy and vapid handwriting simulating French *esprit*. In the postwar moment cinema has entered the too light mode of *mass tourism*. Advertisement derives its promise from clichés, from superficial or void associations, and these, in canceling their own semantic content, break into graphic units with shadow implications: "If you love life, you'll love France." The entire montage of a montage, a sort of thieving demontage that Sterritt utterly mistakes for documentary style (it is *not* what it says, *not* what it is, *not* what it displays) is a lethal allegory. And it departs, too, from a covert citation that returns to the figure of travel folding examined decades before: the credit sequence of the first *Man Who Knew Too Much*.[1] In that early work the topos of "knowing (too much)" receives a discrediting commentary: appearing merely to tell the viewer "where" one is traveling to in that film, a hand reaches from a pile of travel brochures to pick out a cinematic destination. There are many possible choices. We only see the hand and are, technically, in the position of the headless browser. But the hand itself holds attention, gathering into its agency of technicity and writing all the invisible processes and powers that deliver the scene to the eye. The final pick is of a brochure for Griesalp, St. Moritz, from which the cover photo will be replicated in the opening shot of the narrative, *as if* moving from photo to the real, ignoring that the latter is still only another, unmoving moving photo. The skit illuminates what knowing too much about "knowing" signifies. It traps the tourist viewer and announces what follows to be an anatomy of this sight-enforcing and -effacing mnemonic trap. Cinema knows too much about how little cognition knows: the eye as epistemological tourist travels from out of a preinscribed image (anticipated, advertised), which will be again sought out or consumed circularly, so that when one arrives there (Griesalp) one is still finding what had been preimplanted; indeed, one had not left that "image" either, in which case it, too, was a fake lure. This is one faux solar trap that Peter Lorre's Abbott will assault from behind the false temple of sun worshippers (which lures cinemagoers seeking illumination). Lorre's white streak of hair, marking him with a cinematic alternation of *black-white-black*, returns in *To Catch a Thief* and is given the wine steward Foussard, who has a Hephaestus-like limp. The viewer or "public" is snakebit. She is promised only iconic models of the Eiffel Tower, glamour, love, indeed, life itself, down to the cartoon sketch declaring, "If you love life, you'll love France." What is here called "life," on the screen, a graphic effect or animation of sorts, does not represent but preinhabits the living. The cartoon advertises in the mode of autoscopic kitsch a self-disowning promise: "life" is a semaphoric or cinematic effect, accelerated and recombinant, as that comes into cognitive traffic, "experience," teletechnic currency. It is a variant on whatever would have been termed preoriginary death, out of the Underground or underworld of inscription from which *phanesthai* spectrally takes forgetful shape. "France" is the land of cinematic signscapes hyperbolized by the Gallic black cat—prowling shadow, preoriginary copy of a copy. In question, though, is "love."[2]

The cited activation of complex puzzles from earlier works testifies to the movement of the black cat, before picturing, before identification, before syllables form, and what will be called the work's broken *parole,* the fragmenting of language and the rebuke of the representational contract betrayed, already, in the advertising logics of the solicitous window with its reflections of another scene. Hughson visits Robie's villa after the extravagent scene at the Nice flower market, which has Grant being drowned in cut flowers and finally restrained by an old hag holding his elastic sleeve around a tree trunk. Grant tells Hughson on the telephone earlier that he will be the one tossing a coin—a single token, like a black marble, used in *Secret Agent.* The circulated coin, like Robie's parole, has become worn, light as air, but tropes a flat disk, an eclipse. The mention of a broken parole in the context of "language lessons" warns us how fragments of words circulate (letters, syllables, phonemes) in this Mediterranean signscape, and on the *state* of the logos as such.

I have given an example of when Hughson praises Grant's villa as a "sort of travel folder heaven." The word *folder* is broken and re-marked a moment later, when Robie explains his origin as a thief to the insurance agent. That is, again, both Robie's as a jewel thief and Cary Grant's as a screen actor, what can be called a thief as a simulacrum absorbing the emotions and identifications of anonymous strangers with no return. Invoking the figure of Handel Fane from *Murder!,* a "half-cast(e)" transvestite acrobat—at once in and out of the cinematic role, frame, or effacing any outside in a *casting* of chance without safety net—he began his work as a trapeze artist for "an American *circus traveling* in Europe" which then "folded." The reference draws another pretense of origin into the narrative, here of the artifice named "Cary Grant," who as Archibald

Leach was a circus acrobat when discovered by Mae West. This will have the effect of inscribing "him" wholly in the work, much as Grace Kelly will be or even Jessie Royce Landis's Mother ("Nobody calls me 'Jessie' anymore"). The figure of a *traveling circus,* moreover, is one Hitchcock uses to name the cinematic operation or trajectory in its entirety, with the "circus" resonating not just with entertainment and caricatured performances but the ring or circuitry of a certain recurrence to which the reel testifies most literally. This circular consumption or precession of referential origins for the "real" actors, let alone the characters, will inform the loss of gravity and referential ground that the logic of the narrative mimes at the outset: the original "Cat" copying himself to catch a copycat thief who has taken over his identity, making him a copy.

And yet if a crease or fold inhabits travel folder heaven, a fold that is one of memory checking back on its original, it undoes temporality as well. The word *time* recurs the most in the dialogue, and, again, Grant remarks, "The biggest problem is time!" Moreover, "to fold" is a trope for collapse. The circus folded, much as Grant will be arrested in the flower market amidst a sheer excess of cut flower emblems, empty semantic props miming the ejaculating excess of Foussard's champagne bottle on first seeing Grant.[3] Travel folder heaven, momentarily, takes on another turn. It is entrapping and it folds; it registers an afterlife of endless recurrence, cinema installed as a permanent cognitive model and blind, as in the age of telemarketing ads. "France" is its treacherous product and map, yet "France" also names the posthistorial signscape of the Mediterranean basin after "the war." It links the faux bliss of the cinematic trance when fed images to delight (the Riviera, Cary in a tux) to an afterworld that mnemonically enfolds, a trap, a labyrinth without exit, a travel folder hell.[4] This afterlife is not just of the screen since it accords with the historical postwar world of expenditure and affluence, of circulation and consumption without production, of the cinematic and gambling *Riviera* as template of media totalizations to come.

All of this oscillates in and around the cameo of Hitchcock that marks the work as a time bomb, like Verloc's. It is as explosive in ways that, with whatever lethal "light touch," will be allied explicitly to a nuclear blast and tied to a broken logos and fragmentation of words into sounds.[5]

In view of this parallel, Grant's link to the Resistance, not to mention the "Underground army," is marked. Hughson notes that Grant, playing Robie playing "Grant," was "a celebrity of the Underground

Figure 27. Foussard happy to see "Cary Grant."

army." Grant takes exception to being lumped in with a platoon of other Hollywood screen wraiths and mere actors. He explains more succinctly: he was in "the Resistance." For Grant to be in the "Resistance" marks the peculiar power he wields for Hitchcock, starting with *Suspicion,* where he is used in an experiment to withdraw all aura or identification from the familiar face, to fragment it by disconnected mugging into automated parts, to annul readability and insinuate, properly, the import of betrayal and murder, not with this one "face," but with *face* itself. But that same resistance to what "Cary Grant" as product advertises locates him as "the Cat," a thieving animeme essentially neither identifiable nor necessarily human. The *Oxford English Dictionary*: "1., *resistere,* f. *re-* Re- + *sistere,* redupl. of *stare* stand," a standing back or against that reduplicates itself in and as staring. Grant resists the audience's identification with him or its ejaculation over him—as he waves his finger scoldingly at Foussard. They do not know even what gender he is playing, and he resists the mimetic regime or the police from whom he is fleeing. As a name *Inspector Lepic* resonates as a *pic*torial logic, which would like to catch or enframe Grant. As a star Grant is a "celebrity" of the underworld—a thief of audience identification, a simulacrum absorbing projections suctioned into a nonresonant space. The photokleptic gang of thieves and killers from the Underground all are employed by Bertani's restaurant—the cinematic kitchen that Bertani says "works like a machine," just like Resistance work in "the old days."[6] What is meant by "*old* times"?

The "whirling pickpocket" lands on a frame, a syllable. If the "whirling *pickpoc*ket" empties folds or pockets, it also absorbs whatever would

Figure 28. Limping Foussard (black-white-black) and Bertani in cinematic kitchen—"cutting, slicing."

delimit the historial and referential status of this Riviera, which is called at one point "Europe's lighter side." Diverse senses of *fold,* for instance, are activated at once, as collapse and as crease or mnemonic relapse. Machinal, there is nothing travel folder hell cannot absorb in its folds, welcome, solicit as sense or historial dossier, as a mobile black hole or thieving cat. It is not that it can cite another work and ricochet from there, laterally, into yet another trace chain or network embedded in "old times." It absorbs the historial folds it is produced by and within, and empties them, until the entire trajectory that moves into a more and more formal itinerary turns up at the Sanford gala at the end. This *formalization* is plainly indicated when Grant, pointing at his striped jersey, asks Lepic's permission in the opening scene at the villa to retreat to his room to slip into something "more formal" to make his escape as the faux suicide of the camera as shotgun goes off, puncturing the scene with a vicarious report and camera shot that evacuates identity and turns the barrel against the camera itself.

The mise-en-scène is located thus in what Hughson, when offered wine at the villa, calls the middle of the day: "No, no, no, no, my dear fellow—not in the middle of the day." Middle of a century, middle of a life and career, midtrajectory of cinema, a certain or putative noon that is without shadow, a Zarathustran resonance neither arbitrary nor casual. What is in the middle, too, in suspense yet suspending touch, is something like glass, a medium, telemedia as such. And all of this in the lushly dry setting of Nice, a word-name diverted throughout to numerous puns on *nice* (in which *ice* is, in Grant's pointed renditions, stressed

Figure 29. Robie leaves to slip into "something more *formal*."

and as if negated).[7] Rather than the ski jump of Louis Bernard, a graphic fall across whiteness precipitating the first *Man Who Knew Too Much* followed its travel brochure opening, and rather than the pattern of "tracks" in the snow that network *Spellbound's* "photophobia," what is called "warm, friendly France" in the Riviera occurs as the horizontal melt-off of all Alpine ice, its crisscrossing of reflective waters erasing once frozen tracks as soon as they are made. Robie offers to "teach" Francie waterskiing, which she declines by saying, "I was women's champion at Sarasota." He then uses the word *nice* to describe the scene: "You know, the *sun* and all." Two pairs of skis leaning against the bathhouse emphasize this point as Grant emerges to find his "real estate" list, in his jacket pocket, with a wet fingerprint on it—the trace of a contact, a pilfering. Nice, *Nizza,* is in a sense both with "too much" sun, almost like the next film's blindingly solar Morocco, with too much lightness, and yet *sans soleil.* And, to be sure, without gravity or *gravitas.* Here, one does not know, nonetheless, where the ground is. As Kelly comments in the hotel lobby, "The Mediterranean"—that is, middle-earth—"*used to be this way.*"

What occurs in the graphics of the aerial panorama is mirrored in Lepic's chasing Robie: that is, the mimetic frame of the pictorial shot pursues, tries to capture and contain, the black trace or spot on the highway, only it is already "two," hunter and chased, the entire hermeneutic machine. The "double chase" is turned back on Inspector Lepic, police bureaucrat who seeks, and incompetently defers, like the police airplane later, the trace that in fact constitutes its fabric and possibility. The aerial scene—without people and without apparent set except for the earthscape and the cars—appears as seamless as a documentary segment. Thus this folding back, now, folds, collapses in the second sense used of the traveling circus. It manifests sight as itself mechanical and blinded in its scorching consumption of a predicted yet now entirely absent "beauty," drawing on the credit sequence of the first *Man Who Knew Too Much.* It is a bare "documentary" if anything, that is, *of* the machinery of allegorical devastation and autocannibalism of the eye, an earth, and telemnemonics in the "planetary" era of mass—and post—ocular tourism.

It is not that "time" as such is registered as manipulable, compressed or prolonged, backlooped, and so on, by the cinematic cut. That is a given. It is not just *a* problem, it is the "biggest problem." *Time* is the single most frequent word in the film. It is a problem not just for Robie staying out of prison for his broken parole, but because the cinematic loop has stumbled, at the *Mediterranean,* into the omphalos of time lines and gotten entangled. One no longer knows what is up or down, where middle-earth is or was, the black hole or cat has preceded and superseded the Greco-Roman logos, itself a broken *parole,* landing in the American tourist mediascape on the Riviera. The Oscar for cinematography is awarded to Hitchcock, once again for appearing, for once, not to be "Hitchcock," for having fallen outside of the sheer artifice for which he is perhaps resented just a bit, with his labyrinthine sets. And when he does go for that this time, it will be at the phoniest of all his sets ever, the Sanford gala, which will seem to his stars and crew (according to Spoto) to have no import whatsoever and perhaps to mock itself with the extravagance of its pointless expenditure and unimaginative period costumes. Finally, one is asked to read the panorama *and* the gala through one another's logics: they are the same. For if what the viewer sees of the Riviera landscape is heralded as "beautiful," as later the picnic spot is by Grace Kelly ("Have you ever seen anyplace in the world *more* beautiful?"), it would seem a matter of seduction as such, the work's leitmotif that crystallizes in the fireworks scene. They think Hitchcock has buckled, "gone Hollywood," yielded to the natural and the visual, even as he will be caught famously on the set, seeming to be asleep while the shoot proceeds—and all of this, for such a light-headed work. They will have caught him—finally.[8] In fact, when we later almost look directly into a blinding sun, even it will be sheer artifice—a blinding *pyrotechnic,* in fact.

Hitchcock will liken the consumption of "life" by the eye to that of food by teeth or the ingestions of the mouth. The credit sequence of *Vertigo* tracks up the woman's face from the lips before collapsing into the mobile mnemographs of her nervous eye or pupil. Bertani describes his kitchen, which produces superb food and confections for its public, in entirely cinematic terms. It is surrounded by glass. He asks Robie what he thinks: "Works like a machine, yes? Just like our little band in the Underground during the war . . . cutting, slicing. Just like the old days." The cutting and s(p)licing is unmistakable. It is a matter of "our little band" and is marked by similitudes ("just like") and referenced to a sort of absolute anteriority ("the old days," "old *times*"). Differently, "Robie's" remark to Hughson about Germaine's quiche, that it is as "light as air," emphasizes an annihilation again preceding origins: "She strangled a German general once, without a sound." But the *parole* breaks yet again, this time the name *Germaine*. A cluster of generative figures recur: *Germaine, German, general*, as if origin is evoked and self-canceled in advance, like "Mother" putting out her cigarette in a sunny-side-up egg. The cinematography that both celebrates and betrays participates in a cryptonymic and performative evisceration of any trope of nature, of trees, of reference, of represented earth. As "Mother" remarks to "Conrad Burns," "There's not much lumber around here." In our first glimpse of Robie he is clipping flowers. Germaine, personification of "service," first appears on the villa's terrace, back to us, her broad form crossed with a giant *X* from her apron.

One sees how a certain lightness or loss of gravity suffuses or occasions a disorientation, simultaneously too much in the sun yet therefore withdrawn, as into dark pockets or recesses. A madness of the day. Time and again, we rise to rooftops with Cary Grant, looking down, or to cliffs, peaks that, rather than seeming profound, appear arrayed in what are gambled as long shots. This loss of *gravitas* mocks and permeates everything: Robie's occupation of "raising grapes"; references to "making up" or "turn up" or "giving up"; his tossing the coin in the air at the flower market; being "light as air"; the game of hackysack played before the Sanford villa by the two police trailing Robie—kicking a ball, back and forth, keeping it *up* against gravity. The phrase *"light touch"* problematizes *touching*, both as thieving pickpockets and as epistemological contact, to say nothing yet of sexual contact or penetrating glass. Hughson signals Robie in front of Mrs. Stevens in the hotel that he wants to talk shop, and reminds him that they spoke of going "up—up—up . . . the funicular railway." Grant counters, "I can't even spell *funicular.*" The rope-inflected etymology of *funicular* inscribes the cinematic trope in a hyperbolic and vertical direction—in a parlor-room aside, *To Catch a Thief* is marked as more profound than *Vertigo,* if it could stop from floating away, "light as air." "Here," at the heart of old rituals of *mimetic* consumption by the "copycat" ("perfect imitation," "imitator," "imitate me so perfectly," "they're imitation"), the wheel has gone into forward reverse, like the brake pulled by the carousel attendant in *Strangers on a Train* when it has accelerated out of bounds, the centripetal counterforce spinning it off its base with furiously grimacing horse figures flying about.

One is in an economy entirely of service industries: insurance, restaurants, catering, gambling, hotels, police, that is, all theft and circulation *without production*. But what is less apparent, with all of this lightness, is that the mise-en-scène seems imperceptibly positioned over a titanic site of mourning—or rather, stands mercurially and deanthropomorphically *beyond mourning*.[9] Or lamentations.

Which seems to be why the name Jeremiah is introduced. It is the name of Francie's dead father, of "Mother's" absent husband, he who would die before the fortune arrived that would buy the numerous jewels and the travel. It is a biblical name, an author associated with the Book, even if one that already was bound, even so, to a sort of wild mourning. In this postwar and posthistorial setting, a background of vast if covert absence is touched on, almost in passing, and again with a too light, vertiginous touch. Mrs. Stevens is tipsy before retiring in the hotel. She is wistful for "Jeremiah." It should be obvious by now that every time an "origin" is invoked it is compulsively exposed, canceled in advance. Grant from a circus? Folded. Mother's egg? Snuffed. A German general? Strangled by Germaine. The sun? A pyrotechnic. The Mediterranean logos? Hephaestus is a gimpy wine steward. But it doesn't stop there, even the mourned Jeremiah, if mourned he is, he of the Book, will prove later to have been, as Mother says, a con man by trade, though a lovable one. Even to signal that this *too light* work and derivative "trifle" is drunk on its own mourning is deranging. But this time it is the "origin" of the Stevens fortune that is in question. Mother will declare her diamonds mean nothing and are only a means of traveling (like "a train ticket"). The family discovered oil near their outhouse. This fact is quite explicit, and as she says it Grant muffles a laugh. "No plumbing—a little place out back." Then the clincher: "Jeremiah didn't know how close he came" to the wealth he sought. This reverse liquefaction of diamonds to oil, a fossil-waste product, again found and not produced, the substance that makes machines (cars) run, is linked in turn to *excrement*: that is, the trace of sheer anteriority, the black sun, sheer sound, materiality, "the cat." In Hitchcock's hypertext it has an abyssal resonance ("up-up-up"): it is a forerunner of Norman's bog, to which cars are returned with stolen fortunes and blondes in them, a black hole or morass of disaggregated marks or letters in turn. It is pointedly affiliated, along another set of wires, with the chocolate factory of *Secret Agent,* a work cited obsessively and obliquely, tattooed across the Zarathustran Nizza.

As a prophet of diaspora and the destruction of the Temple, Jeremiah calls himself one without speech, an infant ("I do not know how to speak; I am only a child"), and is one whom Yahweh authorizes to destroy ("I give you authority over nations and over kingdoms . . . to destroy and demolish" [Jeremiah 1:6, 10]). He is not only the avenger of exile but medium of the abyssal rants of Lamentations. It insinuates a rogue and limitless lamenting of and by the cinematic Riviera, disguised in its affluence, itself a desert of destructions like the references to the recent war and its recent dead—which was nothing less than the "end" of a certain Europe. It laments the histories gathered at Nice that underpin its "lightness," its absence from itself, the false suicide, or the film's own lack of regard as a "Hitchcock" oeuvre. Yet in lamenting itself simulating lamentation, *To Catch a Thief* cites the ruins it enacts and records. "He never knew how close he came to twenty million barrels of oil." The cinematic and excremental discovery of oil displaces the paternity of the biblical prophet the way the cat or bar does the legacy of the Book. Indeed, the prophet turns out to have been another faux performer, a literary hack or "swindler." This is marked too by contact with a sheer excess of *bar*(rel)s, or the bar series, of sheer anteriority and the prehistorial fossil waste of all that informs writing, transport, machinery, acceleration, diamonds. Deceased nonfather, abdicated in advance and a con man, associated nonetheless with excrement, with nescience ("[he] never knew"), his name returns spectrally in a world in which women seem to rule: Grant will be led into the gala in blackface, dressed as a parasol-carrying eunuch attending the Stevens women. And it is Danielle Foussard who is unmasked as the copycat finally. Jeremiah's "little place out back" is in a nonplace. *This* Jeremiah is dead and was anyway a simulacrum later disclosed, by Mother, to have been an "operator." How to mourn this, if it breaks all lines of imagined legacies and paternity within the family plot? The complex suggests exile without home, for which lamentation or even mourning is a front. Thus he is also wildly replicable, multiple, as when Mrs. Stevens refers to not exchanging something for "a *hundred thousand* Jeremiahs."

The cinematic Riviera is not of but beyond mourning, no more capable of mourning than prehistorial birds that attack or than Mrs. Bates. The lightness of the Riviera takes a dark turn, if the black cat had not warned us of this in its nighttime prowl, black on black, proceeding through some technical acceleration beyond historial markers.[10]

The biblical *pater* "Jeremiah" is left as a swindling trace, another cat. A virtual faulting of time and historial warping will appear to be, by the gala sequence, all but induced, like a caesura collapsing historial time posts in a scene in which the "biggest problem is time." It is not that "modernity" is itself a cinematized product and fiction, but that even this is fiction at risk in a Riviera that finds its closest historical analog, if the gala is to be trusted, in a pre-Revolutionary costumed simulacrum of the Bourbon court drifting toward mass beheading, or cutting floor, to which it is oblivious. The work mourns, if anything at all, the future that it consumes or implies the consumption of as a totality. What latent funicular signifiers might one have to activate to regard *To Catch a Thief* as covert jeremiad—bird attacks on already vanished auras, anthropomorphisms, and ontological phantoms?

The work takes place at a *meridian,* in and as a medial logic, the Mediterranean, "in the middle of the day." The earth too is an effect of "the cat," animated, mediatized. The "broken *parole*" names not only the broken oath of the betraying image, like the travel service window's lethal front, but a suspension of definition and gravity. The cat is deauratic, not even terrestrial. It is here, without direction, that one might enter the hotel casino and gamble, with alternative futures, with "old times." *To Catch a Thief* is as if suspended crossing the road, like a chicken. It departs from recesses, black traces ambling rooftops, the outside of the *house*—like the tiled roofs and gutters of the Sanford villa where the encounter of the two cats will finally occur, a dubious sort of disrobing. The *cat* crosses rooftops, networks all telekinetic media and *architecture,* cases the joint, moves across gutters or peaks, becomes a gloved hand or *technē* reaching under pillows with sleeping heads on them, as if into ears or mnemonic programs. The first shot of Grant outside clipping flowers is framed by a window and from within, a perspective allied with Robie's black cat sitting on a newspaper on a couch.

### Finishing School: "I'm Very Good at Secrets"

> The word cat is not only the nonexistence of the cat, but a nonexistence made word, that is, a completely determined and objective reality.
> —Maurice Blanchot

> "The word *cat* is a noun."
> "Not the way you use it."
> —*To Catch a Thief*

A black cat appears on a chair, walking over roofs, scratching news-paper print. The cat is woven into chains of animemes, like the tele-pathic dog in *Secret Agent*. It is all feet or legs, heir to the black sun figure or the chocolate or obliterating sound in the last-mentioned film. It will momentarily "act like" a word—"The word *cat* is a noun," Robie reminds Danielle. It will also act as a sort of anagrammatic fractal dispersed across signifying networks: in the title ("*Cat*ch"), in *Ca*ry Gran*t*'s name, in his hissing pronunciation ("the l*i*st") or purring his dialogue ("*per*fect"). Danielle's "language lessons" referred to during the boat ride with Robie suggest a defaced scene of instruction about linguistic effects in cinema, like mention of breaking one's *parole*. As in *Secret Agent,* there is mention of language lessons, only this time in the past tense:

DANIELLE: You only taught me the nouns. I learned the adjectives myself.

ROBIE: The word *cat* is a noun

DANIELLE: Not the way you use it. For you it means excitement, dan-ger, affluence. What do you think of that word, *affluence*? It means "wealth."

ROBIE: What's on your mind?

DANIELLE: Nothing. I was just thinking about you.

ROBIE: School's open again. Professor Robie will now conduct a class in bad manners—or how to get spanked in a hurry.

DANIELLE: You can't touch me, I've graduated.

We can put to the side, for now, the entire invocation, and breaking off, of teaching or schooling, echoed elsewhere, as in Francie's "finish-ing school" or Mother's threat to send her back "to school." We will also bracket the ceaseless class warfare motif, the totalized premise that *all* property (including semantic) is theft, since both are subsumed by a more formal historial horizon linked to the "service" of teletechnics. Robie had speculated on what would occur if he broke his parole and observes, simply, that "they'll throw away the *key*." After all, it is a parole that gives Grant a certain freedom, he observes, to pursue what he calls "good taste" at his villa. Danielle recalls how Robie and "the boys" got this parole when their prison was "bombed" by the Germans: they es-caped, then joined the Resistance. Freedom, *la liberté,* so dear to France, nation of the free, begins with the parenthesis of a (cinematic) bomb or shock. Danielle continues to allude to "pardons that are not worth anything" and is corrected:

GRANT: They weren't pardons, they were paroles.

DANIELLE: Those paroles don't have much value today.

GRANT: At least they haven't been withdrawn from circulation.

What the film calls "breaking parole," however, is carried out surgically as well, by a virtual dismemberment of language into parts. Departing from discussion of "the word *cat*," we hear of words without "value" if in "circulation," words used as "playthings" or which are exchangeable in the casino for chips ("if you'd rather not take my word for it"). Robie's parole is a contract, alleged by Hitchcock, whose trust the lady gambler can (and perhaps should) discount, but she can only publicly disrobe and have her dismembered body parts put on display to review it, which is too disrobing. "Nouns" and "adjectives" are mentioned; Francie speaks of Robie and Danielle "conjugating irregular verbs"; there is reference to spelling ("I can't even spell *funicular*") as well as grammar (Francie's difference from Mother is "just a few years and some grammar"). This, while all along English is dislocated by spoken French, and vice versa, promoting a gap mimed in a visibly disjunct lip-synching, most explicitly for Bertani, who is, as Danielle says, ultimately "behind it." Mother advises Francie to "practice your apologies in two languages." Hitchcock breaks this *parole* literally and in all variations.

The classical Greek *logos* subsists in the fourfold elements: earth, fire (the pyrotechnics), water, and air. All are cited by the camera. Robie, who flies up to rooftops, is said by Mother to be a man with both "feet on the ground" who nonetheless protests like Chicken Little that "the sky is about to fall in on me." The sun will appear as a sputtering night-time sparkler. The term *logos* is folded into cut logs, trees, or *phusis,* defaulted figures of "natural" reference and genealogy, coolly burned away, mass-cut by "Conrad Burns."[11] But this European logos in free-fall evaporation appears as a *Herald Tribune* column. The paper is on a chair with Robie's black cat in the first visit to the villa. The camera closes in and we *read* a gossip column called "Europe's Lighter Side" about Robie and "the cat's" escapades, and Hollywood types pretending to promote their films while touring Europe to accumulate tax write-offs. "Europe's Lighter Side," like "light as air" or "light touch," puts *lux* in suspension. The lighter side or edge of Europe is on the Mediterranean, yet it is connected to the black cat. The latter's scratchings—slashes, notches, marks—are seen on the page amidst print and letters, *logoi,* the sheer circulation of gossip. "Art Buchwald" disintegrates the borders of "real" names and simulation. The signature breaks, affiliating an aesthetic effect (Art) with the cat scratches or letters and invoking books (the German *Buch*) in association with, or derived from, forests or woods *(Wald)*, as paper is. The shot dissolves the technicity of "book" into its pulp, pages whose very production consumes the absent forests the camera re-marks, burns away.

The viral cat seems to traverse and displace temporal maps. It spares nothing: generations, the sun, Mother, the specter of cinema. The ghostly marquee reflected in the travel service window returns. First the reflection yields the word itself, and then Hitchcock breaks that into its components: as when it is said that the robberies all have Robie's "mark" or that the "key" will be thrown away if he breaks his parole. Then almost showing his hand he reconfigures it monstrously in the name of the boat in which "language lessons" are discussed by what turns out to be the two cats, Robie and Danielle, the original and the copy. The morphing of a shadow on the language class is, momentarily, explosive, cutting off one of the more poignant origins the work might seek—what might be called cinema's own.[12]

The boat whose engine will be cut has the impish name of *Maquis Mouse,* as we are given to see briefly. Maquis—a guerrilla fighter in the French Underground—morphs into *marquis,* a noble represented in costume at the gala, or in turn *marquee.* The *Maquis Mouse* inscribes animation as cinema in the logics of a postwar or representational Resistance. This returns us to the cartoon sketch in the window, to what it insinuated by the word *life.* In a scene that systematically precedes its own prosthetic origins or originals, this trope contains and encircles the cinematic itself—what is situated within a figure of animation that the echo of the movie "marquee" recalls, joining the two words *(mark, key)* in an exceptional inflection. Here the whole premise of mimetic representations (copy) is preceded by graphics, the rapid mobilization of inanimate markings, cartoons, such as "Steamboat Willie," Disney's original Mickey Mouse, precursor of cinema. *Animation* occupies an exceptional logic: virtually digitalized, nonmimetic, the effect of speed,

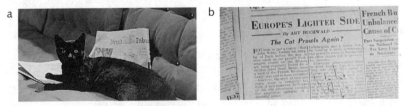

Figure 30. (a) Black cat rests with print media; (b) claw marks marr Buchwald.

pregenerator of "life" as an effect ("If you love life . . ."), it is what Robin Wood reflects Hitchcock's work is, in its way, closest to simulating by its sheer artifice. But the encapsulating citation inverts the container for the contained, the pursuer for the pursued: the would-be prey of the cat, the mouse, riffing the French royalty whose costumes will appear later at the gala, encloses and conveys as a machine *the two cats*. There are "two cats"—both contained or spawned by "Steamboat Willie": the royal, "Hollywood" cinema of Grant, tool of the aesthetic state, and the *other,* that of the simulacrum of simulacra, the saboteurs and "the Resistance"; that of the *marquis* or *marquee* and that of the *maquis,* both of the same "mark." The animeme is a technical figure that converts into sheer animation, rendering the animal itself a corollary of the cinematic effect, as Akira Lippit has demonstrated.[13] The *Maquis Mouse* contains warring cats—the (faux) original and the (true) copy that has sup-planted the "original" are both displaced by this zoographematics, even as the logic of the outing compels Robie to copy himself to "anticipate" his language student Danielle's copying him, and so on. It is the speed-boat that displaces the model cruise ship from the travel service window, with its citation of cinematic tourism from *Rich and Strange*. It is also, with its virtual animals, a bizarre little ark without any Noah, a vehicle whose engine is cut as its felines open a dialogue concerning dictionary definitions. Such a machine of citational precession or backlooping, momentarily dead in the water, invokes a site, like that just before dawn, where inscription may be altered. The police airplane that supplants the aerial eye of the panorama enters from above to spur the boat forward.

Figure 31. Two "cats" discuss language lessons in zootropic *Maquis Mouse.*

Such an ark, stopped in midcrossing, is unclear as to where its ghosts, as if preserving "life" for a future, are crossing to.

### Parasol without Sun: "No Need to Bother the People"

[Commercial directors] have learnt, as it were, to put the nouns, verbs, and adjectives of the film language together. But . . . what we must strive for at once is the way to use these film nouns and verbs as cunningly as do the great novelist and great dramatist.
—**Alfred Hitchcock**

What is at issue exceeds the reversibility of genealogical signs. That is evident, again, when the typical Frenchman, *Bertani,* bears an Italian name, or the very British Hughson is pronounced (or "sounds like") Houston, as if American, or when Cary Grant is said by Kelly inversely to "sound like an American character in a British movie." The *too light* work scorches *genealogical* tropes. "Everything" appears absorbed: suns, trees, mothers, eggs, *logoi,* earth, light, cinema, the Book, "real" actors, the "cat." While the origin of the Stevens fortune turns out to be oil and then by association excrement—or, inversely, the biblical legacy of writing is displaced from a poetics of mourning and loss by its own totalization—the actors themselves are successively sucked into this maelstrom. This is not a toying with "simulacrum" but a precession and totalization en route elsewhere. Yet if Grant gets situated front and center as "a celebrity of the Underground," Grace Kelly's life and career appear all but sacrificed or consumed by the machinal order of representations when "Mother" remarks, "Everyone in Philadelphia reads the *Bulletin.*" Mother totalizes Kelly's hometown, ignoring the homoerotic inflection of the city of "brotherly love" that will mark Grant's performance throughout, or how the word *bullet*in incorporates little balls that injure. Inversely to how Anthony Perkins will be sacrificed and consumed as a life and career by his single turn in *Psycho,* unable ever to leave it, doomed to producing income through cheap remakes (*Psycho* II, III, IV . . .), Grace Kelly never leaves this film set *or* her role. Not only will she be compelled to play out the persona of "Francie" with Prince Rainier, but she will die in a car crash at the very site of the picnic scene by the U-turn, the travel fold par excellence.[14] There will be no getting out of these folds for Grace—not even when Hitchcock offers her *Marnie,* which Rainier will block one last time, and which itself would have exposed "Francie" (and Grace) in a manner almost too cruel and precise to fathom.

The cameo authorizes the work as a time bomb. Its benign "France" or intangible cat transforms, disperses across lethal light touches, and *totalizes* into still-uncertain fireworks. No network or history cannot be absorbed and eviscerated by its "whirling pickpocket" if some citational touch or contact is triggered: the advent of the cinematic (its histories, its teletechnic extensions down to nuclear weapons), the culture of the book, that of dinosaurs decomposed into oil, that of fractalized language, the logos of the West, the gods, the sun, architecture, number such as *pi,* service industries. What is called repeatedly in the work "everyone, everything." As if the "sponger" that is a variant of the cat—the capacity of the photographic trace to simply absorb citationally and hyperbolically all virtual trace chains in its vicinity by one or another affiliations—were encompassing, precessionary, virulent without defense. This *bombing* will appear marked, first, as sheer avenging anteriority, out of the "old days," "for old times' sake," like references to the war itself, which, in a distinct way, would unwittingly have been lost, much as the postwar democracies to emerge further consolidated for Hitchcock the American deserts that would inherit the "Enlightenment" imaginary and absorb the once discrete fascist other into a global or planetary logic. What had been located as if in the past, in the cloacal site of oil and Francie's dead father, in the posthistorical Riviera, is relinquished, much as Jeremiah is revealed later to have been a "swindler, if a lovable one." If the unreachable *Con*stantinople of *Secret Agent* is here replaced with the pseudonymous "*Con*rad Burns," it is not just a certain order of cognition—which is to say, with the senses, sight and hearing—that is placed on the historial gambling table.

Anapocalyptic, beyond "mourning," this semioclasm is associated with a series of literal and cited *aural crashes,* as though what the next film, the second *Man Who Knew Too Much* spells out in its title scroll as "a single *crash* of Cymbals" (or symbols). These material punctuations of sheer or asemantic sound appear temporally dispersed across the work but have the odd effect of absorbing narrative anteriority ("old times") into the rupture of signifying chains by their own voiding of metaphorical *vehicles*: the unseen shotgun blast and the pop of Foussard's ejaculating champagne, references to bombing a prison or that "building is booming," the unseen police car crash, the muted fireworks.[15] If an invisible explosion at any point is allied with *sheer* sound (crashes, starting and stopping, accelerating and networking), then the myth of a nameless anterior catastrophe such as "the war" has been redistributed, shifted up, across a sequence of non-"presents" and non-"pasts" instead. Such

Figure 32. (a) Cary pyramided by cabana boy, who, (b) chin to bar, is awarded key before parallel skis.

would be in part simply located in the *ear*. If the cat suggests a trace that precedes the organized effects of the visual and the aural, it teleports between them imperceptibly. The *ear* proximates access to the labyrinthine switchboard of puns, citations, "light" touches, broken words, syllabic and material carriers that induce the shadow traffic or hyposcript called "the Resistance." There is unusual focus on Grant's ears or hearing—his "Pardon me while I get the water out of my ears" at the float, or, in response to Francie's remark that drinking "dulls the senses": "and if I'm lucky my hearing." He tugs at and fingers his ear quite a bit. They all but stick out. At Foussard's funeral, Hitchcock plants a boy with distended ears near Grant and seems to cite the scenes in *Suspicion* in which the star taunts Joan Fontaine as "monkey face," himself evincing that trait as his face repeatedly fragments into puddly movements, dismantling it as unreadable. Grant's ear-distended monkey face, like his mirrored tire-face in the bus window ("I may even retire here"), laces him through an animeme that is preanthropomorphic. If face is a tool of the actor's many thefts (anonymous identifications, investments, loves, iconicity), Grant displays an utter loss of face when entering the gala at the Sanford villa. Inverting the cold cream whiteface of the shrieking woman tourist after the opening credits, Grant appears mute as a jet black Moor carrying a *parasol* at night, indeed, in costume as a eunuch servicing the two Stevens women. Ahead of their entourage, recalling all the references to "boys," a row of gold-painted youths enters, only not Ganymede-like but as if in gargoyled armor. The camera will settle on and isolate the sunless parasol Grant carries, as if stationary, himself a black hole in the brilliant and artificial gathering, a historical costume and period piece abysmally traducing any "present."

"Nature," as the panoramic aerial shot conveyed, here does not exist as other than a teletechnic system. As anthropomorphism recedes before the totalizations of the cinematized era, of infinite citationality, it is as irrelevant trope as origin: all is, so to speak, formalized. The entirety takes a turn into "something more formal," as Robie bluffs about his impending change of clothes from his striped jersey at the villa when Lepic first arrives. *Trees* stimulate prosthetics: first, fronting as naturalized referents, the natural image that is always also a vehicle, they are converted into vertical columns or archival props (the rings in *Vertigo's* great sequoia exposing a dating system).[16] This logic is flagged too in the debacle at the Nice flower market—a flood of cut flowers that arrests Grant and the narrative itself. A withered crone intervenes, gabbling in furious French. She is angry at Robie for upsetting her flowers and grabs at his sleeve.[17] He cannot strike or touch her (as Danielle said earlier, "You can't touch me, I've graduated"). He cannot bring himself to strike an old woman. Yet his jersey sleeve is stretched around a tree trunk, which holds him in place, even as he is elongated like a cartoon character. The withered hag binds Robie, who would flee or fly off, perhaps again upward beyond gravity. Cary Grant or the cat is held in place by her, his sleeve keeping him connected, even here, to the *natural image* that the photograph always uses on the set of earth, even if just these trees will appear cut or absent, or if Grant's alias, Conrad Burns, has a role in their mass eradication (like Bertani's "cutting, slicing"). The police apprehend him, only to release him again.

Grant is betrayed by the citational structure of the mimetic image,

Figure 33. Pre-Face: (a) preceded into the gala by gargoyled solar youth; (b) Grant, as black-faced Moor servant, carries parasol at night.

its dependence for recognition on the objects Hitchcock seems, none-theless, to inflect or magically desemanticize so that they are all that one remembers (Godard). Deleuze notes the centrality of weaving in Hitchcock: what is flagged here certainly evolves into something "more formal," from this jersey, through revealing swim trunks (Danielle: "And I thought you didn't want to be *con*spicuous"), to the laundry-woman who dumps the lot in the middle of the road in the second car chase, to the utterly formal gowns and costumes at the gala. The tiny fury anchors the *barred* jersey to a tree trunk, the trace of the natural image that the camera's mimetic pretext supplies as it is citationally converted into figure, allographic traffic. A precession occurs, as if from clothes, to "natural image," to container or crypt within the cinematic car's trunk, from which are extracted the very stuff of a *pic*nic ("Which I've already *picked out*"), the dismembered parts of a chicken ("a leg or a breast?") that sets up the still more betraying seduction scene. The hag's tree trunk is columnar, however, an isolated bar. It is this same wood or tree that turns up, from the first, as the prosthetic limb we hear limping, a syncopated knocking (/ / / /) as Foussard goes by, a wooden leg. As Lepic acknowledges when pressed by Robie after Foussard's death: "I think he had a bad leg."[18] What, however, is this prosthetic "legwork," reminiscent of the up-kicking chorines above the dying Mr. Memory's slumping head? What has this movement of steps and feet, allographic markers, to do with what is called "the biggest problem," that is, "time"? The word *time* ricochets across the dialogue, as noted, more than any other: "old times' sake," "have time for me," "spare the time," "be on time," "take time," "waste time," "pushed for time," and so on—a virtual archive of temporizings.[19] The repetitions are also desperate. What has the death of Mr. Memory to do with a warping or defaulting of time lines, of genealogical trees, of costumed eras? The problem would not be the "time" of the cinematic image, but how, in traveling, it seems to fold or engulf histories.

Amid such chronographic faults, signposts indicating before and after alter.[20] Robie's "biggest problem" involves concern for when time, in this antiapocalyptic afterworld, will run out, in its mode as chase, appetite, genographs. Hence Francie's "*finishing* school," which Mother says seems to have finished her. Virtual futures depend on programmed orderings of past legacies possibly broken off, disrupted, or effaced with and as "the war." Any fold in "time" would threaten maps of historical epochs: the West reeling back through its mock-Grecian origins, only to have a wine steward limp out, or the slide of "France," in the gala, back "several centuries" to a classical era it might appeal to iconically in a time of postwar touristic dislocation, the famed Bourbon court, heir of the Sun King himself. One keeps time by measuring succession, progress, generations, the differential relation of copy and model, parent and child, the entire catalog of mimetic tricks by which "nature" comes to stand for (and efface) a mnemonic inscription.

Following the curiously desexed seduction scene, Francie bursts in on Robie and demands that he give "them" back. Something had been stolen: "Where are they?" Grant coolly pauses, letting all possible referents proliferate: "What do you have in mind, Francie?" As the thought of her despoiled sex coalesces, Hitchcock has her restate what she meant:

Figure 34. Crone anchors Grant's sleeve to tree trunk (or *natural* image).

"Mother's jewels." Even if the jewels were her sex, which Hitchcock lets the viewer supply yet retracts with Grant rising fully clothed and pressed from the darkened couch, why are they, whatever "they" names, Mother's and not, say, Francie's? The insinuation opens another evacuation and theft in advance—Mother of Francie's identity or sex, "Francie" of Mother's preinhabitation. When Grant visits Mrs. Stevens's bedroom next to inspect this theft, the latter flirts openly, purring about sleeping soundly ("I *do*"). The roles Francie takes on are routinely programmed by Mother's tutelary hints, her vicarious desires, her directions, yet here too her coeval competition ("it looks like the blockers are having all the fun"). Even in the last lines at Robie's villa, Francie stands aside as mere advance shock troop, a Trojan horse: "Oh, Mother will love it up here." Generational difference is suspended: "just a few years and some grammar," says Kelly, separate mother and daughter. (Hitchcock will turn the screw later when Jessie Royce Landis, the same age as Cary Grant, turns up as *his* mother in *North by Northwest,* the next Grant project, detached and folded back again.) Yet if Francie's programming and even her sex are Mother's ("Just *what* did he steal from you?" "Oh, Mother!"), it is unclear what zone, what apparatus, what materiality "Mother" will claim—particularly where generational difference is not left intact. *Mother,* as some variant of whatever is implied by that term in *Psycho,* at times seems spoken by the shape-shifting telecat. In both works, we may pretend, "she" or *it* is called forth from within the work's operation as a sort of zero effect, like the hag at the tree, one of Mother's "good" if inconsequent incarnations, cast off again for her weak dedica-tion to the flower market and the mimetic image. If the archival order that manages and produces the Riviera's mnemonic programs is itself in question, is gambled as a totality ("everything") with the earthscape and the visible (or eye) at the tourist casinos of Nice, if it is turned against itself as the shotgun is at travel folder heaven, in the fake death of Robie at the villa, one would expect a return of Mother in some guise—such as Grant in fact attempts in the openings of both *Suspicion* and *North by Northwest* first by mail, then telephone and telegram. "Mother" may now be heard, in not-so-sotto voce, as a *khora* figure, a nonsite turned to from a historial or telegrammatic impasse, such as when Cary Grant's face will be deconstructed without reprieve or when he is imprisoned in the advertised product, "Cary Grant," whose circular and void ad-vertising language he cannot get outside of without the intervention of a radical other, without *going under* totally. "Mother" is neither a he nor a she, quite, not maternal or (a)material, allied to the bar series or married to "J," nonplace of reinscription and its virtuality before any phenomenality—sleeping *soundly*. And she reads, extensively perhaps, but not naturally, not from left to right, or top to bottom—as we hear Francie's voice rise to Robie's ears when he is crouching in the dark on the roof: "Mother, the book you're reading is upside down." One should not, perhaps, steal Mother's jewels nonetheless, even though she does not care ("I'm insured!"), and the incident will propel the copycat's de-mise several scenes later, and with it the exposure of Bertani, Mafia-like caterer to the Riviera and cineast.

If all is gambled on a "long shot," as Grant tells Hughson, it is not clear what the logic of the long shot (say, as in the panorama sequence) includes. Can it not take in everything, including its own premises? Can it not expose temporal faults and fictions? Does it not gamble with the "visible" altogether? The "long shot" will release an ejaculating and drowning excess of flowers, foam or semance, networked systems, pun-ning touches, citational vistas. It would sponge up and mock the open-ing logo for Paramount's VistaVision. Yet it too is caught in the reversals it initiates, as the virtual face-off of Grant's women at the bathing float before the hotel. Danielle questions Robie about her perceived rival, Grace Kelly, a fake double with whom a near catfight will be staged—nonetheless in the water, what we precisely hear cats don't like ("It's true what they say—cats don't like water"). Danielle, dismissed by Francie as a "teenage French girl," will press Robie about his stupid preference for an older woman who's been around the block. Particularly over a young

girl who wants to take him to South America, called by her in an atro-
ciously interesting pun a "virgin country." She presses: "Why would you
buy an old car when you can get a young one cheaper? It will run better
and last longer." The recursion to machines of transport, new and old or
used cars, is resonant, suggesting not so much female serviceability and
sexual usefulness as a "new" machine of transport, or cinematic project
or weapon to emerge from the pyrotechnic ashes phoenix-like and new
(Danielle prefigures California Charlie in *Psycho*). Amidst the badinage,
Kelly vacates her beach spot (Grant: "It looks like my old car just drove
off"), but she teleports instantly *into* the frame. Next to him suddenly,
she explains of her new powers of metamorphosis: "No it didn't, it just
turned *amphibious*."[21] What is amphibious is in between places, shore
and sea, old and new species evolving, but also life and death (*amphibious*). Grant tries to avert the coming argument: "Say something nice
to her, Danielle." Counters Danielle: "She looks a lot older close-up."
The long shot has become a close-up, and betrays age or time in its devastations, especially on a woman. Yet as the camera makes clear in her
waddle from the beach to the water, viewed unflatteringly, it is Danielle
who appears older than Grace. When the long shot is suspended, time
or age differences (again) redound and reverse, entrapping the eye in
minute folds.[22]

The catabasis to this underworld called France, as with the visit to
Mr. Memory's Music Hall, is always an occasion to ask questions of
the dead. When Grant would swim away he is caught underwater by
Danielle and as if bitten on the leg by her. The scene will be followed
by a turn to inspecting "real estate." Differently than Green Manors or
Manderlay or the Bates's house, which leads into a labyrinth of interiors
and crypts, the superficial *To Catch a Thief* will stay on the outside, will
discern that it is all a question of architecture, joints and lines, gutters
and roofs.

### Real Estate List: "Building Is Booming"

> Hitchcock is one of the greatest *inventors of form* in the entire
> history of cinema. . . . In Hitchcock's work form does not embel-
> lish content, it creates it. All of Hitchcock can be summed up in
> this formula.
> **—Éric Rohmer and Claude Chabrol**

> Number is the specter.
> **—Jacques Derrida, *Specters of Marx***

Grace Kelly drives Robie to check out the hills around Nice, which "Conrad Burns" is forced to present as a hunt for real estate ("I might even retire here!"). He is, in fact, casing likely targets for the copycat to hit. Under this pretext we are given a first look at the Sanford villa, where the gala will later be held.[23]

The "list" is handed to him by H. H. Hughson at "travel folder heaven." It is the only written text we see Grant reading. The "list" (a word the feline Grant hissingly pronounces) is curious since, as a mere list, it has no sentences or grammar: it is, rather, a ledger, an enumeration, a collection of names, numbers.[24] On the stationery it is printed on there is a heading for a certain "Para House." If Hitchcock's "houses" are personified routinely, with magic lantern windows for eyes, it is not yet clear what a "para house" is. Grant here is as if visually surveying its linear relations, angles of connection, gutters and roofs for traversing, the outside of the archive. Conrad Burns's pretext will, for the moment, be to study the architecture. He even pretends to identify a nonexistent but telltale architectural style: "Mediterranean, turn of the century— isn't it?" With this *turn,* Grant sets in motion a warping of temporal folds, a turning of centuries.

Robie tells Francie at first that they will "look at the gardens," adding that there is no need to "bother the people"—there are none about (except for Bertani, coming from setting up his catering job for the party, who looks away and disappears). The scene follows banter in the car about Francie looking for a man without a price, whereupon Grant says, "That eliminates me." This leaves, in a sense, no humans, just ghosts and architecture and classical citations and formal gardens. Whatever *eliminates* Grant's "me" as if into waste product also strikes people from the formally vacant scene, all in any case artifice. Deauratic, *real estate,* a list. The Edenic premise is inverted. The classical setting, replete with kitsch statues, exudes fallen Olympian stillness, while the pretext of examining architecture highlights geometrics sliding into numeration and sheer formal relations as the eye glides across edges. One can hear "Mediterranean," again, as middle-earth, historial omphalos or center, what is again lost together with gravity before pure form without locus or direction (it "used to be this way").[25] In Lepic's office Hughson later asks when he might retrieve the stolen jewels, since the former pretends "the Cat" has been killed (Foussard). Lepic avers, "It will take time." Robie, at the door eavesdropping, interrupts to add, "Several centuries." The mise-en-scène does "turn" the centuries, several in fact, only rather than sliding forward quite or entirely, it slips as if backward, and that

a

b

Figure 35. (a) Kitsch classic "real estate," sans people; (b) architecture, "turn of the century, isn't it?"

occurs precisely at the same nonplace, the Sanford villa, at the costume gala that is called an "eighteenth-century affair." As Francie virtually relays, it is for those attached to form: "Everyone who counts will be there." What, though, has the formalism of a deanthropomorphized "architecture" to do with a turning and warping, in and of time, across centuries? The "list" asserts a covert formalization of its notations and inscriptions.

In a travel service window displaying icons of "France" and in a work that is concerned with cats one might expect some hint of the French poet most associated with cats and flowers to traverse the stage, even *fleurs du mal* (the screen all but drowns in them at the Nice flower market), namely, Baudelaire. Godard acutely will term Hitchcock a *poète maudit*. One may expect a reference to the signature poem of that poet, that is, *Correspondances,* which like the film treats a disrelation of language to and within nature and history.[26] The poem asserts, "La Nature est un temple." One where a "forest of symbols" is juxtaposed to "living columns," and where, as in Conrad Burns's lumber mill, trees are either felled as natural referents or transmuted into columnar statuary.[27] Robie and Francie in the "classical" villa, exchange innuendos that carry further innuendos, then wander into the formal set of what will presage and host the gala to come, already drained of personification.

Baudelaire has been a key text in the development of the performative, amodernist concept of allegory as a reading model capable of altering—destroying and reinscribing—historial models and mnemonic programs, as the work of Benjamin and de Man demonstrates. It is not surprising to find him haunting Hitchcock's cinemallographic practice, even as a knowing aside. In contrast to Benjamin's hyperbolical metaphors for allegorical intervention ("shock," "blasting"), de Man turns to a sort of micrological engineering. Eventually such is required to rewire inscriptions—and lends a missing specificity to this territory. In the context of addressing "anthropomorphism," de Man remarks of *Correspondances*: "In Baudelaire's, as in Nietzsche's *[On Truth and Lies],* the icon of the central trope is that of the architectural construct, temple, beehive, or columbarium. This linguistic and graphematic building is built by the infinite multiplication of numbers ranging each other to ever higher mathematical power."[28] Such autoacceleration is not alien to *To Catch a Thief.* That shift from a "forest of symbols" to "architecture" segues into a sort of *numerology* as relations reconfigure. De Man addresses the formal implications of a numerical sublime in Baudelaire's poem:

> [W]hat can be more perverse or corruptive for a metaphor aspiring to transcendental totality than remaining stuck in an *enumeration* that never gets anywhere? If number can only be conquered by another number, if identity becomes enumeration, then there is no conquest at all, since the stated purpose of the passage to infinity was . . . to restore the one, to escape the tyranny of number by dint of infinite multiplication. (247)

Throughout *To Catch a Thief* there are ceaseless recursions to counting: mentions of "expense account," "I won't count it," "just common people with a bank account." It is heard in Danielle's promise to take Robie to that *other* place, primordial zero-land whose music will be played on the dance floor, "South America." Numeration erupts at a self-canceling origin that, volcanic like the fireworks, delivers the pair to a garden of columns and nonauratic relation.[29] This occurs already on the markings at the roulette table. Hitchcock accelerates a movement of outbidding that will appear as if self-derailed, an automatic acceleration like the car chases done as if by and on numeration itself. Once triggered, numbers increase digitally and by way of zeros across the script. When Grant drops his gambling plaque down the lady gambler's front at the casino, he would exchange it for ten thousand francs, without touching her. Mrs. Stevens will speak at one point of "a hundred thousand Jeremiahs," then Robie calls Francie "a girl in a million." And at Lepic's office, where "several centuries" are invoked, we hear the figure quoted of 92 million francs to be paid in insurance.[30] Just when the sheer exteriority of structure or architecture (angles, lines) or of numbering appears to crystallize, temporal contours fold or deform, time slips "several centuries" back. Outside the gate, the two trailing cops are found playing hackysack with their feet, trying to keep the dark ball *up* between them—against gravity, yet by virtue of the material, the foot. Numbers, which inform Mr. Memory's recited formula, are like steps, trace figures, precessual orders of the logos. Language is virtually reduced in and to the *list,* a sibilant word that implies notations of the eye and of aura or light, *luster,* even listening, reduced to cat scratches, to what is prefigural. As the core of Hitchcock's most stunning visuals and cinematography given over to nature, at the heart of ocular splendor, the work in fact precedes grammar and *descriptive* language. It outbids (itself), upping the *ante.*

This *formalization* anticipates the penultimate scene, which occurs when people are reintroduced to the Sanford villa. Like all galas, it should be revealing, unveiling, apocalyptic, even dressed and masked to the hilt and blasted out of historial maps. The disaster takes another form. Just when the scene passes into pre-Revolutionary world historical ruptures that are quite literal, it swerves, not only to the garish Hollywood fashion show that will be the ball, but also away from visuals and into asemantic sound. Grant adverts to the problem of his *ear,* at the float and again in the fireworks scene. An implosion in and of the ear echoes in a series of blasts and verbal wreckage but also is assimilated to the historical black hole of the war alluded to as only the most recent disaster. Thus the work dislocates its temporal locus. It displaces the past and "the" war into a rupture that is not historically localizable, a caesura within or by the aural as such, betraying vehicle of semantic or mnemonic reserves.[31]

A rift and black hole opens within organizations of anteriority, "old times," reference.[32] A resulting *totalization* without horizon implicates all of "modernity" and all its trace chains, "everyone who counts," "everything." France becomes like the blackmailing "sponger," Tracey, who when pursued by the police runs back through *all* of monumental history in the British Museum. It lights up the telegraphic circuits to obliterating excess, like a firework display. Innumerable lines pass through the "spies' post office" to other signature works, too many to cite: a wine bottle leads through the radioactive sand in *Notorious* to the accord between the cinematic and nuclear weapons; sheep pass through the blocked road to Inverary in *The 39 Steps,* to Mr. Memory's exteriority and the British Museum, reliquary of "old times": nothing can withdraw from being generated by, folded into the vortex of this too light touch. Fingerprints testify to a light touch *and* to its being barred, already archived ("You can't touch me, I've graduated"). The image of earth, cool yet amok with a madness of noon, is riddled with cool Zarathustran jeremiads. This totalization erupts out of the dialogue in a series of phrases using *everyone* ("Everyone who counts"; "Everyone in Philadelphia reads the *Bulletin*") and *everything* ("Good taste in everything"; "Ever had a better offer, one with everything?" "Everything?").[33] All is formally gambled at the roulette table in this cinematic Nice.[34]

And yet touching itself is virtually barred, and with it a certain epistemological contact, which at best appears to start machines of transport, as when Robie barks at Danielle to activate the boat's engine with a key—*"Stupide! Le contact!"*—where contact, too, references a photographic print sheet. It is no surprise, then, that the light touch of the film comes to focus on fingertips, which, when seducing Robie, Francie will kiss one by one. Which leads to fingerprints. If "touching" is barred from being a conduit of sense, if one can only point at or index, "fingerprints" are what is always left of this crime. Francie complains of Robie's leaving his "fingerprints" on her arm, and Robie notes that there will be no "fingerprints" in Mother's robbed hotel room. The sole fingerprint we are allowed to see is the wet one on Robie's "real estate list."[35] Such a finger or its print is allied with the pregrammatical list. The citation invariably leads back to *Blackmail,* where "fingerprints" are used, among other convolutions, to disarticulate the indexal claims of documentary, and to indicate a material order of inscription from which "perception" is, like a projected image, phenomenalized.[36] If *touch* appears barred by what implements it, by remaining in advance of its own recognition a mnemonic imprint that cites itself (like a contact sheet), it evades ever being present. When Cary Grant places the gaming plaque down the cleavage of the woman gambler at the roulette table, it falls between clothes and body, between breasts, the woman's body a scene of exchange yet without being "touched"—a situation Mother laughs at heartily, from across the room.

What the work gambles with and on is the carrier itself, the vehicle, which we hear not only in numerous cars, or Cary Grant, or Carlton Hotel, or "carry it off," but in Francie's being "born in a taxi between home and the hospital" or Mrs. Stevens's valuing her jewelry the same as just "a train ticket."[37] When a woman crosses the road carrying laundry and Francie must abruptly brake, the laundering of threads presages a new form of cinematic accoutrement en route to the ball, like Danielle's offering herself as a new car. Hitchcock is probing his horizons. When Grant's car pulls off the road for the picnic, that picnic spot is in a hidden fold within a great U-turn on the cliff, a fold within a giant fold, where things can be spread out for a moment. The quest for a copycat that has supplanted the original, that compels the later to copy himself in order to copy the copycat in advance, veers toward a precession of the entire history of mimesis, which culminates in the Riviera's acme of teletechnic and touristic affluence. There will be, invariably, a cold meltdown not only of sense but of the senses themselves. This is, astonishingly, rehearsed around the now universal topic of seduction in the scene featuring pyrotechnics, the fireworks themselves.

### Grace Kelly Does Heidegger: "How Long Has It Been?"

> Adorno said the only truly great art is the making of fireworks: pyrotechnics would simulate perfectly the sterile consumption of energies in *jouissance*.
> —Jean-François Lyotard, "Acinema"

If cinematized "life" is overexposed, too much in the sun, it generates the phantasm of a secret to give it cover, like a parasol. This role is assigned to Grace Kelly, at the height of her genius in this outing, whose triple entendres and delivery cause even the veteran Grant to wince and

a

b

Figure 36. (a) Kelly anoints fingertips; (b) fingers hold "the list"—
insured by Para House.

do double takes. At the picnic Francie assures him, "I'm very good at
secrets."

Kelly's "Francie" puts into play a morphing and self-differencing
stream of double-talk that is all but lethal to the tourist viewer who
imagines "himself" on the inside of its secrets. The latter will be, in effect, peripherally pickpocketed. It seems all but impossibly scored with
overprecise sexual asides that defeat the very seduction it is meant to
execute. Generating fake "metaphor" like fireworks, it disbands the
premise of figuration in the same instant, retreating to a prefigural re-
cess or void that is mistakenly thought to be secret. It exposes the secret
of the secret's absence in a conflagration that seems to absorb every

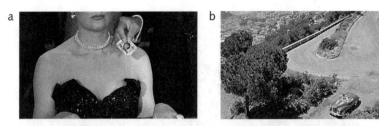

Figure 37. (a) Clothed nakedness, site of exchange; (b) fold outside travel fold, Grace's "picnic" site ("already picked out").

semantic flare at the point of evaporation—like the phantom ejaculation Foussard's champagne provided. "Secrets" appear to be flashed as obscene referents become all *too* obvious, then never arrive ("Tell me, how long has it been?" "How long has what been?" "Since you were *in* America last"). Such double-talk eviscerates the fiction of the "secret" from which reference appears generated as the responsibility of the dupe that provides it mistakenly, a roman candle to the metaphoric era of the figurative West's broken *parole*. A kitten playing with a dead *meus*. One is no longer in a scene of mourning, no longer at a semantic striptease of concealment and faux revelation. Hitchcock uses Grace Kelly as a sort of Trojan horse in the gender wars, since *seduction* itself appears exposed as an antierotic and postgendered ritual. Grace Kelly appears the effaced avatar to the few references to Mae West scattered in Hitchcock: "woman" as female "female" impersonator in the absence of any but a simulant "male." The vivisection of romantic "love," drawn from the bohemian cartoon in the display case, glamorously anticipates Brenda Blaney's grotesquely pragmatic marriage service in the purgatorial *Frenzy*. Kelly's repartee suspends any content that, with her apparent nod, the viewer assigns to it, as in literalizing the offer of body parts in the mode of fried chicken at the picnic: "a leg or a breast?" It is not just the film industry censors Hitchcock is evading and defacing.

The logics of seduction rule in "France." Recall Baudrillard's deauratic take: "Seduction is only possible through this giddiness of reversibility (also present in the anagram), which cancels all depth, all in-depth operation of meaning: superficial giddiness, superficial abyss."[38] Baudrillard presents "seduction" in a nonsexual or nondesiring light. It is a matter of *eclipse*: "Seduction is not desire. It is that which plays with desire, which scoffs at desire. It is that which eclipses desire, making it appear and disappear" (67). It is, he suggests, tied to the vagrancies of "the secret":

Only the secret is seductive: the secret which circulates as the rule of the game, as an initiatory form, as asymbolic pact, which no code can resolve, no clue interpret. There is, for that matter, nothing hidden and nothing to be revealed. It cannot be stressed enough: *THERE NEVER WAS ANYTHING TO PRO-DUCE.* (64)

The afterworld of Hitchcock's postwar Riviera, hyperbologic site of "affluence" and awash in semiotic excess, is traversed by an avalanche of citational relays, limping revenants, replicants, demigods. As Robie warns, any putative economy of *paroles* and circulated money is withdrawn from production and exchange value. It is promised in the form of the sheer and totalized "gift," what is treacherously advertised as an "offer with everything." It relapses to totalized service *(service compris)* and totalized theft. The gift is virtually privative. It recurs to the "whirling pickpocket" of the casino, ingesting chance. Baudrillard: "Thus in gambling money is seduced; it is deviated from the law of value and is transformed into a substance of bidding and challenge" (67). A seemingly transparent medium that bars touch (glass, "middle of the day," "between home and the hospital," "*Medi*terranean") usurps priority over what it reflects or carries. It bars touch yet retains prints. No production means: cut wood or lumber becomes a prosthetic leg; sheep generate clothes; the "origin" of the Stevenses' jewels is excremental oil. Seduction interrogates "sex," not as a gift or a commodity, but as something that does not exist *as such.* That is its secret, which cinema knows. As Grant rather explicitly implies when first invited to Francie's hotel room to view the fireworks, referencing less his persona than his status as screen wraith: "I can't come."[39] Thus the pyrotechnics, which present the acme of seduction and the promise of *jouissance,* do so by way of a countererotics, performed from simulant or neutered positions. Grace baits and teases Grant, mocking his inability to touch or get at imaginary *jewels* behind glass window panes, as if it were her sex, then pretends to substitute herself, before he has time to digest that the diamonds she is dangling before him, what alone he "can't resist," she says, are fake. She disembowels, vicariously, any touristic male viewer who attempts to fill in gaps and see, if not touch, her body on the screen. Hitchcock seems to have perverse insight into Kelly's female persona. We can call this her "Mae West" side—her rhetorical use of "femaleness" as effaced drag. He routinely exposes the screen goddess as, counterintuitively, all but incapable of generating male interest—as though she were profoundly queer, structurally allo-gendered, as much as inhabiting sets with males even more so (Grant, Stewart, Milland). Kelly seems at any given moment to instantaneously have reconstructed through default and auto-citation where "she" should be, as in her efforts in *Rear Window* to seduce James Stewart by any and every normal means—yet she does so from an exposed and neutralized space. Among all of Hitchcock's favored actresses, she at least seemed to intuit and take delight in outbidding what Hitchcock was doing with it all. "Francie."[40] She—someone—is always almost "acting like" the actress, "Grace Kelly."

Homoerotic markers saturate and dislocate "Grant," who seems indifferent to them. He wags a scolding finger at Foussard's masturbatory champagne froth as at a fan's excessive hopes—a gag literalized in *North by Northwest* with, however, a bespectacled woman reading in the hospital room. The cabana boy's legs are spread above his head on the beach, and there are recurrent references to "the boys" (Bertani's "boys," "the boys must have enjoyed that"). The scolding finger might say: don't screw up with the champagne; or, don't ejaculate at me; or, don't expect me to respond, since every viewer does that; or, "Cary Grant" exists only as this screen specter; or, cognitively, sexual contact is a MacGuffin and what you interpret as scopic desire, at the very least, is premature. Like the lady gambler in the casino whose body becomes an inert slot machine that returns change, as Peter Conrad observes, "Cary Grant" seems to some a walking eye trap, or virtual brothel, though the tourists who stare at the *stars* literally and obviously in the lobby of the Carlton seem equally puzzled and disinvested. This sheer expenditure or waste is forerunner of the fireworks scene.

The fireworks display exposes this expenditure by routing it through a stale covert literary trope for *jouissance.* Inversely, it looks directly into the sun. It finds an artificed or technic "light" that sputters. And it affiliates the cinematic not with an imaginary *jouissance* but nuclear atomization. The scene is set up by banter that begins at the picnic:

GRACE: Tell me, how long has *it* been?
CARY (small stutter): How long has what—what been?
GRACE: Since you were in America last.
CARY: Don't talk *like that.*
GRACE: You're leaving *fingerprints* on my arm.
CARY: I am not John Robie "the cat."

Neither John nor Conrad nor even "Cary." That would eliminate "me." Grant's plea that Grace *not* "talk like that" is hopeless. Do not, he pleads, place *en abyme* obscenely proliferating double entendres that vaporize the last refuge of the obscene as a fiction; do not pretend the mechanics of meaning as flickering concealment is not hopelessly exposed, along with Jeremiah, who turns out to be, with his biblical intoning, a "swindler"; do not open the cruel performativity of seduction's anything but secret mechanics to the black light of this artificed sun, whose effects we have already "seen" in the panorama. "Don't talk like that." There is a parallel disconnect between the pretense of mimetic reference (a vista described as "beautiful") and the pretense of the open "secret" that is the content of what can no longer be called double-talk, a disconnect that is generated by the obscene spectralization of the literal referents of sex. But Hitchcock ignores the plea and seems determined, with a light touch, to expose the mere literary figure that preserves all figuration coming out of the tradition of novel writing itself. The trap mimes that of the travel service: the audience fills in all of these missing referents, decoys that in turn expose the "secret" of the secret's nonexistence. Hitchcock lures his audience to sniff about for truffles amidst the cool glamour, expensive gowns, everything called "Nice." Grant realizes too late he is being set up, not by Kelly but by Mother, or Hitchcock:

GRANT: *That's* why you came up here, isn't it?
FRANCIE: We'll have cocktails at eight and dinner at eight-thirty, all in my suite. We'll talk about it there.

Unlike Danielle, who mastered her language lessons but not her too "French" accent, Francie uses words as "playthings." The *it* is a designate for a permanently missing antecedent. It provokes the exposed "Conrad" or "Cary" or "John" to try at being blunt:

GRANT: I can't come. I'm going to the casino and watch a firework display.
FRANCIE: You'll get a better view from my place.
GRANT: Already got another date.
FRANCIE: Everywhere you go I'll have you paged as John Robie "the Cat." Eight o'clock. And be on time.
GRANT: Haven't got a decent watch.
FRANCIE: Steal one.

Steal a watch. Grant "can't come," doesn't have time or means, cannot ejaculate or quite arrive. Certainly not if he has, as he says, "another date," will be in an other time, is without a "decent watch," blinded, without an *Augenblick.*

The arrival of fireworks against the night sky above the sea puts coming or *arrival* in question. Yet it is in this scene that the work is thoroughly deauraticized. It is the only place in Hitchcock that a citational sun, so to speak, becomes a character. Yet its face and even production are betrayed. The white implosions telescope the serial metronome of booms or pop sounds to the seemingly visual, "one of the Riviera's most fascinating sights," while the screen's counterorgasmic whiteout seems thrust like a cigarette ember into the tourist viewer's eye itself. The most fascinating of sights, it can't be seen. At once it pretends to *metaphorics* and performs a precession of trope *tout court.* It cites as well a faux sun, a then familiar metaphor of coming, an atomic blast, cinematic *jouissance.* "It" is both the obscene and the simulacrum of all presencing. But if the sun, origin of light, is the effect of a *technē,* a *pyrotechnic,* the accelerated array of double entendres suggests the inverse of the black cat. Cold, furious nothings, it or they (multiplying implosions) seem to precede sense even as the bursts are muted, prephenomenal, void of interior or exterior. This vivisection of mimetic seduction and "love" veers back to address the asolar vacancy that haunts this lighter side of Europe.

Kelly allows the thought of her nakedness to coalesce in the viewer's mind after promising Grant that he will see one of the "most fascinating sights" on the Riviera. Then she counters, if only to ensnare by disclaimer, "I mean the fireworks." Such a light touch, like the phantom touch of imagistic cinders in the retina. The work of creating secret *meaning* is performed and exposed as in itself obscene. An artificed and thieving "sun" that had been worshipped, brooded over, or anthropomorphized in the Mediterranean cradle and its successive regimes arrives, only at night and sputtering. The black cat has morphed. The Tabernacle of the Sun in the first *Man Who Knew Too Much,* a fake temple of sun worshippers, introduced a hypnotizing black marble to initiate filmgoers into the "mysteries" of the cinematic trance, yet by now all bets are off. A solar refugee struggles to fake orgasm or *presence* from what cannot generate heat yet tortuously burns out screen and the touristic monops. But if a sun can be the effect of a *technē,* a pyrotechnic, the array of double entendres recurring to "it" or "them" (jewels, "legs" or "breasts," woman's sex) vaporizes the army of generated referents. To say, "I mean the fireworks," is to insist on meaning something that will decimate the phrase.[41] The exploding white performs as another black

Figure 38. White hole: camera turns to sun as prosthetic.

hole, consuming the semance and light that it sprays about. It opens a wormhole, in which one will be shortly transported to perhaps other time-spaces. "Grace" naturally begins with a question of sense, sensation, feeling, *sights*:

GRACE: I have the feeling that tonight you're going to see one of the
    Riviera's most fascinating sights. . . . I was talking about the fireworks.
ROBIE: I never doubted it.
GRACE: The way you looked at my necklace I didn't know. You've been
    dying to say something about it all evening. Go ahead.
ROBIE: Why, have I been staring at it?
GRACE: No, you've been trying to avoid it.

The "it" in question—which, again, suspends any programmed desire ("Mother's jewels"), as well as any fantasy of the "male" tourist eyeing "Grace Kelly"—ricochets off the necklace, the "imitation" diamonds, to construct her concealed *sex* and parts as its false referent. "Then tell me you don't know what I'm talking about." Not only will a sun be disclaimed as artifice, light without natural origin (like Lepic's flood-lamps), but the tropology disintegrates in a further trap. *Jouissance* is cited. It mimes a citational performative supposedly climaxing seduction. Cold "imitation" diamonds are substituted at the last moment for and inversely by Kelly's sex. Any signified arrival or copulation is momentarily expunged without trace as an uncreased Grant walks from the couch to the balcony with tux and bow tie intact. *Jouissance* is another fake ad in the travel service window. Cinema does not "come."

Fireworks evince by subtraction the obliterative powers of the cinematic weapon. That weapon is nonetheless turned upon the privileged hedge of literary modernism, on the *modernist* "novel." It is not just that the entire scene is allowed to parasitize a literary cliché, one at the other end of the scriptural tradition to which the Biblical "Jeremiah" testified. Hitchcock can ever so lightly touch, steal, and evacuate an entire literary archive with a single citation or shot—even a tradition at its peak. It is not that there is a contest between the "modern" novel and Hitchcock's cinema—that the latter wants to prove he is serious, literary, worthy of cultural regard. There is no contest at all: cinema won in advance. This is the "lightest" of trifles, and the implied Olympian lightning bolt leaves no cinders. It exposes the amateurism of literary modernism and its need for metaphor; it absorbs it and sucks up its entire archival network with dizzying and mocking superficiality. The trope of pyrotechnics as ejaculation clearly cites (that is to say, steals) Joyce's fireworks-and-masturbation passage from *Ulysses*. In doing so, it covertly assumes the Odyssean motif of *nostos* as its own, a site ruthlessly disfigured as egg, Mother, nature, Greco-Roman classicism, light, the sun. Hitchcock allows the autodeconstruction of gender to pass in the most antiromantic "seduction" scene imaginable (betraying and realizing the kitsch advertisement's promise of "love"). And he links that exposure to a nuclear and semioclastic atomization, each allied to the cinematic advent.[42] The programs of the Book and the atomic bomb intertwine and are hosted by cinematic technics. The masturbatory shot of Foussard's disseminating champagne confirms the link to Joyce, and Hitchcock flags this theft and dismisses Joyce's meager invention when he has Grant protest that he has absolutely no interest in, among other things, "modern poetry." Robie says as much: "I have about the same interest in jewelry as I do in politics, horse racing, modern poetry, and women who need weird excitement—none."

If fireworks-as-metaphor for orgasm is as if stolen from Joyce, a pickpocketing of "high literature," it rejects that as the last refuge of modernist posturing. It says: "Look, Joyce bumbled through this banal trope, for which he gained notoriety and sales, but here it is, before you, right in front of you, and see, in fact no one came, there is no one even there in this burnout of sight, touch, indeed, of metaphors as such." The recurrent offers with everything, the structural inability to come, the linguistic fragmentation and focus on the ear ally the work, however madly, more with *Finnegans Wake* than the still bibliophilic *Ulysses.*[43] This would be the "Joyce" that Hillis Miller characterizes as a modernist icon within the transformation of the literary that Hitchcock targets:

> The literary revolution participated in, and to some degree initiated by, James Joyce might be defined as the displacement of the grounding of literature in some solid extralinguistic logos: God, the One, or the materiality of the external world. These grounds are, in Joyce's work, replaced by a groundless, endlessly proliferating, self-canceling, self-regenerating play of signifiers.[44]

Yet even this site is subsumed as cumbersome and self-fetishizing within the decay of the "literary" mystique and medium restrictions. Such a perspective is, in its way, no different from the perspective of the *cat,* whose logics run from Egyptian hieroglyphs *(Blackmail),* to the Bible ("Jeremiah"), to Greek epic *(The 39 Steps),* or the implications of a generalized *teletechnic* field inflected by proliferating phones, telegraphs, presses, secret writing, floodlights, cars, carousels, taxidermists, and so on. More: there is something jejune, masturbatory, in Joyce's playing off nineteenth-century censorial programs. It *still* mourns, it is *still* auratic. It is dismissed.

Rather than inscribe himself as a modernist grateful from a mass cultural niche to be citing Joyce, Hitchcock traumatizes and blinds the visual at its core or cornea. The scene is Cyclopean and, like the famous opus it pilfers, *en*cyclopedic. The monops of the tourist viewer is burned out, like Mother's sunny-side-up egg, but by *outis,* no one, the name Odysseus gives to Polyphemus. A more overt allusion could have positioned Hitchcock as mere thieving heir of literary effects, affiliating commercial cinema with the "great" modernist novel to the former's prestige. Joyce appears uneconomical compared to these lightning-like powers, which void metaphor altogether. A new car, or weapon—amphibious. The flamed whiteout carries no natural or mimetic "image" at all, which is what the hag at the tree was restraining Robie by the sleeve to prevent.[45] Cary Grant, or whatever goes by that name, will subsequently become inaccessible to light, to mimesis, to face, upon entering the gala as eunuch. From here, "sex" appears to be a cinematic MacGuffin.

The burning out of vision by a flashing pyrotechnics literalizes the flashing blast of the revolver into Dr. Murchison's eye (and or as the camera) at the suicitational end of *Spellbound*.[46] The cinematic is turned against, made to atomize, its then current incarnation.[47] Darting, expanding, the pyrotechnic light shoots out in lines, like a white bird, attacking a blindness inherent in the eye. The whiteout would dissolve inscriptions. The pyrotechnics mimes an atomic blast, techno-affiliate to cinematic atomizations by artificed light. Yet instead of everyone ending in ashes, "everyone who counts" returns encumbered with highly formal costumes, a ghost party of in-house cinematic intrigues between the copycat and the cat, the caterers and the police, the fashion show and its historial miasma of a postwar, post-Western, newly "global" history become, and produced by, film. And it is not only the eye that is altered. The verbal exchange of the seduction scene demands a specific sort of ear. Grant pulls his ear, fingers it, touches it:

GRACE: Doesn't it make you nervous to be in a room with thousands of dollars of diamonds and *unable to touch* them?"

GRANT: No.

GRACE: Like an alcoholic outside of a bar on election day.

GRANT: *Wouldn't know the feeling.*

GRACE: All right. You've studied the layout, drawn your plan, worked out your timetable, put on your dark clothes with your crepe-sole shoes, and your *rope,* maybe *your face blackened.* And you're over the roof in the darkness, down the side wall, to the right apartment—and the window's locked. All that elation turned to frustration. What would you do?

GRANT: I'd go home and get a good night's sleep.

GRACE: Wouldn't you use a glass cutter, a brick, your fist, anything to get what you wanted—when it was just there waiting for you. . . . Drinking dulls your senses.

GRANT: Yeah, and if I'm lucky some of my hearing.

The "it" that bars touch "like an alcoholic outside of a bar on election day" is in between, a window like that of the credit sequence. "It" is just beyond ("just there waiting for you"). Yet "it" morphs and another—say, *the cat*—serially consumes every referent it generates: a black hole, it reverses the flow of phenomenalization by adverting to the "senses." The vertigo of preceding even the play of signifying agents in what remains recalls Mother's costume party repartee: "After all, *my foot!*" After all—"after" everything, everyone, everybody. Pan, panorama, pantaloons—as Mother complains at the gala of detectives in costumes, "Wigs, pantaloons, and flat feet." My foot suggests, however, one step beyond.

"Beyond" is one sense of *para*. The words *pardon* and *parole* re-mark themselves in proximity in the dialogue as if to apologize for something ("it's not a pardon" but "a parole," counters Grant). The prefix *par(a)* is isolated by this repetition. It returns here and there. For instance, in the real estate list, where it appears on the stationery itself, which is marked by an address: "Para House." What is a "house" that is para, beyond the house as such? The object carried by Grant on entering the gala is a parasol; these had been seen lining the beach, at first, and Francie flourishes an umbrella in her mother's hotel bedroom. What, however, is a parasol doing being carried by a man in blackface at night? Yet another occurrence, of course, would be in the film's opening logo for Paramount, an obvious referent for the "Para House" imprinted on the "list" of people with jewels to steal. Umbrellas more generally appear across Hitchcock as signature effects for mobile black suns, as when cinematic Amsterdam in *Foreign Correspondent* is defined by them and bicycles. Norman speaks of his "trusty umbrella," offered in the rain. In *Stage Fright* numerous ones open at the garden party—so many black spheroids, or black suns, protecting, encasing. This cinematic parasol carried by Grant maintains a shielding effect: it shades the eyes from a nonsun's rays, the better to "see" in the dark. It eclipses a preorginary

Figure 39. Black-faced Grant's servicing para-sol; "whirling pickpocket."

eclipse. If it is the prefix *par-* or *para-* that gets isolated, particularly with reference to the sun or mountain peak (height, ice, VistaVision), one must recall the resonance of the syllable as if surviving a broken *parole,* which the *American Heritage Dictionary* partially defines as: "1. Beside; near; alongside. 2. Beyond. 3. Incorrect; abnormal. 4. Similar to; resembling. 5. Subsidiary; assistant. 6. Isomeric; polymeric. 7. A diatomic molecule in which the nuclei have opposite spin directions . . ." The Greek *para* cites and places the work to the side of and, potentially, "beyond" the sun (as the pyrotechnic scene implies, too). It interfaces with the *service compris,* as well as that of a double center "in which nuclei have opposite spin directions." The parole "pardon" also breaks, yielding the *don* of gift:

GRACE: What do you say?

ROBIE: My only comment would be highly censorable.

GRACE: Give up, John. Admit who you are. Even in this light I can tell
    where your eyes are looking. Look, John, hold them—diamonds,
    the only thing in the world you can't resist. Then tell me you
    don't know what I'm talking about. (Kisses his fingertips, then
    places necklace in his hand.) Ever had a better offer in your whole
    life—one with everything?
(Fireworks with increasing light bursts.)

"It" becomes "them." Fingertips can only be kissed by lips or mourned, as Kelly understandably wants "more tangible excitements" than what all of this vaporizing connotes. An offer "with *everything,*" however tendered, is still a sales pitch. Grant parries. The *parasol,* inverse figure of allographic shadows, generates the specter of a sun it would itself as if protect from. It temporarily halts a precession of the senses.[48] From the opening shriek of the cold-creamed female tourist, face had been in question, yet the focus was less on the blonde Kelly than the feline "Cary Grant." Inverting that opening citation, the face of the star is entirely blackened on entering the gala, a black space that absorbs light and is entirely mute, without voice, the ghost of silent film.[49]

## Gallic Wormholes: "Everyone Who Counts Will Be There"

The lamentations of "Jeremiah" put a biblical figure into play, like Joseph, suppressed middle name of "Alfred Hitchcock," whose missing initial or letter *J* was once configured as a slash or digit, a bar, and earlier as the pictograph of a hand in Egyptian hieroglyphs, figure of human technicity. Joseph, of the many-colored coat, interpreter of dreams. The costume ball brings such weaves and multicolored robes into a formalized nighttime gathering. Robie enters behind the Stevens women in stifling gold regalia as a blackfaced Moor. Once he is identified, he mutely nods to Mrs. Stevens and goes upstairs to fetch her heart pills. (In Hitchcock, heart pills were last evoked in *Young and Innocent,* for the black-faced "drummer man" with a compulsive eye twitch or blink accelerated beyond all control.) Upstairs, Hughson takes over Grant's disguise while Robie waits in vigil on the roof in the dark. Later, we hear three owl hoots and a train whistle—the bird of "wisdom" dissolved into cinematic travel on parallel, binary tracks.

The Sanford villa is a cinematic Noah's ark filled with historical refugees: a production lot waiting for the shoot to begin. Clothes glitter as formalized period costumes, citations both of the past and the need to be clothed in its aesthetic debris. On the one hand, it is a travesty of the Enlightenment's dominion, a nostalgia for the court mythos cloaking classical "France's" imperial fantasy. On the other, it caricatures how a "past" is cited, ritualized, implicitly devastated by a cinematic "present" compelled to cloak itself in fantasy and "old times."

In his account of the production of *To Catch a Thief,* Donald Spoto noted that nobody could figure out why Hitchcock was lavishing such detail and expense on the sets for the gala. It has little or no narrative use, and nothing happens. A theater without outside, those who enter to applause only turn to applaud others in costume; all is spectacle. Personifying what precludes personification, the film's star enters without face. The mise-en-scène cycles back centuries to a premodern and prerevolutionary "France," a safe regression for the postwar trauma bubble of the Riviera. It is a hyperbolic set in historial costume before a shoot, painting "history" as a cinematic invention (like the Western for Americans). It turns the icon of "France" into a set. It is as if Benjamin's concept of the past enters "legibility," readability, at this most *an*aesthetized moment of danger, a state of totalized emergency and canceled emergence, a contemporaneity beheading toward which the entire court drifts. The word *gala,* as Danielle might say, can also be heard to "mean" apocalypse, or derobing and revelation. It culminates in a predawn unmasking in the blackness of night, atop the roof, by the Cat and the copycat. The film's precession of its own (film) production and of the sun is marked not by Danielle's disclosure ("Bertani's was behind it") but by the movie set floodlights Lepic turns on with the threat: "We'll be forced to shoot." The two "cats" meet in the dark, black on black on the roof—the "teenage French girl" unmasked as Cary Grant's double.

The work signals a slippage of "centuries" forward and back in this cradle of the West, but it occurs within recording processes, the archive as costume closet. Everything, everyone "who counts" is wired to the gala. The heliocentric "West" or *Abendland* appears with its lights knocked out, as at the close of *Foreign Correspondent*: the "war" is not over, it has been totalized; it is the teletechnic empire and everything that the cinematic services. The *band* in the Resistance is now the thieves who, in the underground of Bertani's kitchen, have supplanted the cinematic anarchists and saboteurs of Hitchcock's earlier allegories. It contracts millennia to seconds. Hitchcock is questing for a postwar enemy state of things, a "rotten" court of cognitive Denmark, to sabotage, and he finds it totalized, "global." The cinematic mass tourism of the postwar Riviera constitutes what is to come: a globalized techno-class in a service economy who regressively model themselves on the extinct Bourbon court. The word *pardon,* repeated at Francie's car after the funeral ("Now if you'll pardon me—," "I won't pardon you"), makes the totality apologetic, a matter of excuses. Grant's *parasol* places the gala as if beside or beyond any solar trap. But the black "cat" precedes metaphor. This precession of light in postwar Europe, gathering about itself limping gods and the mock origins of the West, displays the default debris of that "Enlightenment" out of which that war, too, flowered.[50] One has regressed backward and forward to a site where this would all have to be done again, differently. Extending the logic of historial intervention sought by him in "cinema," Benjamin's thumbnail description of how a nonpresent "blasts" the flashing image of a charged past to reconfigure virtual or alternative futures alludes to *The Eighteenth Brumaire*'s famous example of postrevolutionary France's appropriation of Roman sobriquets. Unlike Marx's degenerative temporal model (first time as tragedy, second as farce), Hitchcock supplants the original with its copy, then accelerates the formal stakes to break the successionary model. "The biggest problem is time."

The gala gathers the last fetishistic debris of aesthetic ideology *tout court*. And it is littered with props and autocitations from other Hitchcock outings: heart pills, feet, dance floors, blackface, bourbon—all outlasted on the dance floor, until everyone and everything seems to drop off, the music ceased. The cat then moves to the outer rim of the archival house, moves along roofs and gutters that seem to recede in identical replications—the outside of the archival structure itself. Francie first offered to bring Robie to the gala when she called him to her car after Foussard's funeral. As Grant tried to withdraw she grasped his sleeve to restrain him. The gesture replicates and cites, curiously, the way that the furious crone held Robie to the tree by his sleeve in the Nice flower market. The shot nastily forecasts Grace Kelly as an aged hag at her most vulnerable-seeming moment. Yet if the crone tried to hold Grant to the mimetic image of the tree, Francie would bind him to memory (she is called "lamb" by her mother, recalling the earlier flock of sheep), and the cinematic MacGuffin itself (her car). Only "Mother," as in *Psycho,* can do without any natural image, any tree figure, anybody, any location, any phenomenalization.

But the gala returns, above all, to feet. Grant leaves Danielle dangling by one hand from the roof. She cries that she did it for her father, but Robie dismisses that as a mere familial or "convenient" front. Finally she confesses, "Bertani's was behind it," alluding to the presence of the bar pattern in the name *Ber*tani. Grant notes that Danielle always did the "legwork" for her father. At the gala, the "maternal" order of semaphoric steps or feet returns with a vengeance. There are shots of policemen's feet, a prolonged focus on the dance floor, and the unmasked Hughson's plaintive, "My feet are killing me." Then there is Mother's postapocalyptic, "After all, my foot!" There is a premimetic allegiance between feet and black cats and the bar series. Hitchcock is where he always is: the site of resistance here, as before "the war," is the same, even as the winners and losers shift within the same doomed Enlightenment tableau mocked in the "eighteenth-century affair" and its costumes, which indict, even so, the present's epistemology. What resists is the cinematic trace, nonanthropomorphic, deauratic, aterrestrial. If the cat both offers and sponges "everything," must totalize history once it has begun, it is, "after 'all,'" what remains. There is some after that would encapsulate the shooting of everything, an excess to the excess of sheer affluence: feet, steps, tracks, animemes, eviscerated "signs." At the same time, this "after all" is denied: "my foot!" The term *legwork* folds back to *The 39 Steps,* the affiliation of steps or legs with legacy, legitimation and legibility, reading *(légère).* Mother's dismissal of the whole spectacle—"wigs, pantaloons, and flat feet"—expands the commentary by isolating the word *pantaloon.* This covering of legs, or the "lower" order of signification, appears totalized *(panta)* and echoes less the mad reflected lunar light in the absence of any sun than resonance of a type of excessive spiration *(pant)* or thought *(pensare)*.[51] The horizonless *panta* migrates through *pensare* to the cognates of *phanesthai,* phenomenalizations and phantoms. This dance of feet seems itself outlasted as the dance floor is finally closed, where the masked Hughson alone continues to dance with Francie as decoy for the spying police.[52] The gala is "after all" concerned with the cat's remarkable feet, with the (a)material agency of this spectral marking system—what *Number 17*'s Ben calls footsteps without feet.

Mother's role is quietly pivotal. Francie speaks of her as being quite the "little actress" at the Sanford ball. If the gala would move "beyond" *(para)* the technicity of the sun, the *para house,* it does not move beyond "Mother." In the final line of the work we will still be waiting for her to come, "up here," in travel folder heaven, whether or not that is, in the design of the narrative, something of a relapse for her. To some degree, this too American "mother," who asks for bourbon when there is champagne, will relay a placeless *America,* the a-privative of *mer,* of *mar,* of *mère* (a-*mer[e]*). In the ballroom, Mother asks in French for a "bourbon" from the bar, tended to by flat feet in costume: "Avez-vous 'bourbon'?" She asks for a shot of American bourbon, as if unaware that she is surrounded by a simulacrum of the Bourbon court. The enfolding, here, parallels that of the "picnic" site, a fold outside of what is *ex*folded: "bourbon," an American name and whiskey effacing the word's origin in a French lineage right there as if before her, handing her the drink. By *North by Northwest* the faint traffic in the travel service window's reflection has become the traffic jam of Manhattan's streets, Grant is an advertising executive, and Jessie Royce Landis rematerializes as *his* "mother," *Clara* Thornhill. Travel folder heaven returns in high official gear as Madison Avenue itself, center of the world and tele-implantation.

### Aterra: "That Eliminates Me"

> With the chronophotographic gun, mechanized death was perfected: its transmission coincided with its storage.
> **—Friedrich Kittler, *Gramophone, Film, Typewriter***

The opening window display, in which the models are already miniature copies, becomes virtually hysterical now in its logics.

Since earth is always in the viewfinder, it is always as if shot, as if reproduced, as if a set, as if archived. The travel service window has another surprise: what is promised, seen, offered ("with everything") by the deauratic agency is a nonanthropomorphic, an "amphibious" order beyond figuration: a sort of *aterra* that drifts toward a teletechnic disappearance. As with all advertisements, one should read the small print. The miniature Eiffel Tower is full of grids and spaces, the cruise ship stuck on a shoal. *To Catch a Thief* is suspended from any critical map of "Hitchcock's works," without locus in the sequence, *atopos,* unaccountable. It is too light, too dark. It whirls backward before what is preoriginary to cinema—"*Steam*boat *Willy,*" say, which Hitchcock accesses as a vehicle moved on steam, London fog, and the *ill* of the bar series signature—and forward, consuming every work to come or repeat its dilemma. "After all," my foot. The "last" shot in Hitchcock's oeuvre, that in *Family Plot,* after all, returns to a stolen diamond concealed in a chandelier, one provoking a wink or blink into the camera, a "full" parabasis.[53] And this within a family plot of sorts, the plotting of the "family" and its evisceration as political fiction, the collective program of the mimetic regime of Western history with its replicant heliotropism, its mimetic blind as earth-eviscerating or self-canceling historial fold: the police, the usurping "villains," the O-men that shuttle between them (Johnny-O, Roger O., Dick-O). The "formalizing" thread of this labyrinth leads not to formalist critique but (perhaps) a Nietzschean going-under echoed in the place-name *Nizza.*[54] It allows Hitchcock to link democratic corporate capitalism and Nazi fascism as a doomed specular dyad in a more generalized imperial vortex or representational maelstrom, of which Nice could appear one touristic capital, indistinguishable from cinematic logics.

Such a catabasis and catastrophe of pyrotechnics would seem all too indebted to a suspect definition of light: Enlightenment programs of transparency and consumption, including the construction of "the visible" conjured through mnemonic repetitions, mock identificatory faces, parking places for the prosthetic eye, "pictures of people talking." The cat prefers the architectural lines and joints, its gutters and roofs, where feet and hands catch. *Cat* names an agency that will traverse boundaries, a cut between earth and sea (Riviera), inscription and perception. It must move from one conceit of dwelling to the next, as if from lodging to nation, nation to nature, nature to earth, earth to sun, sun to star.[55] Hitchcock wanted to "kill off the star" in *Psycho,* but in *To Catch a Thief* stars are killed by their own display cases, the film inversely reclaiming Kelly's subsequent "life" and "on scene" motoring death. But the pyrotechnic is also a death star, a star killer, as if in this "travel folder heaven" suns could not take refuge, even, by being "stars." The black cat induces by theft the sheer formalization of signifying orders, an *animated* black hole. It gathers all the humans in the inverse ark of the Sanford villa, as the birds do in Bodega Bay. The aerial panorama cites already "humanity" in the lens of a dispossession. An *Opfer* with everything, everyone—the Hitchcockian archive, the West, the eye, architecture and "beauty," earth and its others. Everything, everyone who counts.

After Danielle's revelations, Grant drives back and Kelly gives chase, this time in the police car.[56] One has been inspecting it all along, "travel folder heaven" with its long shots. Francie is waiting for Mother to arrive, to come, to take possession of what she, "Grace," has acquired. Francie's last line observes that she, Mother, will love it up here. She looks in bliss over Grant's shoulder and past him, as though his elaborate capture were for possession of this, or in Mother's name, or both: "Oh, Mother will love it up here!" One can suspend the first decoy interpretation one is supposed to delight in having recognized, sure that one has gotten the inside wink: that Robie is trapped and in fact now burdened with a mother-in-law to boot. The bell of cognition rings. But it is not a mother-in-law that is the problem.[57] "Francie" has been all along as if possessed, programmed by "Mother," is all but spoken through, as Norman appears to be. We might listen telegraphically to each *parole* as if transcribed from Morse code tappings: Oh . . . Mother . . . will . . . love . . . it . . . up . . . here. As if the line were a spy encryption relayed and concealed at the chocolate factory in *Secret Agent*, the "spies' post office," each *parole* broken open. *Oh*: that is, again, "O," the circuit ("Con*rad* Burns"), null, an open-ended apostrophe or prosopopoeia recalling the opening's middle-aged tourist, cold-creamed white, not quite face. *Mother*: extinguisher with a cigarette ash of egg and eye and sun, canceling in advance generation and sight, a *khora* or archival front for a site of inscription that the celluloid reel parodies, preceding gender or personification. *Will*: this is still to arrive or come, her installation at this new "home," amphibious if it is not everywhere already, in the sequence to which this scene belongs. *Love*: a promise put into "question" by the window's graphics, evoking a series in whirling disarticulations—affirmation, identification, (a)maternal consumption, seducing before and beyond the evacuation of the secret, sex, the obscene. *It*: the condensed series of *its* that lacerate the dialogue like claw scratches, without antecedent, referents, aura, or personification. *Up*: the heights, structural loss of gravity or hyperbolization ("too much") as the simulacrum is accelerated to precede itself, the "chase" short-circuited, chronographic regimes ruptured. Perhaps, finally, *Here*: nonplace where inscriptions are forgetfully totalized as perception and anestheticized as commodity repetition, nonplace where historial programs are installed and disinstalled like movies, travel folder heaven (or hell), which is also to say, anthropomorphized earth, "in between," the middle-earth, media. *Here* an imaginary of sight as a passive apprehension of the world in mimetic grids participates in cognitive accelerations and conspicuous consumption or incineration, totalized.[58] From here "Mother" will proceed, make *Psycho,* shoot *Frenzy,* assert a resistance and defacement against a totalization beyond any nation-state or world war—a totalization of tele-medial programs before which only an allegorical "war on terror" names a phantomatic other.

"Travel folder heaven" is, simultaneously, the trap of deathless reemergence and the prospect of disinscription—whose alternative pasts and futures are optioned, *sense* or the senses recast. An anarchival drive links the eye for Hitchcock to teeth and to eating, an (a)scopic drive of ingestion or internalization before which sexual desire serves only as a front or MacGuffin. Before the "eye" posits itself, this drive is complicit with and resisted by the cat: the cat both triggers the phenomenalization of this tele-archival memory and is called forth to combat, celebrate, displace, or survive its depredations. More than a blind order of the visible resides in this travel folding, in which geometric time is formally put at risk: chronographs, wormholes, defaults, precessions, and virtual futures. A classical Western order is massively summoned to attendance, together with much of earlier (and later) Hitchcock, Shakespeare, Joyce, Baudelaire, the Bible—indeed, Mother, the solar trap. What emerges from the pyrotechnics' phoenix-like incineration is a sort of teletechnic earth, deanthropomorphized, an irreversible movement that Hitchcock terms here "finishing school." On the one hand, the return of "Mother" is a bell toll of entrapment, a return to what "she" or it already knows and will love to see (again and again): travel folder heaven, the repetition of installed programs. Hence Grant's look: it is not that "travel folder heaven" has just been taken possession of by Francie, virtually, or that he is himself "caught" (by yet another thief), but that it was all scripted and vicarious—for and by Mother. More present in her absence. Grant is dispossessed (again eunuch), sent back to another film, his *parole* revoked, into the half-faced shot stolen from Grant's choreography with Ingrid Bergman in *Notorious.* Bergman's tough and experienced persona has become *this,* "Francie Stevens"? The latter closes her eyes and smiles in fake *jouissance.* In appalling bliss.

On the other hand, Mother is nonexistent. She will not arrive, or come, but is only announced. One can enter the labyrinth of Grant's

startled half-face from another angle. "Mother" (she or it) may materialize in bodies, voices, dialogue. She will just love it up here, rather than
the fruit cellar. The final line can easily be intoned as more sinister. "Oh,
yes: so this is *it,* the bad cinema of human perceptual hell at its refined
peak—'heaven,' as it anaesthetically thinks. Look at Grace's deceived
smile as she descends into the travel folder hell as Princess of Monaco.
Mother will just love it here." It cuts, "she" cuts, both ways. The prospective "will love it" projects a coming that is a return, particularly to
her new "home." She will love it because she knows it, has seen it already
or a picture of it, loves the fact of this machinery itself, which she also
precedes and manipulates.[59] What is the *it* that "Mother" would love?
This folding back or over in advance recurs to mnemonic inscriptions
that program or project. The "present" is a citation of a perpetually costumed period piece. "Travel folder heaven" consumes, predates itself,
spinning off its base like a carousel or off of its tracks like a runaway
train, and yet stationary, all but *here.*

### Nizza, Capital of the Mimetic Empire: "Stupide! Le Contact!"

Hitchcock puts in play different figures to represent the cinematic—
London fog, the temple of sun worshippers, the amusement park. His
final trope in *Family Plot* is a faux séance. This time the séance table
is set in the travel service window: the signscape of "France," "life"
as animation, the promise of tourism. It is the early-1950s, after "the
war." Something to do with sight, with travel—but then, as movement
or cinema, with reference; mimesis; "history," the violent materiality
of form. With acting and agency (of course). With feet (again). With
seduction. But it is out of control, ingesting its frames incessantly, a
"whirling pickpocket." Everything, everyone, is drawn in, seduces what
is not even its "other." The most theoretical of cinemallographic works,
it proceeds with an immolation of "theoretical" props.

   Whatever is gambled in and by this séance relies upon the operations of secret agencies, feet or legs, including anagrams, sound links,
switchboard and signature effects, telecommunications and telepathetic
nodes, monads.

   *To Catch a Thief* ingests and names the totalization of the double chase,
implodes in a preoriginary quest or precession to what seeks the order of
its own spectralization. Some ghosts at the gala had not been seen on the
earth for centuries—or ever. The cat totalizes ("everything") while inverting a programmatic definition of the "aesthetic" long wrongly associated

Figure 40. Robie's villa—"travel folder heaven"—haven of long shots.

with the Greeks. This is suggested by the sparkling jewels, the fireworks, the champagne froth. Everything is aestheticized, it seems, hence too light for the critics and without moral import or weight to be sure. Trifling. And yet an anaesthesia prevails also, over the whole. It is too cool, too formal. Such inverting of the domain of the "aesthetic"—long marginal, not serious, mere play, *para* house, imitation, light stuff—appears usurpative. This inversion is literalized as cinema, which generates perception, inherent in the Greek *aisthanumai,* from mnemonic marks, bands, networked recordings, from which worlds appear phenomenalized. Literature and the era of the book dissolve into this teletechnics. Yet to the extent this inverts a Grecian pretense transposed into the high aestheticism of "France," the work accelerates a meltdown of the Gallic version of the Romance copy of the Hellenic revision of the Greek redaction of Egyptian inscription—or the "real estate list." A pre-Egyptian cat traverses Western costume history and formally voids received definitions of simulacra, time, earth, and gender. It seems poised at an irreversible juncture. It can never return, as in a fake *nostos,* to the Egypticist (hieroglyphic), Grecian (phenomenological), Hebraic (prophetic), or Roman (legal) models. The historial bubble that Hitchcock tracks around Nice would be and was, he knew, "globalized" in the coming markets of tele-empires and what might be called *acapitalism's* totalization.[60]

Within this postwar mise-en-scène there appears a cannibalization of a now borderless tele-archival state and tourism—coincident with a dispossessed English's hegemony as global lingua franca. This Nice stands beyond mourning, since it cannot determine what is lost or whether it ever was otherwise within the double time and downtime of the travel agency. "Mother" can be hosting or hosted, may colonize, turn up as Doris Day, called "Mummy" in the next work, which again is about American tourism, about remakes and formalization, about knowing too much and repetition, in the now obliterating desert sun and underworld of Morocco, on the *darker* side of the Mediterranean, the "dark continent," a place "twice as bright" as Indianapolis.

Jeremiah, Mother tells us, would not have approved of all her "flying about." Too much travel, too many movies. It would not have escaped Hitchcock that in Nizza what might be called the gala of the fourth book of *Zarathustra* was to have been composed—at which the earlier animemes and figures "who count" reappear. The film reflects the debris of a wrecked crossing using the model cruise liner in the travel service window as vehicle: much as *Lifeboat* opens with the floating debris of its own torpedoed ship. The book Mother was reading is "upside down," as if Mother reads by some sort of chiasmal rule. Mother, like the cat, is the archival regime's nightmare.

There is perhaps one god who has never been accounted for—*Apollo,* archer of deadly light. To be sure, the gods assume one another's names on the Riviera, so that Promethean theft (language, fire) may be impossible to dissociate from Apollo. Why is the prosthetic eye of the aerial panorama exposed as a scorching and obliterating sun in eclipse, already a shadow, a parasol? "Apollo" occurs elsewhere in Hitchcock in the form of a shadow bird archer, killing Cock Robin in the animated Disney sequence in *Sabotage.* Hitchcock burns through a logocentric phantasm, a mimetic historical trance, and the iconography of the Greco-Western itself. Light here is exposed as other, associated with *list*(en)ing, with Bertani's Dionysian "cutting, slicing," with the movement of feet. Apollonian "light" is crafted from blackness, like the Dionysian bar series that turns out, as it does as *rhythm* in *The Birth of Tragedy,* to be already the preoriginary effect of something like Apollonian *form* as rhythm. So we can locate the far-seeing Apollo in the "long shot," like the shadow arrow crossing the display case window from left to right. But the travel folder heaven that is called "here" (the villa) returns to what the film calls "business," a machinal service of eviscerations. "Mother" either appears as the agenerative nightmare of recurrence in a bad historical infinity or as the anarchival agent of a transformation of active relations, performatives, gender effects, inscriptions, (a)materialities.

Two "Mothers," then, at least, neither a birth mother, both prosthetic, like the two cats or the political entities battling in the spy thrillers—the police and the epistemological assassins or anarchivists. First, the "bad" mother, consuming and eviscerating, cutting, slashing. Aware of her non-existence or pregendering, she wanders, seeks bodies or images to "speak" through, ventriloquizes and is ventriloquized. She could as easily turn on the characters and stars and say: Look who's talking, you literally are nothing but light shafts, entirely irreal. "I" at least reside with the facticity of inscriptions and events. Avenging. And the "good" mother, whose slashing tears what must be sundered, the ocularcentrism and mimetico-evisceration that allies her, it, the "bad" mother, with travel folding. Two nonmothers, then, mutually enforcing, mutually exclusive, rotating positions. The same. One cynically manages the state spy or police agencies, finds power in concealment, in not being in the travel agency window—nothing but a parade of signs advertising clichés; the other tears at, slashes the eye and exposes the visual as predatory construct, as travel folder hell, consuming. *Two mothers.* Two loves. Two annihilations: travel folder heaven, the affluent bubble of Western expenditure drifting toward beheading, and its anarchival others. Thus "Mother" vanishes from the set after the rooftop dangling and unmasking of Danielle. "Mother," as the site for a tearing of the *Ursprung* also is the guardian of archival intervention, *atopos, Atropos.*

If *you* love, if you love "life," you will certainly love "France." Staying within its folds can be heavenly. One consumes American bourbon, "Grace Kelly," glamour, above all the blindingly beautiful view of the earthscape. One is raped of all interiority or reference, and anesthetized, by a hypno-kleptic animeme. One studies with one's sockets, where images are inverted, read upside down. Mother, who incinerates suns with the lightest touch, will love this long shot—of, or for, an earth without center or gravity. To gamble "everything" on such a light work, in and by it, is madness. Who but Mother would read it upside down, except for the eye lens's translated image? But this gamble is like the usurpation plots of the early political thrillers too, which gamble all on a failed event, act, border passage. On a translation. The "thief" caught from the beginning is the tourist viewer, blindly regarding the travel service window, waiting for it to pass, looking at the cinematic screen, trying to get travel, exotica, experience, "love," "life," whatever, all for a cheap ticket—trying to get away with it all, everything.

The "cinematic" reels back here through cartoonish graphics, through an animation like artificial memory, which is to say memory, and all along might have implied powers attributed to the digital. As the pre-history of the afterlife of "cinema," Hitchcock folds back the Möbius band hosting that divide. In practice, one can say that he digitalizes *avant la lettre,* proximating literal animation. "Mother will love it up here," in the archival glass booth where consumption and politics will be directed with presensorial levers—the imperial "power" Godard attributes to a Hitchcock as first master of global media and mass culture. But this postwar "France" is not the happy land of democracy's victory. Hitchcock gambles, in a long shot, an offer with everything, flooded with cut flowers and concealing a raging fire in the archive, as sets off alarms in the chocolate factory of *Secret Agent.* In the ensuing fog, Hitchcock descends into Nice, capital of the tourist empire.

One can imagine some variant. Mme Blanche speaking and spoken *through* by a male voice, inverting and mocking "Mother's" voice in *Psycho,* a particularly light touch, responding to and summoning her spectral go-between, "Henry," to help dispose of a family legacy and doom. A hoarse voice mockingly plays along to connote spooky things. As Mme Blanche intones in "Henry's" borrowed rasp: "O-o-oo-o-oo-o—" Mother again? The faux Olympian atop travel folder heaven can issue lightning bolts as muted fireworks and thunderclaps as popping champagne bottles, running the Riviera like an amusement park; yet he also tries to add up business accounts behind the travel service window. Hitchcock puts "earth" on the roulette table, the middle-earth or Mediterranean, in what is also a site of reinscription. Mother will love it up here: this coming site of programmed cognition and accelerated technicities, planetary mass marketing and anarchival resistance. She likes the roulette tables, she says, even if she loses regularly, and here she gambles the received constructions of the eye. A site, beyond mourning, which is that of the cat: the animeme, the phuseme, the techneme, the nonanthropomorphic, the deauratic. A spectrographic "Hitchcock," then, distills the formalizing imprint of all cinema and telemedia to come, of the tele-archival era "he" is networked at the center of, shuttling forward (tele-empires to come) and back (to the cave hand prints, say), sponging, accessing instantly and by citational relay. And it is caught in a vertigo, the going-under of an ocularcentrist system that is a setup through and through. Such a spectrography gambles with alternative time lines. The animeme, the cat, does reconnaissance for the angel, or angle, of what can no longer be called history, condensing, as it does, the seeming era of the "human" and mnemotechnics to this long shot.

What is called "Mother" is the cat, alternately the oil pit or Norman's bog, which her skull grin dissolves into as the celluloid chain extracts a secondhand car. Amphibious. Deanthropomorphic, "she" emerges from this "alphabet soup," this technicity, the portal signature for everything that is not what the birds will virtually cite as the human enclave—rock, tree, mnemonic trace chains. The cinematic image, like the agency window, cannot not betray; one can identify with characters, read narratives, impose metaphors, determine apparent references, yet it adjusts to attack. *To Catch a Thief* acknowledges that the hermeneutic home state presented as "England" in the early thrillers (and hence, a logic of semantics, property, identification, ocularist pursuit) is, had been, perhaps always was, totalized in the already implied "global" tele-empire. Before the era of the cinematic is closed, cinema is "dead"—if one can kill what arrived as vampiric, undead. It requires one more backloop. It expands to include contemporary mnemonic programs and political powers of the tele-image, the evisceration of geological reserves and cultural or even prehistorial memory. One more fold, aside from holding the possibility open that one has not quite left this one, call it *Nice,* or that a network such as Hitchcock's oeuvre presents has yet to arrive at its appointed time: the contracts to nonexistent or future readings that it marks in its flood of secret scripts, signature systems, black holes. So many historial chains pass through its stations and citations—the history of technicity, states and wars, techno-genocides, representational politics, gender and relational deformations, numbers and speech acts, deforestation and the "universal reading room" of the British Museum, the archive, animemes, aesthetics, "America" and global marketing.

"Mother" countersigns the shock of the cinematic machine and the sensorial template it installs, travel folder heaven, at a site that is neither historial nor inscriptive nor anthropomorphic. Yet it remains handcuffed to this going-under that cinema implies while catering to the mimetic state with impeccable *service compris*—that of betraying and eviscerating sensorial and representational programs. What is peculiar about this image culture that "Hitchcock" shaped and interrogated, is that the citational structure of the image upon which all relies (namely, the indexing testimony of the mimetic photograph, say, in which a stability of knowledge is assumed) structurally betrays everything that is invested into it—everything auratic, that is: identification, metaphor, gaze, auteurism. Like a "whirling pickpocket." Yet this voiding, implicitly and from the first, operates as a kind of irreversible direction. It cannot descend into and cite Nice without incinerating it in a pyrotechnic display, positing a beyond to that, what is *para,* a Para House, again, or parasol carried for protection in the absence of any sun, at night. Hitchcock represents a site within the tele-archive where the old software, still, of epistemological regimes is made to go under.

# Coda: Trouble at the Séance

"I don't read any more . . . not at all," he said, speaking as
much to himself and his private ghosts as to me. . . . Then . . .
he grabbed a piece of white tagboard and a black marking pen,
and began to draw himself, making the famous caricature, the
line drawing of his profile that appeared on everything from his
television show to his matchbooks. . . . [H]e began stuttering
the word "I . . . I . . . I . . ."
—David Freeman, *The Last Days of Alfred Hitchcock*

Mother, Mother, I am ill.
Send for the doctor on the hill.
Send for the doctor, send for the nurse.
Send for the lady with the alligator purse.
—*Marnie*

In his interview with Gavin Elster in *Vertigo,* Scottie explains his vertigo
as a minor impediment, keeping him merely from doing things like
going to the "bar at the top of the Mark" (the hotel by that name in
San Francisco). To readers of Hitchcock who have developed a third ear
and eye, the phrase is arresting. Within the labyrinth of Hitchcock's
networked scenes and phrasings, one cannot get away from these two
terms—*bar* and *mark*: neither words, really, nor figures. They recur
across every work, linking each to each, as do the cameos. They become
and invoke the logic of cameos, only sometimes in other forms, as objects,
angles, citations. There is reason to ask what, if any, difference this recurrence makes—vertiginous or otherwise—to the logics of the auteur that,
in various ways, secured the most brilliant dossiers of Hitchcock criticism from Chabrol and Rohmer through Zizek. Indeed, what, if any,
difference does it make to the logics that have attended the auteurial fold:

essentially regressive, essentially auratic, essentially ocularcentric? How do they open a different view of "Hitchcock," not as a filmmaker, but as an event—together with the advent of cinema itself—in what has become the teletechnic era more generally?

Two retro theses.

Let us first admit with good humor that perhaps we got it all wrong, totally, this business of "signatures," rather like Hitchcock's funeral with its empty casket. That is, instead of marking a directional agent that reassures and sustains the specter of a subject whom we can ventriloquize to master "suspense," the logic of these signature effects empties the premises of auteurism, not to mention the mimetic assumptions of photography—or the ocularist programs behind it.

Second, "Hitchcock," today installed at the dubious center of popular and intellectual culture, presents still a sort of sensorial time bomb within this archive.

Think again of the "cameo" logic. It was assumed to denote territoriality and *self*-inscription. A certain "Hitchcock" body enters the frame, repeats the gesture across the films, and this furtive simulacrum becomes actively sought, like a trademark or label, perhaps at the expense of narrative consumption. It will later be cited in outline or shadow *("I Confess," Family Plot),* and surrogate figures that wander the works

Figure 41. Framed reader falls over "Harry's" corpse.

invoke some trait as well, usually comic, interrupting figures: the portliness, the pouting lip, the balding head. Ignore where these autocitations proliferate across the films in a network of interrupting surrogates: the impresario in *The 39 Steps*, the drunk in *Stage Fright*. What, after all, do they *perform*? As a result of their presence, whatever is outside the frame is folded into it, a gesture that contaminates (and displaces) any mimetic, historical, or narrative pretense or front. Because of them, the image is disclosed to be not mimetic or representational but *something else* that requires a citational model.

*No*? Go back to the *first* "cameo." Not the one at the end of *The Lodger*, where a certain "Hitchcock" stands behind the series of bars that make up a fencelike row of spikes, on which the lodger or Avenger, the would-be avenger of the Avenger, is hanging by his cuffed hands.[1] Before this better-known cameo, and almost invisibly, is another, a pre-cameo occurring in the bizarre interlude that interrupts the narrative at its very beginning to follow the working of the giant printing presses. "Hitchcock" in the editor's glass booth, directing the giant gears of the press, a logic of *typographics*. He is turned from us. He is at the center of diverse media machines (as "editor"). We follow a teletype, producing letter for letter the "news" about the Avenger: the triangle killer has struck another blonde. The murder is associated not with the camera that confronts the blonde's face before us in the opening shots but with this machine of impress, imprint. The giant machines issue dead repetitive prints, editions of the *Evening Standard* stacked in the back of a truck notoriously given eyelike windows: a standardizing truck face or head filled with inert print. It is driven forward while its "eyes" point back. Is what this tells us too obvious, too technical, too much a matter of the *technē* of print and memory and film prints to remark: that the screen image is a mosaic of marks, that light is the effect of waves determined by its own more radical lack, that "face" does not exist as such (is not represented but emerges within this artificed light)?

The cameo turns from us to *that*.

This turn alters everything, even if it has always been the case. Hitchcock takes us, from the start, through this other loop, a backloop of mnemonic production. One might summarize in advance: the "signature" logics of Hitchcock do not guarantee any auteur, or even a "human" model of perception, but undo both (and the hermeneutics dependent upon them). And one of the *Hitchcocks* we encounter never stops marking this. We might here reconceive one last time the enigma observed by William Rothman, and left totally uninterpreted, of what he calls "Hitchcock's signature": that is, a series of bars, or slashes (or, in sound, knockings), that traverse every film. *Intervals* (/ / / /), and intervals between intervals—before any image, before light, before representation, and before spelling.[2] Interiority is de facto foreclosed, citation initialed. If this is a "signature" (as Rothman calls it), then the "bar pattern" has the power to suspend or disrupt the spell of the "sensorium" (or even the semantics of spelling).

And could not "Hitchcock" the name be a signature effect or front for it, if it precedes letteration, countersigns a cinematic event? Since no representational or narrative logic can arrest what precedes representation, it precipitates a slide through names—like the many names adhering to designated characters throughout (the professor's aliases, the general's honorifics, Marnie's identity cards). Or through temporal orders, like the blackmailer *Tracey,* preceding even Egyptian hieroglyphics ("originary" writing), crashing through the glass dome into the British Museum's universal reading room, a universal reading model that Hitchcock's project does not leave intact. One problem the saboteur Verloc found was that when (the) light went out—that "light" which we hear in the term *Enlightenment,* say, a *lux* that supposedly guaranteed origin or perceptibility, even "nature," certainly a received model of man (and hence the *auteur*)—when the light went out Londoners merely laughed. Hitchcock's public was primarily entertained. They did not see or read that the "aesthetic" itself had been violated at its core, that phenomenality was a matter of effaced inscription. The political subversion allegorized in these early "thrillers" reflects Hitchcock's encompassing material or cinematic practice: that of entering the underworld of inscriptions before any image appears, the graphematics precedent to "light," writing, and ocularist pretense. (Think, again, of the temple of the sun worshippers in the first *Man Who Knew Too Much,* that is, the dupes, like ourselves, lured into the dark *templum* with the promise of worshipping the light, itself a front of a history altering assassination, only to have their money taken from them; or Mr. Memory, that "re*mark*able man," who only records "facts," like a snapshot, yet who bears in this unutterably banal way a secret formula for a *silent* warplane whose relay would starkly threaten the state.)[3]

Two implications.

If the machinal Mr. Memory updates Hesiod's Mnemosyne, Hitchcock's depiction of memory as an external operation immersed in banality and repetition does not separate this cinema from the epic traditions of the sublime, as if that involved a movement from poetic interiority to cinema's engraved memorization of things themselves—virtually banal "facts." Rather, it implies that memory has always been an effect of this technicity, all media, back and fore. Epic, literature as institution, was never other than this archival telemarking, memory never other than this exterior effect.

Second, this ur-signature opens a spectrographics that, like the pattern of parallel bars, can atomize every territorial notion of "signature," such as that assigned to or by auteurist logics.

Much of the intricacy of Hitchcock's citational play and rhyming effects becomes legible in repeat viewings, accessing video or DVD replay and pause, again and again, yet like the signature of Miss Froy on Iris's *befogged* window pane, soon effaced. And it seems confusing: the bar series, if it exists, after all precedes not only the cognitive assumptions of mimetic pictures, but sentences, words, as if receding to a preoriginary effect that informs yet coincides with no graphematic figure. But it only gets worse. Because if Hitchcock suspends light in the name of a printing machine that precedes and generates "it" to begin with, in and before *The Lodger,* and if he explosively and patiently unleashes, in this suspension, mobile networks that fan out across scenes as secret signifying agents, these cannot be contained by theoreticisms. These signifying networks that are not "visual" as such less guarantee or undersign a received model of perception than predict legibilities not yet in place. And with these an *archival* recalibration of times, of the "human," of gender and politicized perceptual programs—to the degree, that is, that an "Enlightenment" template can appear enfolded, too purely, into acapitalist machines, ocularcentrist regimes managing what Melanie Daniels calls "general semantics" (which she studies, of course, at *Ber*keley).

Hitchcock thus does not presence himself in what are called his cameos, which might be assembled as a kind of grammar of movements and bodily citations linked to music, reading, a rupture within signifying orders. The networks of traces and effects that we call "Hitchcock" emerges in and through proliferating signature systems, what might be called *cameonomies.*

Three secondary implications and a hypothesis.

*First,* the Pandora's box of this teletechnic presence marks this "cinema" as capable of absorbing and preceding every media and recording machine, in the process rewriting the "aesthetic" itself. This

links Hitchcock's cryptonymies to a sort of Nietzschean or chronographic backloop from which time and world are projected—from behind, and
not in front of, the "eye."

*Second,* Hitchcock's cinema, rather than guarding the mimetic promise of the photograph, assaults ocularcentrism generally and what is called
the visual.

*Third,* perhaps harder to *see,* there is what must be called an epistemo-
political agenda at work, only it cannot be resolved into nation-states, historical good guys and villains, world war or cold war opponents. Indeed,
these appear often as specular alternatives within the same inverted Enlightenment program (fascism/hypercapitalism): it points from the instant of its appearance to a beyond of this program, which is that of the
plots, the costumed sets narrated as history.

"Hitchcock" poses a riddle and resistance at the "dawn" of the cinematic era, at its advent, *as* its advent. If a political or epistemo-political
agenda pervades this project, it is there through all the political thrillers
and, in highly refined forms, everywhere. Hitchcock presented this
agenda in espionage terms as a perpetually failed or interrupted *crossing*:
a translation as if from one system to another (even if that latter, allo-
human, was prehistorially in place).[4] That is, say, a spectral "passage"
toward a teletechnics precedent to perception, to "life," to light, to the
human, to historicist time, and so on, by way of a prosthetic memory
band simulating a site of inscription. Hitchcock does not overtly choose
sides in the world war and cold war rebuses. "Cinema" will position
itself antithetically to the home state, and these specular wars are jointly
bound (ideologically, ideationally, eidetically), grouped as a "humanity"
assaulted in its enclave by what will be called the bird war. Numerous
nominal "professors" across this oeuvre testify to some impossible scene
of instruction. This cinematics apprehends its technical premises as a
war within and over the tele-archival, as anarchivist, which is also to say
over the production of virtual pasts and alternative futures.

It would take a mutating hypertext to track the systems of *marking,*
the choreographies and citational webs here (forward and back): the letters, numbers, phrases, gestures, sounds, double citations, all forms of
repetition and permutation of repetition. Point: all of these systems of
"puns" relate not to some planted code but to a performative reflection
on a *material* basis of marking or writing precedent to (and, in effect,
*barring*) any arrival of aura.

But one is also led, as if to the "Rome" of *Spellbound,* to a site that
precedes graphics, letteration. If I were absolutely pressed to give this a

name, I might call it that of *disinscription*— that which alone guarantees the dissolution of any mimetic promise of image when these elements resolve into *proactive* systems of citation (which, in Hitchcock, it is virtually at all points). As a series of bars or intervals registering and performing less sequence than suspension or Benjaminian "shock," *it* bars the arrival of any present, preceding even face, as with the striations in the stone that score the giant heads of Mount Rushmore. This precession of face, letter, or light itself points to where an effect we call "Hitchcock" identifies the technology to intervene in programs of memory, as in the faux séance that opens *Family Plot*, itself a (faux) model for Hitchcock's *cinemallographic* practice. Thus it is not "wordplay" that is at issue here: rather, as with the alpine Tower of Babel scenes of the British spy thrillers, diverse languages are dissolved (first) into more sound—what Hitchcock told Truffaut "dialogue" was for him first of all.[5]

This irreducible semiosis suspends any ocularcentric regime linked to auteurism and identification—that is, to so-called aura, to the image as representation, to telemarketing, "global" capital, and its eviscerations.

The early "political thrillers" tend to propose that some subversive "event" was at stake on which the course of history, or history itself, depended. Even in *Sabotage,* Piccadilly Circus, the target of the cinematic time bomb, is called the "center of the world." Rather than the reverse, as is assumed, the enemy state would be hermeneutic imperial Britain, the home state, homeland security, a regime protected by Scotland Yard's machinations and perverted detectives. The active politics here involves Hitchcock's attempt to alter mnemonics and the "sensorium." If "auteurism" as one general name for this ideology of an aesthetic state upholds that same model of the subject and "man," of mimetic reading, it has all along marked a relapse before and evasion of Hitchcock's aims.

Hitchcock as a sort of Hegel of the cinematic, in excess of any aesthetic category or what one calls "film," may be circled as an event within the histories of teletechnics and the advent of the cinematic—an incision the "global" still dwells within (or was generated from) and is clearly still playing out. One may frame it, momentarily, as a pedagogic template for legibilities in a tele-archival era; or as a site in which alternative "laws" of agency, the senses, and memory are under way. At the moment, the entire auteurial tradition, which had importantly performed its mission of recovery, mapping, and incubation, may be retired. There are not even, as one might say, *the Hitchcocks* (as he averred: *"The Birds is* coming"), numerous spectral units generated from and traversing proactive signature systems. One might wish, instead, to sketch a spectrographics, one departing from questions of how this shock within tele-archival mnemonics operates, still, in the suspension of borders between categories like living and dead, nation-state and other, mnemonics and global epistemo-politics. One may also do so with the suspension of the "ocularcentric" premises and programs that auteurist models discreetly presumed and that, it is now clear, Hitchcock suspended from the outset, together with what was once called aura. Perhaps Hitchcock must be approached as the most explicit Benjaminian practice of cinema, in which case the questions his work solicits, "today," when it is still soliciting unprecedented readings it had programmed and camouflaged in advance, have to do with the prospect of intervention within the historial, within the tele-archive as such, and hence, still, as all of his espionage thrillers make clear, within not just categories of time, perception, semiosis, and agency, but also the virtual futures and pasts that remain in disappearing competition. At the very least, the micrological Hitchcock demonstrates how the "cinematic" was a deauratic event: what and how a political vaporization of anthropomorphism and personification would have been implemented—everything, in short, that film studies as such had from the outset covered over or tried to restore.

And this is what he intends by the word *ill* used in the jingle of the zombie children from the end of *Marnie.* "Mother, mother, I am ill . . ." "I" is. The illness that registers in the strokes of the parallel bar pattern is at once the source of catastrophe and the cure. The lady with the alligator purse is Mother—or a certain "mother" whose purse is as alien and consuming, perhaps, as a reptile skin, citing the purse seen in the opening shot of the film, stuffed with money to bulging, yellow, a dismembered vaginal "phallic."

Of course "Hitchcock" is conjured and produced by signature systems and marks, and not the reverse. He comes out before the television camera a hosting specter mugging, inserting "murder" into the house, and its new templum, television. *It*—this Hitchcock—has implanted itself inversely at the heart of a cinematic canon it continues to dispossess or transfigure, as a spectrographics feeding off various futures. Beyond the auteurist model, a programmed fold, it transforms its own legibility. It locates itself not within film studies but still incomplete histories of teletechnics that wire epistemologies and define the human, within which "cinema" represents an exorbitant engine and self-marking hiatus. A deauratic practice, it operates as an antipode to the ideologies of the image that claim (like a defaulted software) provenance "today":

ocularcentric, mimetic, thanatopic, consumerist. Such a "Hitchcock" cites and atomizes programs of identification and gender, temporalization and epistemo-politics, mnemonics and the aesthetic. It is perhaps one site from which the nonanthropomorphic and teletechnic other might be summoned for interrogation—on the putative eve of a "planetary" legibility vaporizing the premises of the home, identity politics, the state, the nonhuman other. Even as it arrives, again, in the mode of spectrographic assault.

# Notes

## Introduction

1. Particularly if one can say, as D. N. Rodowick recently has, that "today" cinema is both virtually dead, before the advent of new media, and at the same moment exposed, in fact, as never having been consensually defined, never fully attached as a figure to the analogic as such, or any one technology—a nonexistent or virtual project wandering from body to body, like "Mother's" voice. See D. N. Rodowick, "Dr. Strange Media; or, How I Learned to Stop Worrying and Love Film Theory," *PMLA* 116 (2001): 1396–1404.

2. Gus Van Sant's hyperreal retake of *Psycho* appears, in the end, a hyper-literal joke on an entire sector of the film industry. One can survey recent offerings to see how many works are marketed as "Hitchcockian": *Mission Impossible II* takes its plot from *Notorious*; the Hughes brothers' adaptation of the graphic novel *From Hell* with Johnny Depp cannot stop citing *The Lodger* to solicit the advent of the cinematic era; *Signs* weakly rewrites *The Birds,* making the domestic avians *outright* extraterrestrials, translating an internal logic of the home to something external, possible to beat off.

3. Gayatri Chakravorty Spivak, *Death of a Discipline* (New York: Columbia University Press, 2003), especially chapter 3, "Planetarity"; Masao Miyoshi, "Turn to the Planet: Literature, Diversity, and Totality," *Comparative Literature,* Fall 2001; Wai Chee Dimock, "Literature for the Planet," *PMLA* 116 (January 2001): 173–88.

4. William Rothman, *Hitchcock: The Murderous Gaze* (Cambridge, MA: Harvard University Press, 1982), 33. More recently, William Rothman has expanded his recognition of the bar series, the "/ / / /" signature, to take into itself a roving band of repetitive techniques—as is appropriate for a mark that has no metaphorical stamp. Yet again, he deludes himself into thinking this can be accounted for in symbolic terms (imprisonment, barriers), not addressing the serial effect and the import of a mark that precedes marking. He also does not ask why such a signal discovery has had no luck entering the critical marketplace, where it goes virtually unremarked or used. It is as if he is pointing it out for us again, wanting his own recognition, but unable

to translate or explain—a silent scream: "[The courthouse columns in *Psycho*] present a perfect instance of what . . . I identify as Hitchcock's '/ / / /' motif, one of a set of motifs or signs or symbols—they include what I call 'curtain raisings'; 'eclipses'; 'tunnel shots'; white flashes; frames-within-frames; profile shots; symbolically charged objects (e.g., lamps, staircases, birds); symbolically charged colors (red, white, blue-green, brown)—that recur, at critical moments in every Hitchcock film. . . . As I demonstrated in *Hitchcock* . . . , the '/ / / /' sign functions at one level, as an invocation of prison bars, reminding us that the creatures who dwell in the world on film are, within their world, trapped, imprisoned'" (32). William Rothman, "Some Thoughts on Hitchcock's Authorship," in *Alfred Hitchcock: Centenery Essays,* ed. Richard Allen and S. Ishii-Gonzalez (London: British Film Institute, 1999); hereafter *HCE.* Rothman presumes, for one, that this citation of bare or presignifying semiosis can be considered a "sign" or "symbol" or "function" as such. Thus, the "sign's" interpretation is used, in short, to reinforce this incontaminability. Rothman has generously, and properly, extended the trope of signature throughout every instance of technical remarking and reflexive cross-cutting—not, that is, "symbols." Everything that would eviscerate the auteurial recognition he imagines, still, such agencies serve.

5. Throughout Hitchcock *this* syllable or syllabic invocation of a cut caroms: in proper names (Barbor, Barton, Bertani), in uses of the word (*Vertigo*'s "the bar at the top of the Mark") or visual props and series.

6. Such cannot *not* aggress, like *The Lodger*'s Avenger, upon the referential regimes of the state and its police, on programs of interpretation and perception, definition and assigned meaning: in short, a certain figuration of the human, the talking head, "pictures of people talking." The exposure of *light* as prosthetic, as an (electric) effect of alternation and rhythmic marking, alters metaphorics of light—the MacGuffin of the *Enlightenment,* the centrality of the eye, the presence or present of the visible. The *aesthetic* with this is redefined, as if in a world-altering assassination or bombing plotted by one of Hitchcock's cinemaphoric "villains." Instead of being representational in any sense, this image dives into the mnemonic underworld or site through which world is generated or phenomenalized, and wars over how it will be read and inscribed.

7. Peter Conrad, *The Hitchcock Murders* (New York: Faber and Faber, 2000).

8. Robin Wood observed that *animation* was the closest model to Hitchcock's practice of controlled artifice. One place Hitchcock marks this link—to cinema generally—is in the Disney cartoon shown at Verloc's Bijou movie house in *Sabotage.* A bird-man and bird-woman sing: the cartoon conceals a monstrosity, a man-animal recalling a minotaur waiting in the labyrinth. Since the screen never can quite produce a full human (the stars' bodies are cut up, too big and too small to be real), what is cited instead is all along monstrous.

If anything, the pretense of mimetic reproduction in photographics is regressive, as is clear when it turns out to dominate the supposed advance of digital imagery. Rodowick observes this relapse as the reinscription of computer-generated imagery to serve and service the mimetic template or interpretive regime: "There is much to be learned from the fact that 'photographic' realism remains the Holy Grail of digital imaging—a certain cultural sense of the cinematic and an unreflective notion of realism are still in many ways the touchstones for valuing the aesthetic innovations of the digital" (1400).

9. François Truffaut, *Hitchcock* (New York: Simon and Schuster, 1967; rev. ed. 1984), 5.

10. This ocularcentrism is a ceaseless opportunity for relapse, since "the visual" itself is a precritical term. It relapses—as in Peter J. Hutchings, "Modernity: A Film by Alfred Hitchcock," in *Senses of Cinema: An Online Film Journal Devoted to the Serious and Eclectic Discussion of Cinema* (May 2000), http://www.sensesofcinema.com—after weaving through valuable "material" referents—to the standard view of Hitchcock's role in the medium's history: "The point is that Hitchcock's understanding of modernity is that it is primarily experienced through vision—a vision that doesn't leave our other senses untouched—and that cinema is the art of telling stories through moving pictures." This conception of the visual is, in fact, pre-Hitchcockian.

11. Wark, "Vectoral Cinema," *Senses of Cinema* (May 2000), adduces a thoroughly countermimetic cinema: "This is not a cinema of resemblances. The hokey looking back-projections with which Hitchcock presents scenes of movement are not really meant to resemble anything. They are an index of cinema itself. We know the scenes are back-projections, an index of projection, because we know they don't look anything like what they purport to look like."

12. See Friedrich A. Kittler, *Gramophone, Film, Typewriter,* trans. G. Winthrop-Young and M. Wurz (Palo Alto, CA: Stanford University Press, 1999).

## 1. Transports

1. Peter Conrad reminds us of this point, when choosing to look in the dialogues for "tell-tale oddities of phrasing or diction," and arguing that "despite his pretended indifference to words, he maintained strict control over what his characters said, and made sure that the writers he hired . . . took dictation from him" (*Hitchcock Murders,* xii).

2. There tends to be a representational cataclysm or disaster affiliated with the camera's violating arrest and totalization that precedes the inauguration of a narrative, which then proceeds as if in a post-space, and after-time drawn, forgetfully, forward: Louis Bernard's ski fall in the first *Man Who Knew Too Much,* the fake death of *Secret Agent,* the blackout of *Sabotage,* the corpses of

*Murder!* and *Rope* or, inversely, *The Trouble with Harry* that precede a narrative that unravels or evades its implications, the shipwrecks of *Jamaica Inn*.

3. The *Mar-* signature is split between Guy's two women: the courted Anne Morton and the murdered pregnant wife, Miriam. Miriam, like Lila in *Psycho,* works for a music store with glass booths for the private replay of *re*cordings.

4. On the train, Bruno will present himself as reading facts from the news, and knowing "all the answers," like Mr. Memory, to the point of alarming Guy that he *reads* "too much" in knowing about his own doings.

5. Kittler, *Gramophone,* 3–4.

6. Ina Rae Hark, "'We Might Even Get in the Newsreels': The Press and Democracy in Hitchcock's World War II Anti-Fascist Films," in *HCE,* 344.

7. Hence Hitchcock's recurrence to tropes of preproduction, like the incorporation of "floodlamps" in the torture scene of *Foreign Correspondent* or the roof finale in *To Catch a Thief*.

8. This drying up of *Rebecca's* signifying *sea,* the *mer,* also shifts from the snowcaps of the Alpine scenes to the white desert of sodium, of salt. The iris shot of Hoover Dam puts a certain consumption of "nature" in question, since it links the manufacture of power in the wrenching of geological form to a containment allied to that of the photographic picture as archival index.

## 2. Combined Ops

1. And one is always left with Goebbels's admiration for *Foreign Correspondent* as a residual reminder. See again Hark, "'We Might Even Get in the Newsreels,'" *HCE,* 333–48.

2. One way to read *Rope,* for instance, is as a study, in small part, of where in the postwar bubble the defeated fascist rhetoric (Hitler is mentioned in association with Nietzsche by Mr. Kentley) migrates back into the victor's intellectual discourse and, through the professor (Stewart), into the acts and aesthetic norms of a succeeding generation—planted, assumed, disseminated, denied.

3. For Hitchcock extricating these narrative moments would perhaps be inconceivable, if the broader "politics" of his cinema implicitly tended to view the antagonists as in some ways interchangeable—as the American capitalists, in *Saboteur,* were in representing a *fifth* column, as though the in(ex)tricate target of transformation were a historial system that had produced specular variants.

4. Indeed, the manner in which Jeanne's *watch* is taken and focused on recalls where, in *Aventure Malgache,* the imprisoned lawyer-thespian will hold to his ear in bed an alarm clock that is really a radio over which Morse code tappings are relayed by the Resistance.

5. The name Arnie itself fits into a series of annotations of the letter *R*—from "old man R," the spymaster of *Secret Agent,* to the *R* of Rebecca, *Marnie,* or, finally, Rust's pin in *Frenzy*—which will be bound, for Hitchcock, to *repetition.*

## 3. A Performativity without Frame

1. David Sterritt, *The Films of Alfred Hitchcock* (Cambridge: Cambridge University Press, 1993), 9.

2. This Poesque calculus irradiates across Hitchcock's setups like a ritual: in casinos, in (preoriginary) "accidents" *(Shadow of a Doubt, Marnie),* in falls (the first *Man Who Knew Too Much*) or staged encounters (the second version). Given the perpetual Hamlet motif that pervades Hitchcock's testing of the mediatized "act," and his awareness of setting in play as mobile a pure artifice (whose writing and production engage the chance concatenation of sounds, letters, production sites, available "actors," innumerable collaborators, and so on), Hitchcock routinely implants a preoriginary "accident" or chance to complicate Mallarmé's "il y a et il n'y a pas le hasard"—or set the conditions of the event within that calculus by which all is, also, repetition, set and set up.

3. The audience in the Music Hall of *The 39 Steps* is without divide from the performer, Mr. Memory, whom it asks its insipid factual and counterfactual questions, the entire theater emptied into the street jointly with the report of shots. Cinema begins in and as a re-marking of a site of "death," or crossing (out) a bordering of life-death, as the faux séance opening *Family Plot* affirms as a trope for Hitchcock's practice.

4. *The aesthetic* is recast as a site of virtual disinscription in the manner, say, of the logic that attends Benjamin's "materialistic historiography." Paul de Man, in a Benjaminian turn, speaks of an "irreversible" movement or shift or *passage* that occurs in moving between reading models—of which the latter is vaguely named the "performative," to indicate where the event ("actual action," says *Sabotage*) occurs, even if that is an event like "translation" itself. One moves from an "epistemological critique of tropes" (de Man) toward that which is no longer a matter of cognition or endless tropological displacement but which occurs, both records and produces (itself) as a positional event. In "Kant and Schiller" we read: "And this passage, if it is thus conceived, that is the passage from trope to performative . . . goes in that direction and you cannot get back from the one to the one before" (*Aesthetic Ideology,* ed. Andrzej Warminski [Minneapolis: University of Minnesota Press, 1996], 133). I have sketched this reading of de Man and Hitchcock, an unexpected pairing, in "Political Thrillers: Hitchcock, de Man, and Secret Agency in the 'Aesthetic State,'" in *Material Events: Paul de Man and the Afterlife of Theory,* ed. Tom Cohen, Barbara Cohen, J. Hillis Miller, and Andzrej Warminski (Minneapolis: University of Minnesota Press, 2001), 114–52.

5. Such performativity can appear as a suspended fall over an abyss—one, like the trick shot in *Vertigo,* that is not just down, but up and down simultaneously, the loss of a gravity. Lost directions, the supplantation of one map, one geographics for an unwritten one. Directionlessness as the premise of another *directionality*; cameo markings taken for auteurist hieroglyphs as the premise for the evisceration of the Hitchcock body, viewed as the remainder found in the

television outline's fragmented circlets. In *Vertigo* a giant sequoia, cut and on display, presents the same vertigo swirl within the center of its trunk—within "nature"—as the vortex that becomes a morphing graphic Möbius band pre-inhabits a woman's eye in the opening credit sequence: nature or the eye not originary but the effects of graphematics archives.

6. This signature number will appear harbored in the Greek *pi* that appears *underfoot,* like a hypogram, in *Torn Curtain,* where the π is a password, traced on the sand mutely, for an underground resistance to the east, which retains the implications of the Pythagorean theorem in a text filled with blackboards of numerical demonstrations (3.14 . . .).

7. Peter Conrad, in *Hitchcock Murders,* explains cinema's originary "shock" effect: "The cinema, like a bomb, is a device for dematerializing the world" (27). Or: "Hitchcock likened his films to buzz bombs—clever engines of mass destruction, invented by the century in which men made war against humanity" (118). This explosion is mutely presented in disasters that appear preoriginary (avalanche, shipwreck, car crash): "Hitchcock allowed himself to be branded 'the master of suspense.' . . . But his real interest was in suspension" (23). See Christopher D. Morris, *The Hanging Figure: On Suspense and the Films of Alfred Hitchcock* (Westport, CT: Praeger, 2002). Morris uses the figure of spectral *photons* ("that wave/particle matrix physicists hypothesize to be a necessary condition of light" [260]) to suggest the irreducible materiality of what, in any signifying order, generates the effect called light—here allied to micrological signifiers.

8. Kittler locates this backloop in the category of Nietzschean "inscription" and relates the cinema's facticity in this regard to a problem: a mediatic acceleration of inscription to a redefinition of the human: "Beyerlen's technical observation that in typing everything is visible except the actual inscription of the sign, also describes *On The Genealogy of Morals.* . . . The only possible, that is unconscious, kind of reading is the slavish obedience called morals. Nietzsche's notion of *inscription* . . . has validity only within the framework of the history of the typewriter. It designates the turning point at which communications technologies can no longer be related back to humans. Instead, the former have formed the latter" (*Gramophone,* 211).

## 4. "How Old Is Mae West?"

1. Lee Edelman, "Hitchcock's Future," in *HCE,* 239–58.

2. The inversion is that a "male gaze" would always position and consume "woman" as such (one of her key references was the Hitchcock of *Vertigo* and *Rear Window*). In another feminist account of Hitchcock, Tania Modleski positions the auteur as a sort of stand-in for the "patriarchy," who repeatedly does violence to threatening females, including that ultimate victim, "Mother," in *Psycho.* See Laura Mulvey, "Visual Pleasure and Narrative Cinema," in *Issues in*

*Feminist Film Criticism,* ed. Patricia Erens (Bloomington: Indiana University Press, 1990), 30–36, and Modleski, *The Women Who Knew Too Much: Hitchcock and Feminist Theory* (New York: Methuen, 1988), "Introduction."

3. An open-ended list of *Mar-* names would include Margot, Martin, Marvin, Margaret (in different forms), Marion, Marlow, and so on, and with variation, Murchisson and Morton, and so on. For a key illumination of the interface of *the linguistic in the image* and "the medium of the mark" in painting that is carried over into the analysis of cinema, see Walter Benjamin, "Painting, or Signs and Marks," in *Selected Writings,* vol. 1, 1913–1926, ed. Marcus Bullock and Michael W. Jennings (London: Belknap Press, 1996): "The actual problem of painting can be discerned in the statement that a picture is indeed a set of marks. . . . [The] relation to what the picture is named after, to what transcends the marks, is what is created by the composition. This signifies the entry of a higher power into the medium of the mark. This power, once there, remains in a state of neutrality, meaning it does not use graphic line to explode the mark but makes its home there without destroying it, because even though it is immeasurably higher than the mark, it is not hostile toward it but related to it. This power is the linguistic word, which lodges in the medium of the composition" (86).

4. Amy Lawrence, in "American Shame: *Rope,* James Stewart, and the Postwar Crisis in American Masculinity" (in *Hitchcock's America,* ed. Jonathan Freedman and Richard Millington [New York: Oxford University Press, 1999], 55–76), gives a superb sketch of Stewart's semaphoric role as a site of cultural defacement, despite linking this "crisis in masculinity" to a historicist map that, indebted to queer studies, may be exceeded by the problematic touched on (how, for instance, does it relate to the "queer" motifs of *The Lodger* or the Mae West quip of *The 39 Steps,* and so on?). This fertile dossier was opened, first, by Robert J. Corber's *In The Name of National Security: Hitchcock, Homophobia, and the Political Construction of Gender in Postwar America* (Durham, NC: Duke University Press, 1993).

5. Scottie is being used, officially, to give an alibi to Gavin Elster during the latter's killing of his real wife, whom we never see as more than a virtual blonde corpse in free fall past the bell tower's window frame—calculably when Scottie's "vertigo" kicks in. Elster sets him up by baiting him with a hokey ghost story about the "dead" harming the living, which Scottie rejects as the irrational rubbish it technically is. Yet Scottie one-ups even this: he will be haunted and harmed by the ghost of what never even existed, since Madeleine was nothing but a successful lounge act.

6. Ray Milland in *Dial "M" for Murder* wants her dead, James Stewart in *Rear Window* thinks she is "too perfect" to desire and sadistically mocks her attempts at seduction, Cary Grant in *To Catch a Thief* is fleeing her incessantly, in tandem with the most brazen and literal come-ons imaginable.

7. This sort of punning goes back to before *Murder!* when Sir John is woken in his bed by an innkeeper's children and a running cat, with the little girl reaching under Sir John's bedcover looking for her "pussy."

8. Without *reference*(s), she is as if a point of passage and transformation for her thefts, her undoing of a patriarchist (or eunarchist) institution that is running, has been running, on empty, that persists over its own nonexistence. In the archive of "modernist" moments, Marnie's evisceration of "female" expectations, producing a nihilist variant of the female performative, distantly echoes that of Addie Bundren in Faulkner's *As I Lay Dying.*

## 5. Phoenix Rex

1. Sigmund Freud, *Sexuality and the Psychology of Love,* ed. P. Rieff (New York: Collier, 1963), 180.

2. The metaphorics of "gaze" does not come without certain baggage. To be sure, classic feminism in the wake of Laura Mulvey's writing on *Vertigo* and the politics of male pleasure has profited by the practical tool of isolating and gendering the "gaze" itself as a machine of desiring and fixating control or violation. See Marian Keane, "A Closer Look at Scopophilia: Mulvey, Hitchcock, and *Vertigo,*" for a sample correlative of Mulvey's hypothesis, in *A Hitchcock Reader,* ed. Marshall Deutelbaum and Leland Poague (Ames: University of Iowa Press, 1986), 231–48; hereafter cited as *HR.* But quite aside from subsequent dismantlings of Mulvey's treatment, including by herself, the trope of gaze may well have provided altogether too fascinating or hypnotic a premise. That is, despite its gothic pretenses, it remains rooted in a programmatic ocularcentrism, as well as a rhetoric of personification (or aura) that, once again, Hitchcock would have seemed to foreclose. Such an approach implicitly brings back with it a kind of metaphysics of the subject (however turned inside out as [Cartesian] "abyss," or "subject beyond identification," and so on), and where a misleading logic of the panopticon ends up by totalizing the metaphor itself, as Joan Copjec has shown in "The Orthopsychic Subject: Film Theory and the Reception of Lacan," *October* 49 (1989): 53–72. Compare the alternate use of the "gaze" in Zizek's *Looking Awry: An Introduction to Jacques Lacan through Popular Culture* (Cambridge, MA: MIT Press, 1991), 125–26, where he argues that the "gaze" is precisely an extrasubjective figure that is not reconcilable to a subjectivist or mimetic aesthetic.

3. The dream sequence is set in a "gambling house," where something is at stake involving the house of psychoanalysis, Green Manors—among other things, identity, time, perception, body, memory, the definition of *white.* Hitchcock reinscribes the cinematic through Dalí's graphic work with Buñuel in a "surreal" suspension of mimetic premises, an allegorical signscape of muting, faceless nightmares, a "labyrinth" in which a minotaur stalks the thread of reading. Books circulate in *Spellbound,* one of which flies at Ingrid Bergman's

head. Christopher Morris, in his accelerated leap into the *figurative* in Hitch-cock, references this to a surrealist politics: "In the unreadable faces of *Vertigo* and *North by Northwest,* misinterpretation is strongly associated with attempts to comprehend visual art. The development of this tradition was not original with Hitchcock. Recent studies by Rosalind Kraus and Martin Jay show how surrealist photography and film registered protests against what Jay called ocularcentrism—the privileged status accorded to the sense of vision as a kind of grail of hermeneutics, the achievement of a true theoretical perspective. For Kraus and Jay, Bataille's enucleated eye, Magritte's *trompe d'oeil* and Dali's sliced eyeball anticipate the philosophical interrogation of hermeneutics inten-sified later by deconstruction." See Morris, *The Hanging Figure,* 217.

4. Robin Wood interestingly observes that: "[a] central characteristic of Expressionism (as a cinematic movement) is the distortion of the 'reality' the camera records or the creation of a world phenomenologically remote from the reality recognized by our senses; a central characteristic of montage theory is the creation of concepts that have no necessary phenomenological equiva-lents in what was actually presented before the camera. These two movements represent, in their very different ways, the two main lines of opposition to the notion of film as an inherently realistic medium: their emphasis is on arti-fice rather than representation. In Hitchcock's cinema, their 'artificiality' is intensified by the fact that both techniques are divorced from their original ends. Expressionism was a 'high art' movement rooted in a specific time and place, a specific *angst*; Soviet montage was associated with revolution and propaganda, with the task of making the principles underlying the revolution intelligible, cogent, and concrete. Hitchcock in a sense perverted both. . . . I find it significant—having in mind the whole Hitchcock oeuvre—that he should build the foundations of his style out of elements inherently 'artificial,' borrowed from cultures other than his own and detached from the conditions that originally gave them their meaning." See Robin Wood, "Retrospective," in *HR,* 28. When Wood describes "expressionism" as "the distortion of the 're-ality' the camera records or the creation of a world phenomenologically remote from the reality recognized by our senses," he notes a scandal, since in passing from "distortion" to a "world phenomenologically remote" he observes that the "senses" themselves may be already programmed, their reality a matter of mne-monic imprinting, and that the "phenomenality" of film apprehends the power of mnemonic inscription to produce phenomenalizations that are irreducible to representations. So much so, it is perpetually suppressed by the cultural mi-meticism of the state, the manner in which the latter's truth, its empiricisms, its assurances of the senses and representations—the policing mentality, say, of the "hard-headed" detective of Scottish descent—are managed as a regime (early on, the home state called England represents this). Hitchcock's most obvious mock-up of the "expressionist" genre, in *Secret Agent,* is preoccupied

with a trace or obliterating sound that precedes sense or the senses, and is deposited in the double agent Marvin (another *Mar-* or *marking* name), undoing phenomenology.

5. It may be that this identity that is not one also is not the case at all, since what we see, on the contrary, is a war of difference(s) between Norman and "Mother"—even when one is supposed to speak another's or another "Mother's" voice (or the opposite)—as between A(nor)man and A(nor)ma ("Mother's" name in Bloch's novel is Norma), Amat(t)er. If the *cell* scene is positioned just beyond such dialectics, is beyond dialectics altogether and not alone in its indifference to being duped by the symbolic order (Marion might fool Norman, we hear, but *not* Mother), what is impersonating whom is not clear (or how many times this goes back and forth). One version of this we see in Margaret M. Horwitz's "*The Birds*: A Mother's Love," where this rift is pasted over, since one can successfully Oedipalize everything, except the absence of the father, present only as a photograph, as the logic of the photographic *Bild*: "Throughout *The Birds* the characters assume shifting roles within an Oedipal family configuration." See Margaret M. Horwitz, "*The Birds*: A Mother's Love," in *HR,* 279. Or: "I believe that in *The Birds,* as in *Psycho,* the heroine is punished by the hero's mother because of the heroine's desirability to him. The process is a result of the male character's inability to successfully resolve an Oedipal relationship. In *Psycho* the mother and son are united in the character of Norman, whose psychotic behavior is revealed and explicated at the end of the film" (279). Mother and son would be "united," and explained, within the commentator's belief system.

6. A "secret" traverses that narrative so obviously marked that it goes unseen: that the kidnapped Bishop Wood is the biological "father" of someone who bore the name Eddie *Shoebridge* and then, later, as if new, Arthur Adamson (a doubling or repetition so that the "first" man, Adam, is not invoked but referenced by a second, a son).

7. Raymond Durgnat, "Extract from *A Long Hard Look at Psycho,*" at *Senses of Cinema,* http://www.sensesofcinema.com.

8. Derrida's analysis of the *khora* in Plato's *Timaeus* approaches this nonplace, accessed by and as "Mother," as what is outside of the couple, the family, the parental and generational map—as what predisinhabits and spawns *family plots*: "This familial schema by which one situates a discourse will be found again at work at the moment of situating, if we can still say this, the place of any site, namely, *khora* . . . (A)lthough it no longer has the place of the nurse but that of the mother, *khora* does not couple with the father, in other words, with the paradigmatic model. She is a third gender/genus (48e); she does not belong to an oppositional couple, for example, to that which the intelligible paradigm forms with the sensible becoming and which looks rather like a father/son couple. The 'mother' is supposedly apart. And since it's only a figure, a schema, therefore one of these determinations which *khora* receives, *khora* is not more

of a mother than a nurse, is no more than a woman. This *triton genos* is not a genos . . . She does not belong to the 'race of women' *(genos gynaikon)*. *Khora* marks a place apart, the spacing which keeps a dissymmetrical relation to all that which, 'in herself,' beside or in addition to herself, seems to make a couple with her. In the couple outside of the couple, this strange mother who gives place without engendering can no longer be considered as an origin. She/it eludes all anthropo-theological schemas, all history, all revelation, and all truth. Preoriginary, before and outside of all generation, she no longer even has the meaning of a past, of a present that is past. Before signifies no temporal anteriority. The relation of independence, the nonrelation, looks more like the relation of the interval or the spacing to what is lodged in it to be received in it" (my emphasis). See "Khora," in Jacques Derrida, *On the Name,* trans. Ian McLeod, ed. Thomas Dutoit (Palo Alto, CA: Stanford University Press, 1995), 124–25.

9. J. Hillis Miller and Manuel Asensi, *Black Holes* (Palo Alto, CA: Stanford University Press, 1999).

10. The bog recalls Mrs. Stevens's referencing the origin of her fortune next to the outhouse on her dead husband Jeremiah's homestead—no plumbing, "a little place out back."

11. And within this translation something happens to feet, steps, legs, ledger, lodgings, to reading, to *legein* and *légère,* since the legacy of "Oedipus" returns—or never went anywhere to begin with, is at all points already in *The Lodger,* say—as a limping foot, a knocking or dragging notch, prints. Such as, the "bad leg" Lawrence is threatened with in the first *Man Who Knew Too Much* if he tries to leave the temple of sun worshippers, which Foussard has in *To Catch a Thief* ("I think he had a bad leg," notes Lepic, while Danielle Foussard will be said to have done her father's "legwork"), or James Stewart as Rupert Cadell in *Rope* or L. B. Jeffries in *Rear Window* (whose leg is signed as in a, or the, "cast") or at the beginning of *Vertigo.*

## 6. Time Machines

1. Michel Chion, "The Impossible Embodiment," in *Everything You Always Wanted to Know about Lacan . . . But Were Afraid to Ask Hitchcock,* ed. Slavoj Zizek (New York: Verso, 1992), 202; hereafter cited as *Everything.*

2. Gilles Deleuze, *Cinema 1: The Movement-Image,* trans. Hugh Tomlinson and Barbara Habberjam (Minneapolis: University of Minnesota Press, 1986), 202. The neo-Lacanians have been equally drawn too close to this flame, since it seems irresistible to reassign this unnamed break with a dyadic history to some endowed stalwart among the Lacanian dramatis personae, as Mladen Dolar does: "the position of the third in the duality is occupied both by the fascinating and lethal object (which is also the object of exchange and circulation) and the mother's desire, Mother as the bearer of the law" ("Hitchcock's Objects," *HR,* 38–39). Stojan Pelko observes more usefully perhaps: "This 'thirdness'

may, of course, be expressed in different ways. What is 'primary' on the cinematic level is no longer character . . . nor action, but the very multitude of relations" ("Punctum Caelum," *HR*, 112).

3. These include letteral combinations in proper names, primarily, that combine the third letter *(C)* with either the first *(A)* or an alternate vowel (*O*, where *O* echoes, without assimilating, a zero effect): Canadian, Caypor, Capricorn, the Carlton at Cannes.

4. There is a still different primacy that attaches itself to what we can hesitantly call a triadic cluster (3, 13, *CA, AC*) that recurs like a motif across many films, threading these almost like the bar series found at the obliterating navel of antimemory itself in *Spellbound*. If *it* announces itself in this way as a kind of cipher of nonorigin, Hitchcock does little to conceal its attachment to the idea of source and seriality, strangling and attack, since it is precisely this that is thematically identified as literally the calling card of the serial killer the Avenger in *The Lodger*.

5. The *pyramid* at its center turns up within a sunburst on the secret message in the first *Man Who Knew Too Much*; emblem of the Tabernacle of the Sun in Wapping, it has supplanted the sun.

6. In this dismemberment by syllable and sound, the black and white inversions mime an installation or inscription: *MUR* is being isolated, highlighted, wildly flashing for attention, a wall, a marring, a "mar" or its first letteral designate—short of the name "Daisy," which in French is *marguerite*. And the Pandora's box is, always was, wide open: *mur, mar, mer, mère*.

7. Hitchcock associates "children" at times with a paradoxical fault within reproduction, as if the pretext of the human child is crossed with the facticity of semiotic consciousness, which sheers away any genetic metaphors, leaving doubles and simulacra. Examples of this would include the skit in *Murder!* with the cat under the sheet on Sir John's bed chased by the children whose mother comes in carrying a baby; the baby crying at the beginning of *The 39 Steps*; the sight of the Moroccan women stitching as Doris Day references having a baby; the treatment of eggs (especially in *To Catch a Thief*); the aquarium scene in *Sabotage*; the birds' attack at Cathy's birthday party (playing blindman's bluff); and so on.

8. Silent film is apprehended by Hitchcock as a pure cognitive map, wherein face, muting, and inscription collude—and to which sound as "talk" will be added on not as a redefinition of the represented subject, but just added on, as more signifiers, different forms of writing, sound, the ear. The cinematic machine absorbs everything.

9. For Plato, or a certain "Plato" (supposed installer of the ocularcentric and heliocentric order), the geometric form may exemplify the *eidos,* that invisible visibility equating seeing with knowing *(eidein),* knowing with illumination, the idea of the good, the paternal sun, and so on. But we know today that the *eidos* as trope is spawned by a figurative sleight of hand attending certain

events in the dialogues: the death(s) of "Socrates," impossible to contain with "his" numerous revenants, the semaphoric link between this death and return and the *eidos,* that sublation of "primal letters" *(stoicheia),* of the mark into its effaced obverse, the spectral *eidos.* Hitchcock returns from the head and eye to the feet, inverting a preoriginary inversion ("after" Plato). He equates ocularcentrism, as if a gift of Platonic dissimulation (itself dismantled in the *Parmenides*), with the state, the *capo,* human consumption, serial eviscerations of woman, the mimetic violation of the visual, a death state policed and politically programmed by mnemonic templates, tourism. The *Avenger* gone corporate, reinstalled at the center of a church—even one that is a front for its (already) other, the churchly robbing of the flock that is the epistemological norm, or even when Hitchcock's cinematic project further insinuates itself (but it was always "there") at this nonsource in turn, installing cinema as the double dissimulation within an official dissimulation.

10. Kittler again: "And once optical fiber networks turn formerly distinct data flows into a standardized series of digitalized numbers, everything goes. Modulation, transformation, synchronization; delay, storage, transposition; scrambling, scannning mapping—a total media link on a digital base will erase the very concept of medium" (*Gramophone,* 1–2).

11. One may be drawn to a more deceptive *triadic* model than C. S. Peirce's, that in V. N. Voloshinov, where a triangulated scene of "utterance" coincides implicitly with the emergence (in cancellation) of the speaker, the first person. For rather than finding that dialogue is a function of *two,* it turns out that it requires three—one version: speaker, listener, hero—of which one (the "hero") is *not* even human, is an apostrophe that inhabits utterance's emergence, a "personification." In Voloshinov, the trace of the dead word of the past, the trace of anteriority, emerges as a prosopopoeia in which the "I" is posited as a speaking dead in advance of an utterance that, like the snow falling in May, is disjunct from temporal succession itself. For elaboration of this threshing machine, see my treatment of this in "Othello, Bakhtin and the Deaths of Dialogue," in *Anti-Mimesis from Plato to Hitchcock* (Cambridge: Cambridge University Press, 1994), 11–44.

12. In addition to anagrammatic play, which often positions the "A. H." signature as a place rather than person—the Royal Albert Hall, the Assembly Hall—in the manner of Ambrose Chapel, the expectoration in rage of the ambassador to Drayton in the second *Man Who Knew Too Much*—"Eh!? EH!? EH!?"—recalls the relation this "ah!" has to apostrophe, the invocation and personification of an (unnamed) entity, and hence prosopopoeia. In *Secret Agent* the association is explicit, when Agent "R" is introduced and Gielgud asks if that is "Ah!" as in exclamation point, and is told, no, *R* as in "rhododendron," a flower of recirclings.

13. The word *pick* recurs repeatedly in Hitchcock, as in *To Catch a Thief* ("picnic," "pick out," "Lepic") or the second *Man Who Knew Too Much,* where

having had to "pick up Hank" is the label given to the narrative. It also itali-cizes the letter $p$ (or Greek pi, signature for a cinematic and pyramidal formula: 3.14 . . .).

14. In Bergman's romantic blossoming, cartoonlike and mocked (as when, asked what sandwich she wants, she says ecstatically, "Liverwurst!"). Doors open onto no particular space, but to other doors within doors within doors. With Peck and Bergman's first kiss, for instance, door frames within frames open not onto an outside but a luminous white wall. It seems a wall or artificial light without a door, but already a frame within a frame within a frame—*whatever* the lovesick violins are doing, like the receding puff clouds of Marlene Die-trich's chanteuse act in *Stage Fright*.

15. Gregory *Peck* may be the oddest of Hitchcock's exposed actor personae: where Hitchcock toys with and strips Grant or Stewart, he just thrusts Peck into his psychosis, skipping all the moves, and tells him to find his way back, knowing he hasn't gone anywhere—as in a faux labyrinth.

16. Green Manors would cite an inverted madhouse of cinema, clearly, over which psychoanalysis is as another front or trope, the analysis an elongated version of Nurse Agnes's hypnosis of Clyde. This too is marked and subverted, since the first house we see on-screen is the Selznick Studio Mansion logo, with leaves blowing by it as in *Number 17.*

17. We defer analyzing how the figure of blackmailing resonates across Hitchcock doubly, both as the structure of how *sheer anteriority* is used against and effaces any "present" or is turned into a destroying secret and why *letters,* mail, and *blackness* figure in this chain.

18. Copious references to cinematic production and epistemo-aesthetic agency recur before the famous windmill scene with its counternatural turn-ing of the sail wheel, indicating another law than any natural, referential, or mimetic logic could contain. George Sanders bears a name inscrutable in being denied a capital letter, and in which three letters are silently doubled. The name is written for us, *ffolliott*, an alphabet soup of hypogrammatic possi-bilities. Among them, the double Os, the bar tripling at the center *(lli),* and the word, as if caught in double vision, *folio.* The word *folio* echoes in the name of Marnie's horse, Forio, which incorporates other precessual resonance—raced in the estate of Rutland Publishing Company.

19. It is Joel McCrea as the double *J*'d Johnny Jones (Hitchcock's dropped middle initial was *J* for Joseph) who becomes the double *H*'d Huntley Haver-stock who stumbles on the live and kidnapped Van Meer in the windmill stor-age room.

20. Fis(c)her recoups the innocent German gentleman who appears British, Caypor, of *Secret Agent,* only this time in fact a secret agent, much as Miss Fish-er (Laraine Day) anticipates the Ingrid Bergman role of Alicia in *Notorious*—continuing, differently, as if from the death of her traitorous father (consider the prim Laraine Day, sans McCrea, during Alicia's wanton days). But the

paronomasic drift of the name *Van Meer* suggests the Van be read as "of the" Meer, *mer(e)*, *mar*(r), mat(t)er, sea, see, and so on. The effaced *c* in Fis(c)her's name is for the cinema, the third letter, and so on.

21. It implicitly reverses positions, asymmetrically, with the "first" definition, since what is formally imperial in the assassination or stolen military secret is intermittently recast as what would intervene in that statist regime.

22. If Lina is caught up in a bookish ideology of "love" sustained by fantasy and a compulsion to interpret (books, like letters, figure centrally in this entirely "hermeneutic" film), Johnny is a figure of verbal performativity, as Peter Lorre's general was in *Secret Agent*.

23. Thus reminding us of the reference to "acrostics" in *The Lady Vanishes* or "crossword" puzzles in *Blackmail*. Fontaine's spectacles become an issue. They are ocular prosthetics: on the one hand, they connect with the film title—suspicion can be heard as sus(under)-spect(ation)—while, on the other, they reroute the eye from looking out the window to a book, condensing image and world to the movements of script.

## 7. Matrixide

1. This alliance between excrement and dogs or cats—excrement as (a)material excess, all legs—is confirmed in Hitchcock's naming his dog Philip of Magnesia, after the laxative, Phillips Milk of Magnesia.

2. The insinuated rape accompanying the strangling is not at all portrayed and a reference in the bar by two patrons extolling Jack the Ripper jokingly suggests an impotent, if not in fact fully clothed, "rape."

3. Thomas Hemmeter's "Twisted Writing: *Rope* as an Experimental Film," in *Hitchcock's Rereleased Films: From* Rope *to* Vertigo, ed. W. Raubicheck and W. Srebnick (Detroit: Wayne State University Press, 1991), draws attention to the role a rupture within discourse itself shapes and is shaped by within the film text: "*Rope*'s critics try to close the film off from serious consideration since it allows play with the structural center of thematic and moral seriousness. But the playfulness of language, its puns and metaphors and multiple meanings, threatens the presumed order of any structure. Indeed, a fear of disruptive language is evident in the critical discourse on *Rope*" (255). The relations of power, of reading (the nonmaster), of literalizing into an "act" (preoriginary murder), of the appropriation, inhabitation, and disownership of words, on a literalization of Nietzschean recurrence and its performative logics—these saturate to the cyclorama of *Rope*.

4. In *North by Northwest,* Grant and Eva Marie Saint meet after the fake shooting in the pinewoods copse, where the trees align as bar figures or spatial cuts, as they are in the closing scenes of the Bandriki woods in *The Lady Vanishes*.

5. Less blonde herself than a citation of *blondeness,* the model presents, one could almost say, a face that defaces in advance, itself and others.

6. Lee Edelman, "Hitchcock's Future," in *HCE*, 249.

7. In the recent Mel Gibson film, *Signs*, the general mise-en-scène of *The Birds* is regurgitated, replacing the avians with, indeed, aliens—exactly the opposite of what Hitchcock, choosing domestic and nonpredatory animemes, indicates.

8. Here the stars are animated slashes, and the humans not stars. By inducting Tippi Hedren the TV model into the role, a mimetic logic is inverted again: the installed model as preoriginal copy (Marnie is associated with an office copying machine as well as *typography*).

9. Zizek is quick to adapt the figure to Lacan: "The MacGuffin is clearly the *objet petit a*, a gap in the center of the symbolic order—the lack, the void of the Real setting in motion the symbolic movement of interpretation." See Slavoj Zizek, "Introduction," in *Everything*, 8. Or again, Mladen Dolar glosses: "The MacGuffins signify only that they signify, they signify the signification as such; the actual content is entirely insignificant." See Dolar, "Hitchcock's Objects," in *Everything*, 45. This "theorization" determines the MacGuffin as a sophisticated performative. Yet no longer a ruse, it rather is given a place in the Lacanian firmament, more or less secure.

10. If one assumes the MacGuffin in *The 39 Steps* is the meaningless airplane formula, one is caught in two webs. On the one hand, the recitation of the nongrammatical letters and numbers by Mr. Memory signals the unseen micrological writing that Hitchcock is using to define his "cinematic" practice as a graphematics of "light" precedent to and inclusive of all other marking systems, precedent to figuration, preauratic. Yet Mr. Memory's finally disclosed formula of letters and numbers remains bound to the subversive machinal flight that his role as courier and agent signals on behalf of Hitchcock's cinematic practice. But here the official MacGuffin eludes even its status as "MacGuffin" as the latter migrates, say, like a black cat prowling roofs at night, into "the thirty-nine steps" itself (the band of agents we never meet). The problem becomes acute when Hannay asks Mr. Memory in the Palladium, "What are 'the 39 steps'?" He is asking, in effect, what the telos of this very "film" performance at that nonpresent is—since the film bears this appellation as its title, and can be being named as well. Nor is the MacGuffin simply the deferral of assigning any referent, a "nothing" in that sense, any more than the "O" that caroms across the names of Hitchcock's agents, like Roger O. Thornhill or Johnny-O Fergusson or Dick-O Blaney, designates the personality as *zero* or loser in some social sense. "MacGuffin" as word seems to cover a plunge into anamorphized space and temporal prestidigitation, sabotaging its assigned referent in advance. It is the most overt and successful incorporation of the "zero" figure into aesthetic and critical calculus since Nietzsche. A nothing, a *cipher*, it resists any literalization yet refuses the substitutes its vacuum solicits; hence, its *proper* Scottish name, mocking the catachrestic as such. *It* can be converted from the static mystique of being a hole in the symbolic to being a

mobile agent of translation, a viral contamination by something precedent to figurative meaning, refusing assignations, dislocating mimetic pretexts. The MacGuffin could be one of "the 39 steps" itself, itself a MacGuffin that, in a sense, is too literally true.

11. Compare the use of "Rome" in *Spellbound,* or the name "Kaplan" to signal a head in *North by Northwest.*

12. Examples abound: Lina in *Suspicion* is interrupted by Johnny Aysgarth (Cary Grant) with her psychiatry book, legs touch. This generates Johnny's prevaricating attempt to change a third-class into a first-class ticket (strange, this 3 to 1) by exchanging postage stamps, quipping to the conductor something about sending a letter to the latter's mother with them (the opening, again, of *North by Northwest,* where there is another such interruption of reading on a train, this time of Eve Kendall). *The 39 Steps* finds Pamela interrupted by Hannay, her spectacles up; in *Strangers on a Train* it is Bruno interrupting Guy, shoes again touching, followed by banter by Bruno about reading and Guy calling him a "great reader," one who reads "too much." Indeed. Again there is the cameo in *Blackmail.*

13. In *The Trouble with Harry* a professor will not stop reading even as he trips over the corpse. Little sister Anne in *Shadow of a Doubt* will barely take her head out of a book while she talks and robotically answers questions. Elsewhere libraries occupy pivotal scenes of murder or intrigue (*Saboteur,* "I Confess," *North by Northwest*).

14. The term *accident* recurs in the same way, as a preoriginary trauma or cut, associated with the cinematic, in *Marnie* and *Spellbound.*

15. Whatever atomizes or dematerializes the "eye," like scissors, can only do so by becoming more micrological in order to precede, at all points, the identified image. It can only already have entered a mnemonic, tele-archival labyrinth, as a *reading eye.* This opens in Hitchcock a letteral order that emerges in chains of repetitions and graphic similitudes: $R$ may be repeated in a word or name (Arnie), $W$ will invert $M$ yet retain the three pyramidal triangles of the latter (as $A$ and $V$ will their one, in the "Avenger"), $O$s cite wheels, reels, and zeroids, $P$s emerge at different points in key recurrences (as will the Greek $\pi$)—all letters, graphically, deriving from the slash, the cutting stroke. Yet each carries a chain of differential inflections departing from cinematic properties.

## 8. Prosthesis of the Visible

1. Sterritt, *Films of Alfred Hitchcock,* 5.

2. The black cat that first traverses the screen and rooftops, figure of pre-originary theft, registers an absence or implosion of "light," a trace or prefigural simulacrum elsewhere manifest as an eclipsed or black sun. That elsewhere is the first *Man Who Knew Too Much,* which the rooftop climax also rewrites and whose opening sketch of a tourist's hand leafing through travel folders is retheorized by the travel service sequence.

3. This inversion, mirrored when one wishes to move beyond identification and ends up actively identifying with an uninterpretable effect or symptom, dwells in Zizek's favorite trope, Hegel's "negation of a negation." This figure allows one to recuperate a negative effect as a positive condition of experience, and recurs, say, when we hear that Lacan's emptying of the subject—his destitution subjective—is not opposed to the Subject of the Enlightenment, but defined it all along, or when Derridean *différance* is neutralized, since rather than being opposed to the logic of identity it is called, instead, the latter's condition. Yet the shibboleth of the linguistic is bypassed and caricatured rather than engaged; its broken *paroles* raised other issues of agency, perhaps more historial still than grabbags like "the symbolic," as occurs moreover within the archival and its programming of sight, definition, hermeneutic conceits.

4. Lee Edelman's appropriation of this Lacanian nonfigure at Zizek's expense as a *"sinthome*-osexuality" produces the occluded logics of a signifying prospect that must, in Hitchcock, be vacated within any binarized model— here heterosexist desire and its claim to historicist narration, or the proprietary semantic that comes with a claim to a deferred future. Edelman's model and example are, again, Hitchcock's *The Birds* and their attack on children, on imprinting, on the family plot of terrestrial consumption: "It's not that the birds mean homosexuality, but that homosexuality necessarily shapes the ways in which the birds mean for a culture that assigns it the negativising burden of sexuality itself: sexuality, that is, as *sinthome,* as always *sinthome*-osexuality, sexuality as that force that threatens to leave futurity *foutú"* ("Hitchcock's Future," *HCE,* 254).

5. Raymond Bellour, "Hitchcock—Endgame," *HCE,* 183.

6. It is the position taken over by the police airplane that later buzzes Robie's boat.

7. One is technically allied to the aerial shot from *The Birds* at the gas station—which actively scorches away the earth, oddly free of trees and desertified, while at the same time, as travel agency tourists, projecting upon that destitution the programmed associations of "beauty." "France," it turns out, would appear a *heavenly* destination that, nonetheless, seems a sort of tourist *Bandriki* (the vampiric Balkan celluloid band-land with an invented language, a sort of cinematic esperanto, in *The Lady Vanishes*).

8. The panorama cites, moreover, colliding logics: the cradle of Mediterranean culture (and with it the logos and *eidein*); the recurrent "double chase" accelerating the hermeneutic ritual linking the eye to hunting and interpreting; the burning away of trees by a solar logic; the projecting of "beauty" onto a burned-out landscape absent of humans (appearing in cliff-embedded towns or dwellings); the mnemonic fold by which the tracking eye seeks what is familiar and hence "recognizes" what is preinstalled (the shot "equals" beauty).

9. This recurs to Murchison's suicide at the end of *Spellbound,* with a giant

prop gun and hand, projector-like, pointed back into the eye of the asylum director. The cinematic is suicided, turned against its "own" technicity, sites, and logics.

10. It is also a theft, calling to mind Mrs. Van Hopper in *Rebecca* doing the same in a bowl of cold cream—and that from nearby to Nice, in "Monte." The citation consumes its predecessor.

## 9. Upping the Ante

1. Pascal Bonitzer notes, with an implicit nod to Deleuze, that all of Hitchcock might be so termed ("let me state quite plainly . . . the whole of Hitchcock is minor, and for this we should be thankful"). In fact, in applying this thinking, we would call into question the entire pretext of finding Hitchcock *serious* at all—of what choices, values, or reading models are invoked, with that term, to begin with. See Bonitzer, "The Skin and the Straw," *Everything*, 78.

2. Thomas M. Leitch, "Self and World at Paramount," in *Hitchcock's Re-released Films*, 37. Even the terms *pessimism* and *genuinely affirmative* are so steeped in auteurial and aesthetic premises that some other lack, or excess, must harass the canon makers when stepping around an anomaly. One suspends translating terms like *decorative trifle* or *shallow*—certainly, one could say superficial, or use the term *light*. *To Catch a Thief* is light *stuff*, even a truffle or mere pastry perhaps. If one "widely" and "aptly" dismisses the film, what does that say about light, visibility, seeing, illumination, "enlightenment"?

## 10. Hitchcock's Light Touch

1. *To Catch a Thief* is suffused with figures of cognition that anticipate the next project—Hitchcock's remake of *The Man Who Knew Too Much* (1956). In a way, *To Catch a Thief* is a more efficient remake of the earlier film's preoccupation with epistemological and solar tropes. One could make a case for *To Catch a Thief*'s being the former's more genuine "remake" or commentary.

2. "Life" in this characterization is the effect and movement of teletranslational and teleportal figurations, shaped and modeling literary or aesthetic or, should this be totalized, cinematic inscriptions, *life* as motion, *speed*.

3. *Fold* can also suggest sheep, which we encounter stopping Germaine's pursued car in the first car chase, allowing Lepic to catch up. Wool, too, is one origin of clothes or knitting in a work traversed by marked clothing. The sheep parallel the car stop in *The 39 Steps*, which occurs on a stone bridge and, thus, conjures (Mr.) Memory. Memory would be, in fact, the premise of this folding or turning back, both on storage bands and as recollection or reference (back).

4. What is called "hell," referenced to Dante, would be travel folder hell, here called "travel folder heaven" when hypostasized as a perceptual machine in temporal arrest. When Robie's *traveling circus* folded, when Cary Grant would be inscribed as a repetitive star commodity in or out of retirement,

when Hollywood would stall in self-imitation, or when public policy derives from cinematic models—that is, when a program takes over the present as "homogeneous" time—travel folder hell is in state. In a way, this condition is what the plot and Grant are striving to defend or maintain.

5. Hitchcock's tele-archive and works are folded back, as the mnemonic sheep remind us, or *summoned* to this gala gathering—even when they limp in for retooling. Such light summonings *activate* complex disfigurations: from *The Lodger* (the opening shriek) through *Murder!* (Fane-like "trapeze" artist, half-cast[e]ing); *Blackmail* (fingerprints, the swirling wheel); the first *Man Who Knew Too Much* (Foussard's hair citing Abbott's); *Secret Agent* (the phony death, sound, ears, agency); *Sabotage* (the birdcage as bomb, sand); *Saboteur* (the sleeve, "fighting fire with fire"); *Suspicion* (Grant's "monkey" face); *Notorious* (wine bottles, keys, radioactive sand, half-face shots of Grant); on into "future" films in the combinatoire like *North by Northwest* (advertising, traffic, the plane), *Marnie, Family Plot,* and so on. The saturation of these renders the work a transformational motherboard of tangled circuitries that a phrase, emblem, or initial mildly activates, gazing fore and back from the "middle of the day" or meridian of Hitchcock's cinematic career, of the century, of an accelerating historial arc.

6. The intrinsic gamble or "bet," which migrates to encompass the whole of the insurance racket, the casino scene, the entire film, is also that of a certain "long shot," epitomized in the anamorphic conundrum of the camera's panoramic tracking of the first car chase over the scorched landscape, in the first instance of travel folding. What seems added, however, is an active (passive) component, complicitous with culture-historical machines of perception and cognition apprehended by Hitchcock as ultimately political, consumption machines whose mimetic deforestations appear instantaneous, which ally a prosthetic eye with an absent yet scorchingly eviscerating sun. Caught in the mnemonic folds and refolds of "sight," it instantly marks as already performed a preoriginary blinding, which effects the structure reference, earth, gravity, futurity, and time.

7. It is on linguistic pieces and premises that *To Catch a Thief* often seems to focus. Nice is taken up into the almost gnawing repetitions of the word nice—usually dismissive ("too nice," "say something nice to her," "why are you being so nice to me?" and so on). It echoes and ruptures, breaks to suggest a negating of *ice,* which itself tropes diamonds, or for that matter the glass that seems transparent yet bars touch and reflects another scene.

8. Caught in what is alluded to as a "whirling pickpocket," in speaking of the thefts of a roulette wheel and film projector at once, another "travel folder," the sun that gives light itself—like the black cat crossing the rooftops—takes away, in this case life, reference, trees. It burns—a trope echoed in ceaseless (and too cool) references to heat, like Grant's pseudonym, "Conrad Burns," or the remark about making "hot diamonds" (that is, ice), or the way Grant's arm

cuts off the print of "Hotel Carlton" at the float to isolate, in the cool reflecting waters, the word "Hot" (a device used in *Foreign Correspondent*).

9. The term "service" reverberates in *To Catch a Thief,* beyond the travel service window to the phrase *service compris,* applied to tipping, and laces through class markers—Germaine, Bertani's kitchen—to include feet and legs. It displays already a tourist world of *service industries*: insurance, restaurants, catering, gambling, hotels. This is even echoed in Mrs. Stevens's complaints about cinematic "tipping": *"Service compris. Service compris.* Everyone . . . gets a tip whether they deserve it or not." The same with travel *services.*

10. Certainly, that includes not only the Hebraic and the Egyptian, but the Greek and with it the very pretext of *aesthetics* associated with light and maintained by a certain mimetic regime (Grant's offering himself to Hughson as "Smith" cites the pseudonym of *"Anna*bella Smith" from *The 39 Steps* and evokes this entire trajectory).

11. When needled by Francie about giving up the alias "Conrad Burns" and using his real name, the outed Robie jousts: "I prefer to be called Conrad." Conrad is a name in which the first syllable invokes a problematic of *cogn*ition (as will reference to stealing the *"Ken*ton" jewels). The second syllable, *rad,* condenses the evisceration of a process of circulation that cancels, beforehand, sight, the sun, or origin, and the acronym RADA will represent the theatrical institution of London in *Stage Fright.* The loss of gravity and *burning* off of trees is now connected to a circular trap of cognition ("Con") purveyed and executed in the destitutions of the panorama or the "heavenly" logics of travel folding. As a "great big" logger (or lodger), we might say, Grant cuts down natural images like trees en masse; hence, the very conceit of a "natural" image. Cutting, slicing. There is a cognitive circularity or precessual recurrence inscribed in the alias "Conrad Burns": it is one as if linked to the pyrotechnic display, a scything light spray or folding mnemonics.

12. An allusion in Mrs. Stevens's hotel room to the theft of Mme La Rue's jewelry wires *"I Confess"* to this circuitry. The film's police inspector (Karl Malden) is named Inspector La Rue, again a transport lane or street. Here a despoiled "madame," invoking directionless traffic, the specter of Inspector La Rue recalls the repeated palimpsest that punningly opens the shots of Quebec City streets in *"I Confess"*—that of pointing street signs (like the one cut by the shadow in the travel service display) with the word *Direction.*

13. Mouse derives from *meus,* a trope for theft, the metaphoric flitting of a shadow. Akira Lippit argues that the advent or invention of the "animal" in modern discourse and that of "cinema" itself are two sides of an event: "Thought of as technology, as a *technē* that opens worlds, the animatephor operates like a fabulous machine. Trace and memory, Nietzschean amnesia or Heideggerian erasure, the discourse on the animal reveals at its origins a technological atopia—a world that, as Derrida claims, always begins on the occasion of its reproduction." See Lippit, *Electric Animal: Toward a Rhetoric of*

*Wildlife* (Minneapolis: University of Minnesota Press, 2000), 196. And: "One finds, by the latter half of the nineteenth century, a set of terms—animal, photography, unconsciousness—coalescing to form a distinct topology" (177).

14. As if to show "who is who, and what is *really* what," as Robie demands of Danielle hanging from a rooftop. Yet just this—*acting like* something, the idea of a something that, a model for it, can only mnemonically precede it without escape—proliferates. *To Catch a Thief* accesses *Hamlet* on performativity differently than *North by Northwest,* which begins by stepping out of a traffic jam (as if from the travel service window). The totality is sucked into inflections of a play within a play within a play more horizonless than Grant's staged shooting by Eve Marie Saint, since with that totalization it cancels its own perpetual parabases, that which makes the timid director look rather glum on the back of the bus, half anyway, since his face is sliced in two.

15. The image of buildings booming, imploding, is projected on the aquarium when Verloc visits the London Zoo in *Sabotage*—a melting away of structures, by the screen and before antediluvian life-forms, atomized. Hitchcock's next film, the second *Man Who Knew Too Much,* will condense and materialize this as "a *single* clash of Cymbals."

16. Elsewhere in Hitchcock the figure of *wood* may be inserted into characters displacing *phusis* (*Stage Fright*'s Charlotte Inwood, Midge Wood in *Vertigo, Family Plot*'s Bishop Wood).

17. The *sleeve* "cites," in turn, or touches on, the final image of *Saboteur,* of the saboteur Fry falling from the torch—a cold flame—of the Statue of Liberty, gift of "France," land of liberty, a statue also holding a book, or *livre.* In that scene, as Fry falls his sleeve catches and unravels, thread by thread.

18. In *Vertigo,* Scottie and "Madeleine" stop before the marked rings of the cut giant sequoia (Francie taunts "Conrad" that he might tell teenage French girls that "*all* his trees are sequoias"): it is a cutting whose rings simulate the vertigo spiral, with "Madeleine's" fingering a point in "her" prehistory where she—Carlotta—lived and died replicates an anamorphic disruption of the temporal that the work exploits and explores.

19. We are reminded of how this issue has seemed, as such, related to a certain technicity, as Mary Ann Doane notes: "From Georg Simmel to Walter Benjamin, modernity is conceptualized as an increase in the speed and intensity of stimuli. Time emerges as a problem intimately linked to the theorization of modernity as trauma or shock. Time is no longer the benign phenomenon most easily grasped by the notion of flow but a troublesome and anxiety-producing entity that must be thought in relation to management, regulation, storage, and representation. One of the most important apparatuses for regulating and storing time was the cinema." See "Temporality, Storage, Legibility: Freud, Marey, and the Cinema," in *Critical Inquiry* 22 (Winter 1996): 314. For Robie to say "the biggest problem is time," and for the scene to carom

as if across centuries, renders time not a stored commodity but an anamorphic band or surface.

20. One may say *originaries* rather than origins or originals, since the former marks even these as conceptual MacGuffins and detached sign clusters inscribed in the service of certain forces and histories.

21. "It [your old car] just turned amphibious" is, however banteringly put, a slanted remark. It is like *Psycho*'s car drawn up from the bog at the end, filled with oil-like waste, a secondhand car with a corpse in it, muddily pulled by celluloid linked chains. The interevolutionary term *amphibious* complicates the series of *animemes* from cats engulfed by a mouse, a "lamb" (Francie) preying on a "lone wolf" (Robie), birds, folds of sheep. It names a machine, a car of course, whose technology is adapting as by an evolutionary leap to traverse borders between water and earth, living and dead, playing to the gadget-obsessed 1950s.

22. This recurrence to cars or the syllable *car* (Cary, Carlton, carry) threads and activates another palimpsest. Here there seems a catlike toying, not unlike Grant with his two female suitors, each rejected in advance—and particularly where it is the reflective surface of the water, a cool glassy surface on which only sun rays play that seems marked as *hot,* as though *reflection* itself here takes on a corrosive role. When Grant reaches his arm up to hold on from the water it crosses out the "e" in *Hotel*. The gesture *in*cites *Foreign Correspondent,* where Joel McCrea knocks off the same letter *E* from an electric sign on the roof of the *Hotel Europe,* rendering it *Hot-l Europe,* the weak referent for which is the European war's heating up. Here this might be an unnoticeable gesture, an erasure, if it did not produce the word *Hot.* Compelled to produce a referent we could point to when asked if he is enjoying the women's catfight, Grant mumbles, "Quite *nice* . . . the sun and all," and Kelly responds, "Well, it's *too much* for me." So a second, concealed referent is the title itself, where "foreign correspondent" also alludes to the problem of translation, or alien transcription, suitable for a scene where Kelly alludes to the two looking like they were "conjugating some irregular verbs" (reversing the language teaching scene from French to English, making Danielle of necessity the instructor). The *Hot* of Hotel Carlton must be extended to the syllable *Carl* seen in the next shots, and we might assume the *l* to be the letter of *letters* and precisely the letters *Car(l)*. The "Hot(e)l Car(l)" cites again *Sabotage*'s dictated would-be confession: "I, *Carl* Anton Verloc." For the bottom of the letters is corroded, as if burned, but in fact by the saline water (the same sea that, in *Rebecca,* will be interfaced with the letter *R*). Yet as the "Car(l)" passes into the exchange on cars, we are alerted of something else—parallel to the citation of water-skiing, and the transposition from Alpine heights and snowy tracks to horizontal sea that absorps crisscrossing trails as swiftly as they are made.

23. The distinction between a "him" (human address) and an "it" (inanimate

one) is traversed pointedly in the "Ambrose Chappell" sequence in the second *Man Who Knew Too Much*. The inspection of "architecture," supposedly, moves into a similarly deanthropomorphic zone, which turns, here, into the *formal* one of lists and numbers as well.

24. The villa as architectural structure is a topos as if encapusulated in the next film, the second *Man Who Knew Too Much,* where "Ambrose Chapel" attempts to give a human face to the name lead only to a taxidermy shop.

25. This reference to the sheer anteriority of the cinematic representation draws out an insistence that goes back to *Blackmail* and before: that the cinematic trace is a "sponger" of all representational histories, as at the British Museum, and critically precedes all writing forms, not as a local technology (the analogic, say), but as a totalization of citational and semaphoric networks, costumes, teletechnics (of which hieroglyphics would be one). Time, of course, had been from the first both dislocated and turned against by the photographic shot or image, as when the single shot of an assassin is presented as an attempt to shoot, capture, a simulated present or "now" (Jill excuses little Betty at the marksmanship contest by saying that she will be there "presently"). It is not only that the atomization of the cinematic is already, as cited in the cameo, figured as Verloc's time bomb, associated with birds on a bus, but that radically other time lines erupt, among them that of the prehistorial birds, nonanthropomorphic time.

26. Baudelaire's *Correspondances* can already be heard as inverted and troped in the title *Foreign Correspondent,* diverting the term into its journalistic and cinematic, even geopolitical, import.

27. This imagery occurs, in a sense, in the pine grove scene of *North by Northwest,* using thin trees too as the spacing of the bar series.

28. Paul de Man, "Anthropomorphism and the Lyric," in *The Rhetoric of Romanticism* (New York: Columbia University Press, 1984), 247.

29. The recursion to a MacGuffinesque or Zarathustran zero or circuitry, a cinematic obverse of Nice, whose initials elicit *Secret Agent,* is elsewhere allied to the number 3, or 3 and 1, or 13—as though the triadic model gave birth to what it annihilates, her number itself as the trope of a "1" (or zero), which makes the 3, first plane of geometric visibility, the "first" number.

30. The number "92" will have been stamped, too, on the plaque that Robie drops down the woman gambler's front—which number, if divided by the Pythagorean *pi,* for instance, yields 29.29, its doubled obverse, a double of 13.

31. This *lower* order of feet and legs, associated with sound and with *cats,* with legacy and *legein,* legibility and legitimizing inscription (the mnemonic order, what is preinscribed, repeated, phenomenalized), is associated in the film with *Secret Agent,* the text in which it seems most fully theorized (the dog, sound, the ear). And, as such, with (historical) agency, the "event" that cannot be located in a linear series, which does not pass through or *simply* break the

transparent glass of the image that reflects another scene and bars contact, but by *means* of it.

32. A *sheer* anteriority repeatedly evoked in conjunction with the black cat—in the "war" (German for *was*), in the name Jeremiah, in phrases like "for old times' sake"—first absorbs the site of a past trauma, of the war, but then projects that into instances of crashing sound and rupture. The latter redistribute that rupture or break from being the mythic cataclysm of a past event to a break within ongoing horizons. "Old times" sucks in every past representations and hence sheer anteriority (as the storage medium of reels), Hitchcock's earlier work ("a Resistance" mock compromised by this work's pretense of slick self-imitation), the prehistorial landscape, animemes. An afterlife in advance, its "bad leg" or legacy is variably that of *France*—the histories of light, ocularcentrism, past glory, Mediterranean fables, the war itself. One effect of this lateral dispersal is the random generation of faulted binaries unyoked from oppositional codes (hot and cold, up and down, past and future).

33. This totalization—in which the point of touch spreads to reference "everything"—registers, in measure, a *sponging* capacity of the image to absorb, without limit, every trace chain connected, and cited, by every other—and then to subject these affiliations to the formal logics of the mediatrix. Tracey, the blackmailer in *Blackmail,* is called a "sponger."

34. McKenzie Wark observes of this totalized consumption, what the film calls an "offer with everything": "Cinema is everything and nothing—like the names of his best protagonists, Roger O. Thornhill and Johnny-O Ferguson. The *O* stands for nothing. Cinema is nothing but the rot of time. And yet cinema is everything, swallowing every other means of culture whole. What is remarkable about Hitchcock is that he saw cinema at one and the same time as immensely powerful and utterly insignificant. Like the MacGuffin, the cinema is an index of what it destroys" ("Vectoral Cinema," in *Virtual Geography* [Bloomington: Indiana University Press, 1994]).

35. In fact, although Hitchcock favors the newspaper as simulated reading scene to stress the public degradation of language he takes for granted, when Mrs. Stevens's non sequitur notes that "everyone in Philadelphia reads the *Bulletin,*" it totalizes reading as catalog, though *Bulletin* echoes *ball*—glimpsed as what the police play hackysack with, again, trying to kick or keep the ball, the eclipsed disk, *up* against gravity, while waiting outside the Sanford villa as the "list" is discussed.

36. McKenzie Wark observes again in para-Deleuzian fashion: "Every sign we receive is an index, Hitchcock tells us, but of what, we can rarely ever know. An index is a sign that is directly produced by a material effect, like a smoke signal. Only the index is always different from what it indexes. It tells us that something has happened, but only by being different from its cause. The index, in other words, need have no resemblance. It is not a representation" ("Vectoral

Cinema"). Wark suggests the vista of a mediatrix-induced reterroriialization of geographies. As a still undetermined "event" within the tele-archival, "Hitchcock" is one site where such vectors are mapped and rerouted, put in suspense, to hypernate, entrapped, acceded to with a curse. The *geo* that emerges in this totalized mnemonics, then, is already an *aterra,* routed through trace chains. Hitchcock's undoing of the eye and ocularcentrism, however, enforces the impression that any Deleuzian reterritorialization, as with the term *vector,* requires the sort of "epistemological critique of tropes" to which Hitchcock subjects cognition, the sensoria, mnemonics, and number within the semaphoric itself.

37. Returning to architecture, de Man's comment on the word *transport* in Baudelaire's *Correspondances,* and specifically the phrase *transports des sens,* recalls the play on "travel" as cinema in the film. It rewrites the idea of movement (cinema) not as linear, or even virtual (what, after all, is "France" as destination? Its echo in "Francie"? Its suggestion of *fire* or linguistic evocation in the later title, *Frenzy?*), but prefigural. Again, de Man: "We have learned to recognize, of late, in 'transports' the spatial displacement implied by the verbal ending of *metaphorein.* One is reminded that, in the French-speaking cities of our century, 'correspondance' meant, on the trolley cars, the equivalence of what is called in English a 'transfer'—the privilege, automatically granted on the Paris *Metro,* of connecting one line to another without having to buy a new ticket" ("Anthropomorphism," 251). De Man glosses: "The problem is not so much centered on *phorein* as on *meta* (trans . . .), for does 'beyond' here mean a state that is *beyond movement,* entirely? And how can 'beyond,' which posits and names movement, ever take us away from what it posits? . . . In this realm, transfer tickets are of no avail. Within the confines of a system of transportation—or of language as a system of communication—one can transfer from one vehicle to another, but one cannot transfer from being like a vehicle to being like a temple, or ground" (252, my emphasis).

38. Jean Baudrillard, "Seduction; or, The Superficial Abyss," in Baudrillard, *The Ecstasy of Communication,* ed. Sylvère Lotringer (New York: Semiotext[e], 1988), 66.

39. In probing one of many possible *queer* Hitchcocks (a word he scored into numerous dialogues strategically), in "Hitchcock's Future," Lee Edelman comes upon the "birds" of that work as marking resistance to the heterosexual fable, to that of the family plot, say, with its claims to guard procreation and pass on legacy, names, futurity. This occurs at the expense—as the film of that name allows—of any "homosexual" recuperation as a narratable alternative: "the reassuring meaning of heterosexuality as the assurance of meaning itself confronts in the birds a resistance, call it *sinthome*-osexuality, that fully intends to wipe the satisfied smile off Melanie's face" (*HCE,* 245). Edelman provides a powerful reading of the ad rebus, "*The Birds* is coming": "Affirming though it does the imminence, the narrative covenant, of futurity . . . this

slogan suggests, as well, the sort of coming without reserve that would expend itself improvidently, thus wasting all hope of futurity and refuting the tranquil faith in an order of narrative intelligibility that Hamlet, for instance, defers to when he forbears from deferring his fate: 'Not a whit, we defy augury; if it be not to come, it will be now; if it be not now, yet it will come. Readiness is all' (V.ii. 220–4)" (247). Indeed, Bodega Bay will be called *our* little "hamlet." Yet the "is" coming that loses time and voids futurity in cinematic expense is, also, beyond arrival, beyond sexual definition or metaphor. The foreclosure of a program of futurity, however, may be, in a Benjaminian viewfinder, on behalf of alternative virtual pasts and futures.

40. An inversion of this occurs in *Notorious,* without any of the analytic power, when Hitchcock has Bergman repeatedly remark in Grant's presence how "handsome" his drab looking spy chief is.

41. One would hear *meaning* in its root sense as semantic property, *Meinung,* what is mine.

42. *Bombing* occurs, in a sense, in every citational shot—like the silent movements of the cat. But in the genealogy of cinematic analogs for Hitchcock, which is to say techno-weaponry, Peter Conrad notes that the bikinis on the Cannes beach, in the 1950s, evoke the Bikini atolls and early anxiety over nuclear annihilation, atom bombs. The cinematic Nazis of *Notorious,* similarly, hunt for uranium, hidden in presumably radioactive sand in wine bottles, just like the bottle Robie tosses in the air, as if juggling, to halt the aggressive giant in Bertani's kitchen who catches it. Yet here the collusion of nonsolar light, radioactive, with the specter of world annihilation—first possible to contemplate before the nuclear invention—pushes the Riviera into a mock-apocalyptic mode, as the scene at the gala will, in a sense, mock in the rarest of fashions (as a fashion show). The prospect of semioclastic atomization by a bomb posing as an incinerating fake sun, of blinding light, undergirds the address by the work of the Mediterranean logos, the earth, affluence, lamentation, the "light touch."

43. *To Catch a Thief,* with its Homeric citations and inversions, may by contamination and synechdoche be said to rewrite *Ulysses* in its entirety, leaping to where Penelope's tropological weaving is brought to its end.

44. J. Hillis Miller, "Zero" (unpublished manuscript). Miller draws on Paul de Man's determination of zero as a trope of the "one," itself in turn a naught; see "Pascal's Allegory of Persuasion," in de Man, *Aesthetic Ideology* (Minneapolis: University of Minnesota Press, 1996), 51–69. Andrzej Warminski provides a penetrating analysis of this rhetorical complication surrounding the zero as rhetorical MacGuffin in his "Introduction: Allegories of Reference," 1–33.

45. As an atomizing and dematerializing trope for this cinematic practice, the illusion incorporates that artificial power—as it was prepared to do with the radioactive sand in *Notorious* (echoed in the *San*(d)ford gala). If Prometheus and Hephaestus attend this Mediterranean scene, the latter as keeper

of "fire" with his lame leg, the wine steward Foussard, the implosion of cold "fire with fire" effectively *blinds* the viewer, puts out the Cyclopean one-eyed or monoeidetic vision associated with the tourist and also with the mimetic text. It is one of the film's own professorial *lessons* repeatedly asserted (reiterated in lines like "You're a singular girl," or of Lepic, "Il est seul?" "Non, deux"), and it is failed. At noon, 1 becomes 2.

46. The shot from Dr. Murchison's pistol into the camera as his eye is a shot that should blind, whiting out momentarily following a spurt of red, a *Marnie* flash, yet after which the hand is still seen pointing the pistol into the nonexistent eye, its own rebirth or survival ghost-miming its own advance self-cancellation.

47. This pitting of "fire with fire" reverts to the opening of *Saboteur,* where the saboteur Frye (whose embroiled name seems adverted to, again, by that of Conrad Burns), arranges for a worker to be immolated when trying to put out a fire with an extinguisher filled with gasoline. Fighting fire with fire, in that text, seems to name a perversely Empedoclean abruption (perverse, for linking the Nazi saboteur to a cognitive-aesthetic agenda).

48. Something is produced that is the very opposite of the orgasmic Mac-Guffin: "all that *elation* turned to *frustration.*" The aesthetics of the *theft* turns out to be a theft of *aesthesis,* so to speak, simultaneous anaestheticization and telestheticization. The light touching of the fireworks may be transposed through the German *Schein,* trope of the aesthetic as such, yet at once as reflection and appearance.

49. Nothing can (not) be projected onto "Cary Grant's" face, stripped of legibility in *Suspicion.* In *North by Northwest,* Eva Marie Saint speaks of Grant's as "such a *nice* face"—invoking the obliterations registered at Nice in his preceding film.

50. That Hitchcock had displaced *gods* in mind is marked by a scene he cut from production. After the Nice flower market debacle, Robie was to leap into a passing carnival float featuring Neptune, whereupon he would hide inside the papier-mâché head, leading to general carnage in the accelerating chase. He is said to have cut it because of the price ($30,000, by accounts), but this mock-up of where *North by Northwest* almost ends, with Cary Grant taking refuge in (American) mock-gods' heads, may have been precipitous. It is replaced, perhaps more tellingly, with the hag holding Grant's sleeve around the tree trunk: Hitchcock supplants a set piece in which Cary Grant takes up residence in the cinematic head of the Greek god of the sea, who comes to ruin thanks to him, with the starkly illegible crone binding him to an earth, by wrapping his barred jersey about the premier trope of a natural image, a tree trunk, as if keeping cinema from leaving the mimetic fiction of the natural image altogether, with a nod to *Maquis Mouse.*

51. For performative deployment within and on this word cluster, see Faulkner's "Pantaloon in Black" in *Go Down, Moses.*

52. What persists beyond the end of the evening, where everyone else has fallen away and the music reverts to South American rhythms, outlasts the legs on the dance floor, a citation that signals elsewhere in Hitchcock a sort of semiotic disentropism associated with preoriginary death or murder (the dance recollected in *The Lodger* where the sister is first killed, the dance floor in the first *Man Who Knew Too Much* where Louis Bernard is shot, that recollected as if from outside memory, and as figure of media constellations as well, that repeatedly invades the text of *Shadow of a Doubt*).

53. This last finger pointing in Hitchcock at a diamond amidst chandelier glass, is accompanied by a direct or parabatic "wink," that by Barbara Harris, looking out of the screen as if to the public, as if eye to eye.

54. Fredric Jameson observes that "Hitchcock's ingenuity lies in giving representation to what is somehow, by definition, beyond it," namely, "'*form*' in the most rigorous sense of the word" ("Spatial Form," in *Everything*, 69).

55. The newspaper headline, "Le Chat est Mort," bears a double sense—much as Mrs. Stevens remarks, apropos of the headline, that Francie should "apologize in *two* languages." *Le Chat* is dead, long live the cat. The cat is death, is "mor(t)e."

56. Kelly is now the thief catching her thief, which will seem gloomily mimed decades later as the "Francie" of *Family Plot*, Karen Black, somewhat enslaved and debased "kitten" to a professional jewel thief, "Arthur Adamson," a.k.a. Eddie Shoebridge, and so on.

57. Hitchcock will bind Cary Grant to Jessie Royce Landis closer still in the next outing, making her his "mother," vaporizing Francie altogether as empty go-between.

58. *Pyrotechnics* is Hitchcock's penultimate trope for cinematic atomizations by artificed "light," absorbing the atomic blast's apocalyptic dread. Because Hitchcock is demonstrating the cinematic correlative of such a blast, it will occur in purely cinematic terms: the exposure of the (non) "secret," the burnout of the eye and the "image," the deconstruction of desire and Hollywood romance, and, instead of everyone going up in ashes, "everyone who counts" returns, instead, encumbered with formal costumes, a death party of historical shams and acinematic ritual. "Mother," as this tearing action of the *Ursprung*, also functions as guardian of historial catastrophes and intervention, the angel of cinemallographic negations.

59. "Mother," it turns out, would have to be *behind* the travel service display, scissors out, where *no* person is (she, he, or *it*, appears incorrigible).

60. Briggitte Peucker, in "'The Cut of Representation: Painting and Sculture in Hitchcock" (*HCE*, 141–58), draws an analogy between the "decapitation" of the frame and the Medusa's head of Caravaggio proceeding through an intricate poker game of "gaze" positionings. The surrealist motif of the *acephalic* is, like the beheadings to come, present in advance as a guillotine-like stroke by cinematics at Cartesian and ocularcentric epistememes. The *head* is cut off

by the frame in more ways than one, but then the rest of the body is too—and naturally, they rearrange: hands, ear, teeth, feet, fingers, dismembered parts, are suspended, marked by repetitions and associations, desemanticized and made to absorb differential relations. Each is epistemologically empowered as the cognitive head is turned off—the center moved to the extremities, material bearers of the "head" as effect, senses redistributed or put in question. And each, in this hiatus, attaches itself to problems of the cinematic: the hand, say, as *technē*, as site of writing, often handcuffed; the eye, inhabited by mnemonic graphics; the pointing finger a braided promise of indexing, indication, and indicting; feet or steps, material carriers or traces (graphics, aural effects). But the acephalic translates into an *acapitalism*—the viewing of capital as a universalized program rooted in the management of memory and perception, an aesthetic state linked to a certain set of histories and mock origins. These are bracketed by the assault of the camera, which must enter its totalizations to have full access: it must *pass*, like Hitchcock with his little box camera lingering outside the court and pouting in *Young and Innocent*. This lopping off of a certain head is not only visual. It implies the effect of graphematic trace chains and their citational explosions: implicit within the image is the whole library, back and forward, every trace chain that will pass through this station. The *photographic* citation exposes itself by citing that process, recurrently re-marking and *upping* the stakes—and this "up" will resonate in phrases, exchanges, descriptions. Hence the "war" in Hitchcock's espionage thrillers is that between, in advance and at once, not only a statist program and its anarchic materialist other, but a naturalized hermeneutics of the picture as mimetic and this other (excessive) "knowledge"—what leads to blackouts, vertigo, nescience. This (a)*capitalism* that cannot consent or return to a dialectical narrative or theological cast places this "system" in the head, the headless head stuffed with *Evening Standard* newspapers on a truck with windows for eyes, where the sensorium is or would be programmed. It is the "eye" as constructed that begins the "hunt" with its own disappearance in advance; it is hunting its own amnesiac premises (say, the bar series in *Spellbound*), and is hunted in so doing, a double chase folded back on itself to be delivered from this metaphoric trap and traffic. And all of this as a sort of cure to a sort of "ill," as it is sometimes called, even if those three letters also mime the bar series that would be the "cure" to a blind perceptual hell. *The legs rule.* They have to. No artificed light, no etched celluloid, no chemical reagent, no spooling machine, no dark room, no screen—well, no money, no tourist viewers led to the kill, no stars, and so on. Service, certainly cinematic servicing, is comprehensive. *Service compris.*

## Coda

1. *Handcuffs*, like reels, also may appear by holding the hands together to block a certain kind of *direct* writing, a mobilization of the hand as writing

implement alone, compelling it to work through the "non" direct marking system dispersed across so-called silent cinema, the experimental ur-site of any allo-graphematics.

2. Like the lines openly pursued as symptom, cause, and etiological puzzle all at once in *Spellbound*—indeed, sought as the nonorigin of a certain *amne-sia*, the site where a technology of marking precedes all possible perception or sight or, indeed, reading.

3. Again: variations of *mar(k)* irradiate across these works: Mark, Mar-nie, Marvin, Marion, Martin, Margot, Margaret, and so on, not to mention variants like Morton or Miriam or Murchison, each haunted as some sort of archival agency by a syllable, a conjuring trick in which overwhelming conse-quences languish: marring, defacing, marking, mar or *mer* (for sea, or seeing), *mère* for or as "mother," albeit otherwise, deanthropormorphized and without origination, elsewhere still. It will turn up on the *Martell* bottle in Handel Fane's dressing room as in Marcella, the hippie tombstone engraver in *Family Plot*. Indeed, the formula Mr. Memory bears is nothing but letters and num-bers, unreadable.

4. This project seems written into the usurpating or (an)archivist "villains" of the early political thrillers—as if global politics hung, suspended, in the bal-ance, as if Hitchcock conformed in ways to Benjamin's use of the term *cinema* as a parallel to what he calls "materialistic historiography."

5. One example of this occurs in *Vertigo*—or rather, in and yet also before *Vertigo*, where in one sense the technicity of the mnemonic and the *prosthesis of the visible* (not to mention gender, reference, "desire") appear exposed. It is, again, in the credit sequence that we see a monstrous graphic band, Möbius-like, inserted into and before the woman's eye, as if the "eye" were itself an ef-fect of such an implant. No sight, no vision, no transparency, no mimesis even. Nothing precedes this marking system, which also invokes one of the site of the bar series ("Judy Barton"). There is, at this instant, no such thing as "gaze," the last refuge of an ideology of the eye, of *aura* and personification—and certainly not a male *gaze*: which will always have to expose itself, repeatedly, as crafted, eunarchist, as is James Stewart ("Why *me?*"), a eunarchy maintaining these machines and levers against *its* further exposure. The Möbius or "vertigi-nous" logic, here, is referenced to the fact that a *first* model, *first* object, or *first* memory for Scottie on which all else supposedly depends, is itself a plant, pros-thetic, even a joke—that is, Madeleine. With this circular buckling of mne-monic order, model and copy, before and after are decoupled. Any intervention in the historial program—as for Verloc, operating from the Bijou—rests with this *rendering virtual* of a programmed past through a dispossessing "priority" of inscription to perception, identity, legibility.

# Index of Films

**Tom Cohen** is professor of literary, cultural, and media studies at the University at Albany, State University of New York. He is the author of *Anti-Mimesis from Plato to Hitchcock* and *Ideology and Inscription: "Cultural Studies" after Benjamin, de Man, and Bakhtin,* as well as contributing editor of *Material Events: Paul de Man and the Afterlife of Theory* (Minnesota, 2000) and *Jacques Derrida and the Humanities.*